Gail Kaciuba, Ph.D
Midwestern State University

Study Guide
To Accompany
Cost Management
Measuring, Monitoring and Motivating Performance

Leslie G. Eldenburg, Ph.D
University of Arizona

Susan Wolcott, Ph.D
WolcottLynch Associates

WILEY
JOHN WILEY & SONS, INC.

Cover Photo: ©Markus Amon/Stone/Getty Images

To order books or for customer service call 1-800-CALL-WILEY (225-5945).

ISBN 0-471-65565-1

Printed in the United States of America

10 9 8 7 6 5 4 3 2 1

Printed and bound by Malloy

TABLE OF CONTENTS

Chapter 1   The Role of Accounting Information in Management   1-1
              Decision Making

Chapter 2   The Cost Function   2-1

Chapter 3   Cost-Volume-Profit Analysis   3-1

Chapter 4   Relevant Costs for Non-routine Operating Decisions 4-1

Chapter 5   Job Costing   5-1

Chapter 6   Process Costing   6-1

Chapter 7   Activity-Based Costing and Management   7-1

Chapter 8   Measuring and Assigning Support Department Costs   8-1

Chapter 9   Joint Product and By-Product Costing   9-1

Chapter 10   Static and Flexible Budgets   10-1

Chapter 11   Standard Costs and Variance Analysis   11-1

Chapter 12   Strategic Investment Decisions   12-1

Chapter 13   Joint Management of Revenues and Costs   13-1

Chapter 14   Measuring and Assigning Costs for Income Statements 14-1

Chapter 15   Performance Evaluation and Compensation   15-1

Chapter 16   Strategic Performance Measurement   16-1

Chapter 1

The Role of Accounting Information in Management Decision Making

√ Study Checklist – Monitor your progress

☐	1. Read the chapter in the text
☐	2. Review the learning objectives below
☐	3. Read the overview of the chapter
☐	4. Read the chapter review for learning objectives 1 - 3
☐	5. Do Problem Set A and check your answers
☐	6. Read the chapter review for learning objectives 4 - 6
☐	7. Do Problem Set B and check your answers
☐	8. Do the End of Chapter Exercises in this study guide and check your answers
☐	9. Do the homework assigned by your instructor

CHAPTER LEARNING OBJECTIVES

After studying this chapter, you should be able to answer the following questions:

Q1. What types of decisions do managers make for an organization?
Q2. What is the role of accounting information in management decision making?
Q3. How do uncertainties and biases affect the quality of decisions?
Q4. How can managers make higher-quality decisions?
Q5. What information is relevant for decision making?
Q6. What is ethical decision making, and why is it important?

OVERVIEW OF CHAPTER

This chapter reviews the types of decisions managers of an organization must make, and how they use accounting information to do so. Various types of biases can affect the quality of managers' decisions, because decision making occurs under uncertainty. It is important to learn the types of uncertainties that managers face, and how they can learn to make higher-quality decisions and resolve ethical dilemmas.

CHAPTER REVIEW: Learning Objectives 1 - 3

Q1: What types of decisions do managers make for an organization?

Managers must first determine:

- the organizational vision,
- the organization's core competencies,
- the organizational strategies, and
- the organization's operating plans.

The *organizational vision* is the entity's core purpose and ideology. A discount clothing store and an elite fashion boutique have different organizational visions, which had to be decided by management before any other decisions could be made. The management of an organization also must determine the entity's *core competencies*, which are the organization's relative strengths. The discount clothing store, for example, may have decided that its strengths are its relationships with suppliers, while the boutique fashion store may have decided that its strengths include the loyalty of its customer base.

After managers determine the organization's vision and its core competencies, they must determine the *organizational strategies*, which are the ways they will use the core competencies to achieve the organization's vision. These strategies are long-term in nature. The short-term plans to implement the organizational strategies are called *operating plans*. To maintain its relationships with suppliers, the discount clothing store's organizational strategies may state that special offers for large lots of merchandise should always be accepted, while its operating plans may include procedures for daily monitoring of the placement of merchandise so that sales of these bulk purchases are maximized.

Q2: What is the role of accounting information in management decision making?

Managers must monitor daily operations to ensure that actual results are in line with the short-term operating plans and the long-term strategic plans of the organization. They need accounting information to do so. The accounting information system measures the results of operations and managers compare these actual results to the operating plans in order to motivate desirable performance by employees. Good performance should be rewarded so that it will continue, and poor performance must be investigated so that the reasons for the poor performance can be corrected.

Managers need financial accounting information to prepare reports used by decision makers external to the business, such as existing and potential creditors and investors, the Internal Revenue Service, and others. Managers need cost accounting information so that they can control the costs of the entity's products or services. The process of controlling costs while pursuing the organization's long-term strategic goals is called *strategic cost management.* Sometimes managers use financial and nonfinancial performance measures created specifically to measure progress towards long-term goals. This is known as the *balanced scorecard* approach.

Recent improvements in information systems software now allow managers to collect and organize information to assist them in collecting and using information. *Business intelligence* systems integrate the accounting and other information systems within an organization as well as with its suppliers and customers.

Q3: How do uncertainties and biases affect the quality of decisions?

Decision making occurs under uncertainty, so managers must use judgment when obtaining and using information for decisions. Uncertainties inhibit management's ability to describe a problem accurately, identify viable alternatives, foresee the outcomes of the various alternatives, and anticipate business conditions in the future. For example, the discount clothing store manager cannot know how well a particular item will sell when it is purchased from a supplier.

Managers must be careful that this judgment is free from preconceived notions, or *biases*. If a manager is biased, he or she may be less able to recognize uncertainties, appropriately analyze alternatives, consider alternative points of view, critically evaluate priorities, or make improvements to the decision-making process. The manager of the elite fashion boutique, for example, may have a bias towards evening gowns when in fact the store's female customers are more interested in high-quality tennis outfits. The manager's bias may prevent her from recognizing the interests of her customers.

PROBLEM SET A (Learning Objectives 1 - 3)

Matching: Match each term with its definition by writing the appropriate letter in the space provided. Use each term only once. The solutions are at the end of this chapter.

List of Terms

A. Actual operations	F. Decision quality	K. Organizational strategies
B. Balanced scorecard	G. Financial accounting	L. Organizational core competencies
C. Biases	H. Management accounting	M. Strategic cost management
D. Uncertainties	I. Operating plans	N. Business intelligence systems
E. Cost accounting	J. Organizational vision	

Definitions

_____ 1. a method for determining the cost of a project, process, or thing

_____ 2. actions taken and results achieved

_____ 3. approach for translating organizational vision into measurable objectives

_____ 4. core purpose and ideology

_____ 5. guidelines for day-to-day activities

_____ 6. issues and information about which we have doubt

_____ 7. preconceived notions adopted without careful thought

_____ 8. process of gathering, summarizing, and reporting financial and nonfinancial

information to be used internally

_____ 9. process of preparing and reporting financial information to be used externally

_____ 10. reducing costs while strengthening the organization

_____ 11. software that integrates information within an organization and between suppliers

and customers

_____ 12. strengths relative to competitors

_____ 13. tactics used to achieve organization vision

_____ 14. characteristics of a decision that affect the likelihood of achieving a positive outcome

CHAPTER REVIEW: Learning Objectives 4 - 6

Q4: How can managers make higher-quality decisions?

To make higher-quality decisions, managers need good information. They need to reduce their uncertainty about the information and make sure that the information they receive is complete, timely and relevant to the decision at hand. The reports they receive must be complete, readily available, and easy to understand. They must use a decision-making process that is focused and free from bias. Exhibit 1.9 in the text is an excellent summary of the path to higher-quality decisions.

Managers must have a decision-making process for addressing *open-ended questions* (those with no single "correct" decision). One such process is the Steps for Better Thinking model. Every chapter in this text book uses this model, and homework questions in the text are coded as to which step (skill level) is required to answer the question so that you can develop the skills you will need to make higher-quality decisions. The elements of the Steps for Better Thinking model are as follows:

- <u>Foundation</u>: Managers must possess the knowledge and basic skills needed to address a problem.

- <u>Step1-Identifying</u>: Managers must be able to identify the problem at hand, the information that is relevant to the problem, and the uncertainties embedded in the information presented to them.

- <u>Step2-Exploring</u>: Managers must be able to interpret information, and recognize and control for their own biases. They must be able to organize information and interpret it in a variety of ways.

- <u>Step3-Prioritizing</u>: Managers must be able to analyze information, prioritize the alternatives, and implement their decisions.

- <u>Step4-Envisioning</u>: Managers must be able to monitor their decision and adapt it to a changing environment.

Q5: What information is relevant for decision making?

Information is *relevant* if it is about the future and varies across the alternatives under consideration. For most of the decisions that managers make, part of the information includes the cash flows of the alternatives. Cash flows that can be avoided if the decision is not made are called *avoidable*, or *incremental*, cash flows and are relevant to the decision because they differ across the alternatives. *Unavoidable* cash flows are those that occur regardless of which alternative is chosen and are hence irrelevant to the decision.

Q6: What is ethical decision making, and why is it important?

Ethics deals with the ability to distinguish right from wrong. In order to practice ethical decision making, an individual must first recognize an ethical dilemma when it arises. He or she must be able to see the problem from other points of view, and consider the impact of the decision on other stakeholders. He or she must compare his or her behavior to some standard or moral code, and work towards improving his or her own ethical behavior as well as the ethics of the organization. Refer to exhibit 1.11 in the text for a review of the process for making more ethical decisions.

Since accountants are the preparers and interpreters of information that others use for decisions, it is particularly important for them to practice ethical decision making at all times. Both the American Institute of Certified Public Accountants (AICPA) and the Institute of Management Accountants (IMA) have ethical codes of conducts for their members. The IMA's standards, for example, state that practitioners of management accounting and financial management have a responsibility to:

- maintain a high level of professional competence,
- maintain the confidentiality of disclosures,
- maintain personal integrity, and
- communicate information fairly and objectively.

The IMA's standards also include guidelines for resolving ethical conflicts.

PROBLEM SET B (Learning Objectives 4 - 6)

<u>True-False</u>: Indicate whether each of the following is true (T) or false (F) in the space provided.

_____ 1. Irrelevant cash flows are those that differ across the alternatives.

_____ 2. Unavoidable cash flows are always irrelevant to a decision.

_____ 3. An internal report is any document that was prepared internally.

_____ 4. An external report presents information for the use of decision makers outside the organization.

_____ 5. The Foundation element of the Steps for Better Thinking model is that management must know the answers to questions they are asked.

_____ 6. Step 1 of the Steps for Better Thinking model states that decision makers must be able to identify the problem and the uncertainties in the information.

_____ 7. If a manager can rank a series of alternatives, then he or she is using a Step 2 skill in the Steps for Better Thinking model.

_____ 8. In the last step of the Steps for Better Thinking model, a decision maker must be able to see what could go wrong with the decision he or she made.

_____ 9. Incremental cash flows means the same thing as avoidable cash flows.

_____ 10. A performance report prepared for the board of directors is an example of an external report.

_____ 11. A schedule that compares last month's actual results to the budget is an example of an internal report.

_____ 12. A corporation's income tax return is an internal report.

_____ 13. A company is deciding whether to purchase Machine A or Machine B, both of which have a purchase price of $100,000. The cost of the machines is not relevant to this decision.

_____ 14. While deciding whether to purchase Machine A or Machine B, a company spent $1,200 investigating the characteristics of Machine A and $1,500 investigating the characteristics of Machine B. The cost of these investigations is relevant to this decision.

_____ 15. While investigating whether to purchase Machine A or Machine B, a manager learned that the expected maintenance costs are $1,900 per year for Machine A and $2,500 per year for Machine B. The expected maintenance costs are relevant to this decision.

<u>Fill in the blank:</u> Review the IMA's Ethical Standards and exhibit 1.11 in the text. Then use the word list below to complete the following sentences. Any word may be used more than once or not at all.

Word List		
conflicting interests	stakeholders	competence
confidentiality	integrity	objectivity
employees	stockholders	creditors

1. A member of the IMA must be able to prepare complete and clear reports. This is part of his or her responsibility to maintain _____.

2. Members of the IMA cannot use information learned in the course of their work for unethical advantage, because they have a responsibility to maintain _____.

3. In order to maintain their _____, IMA members must fully disclose all information that could be relevant to a decision maker.

4. Ethical dilemmas arise when there are _____ of the various _____.

5. Members of the IMA must perform their professional duties in accordance with relevant laws, regulations, and technical standards as evidence of their _____.

6. The parties affected by a business decision are known as the _____.

7. _____ are a stakeholder in nearly every business decision that affects profits.

8. A decision to close a division that has been operating at a loss can have a positive impact on _____.

9. A decision to close a division that has been operating at a loss can have a negative impact on _____.

10. A decision to fraudulently complete a loan application probably most negatively impacts _____.

END OF CHAPTER EXERCISES

<u>Multiple Choice</u>: Write the letter that represents the best choice in the space provided.

_____ 1. Decision quality:
   a. refers to a decision that had a positive outcome
   b. refers to the characteristics of a decision that affects the likelihood of achieving a positive outcome
   c. is reduced by uncertainty and bias
   d. both (b) and (c) are correct

_____ 2. Which of the following statements is false?
   a. managers must determine the organizational vision before further planning can occur
   b. organizational strategies should take advantage of the organization's core competencies
   c. operating plans are long-term in nature
   d. organizational core competencies are an organization's strengths relative to competitors

_____ 3. Which of the following statements is true?
   a. managerial accounting and cost accounting are the same thing
   b. managerial accounting prepares reports used most frequently by external decision makers
   c. cost accounting information is used for both management and financial accounting
   d. preparation of the entity's income tax return is an example of a cost accounting activity

_____ 4. All of the following are examples of external reports except:
   a. tax returns
   b. credit reports
   c. financial statements
   d. budgets

_____ 5. All of the following are examples of internal reports except:
   a. cash flow analyses
   b. news releases
   c. analyses of supplier quality
   d. product mix analyses

_____ 6. If a manager is deciding whether to repair equipment or replace it, which of the following is irrelevant to the decision?
   a. the cost of the repair
   b. the original cost of the equipment
   c. the warranty period for the repair
   d. the expected life of the equipment if it is not repaired

_____   7. Lori is deciding whether to go to school full-time at the local community college or get a full time job. Which of the following is not relevant to her decision?
   a. tuition costs
   b. potential salary she could earn in a full-time job
   c. cost of books
   d. the monthly rent on her apartment

_____   8. Relevant cash flows are
   a. unavoidable
   b. incremental cash flows
   c. constant across alternatives
   d. those that occurred in the past

_____   9. Which of the following is not one of the steps in ethical decision making?
   a. identify the ways you might get caught doing something unethical
   b. identify the stakeholders to the decision
   c. identify the ethical dilemma
   d. identify the effects of the decision on the stakeholders

_____   10. Which of the following statements is false?
   a. Strategic cost management focuses on reducing costs as well as strengthening an organization's strategic position.
   b. The balanced scorecard is a formalized approach to strategic cost management.
   c. The balanced scorecard may include both financial and nonfinancial measures.
   d. Cost accounting information used for strategic cost management includes only measures of costs.

Exercises: Write your answer in the space provided.
1. While interviewing for his first job after college graduation Joe flew to New York City. He interviewed there with Co. A and Co. B. Since the two firms don't know about the other firm's interview, Joe could submit a claim for a reimbursement of his $880 travel expenses to both firms. He really needs the money. Use the process shown in exhibit 1.11 in the text to discuss Joe's decision. What given information is not relevant here?

_____

_____

_____

_____

_____

_____

2. Stan is the manager for Take Two Videos, which rents video games and movies on VCR and DVD. The store next to his has become vacant, and he is trying to decide whether to expand his store into that space. It would allow room for a section for customers to try out games before renting them, and buy and sell used video games. Stan keeps up with all the video game magazines and has made sure that Take Two has several copies of every new game released. Discuss what information Stan might need to obtain in order to make this decision. Which information carries the most amount of uncertainty? Is there any way to reduce this uncertainty? What biases might Stan have that he needs to take into account in this decision?

_____

_____

_____

_____

_____

_____

_____

_____

_____

3. Jennifer, who lives near Champaign, Illinois, is trying to decide whether she should take the shuttle bus or drive to a conference at a hotel in Chicago. While she's away, Jennifer will pay $25 to have a house sitting service come in to feed her cat.

    If she takes the shuttle bus, it will cost $50 for the round-trip ticket plus $40 for taxi fares in Chicago. If she drives, she expects her total mileage to be about 180 miles. Jennifer has estimated that it will cost about 80¢ per mile to operate her car, using the calculations below and an estimate of 500 miles for her average monthly mileage.

Cost category	Monthly Cost
Gasoline and oil	$ 75
Maintenance and repairs	45
Depreciation on the car	150
Car insurance	75
Cost of her garage at home	55
Total monthly costs	$400

    Jennifer calculated the cost of her garage as a percentage of her home expenses including property taxes, insurance, depreciation, mortgage interest, etc. She allocated these costs to the garage based on the square footage for the garage as a percent of the total square footage for the garage and living quarters.

    a) List the cash flows in Jennifer's cost per mile that are unavoidable.

    _____

    _____

    b) List the relevant cash flows for this decision.

    _____

    _____

    _____

    c) What alternative is least costly? Show computations to support your answer.

    _____

    _____

    _____

    d) List two factors that may be relevant but not measurable in dollars. _____

    _____

SOLUTIONS TO PROBLEM SET A

<u>Matching</u> (See GYL 1.1 in the text if you got any wrong)
1. E
2. A
3. B
4. J
5. I
6. D
7. C
8. H
9. G
10. M
11. N
12. L
13. K
14. F

SOLUTIONS TO PROBLEM SET B

<u>True-False</u>

1. F   Cash flows that differ across the alternatives are relevant.
2. T   Unavoidable cash flows do not differ across the alternatives.
3. F   A report prepared internally for use by those outside the organization is an external report.
4. T   This is the definition of an external report.
5. F   The Foundation element of the model is that decision makers must possess the knowledge and skills to address questions, not that they will know the answers to all the questions they are asked.
6. T   See exhibit 1.10 in the text.
7. F   Ranking alternatives is a Step 3 skill.
8. T   The ability to see how the future may impact your decision is a Step 4 skill.
9. T   See GYL 1.2 in the text.
10. T   See exhibit 1.7 in the text.
11. T   See exhibit 1.7 in the text.
12. F   See exhibit 1.7 in the text.
13. T   The $100,000 does not differ across the alternatives and hence is irrelevant.
14. F   The cost of the investigations occurred in the past and is irrelevant.
15. T   The expected maintenance costs will occur in the future and differ across the alternatives.

Fill in the blank (refer to the IMA's Standards in the text if you got any wrong)
1. competence
2. confidentiality
3. objectivity
4. conflicting interests, stakeholders
5. competence
6. stakeholders
7. stockholders
8. stockholders
9. employees
10. creditors (even though integrity would also be a good answer here!)

SOLUTIONS TO END OF CHAPTER EXERCISES

Multiple Choice

1. D
2. C   Operating plans are short-term in nature.
3. C
4. D   Budgets are prepared for internal use; see exhibit 1.7 in the text.
5. B   See exhibit 1.7 in the text.
6. B   The original cost of the equipment occurred in the past and doesn't change whether the equipment is repaired or replaced.
7. D   Presumably Lori will live in her apartment under either alternative.
8. B   Incremental and avoidable cash flows is the same concept; these cash flows are always relevant to a decision.
9. A   See exhibit 1.11 in the text.
10. D   Cost accounting information includes financial and nonfinancial measures.

Exercises
1.   The problem is that Joe could probably get away with an action that will provide him with $880, which might be tempting. The stakeholders in this decision include Joe, the two companies, and probably Joe's family and his college. There are no benefits to any stakeholders except Joe if he decides to double-bill his expenses. It costs the two companies $440 each more than it should for Joe to do this. The negative impact to Joe's family and friends is the disappointment they would have in him if they were ever to find out what he did. The negative impact to Joe is that he would always know he sold his integrity for a mere $880. Joe is an alumnus of his college, and it is a poor reflection on the school to have alumni that would behave this way.

The irrelevant given information is:
- the two companies don't know about the other firm's interview (because Joe should arrive at the ethical decision even if there were no chance of getting caught)
- Joe really needs the money
- the travel reimbursement is $880

2.   Stan needs to determine the cash flows surrounding the decision.
- The rent for the new space probably has the least amount of uncertainty. If Stan doesn't know this amount already, he can just ask the landlord what it will cost.
- The monthly operating costs of the new space can probably be estimated with a reasonable degree of certainty. Costs such as utilities can be estimated from his existing utility cost information. Costs such as hourly wages for the workers in the new space partially depend on how busy the new area will be and are less certain.

- The monthly cash inflows from the expansion have the most uncertainty because Stan can't be sure of the customer demand for these new services.
- Stan can reduce some of the uncertainty surrounding the cash flows that depend on customer demand by doing a survey of existing and potential customers about their desire for the new services Stan wants to offer.

There is other financial information that Stan should try to obtain in order to make this decision. For example, how will the new space impact existing customers? Will he lose any of his video rental business because the new space will change his store's image? If possible, Stan should also obtain as much information as he can about the competition in the area for game rental and exchange facilities.

It seems that Stan may be a bit of a game fanatic himself, so he should take care that this bias does not affect his decision making.

3.   a) Unavoidable cash flows are costs that Jennifer will incur no matter how she travels to Chicago: house sitter ($25), car depreciation ($150), car insurance ($75), and garage costs ($55).
   b) Relevant cash flows are cash flows that can be avoided if Jennifer takes the shuttle, which is the gas and oil costs and the maintenance and repair costs that are incurred solely due to this trip.
   c) Cost per mile to drive = gas and oil ($75/500 = $0.15 per mile) + maintenance and repair ($45/500 = $0.09 per mile) = total cost of $0.24 per mile, or $43.20 total ($0.24 x 180 miles). Jennifer should drive because it would cost $43.20 to drive versus $90.00 for shuttle and taxis. Jennifer would save money by driving.
   d) Here are several possible factors: (1) Perhaps Jennifer does not like to drive, particularly in Chicago; (2) Taking a shuttle would take extra time because Jennifer would have to be at the bus station at least 15 minutes before the shuttle leaves, and she would have to wait for taxis in Chicago; (3) Jennifer could read on the shuttle and be better prepared for the conference; and (4) Perhaps Jennifer believes that it is unethical for environmental reasons to drive a car when she can take a bus.

Chapter 2

The Cost Function

√ Study Checklist – Monitor your progress

1. Read the chapter in the text
2. Review the learning objectives below
3. Read the overview of the chapter
4. Read the chapter review for learning objectives 1 - 2
5. Do Problem Set A and check your answers
6. Read the chapter review for learning objectives 3 - 7
7. Do Problem Set B and check your answers
8. Do the End of Chapter Exercises in this study guide
9. Do the homework assigned by your instructor

CHAPTER LEARNING OBJECTIVES

After studying this chapter, you should be able to answer the following questions:

Q1. What are different ways to describe cost behavior?

Q2. What is a learning curve?

Q3. What process is used to estimate future costs?

Q4. How are engineered estimates, account analysis, and two-point methods used to estimate cost functions?

Q5. How does a scatter plot assist with categorizing a cost?

Q6. How is regression analysis used to estimate a mixed cost function?

Q7. What are the uses and limitations of future cost estimates?

OVERVIEW OF CHAPTER

This chapter examines how costs behave with respect to changes in activity, and how managers use their knowledge of cost behavior to estimate future costs. Linear cost behavior is covered, as are certain types of nonlinear cost behavior, including the learning curve. Methods of estimating costs are reviewed, including two-point methods and regression analysis. Various cost terminology is introduced, including terms that describe how costs are assigned and categories of costs used in decision making.

CHAPTER REVIEW: Learning Objectives 1 - 3

Q1: What are different ways to describe cost behavior?

A *cost object* is any thing or activity for which we need to measure costs. One way to categorize costs is according to whether they are easily traceable to the cost object.

- *Direct costs* are those that are easily traceable to the cost object and *indirect costs* are those costs that are not. Whether a cost is direct or not depends on the cost object defined, the bookkeeping system in place, and the technology available to capture information. For example, when a CPA firm computes the cost of a particular audit, whether or not copying costs are direct depends on the copy machine's ability to capture information about which client's copies are being produced.

- In manufacturing, when the cost object is defined as the product, the direct costs are the direct materials and direct labor costs. Indirect manufacturing costs are known as *manufacturing overhead*, or simply *overhead*.

Costs can also be categorized as to how they change when the activity level increases, which is known as *cost behavior*. A *cost driver* is defined as a measure of activity that, when increased, causes total costs to increase. If costs are linear, then:

- *Total variable costs* are defined as costs that increase in proportion to increases in the cost driver. This means that variable costs per unit are constant as the cost driver changes.

- *Total fixed costs* are defined as costs that don't change as the cost driver changes, which means that fixed costs per unit decrease as the cost driver increases.

- The cost function is defined as TC = F + V x Q, where TC = total fixed costs, F = total fixed costs, V = variable cost per unit, and Q = volume of the cost driver. F is the y-intercept of this linear function and V is the slope.

- Costs with a fixed and a variable component are known as *mixed costs*. For example, if a store pays rent of $20,000 per month plus 2% of sales revenue, then the store's rent is a mixed cost.

Although we often assume that costs are linear, this assumption doesn't hold for many types of costs.

- We define the *relevant range* as the range of the cost driver for which our cost assumptions hold. Some costs are nonlinear over a large range of activity, but are linear within different ranges of the cost driver.

- A *stepwise linear cost* is a cost that is fixed at one level for a range of the cost driver and fixed at a different level for another range of the cost driver. If a manufacturer must hire one factory supervisor at $40,000/year for each 8 hour shift, then factory supervisors' salary costs are stepwise linear because they will be fixed at either $40,000, $80,000, or $120,000 per year, depending on the number of shifts.

- A *piecewise linear cost* is a cost where the variable cost per unit is constant at one level for a range of the cost driver and constant at another level for a different range. If a manufacturer pays $8/lb for its materials when it purchases quantities between 0 and 1,000 lbs, but pays $7/lb when it purchases more than 1,000 lbs, then materials costs are piecewise linear.

- Whenever a cost function shows variable costs per unit that decrease as activity increases, we say that the cost function exhibits *economies of scale*.

There are other terms for costs often used in decision making.

- *Marginal cost* is the incremental cost of producing the next unit. When costs are linear, marginal cost and the variable cost per unit are equal.

- *Discretionary costs* are fixed or variable costs that may be altered during the period, at management's discretion, such as advertising expenditures.

- An *opportunity cost* is the benefit given up when one alternative is chosen over the next best alternative. If you are attending college full-time, the wages you would otherwise be earning are an opportunity cost of attending school.

- A *sunk cost* is a cost incurred in the past. No decision made at this point in time can change the fact that the cost was already incurred. In Chapter 1 we learned that past costs are irrelevant in decision making.

Q2: What is a learning curve?

When an organization first begins to produce a new product, workers are still learning the new production process. The *learning curve* is the relationship between cumulative average hours per unit and the cumulative number of units produced. An example is shown in exhibit 2.8 in the text. It shows the rate at which the labor hours used to produce a product decrease as more units are produced.

- The cumulative average-time learning curve is $Y = \alpha X^r$, where Y = the cumulative average labor hours, α = the number of hours used to produce the first unit, X = the cumulative number of units produced, and r = the rate of learning. The parameters α and r are estimated based on past experience with similar products.

- The rate of learning, r, is based on the company's estimates of the percent of learning that occurs, where $r = \ln(\text{percent learning})/\ln(2)$, and ln is the natural logarithmic function. The "percent of learning" is the measure of the change in the cumulative average time per unit (or batch of units) that occurs each time production doubles. For example, if the cumulative average time for the first two units is expected to be 90% of the time spent on the first unit, and if the cumulative average learning time for the first four units is expected to be 90% of the cumulative average time for the first two units, then the "percent of learning" is 90%.

Demonstration problem-Learning curves
Carole's Kit Cars is producing a new line of single-person electric cars for commuters who need to travel less than 5 miles to work. The first car produced took 120 labor hours. Carole estimates that the percent of learning for this new car is 90%.

Required:
Compute the average number of hours per car it should take to produce 20 cars, and the total number of hours 20 cars should use.

Solution to demonstration problem
First, compute the rate of learning:

$r = \ln(\%\ \text{learning})/\ln(2) = \ln(0.9)/\ln(2) = -0.10536/0.69315 = -0.152.$

Then compute the cumulative average time to produce 20 cars, Y, where $\alpha = 120$, $X = 20$, and $r = -0.152$:

$Y = 120 \times [20]^{-0.152} = 120 \times 0.6342 = 76.1$ average hours per car.

The total hours expected to make 20 cars then, is:

Total hours for 20 cars = [76.1 hours/car] x [20 cars] = 1,522 hours.

PROBLEM SET A (Learning Objectives 1 - 2) Before answering the questions in this problem set, review the terms listed in Guide Your Learning (GYL) 2.1 and GYL 2.2 in the text.

Exercises: Write your answer in the spaces provided:

1. Jim's Jungle Gyms is producing a new line of high-end backyard playgrounds. The first playground produced took 80 labor hours. Jim estimates that the percent learning for this new playground unit is 85%. Compute the average number of hours it should take to produce 50 playgrounds, and the total number of hours 50 playgrounds should use.

_____

_____

_____

_____

_____

2. Match the graphs below to the correct description of costs. Use each graph only once.

Cost descriptions

G 1. Total property taxes are $5,000 unless you hire more than 50 people, in which case the city will not charge any property tax.

B 2. Supervisor salaries are $50,000 for 0-1,000 units and $70,000 for over 1,000 units.

C 3. A consultant charges $100/hour for a project but capped his fees at $100,000.

A 4. The rent on the office building is $10,000.

E 5. Direct labor costs $22 per hour including benefits.

D 6. Salespersons earn $30,000/year plus a 4% commission on sales.

F 7. Materials cost $13/gallon for under 1,000 gallons and $11/gallon for over 1,000 gallons.

H 8. The rent on the store is $3,000/month plus 2% of sales exceeding $20,000 in a month.

<u>Matching</u>: Match each term with the **most appropriate** definition or example. Since there can possibly be more than one term for each definition or example, the bold font is a hint. Use each term only once.

List of terms

A. Cost behavior	H. Fixed cost	P. Percent of learning
B. Cost driver	I. Indirect cost	Q. Piecewise linear cost
C. Cost function	J. Learning curve	R. Rate of learning index
D. Cost object	K. Marginal cost	S. Relevant range
E. Direct cost	L. Mixed cost	T. Stepwise linear
F. Discretionary cost	M. Opportunity cost	U. Sunk cost
G. Economies of scale	O. Overhead cost	V. Variable cost

___C___ 1. **$5,200 for hall rental and musicians plus $12 for each person** invited to the wedding.

___A___ 2. **How total costs change** with respect to changes in activity.

___B___ 3. **Number of people invited** to your sister's wedding, if the cost being considered is food.

___O___ 4. The **cost object** is a batch of widgets manufactured, and the rent on the **factory** is $3,000.

___I___ 5. The **cost object** is the 2003 income tax return for Mr. Smith, and the **rent** for the tax department's offices is $8,000 per month.

___E___ 6. The **cost object** is the tax department at a CPA firm, and the **rent** for the tax department's offices is $8,000 per month.

___L___ 7. The **cost of your room and board at school**, if it costs $1,200 plus $4 for each meal you eat in the cafeteria.

___K___ 8. The cost to produce the **101st unit less the cost to produce the 100th unit**.

___J___ 9. The **relationship** between cumulative average labor hours per unit and the cumulative number of units produced.

___T___ 10. Total fixed costs are **$150,000 if you produce between 0 and 100,000 units, but they are $200,000 if you produce between 100,000 and 200,000 units**.

___S___ 11. Total fixed costs are $150,000, but only if you produce **between 0 and 100,000 units**.

___G___ 12. A cost function shows **variable costs/ unit that decrease** as activity increases.

___D___ 13. You are **interested in knowing** how much your parents are spending on **your sister's wedding**.

___Q___ 14. You could buy a 10-pack of pencils for **10¢ each**, but in a 20-pack, they cost **8¢ each**.

___F___ 15. You decided to skip work and go to the movies, and **the movie cost $9.**

___M___ 16. You decided to skip work and go to the movies, and you **could have earned $40 in tips**.

___U___ 17. You **spent** $100 on food last week, when you could have eaten at your parents' house.

___P___ 18. You spent 2 hours building your first model, but you spent **90% as many hours** on your next one.

___R___ 19. You spent 300 hours studying for cost accounting the first time you took it but this time you only spent 90% as many hours; **ln(0.9)/ln(2)**

___V___ 20. Your parents are going to spend **$12/ person for the food at** your sister's wedding.

___H___ 21. Your parents are going to spend **$4,000 to rent the hall** for your sister's wedding.

CHAPTER REVIEW: Learning Objectives 3 - 7

Q3: What process is used to estimate future costs?

Before cost estimation begins, one must first know the cost object and the purpose for estimating the cost. If the cost itself is not relevant to the decision at hand, then the cost should not be estimated, of course. When estimating discretionary costs, past costs might be not be helpful in predicting future costs. If it is determined that past costs will be helpful in estimating the costs, then we estimate the past cost function, and update it for changes that we know about, using the techniques described in learning objectives 4 through 6.

Q4: How are engineered estimates, account analysis, and two-point methods used to estimate cost functions?

There are 3 categories of methods discussed in this section of the text that can be used to estimate cost functions.

- The *engineered estimate of cost* method uses engineers and accountants to analyze the activities necessary to produce the product or service whose cost is being estimated, determine the cost behavior of each activity, and measure the costs of each activity.

- The *account analysis* method uses a review of the costs in the accounting system over time to determine whether the cost is fixed, variable, or mixed. If the cost is mixed, then either a two-point method or regression analysis can be used to separate the fixed and variable cost components.

- In the *two-point method*, any two observations of the cost and its associated level of activity are used to separate the fixed and variable components of a mixed cost. The *high-low method* is a two-point method where the two data points used are the observations with the highest and the lowest levels of activity. Two-point methods are often inaccurate because they use only two data points, even if more information is available.

Demonstration problem-Two-point method

Bill's Bracelets, a jewelry store, wants to estimate its cost function. Bill tells you that last January they sold 1,100 bracelets and total costs were $192,000. In April they sold 1,500 bracelets and total costs were $240,000. Determine the total fixed costs and the variable cost per bracelet sold for Bill.

Solution to demonstration problem

First estimate the variable cost per bracelet sold, using the formula for the slope of a linear equation:

Slope = rise/run = increase in total costs/increase in activity
= [$240,000 - $192,000]/[1,500 bracelets – 1,100 bracelets]
= $48,000/400 bracelets
= $120/bracelet = variable cost per bracelet.

Next, use either of the two data points to determine the total fixed costs, using a linear cost function:

Total costs = total fixed costs + [variable cost per bracelet] x [# bracelets]
$192,000 = total fixed costs + [$120/bracelet] x [1,100 bracelets]
$192,000 = total fixed costs + $132,000, so total fixed costs = $60,000.

Q5: How does a scatter plot assist with categorizing a cost?

Scatter plots help identify cost behavior when there is only one cost driver. In the scatter plots below, the y axis is total cost and the x axis is the number of units produced. The scatter plots below indicate several examples. The dotted line represents the assumed relationship between total costs and units produced.

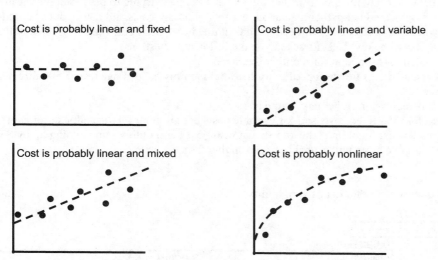

Cost is probably linear and fixed

Cost is probably linear and variable

Cost is probably linear and mixed

Cost is probably nonlinear

Q6: How is regression analysis used to estimate a mixed cost function?

Regression analysis is an arithmetical method for finding the "line of best fit" and is easily performed using many different software packages, including Excel. In simple regression, there is only one X variable (cost driver) and the software output provides an estimate for the intercept (total fixed costs) and the slope (variable costs per unit of the cost driver). The output also provides statistical information as to the goodness of fit for the line as well as the statistical significance of the estimated intercept and slope coefficients.

SUMMARY OUTPUT

Regression Statistics

Multiple R	0.84127
R Square	0.707736
Adjusted R Square	0.701647
Standard Error	1409.37
Observations	50

	Coefficients	Standard Error	t Stat	P-value
Intercept	26956.8457	468.54324	57.53331	0.000021
Units	0.25960981	0.0240798	10.78123	0.06189

In the partial regression output from Excel on the left, there were 50 observations of total manufacturing costs and the units produced. The line of best fit has an intercept of 26,956.85 and a slope of 0.2596. That is, the estimated cost function is:

Total mfg costs = $26,957 + [$0.2596/unit] x [# units].

The adjusted *R* Square measures the line's goodness of fit. It shows the percentage of variation in the Y observations explained by the regression line. Here, 70.16% of this variation is explained; this is also called the *explanatory power* of the model. The *t*-statistics, and the *p*-values, measure the statistical significance of the two coefficients. In general, a *t*-statistic greater than 2 or a *p*-value less than 5% (or maybe 10% for some decision makers) indicates that the estimated coefficients are statistically significantly different from zero.

Running a regression using Excel is very easy, and the demonstration problem below concentrates on interpreting the output.

Demonstration problem-Simple regression
Deanna's Dishes makes serving platters from sterling silver. Deanna is trying to plan total overhead costs for next year. You helped her gather data about her total monthly costs and direct labor hours for the last year, and you regressed total monthly costs against the direct labor hours used for the month. The regression output is shown below. Deanna asked you the following questions:
a) What is her estimated cost function for monthly overhead?
b) What does the estimated cost function predict for her total monthly costs if she uses 5,500 direct labor hours in a month?
c) How well does this regression fit her past cost data?
d) Are the estimates for total fixed costs and for variable costs per DL hours statistically significant?
e) What is the estimated cost function if she knows that next year her monthly rent is going up by $3,000 and that her variable costs will probably be 5% higher than last year?

Required:
Answer Deanna's questions to the best of your ability.

SUMMARY OUTPUT

Regression Statistics					
Multiple R	0.9931				
R Square	0.9863		Standard		
Adjusted R Square	0.9849	Coefficients	Error	t Stat	P-value
Standard Error	5101.2	Intercept	91034	3139.578	28.99564	5.5493E-11
Observations	12	DL Hours	11.433	0.426585	26.80222	1.2075E-10

Solution to demonstration problem
a) The estimated cost function is:
    Total monthly overhead costs = $91,034 + [$11.433/DL hour] x [# DL hours].
b) If Deanna uses 5,500 DL hours in a month, then total monthly overhead costs are estimated as:
    Total monthly overhead costs = $91,034 + [$11.433/DL hour] x [5,500 DL hours]
        = $91,034 + $62,882 = $153,916.
c) The explanatory power of this model is 98.49%, which is really excellent. You explain to Deanna that, for cost estimation, an explanatory power of 70% is often considered a reasonably good fit.
d) First you need to explain to Deanna that Excel uses scientific notation for very small numbers. For example, 1.3E-5 is 1.3×10^{-5}, or 0.000013. A p-value less than 0.05 is generally used to indicate that the coefficient is statistically significant. Given the very low p-values for the estimate of fixed costs and for the estimate of variable costs per DL hour, both coefficients can be considered highly statistically significant.
e) The regression equation was based on past costs, but can be adapted because Deanna has a good estimates of expected changes in total monthly fixed costs and her variable costs per DL hour. The revised estimated cost function is:
    Total monthly overhead costs = $91,034 + [$12.005/DL hour] x [# DL hours], where
        12.005 = 1.05 x 11.433.

Sometimes it is appropriate to use more than one cost driver. Regression analysis with more than one cost driver is called *multiple regression analysis*. For a discussion of multiple regression analysis and other issues in using regression to estimate cost functions, refer to Appendix 2A of the text.

Q7: What are the uses and limitations of future cost estimates?

Managers need to estimate future costs for routine planning purposes as well as for non-routine decisions. However, they need to remember that the estimates they use are just that; the future is, of course, unknown. There may be additional uncertainties about the estimates of future costs because:

- managers may have misclassified the cost behavior, or

- an inappropriate cost driver may have been chosen, or

- cost behavior in the future may not mimic cost behavior in the past, or

- the past cost information used to estimate the future costs may have been inappropriate or contained errors, or

- information from outside the accounting system may have been used, introducing another set of concerns about the quality of the information used to estimate future costs.

PROBLEM SET B (Learning Objectives 3 - 7)

Before answering the questions in this problem set, review the terms listed in Guide Your Learning (GYL) 2.5 in the text. Check your answers against the solutions at the end of this study guide chapter.

<u>True-False</u>: Indicate whether each of the following is true (T) or false (F) in the space provided.

_____ 1. The engineered estimate of cost method of estimating costs includes an analysis of the activities necessary to produce the final product or to render the service.

_____ 2. The high-low method of estimating a cost function is an example of a two-point method.

_____ 3. A scatter plot shows the estimated cost for various levels of activity.

_____ 4. A two-point method of estimating a cost function is more free of uncertainty because it uses only two data points for past costs.

_____ 5. Multiple regression analysis is a procedure for estimating more than one cost function at time.

_____ 6. Both simple and multiple regression estimate a single cost function.

_____ 7. The account analysis method of estimating costs can be used with either a two-point method or regression analysis when estimating a cost function.

_____ 8. The high-low method may mis-estimate costs because it uses outliers in the calculations to separate a mixed cost into its fixed and variable components.

_____ 9. If future cost behavior will mimic past cost behavior, then using past costs to estimate the future cost function should be free from uncertainty.

_____ 10. A *p*-value of 92% for the intercept term in a simple regression means that it is likely the company doesn't have any fixed costs.

<u>Matching</u>: Match each term with its definition by writing the appropriate letter in the space provided. If you get any wrong, go back to GYL 2.5 to locate a page reference for the term's definition in the text. Use each term only once.

List of Terms		
A. Adjusted *R*-square	F. High-low method	K. Engineered estimate of cost
B. *p*-value	G. Two-point method	L. Account analysis method
C. *t*-statistic	H. Scatter plot	M. Average cost
D. Simple regression	I. Intercept	N. Cost function
E. Multiple regression	J. Slope	

<u>Definitions</u>

_____ 1. A statistical procedure for estimating a cost function with one cost driver.

_____ 2. A graphical display of the observations of past costs and past cost driver levels.

_____ 3. A method of separating a mixed cost into its fixed and variable components that uses total costs at the highest and lowest volume levels.

_____ 4. A method of estimating cost of a cost object that analyzes the activities necessary to produce the cost object.

_____ 5. In the results from a regression analysis used to estimate a cost function, this is interpreted as total fixed costs.

_____ 6. In general, if this is larger than 2, you can be confident that the true coefficient being estimated is not zero.

_____ 7. In the results from a regression analysis used to estimate a cost function, this is interpreted as variable costs per unit of the cost driver.

_____ 8. A method of separating a mixed cost into its fixed and variable components that uses any two observations of total costs.

_____ 9. This shows the goodness of fit for a regression equation.

_____ 10. A method of determining past cost behavior that is used before a two-point method or regression analysis.

_____ 11. An algebraic expression that shows how total costs change as the cost driver changes.

_____ 12. This shows the probability that the true coefficient being estimated is equal to zero.

_____ 13. A statistical procedure for estimating a cost function with more than one cost driver.

_____ 14. This is the fixed cost per unit of the cost driver combined with the variable cost per unit of the cost driver.

END OF CHAPTER EXERCISES

<u>Multiple Choice</u>: Write the letter that represents the best choice in the space provided.

_____ 1. Fixed costs
   a. do not vary in total within the relevant range
   b. do not vary on a per-unit basis within the relevant range
   c. vary on a per-unit basis in direct proportion to changes in the cost driver within the relevant range
   d. vary in total as the cost driver changes within the relevant range

_____ 2. Variable costs
   a. do not vary in total within the relevant range
   b. do not vary on a per-unit basis within the relevant range
   c. vary on a per-unit basis within the relevant range
   d. both (a) and (c)

_____ 3. The approach least likely to be used to estimate overhead costs is
   a. account analysis method
   b. engineered estimate of costs
   c. a two-point method
   d. a scatterplot

_____ 4. Which of the following could be defined as a cost object?
   a. a single unit of product in a manufacturing process
   b. a batch of products in a manufacturing process
   c. a business process, such as managing accounts receivable
   d. all of the above could be defined as cost objects

_____ 5. Which of the following statements is false?
   a. A cost can be defined as a direct cost if the bookkeeping system can keep track of how much of the cost was consumed by the cost object.
   b. Whether a cost is direct or indirect cannot be determined until the cost object has been defined.
   c. If the cost object is a batch of 1,000 units of production, then factory property taxes could be a direct cost if the bookkeeping system is detailed enough.
   d. Some indirect costs might have been considered direct costs if a company had better technology for capturing information.

_____ 6. The total cost of salaries of production supervisors, where 2 supervisors are needed for each 8-hour shift, where the relevant range is 0 units to the number of units that can be produced at full capacity using 2 8-hour shifts is a
   a. fixed cost
   b. variable cost
   c. piecewise linear cost
   d. stepwise linear cost

_____ 7. The total cost of materials, where the supplier charges $9/lb if 0-1,000 pounds are purchased, $8/lb if 1,001-2,000 pounds are purchased and $7 if 2,001 or more pounds are purchased, is a
   a. mixed cost
   b. variable cost
   c. piecewise linear cost
   d. stepwise linear cost

_____ 8. The rent on a store, where the landlord charges $1,200 per month plus a percentage of sales revenue, is a
   a. fixed cost
   b. variable cost
   c. mixed cost
   d. stepwise linear cost

_____ 9. The depreciation on a factory machine is a
   a. fixed cost
   b. variable cost
   c. mixed cost
   d. stepwise linear cost

_____ 10. Which of the following statements is true?
   a. Opportunity costs are never relevant for decision making.
   b. Discretionary costs are never relevant for decision making.
   c. Marginal costs are never relevant for decision making.
   d. Sunk costs are never relevant for decision making.

_____ 11. If firm A has a learning curve with 90% learning and firm B has a learning curve with 80% learning, then
   a. firm A has more experienced workers
   b. firm B will be more cost efficient over time
   c. firm A workers learn more quickly
   d. firm B has less experienced workers

_____ 12. A firm's production is expected to show an 85% learning rate. The first unit took 200 hours to produce. The second unit will take
   a. 170 hours
   b. 140 hours
   c. 200 hours
   d. 289 hours

_____ 13. A high adjusted *R*-square for the regression of a cost against a cost driver
   a. indicates that the predicted linear relationship between the cost and the cost driver is probably correct
   b. indicates that the relationship between the cost and the cost driver is probably linear
   c. indicates that the cost driver explains a high percentage of the variation of the cost
   d. indicates that the cost driver is statistically significant

_____ 14. A *p*-value of 1% for the intercept term in a regression of a cost driver against a cost
   a. indicates that the true fixed costs are statistically significantly different from zero
   b. indicates that there is only a 1% chance the true fixed costs are zero
   c. indicates that the variable costs are immaterial in this cost function
   d. both (a) and (b)

_____ 15. A *p*-value of 89% for the slope coefficient in a regression of a cost driver against a cost
   a. indicates that the true variable costs are statistically significantly different from zero
   b. indicates that there is only an 11% chance the true variable costs are zero
   c. indicates that the relationship between the cost and the cost driver is nonlinear
   d. none of the above

_____ 16. The difference between simple regression and multiple regression is that
   a. simple regression is easier to do in Excel than multiple regression
   b. simple regression is only performed once when estimating a cost function, whereas multiple regression is performed more than once
   c. simple regression uses only one cost driver but multiple regression uses more than one cost driver
   d. simple regression is for estimating only one cost and multiple regression is for estimating more than one cost

_____ 17. A regression of total selling expenses against number of units sold yields an intercept of 178,024 and a slope of 12.3. This indicates that
   a. total fixed selling expenses are predicted to be $178,024.
   b. variable selling expenses are predicted to be $12.30/unit.
   c. total selling expenses are predicted to be $190,324 when 1,000 units are sold
   d. all of the above

<u>Exercises</u>: Write your answer in the space provided.
1. Willis Widgets, Inc. is trying to estimate its overhead cost function, and believes that machine hours is a good cost driver for total overhead costs. You are given observations of total overhead cost and total machine hours for the first 8 months of this year.

Machine hours	Total Cost
180	$5,680
210	$6,090
590	$11,400
550	$10,310
420	$8,720
340	$7,650
100	$3,210
470	$9,330

a) Draw a scatter plot for these 8 observations.

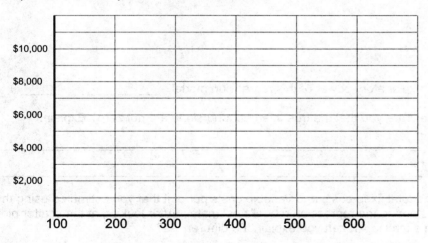

b) Use the high-low method to estimate the cost function _____

c) If Willis expects 600 machine hours in September, what is your estimate of total overhead costs for that month? _____

2. Suppose you used a software package such as Excel to regress total overhead costs against machine hours for Willis Widgets from exercise #1 on the prior page. The partial output is shown below.

SUMMARY OUTPUT

Regression Statistics	
Multiple R	0.987581
R Square	0.975315
Adjusted R Square	0.971201
Standard Error	457.8638
Observations	8

	Coefficients	Standard Error	t Stat	P-value
Intercept	2515.393	379.4092	6.629763	0.00056781
Machine hours	14.77862	0.959838	15.397	4.7444E-06

a) What is the estimated cost function? _____

b) If Willis expects 600 machine hours in September, what is your estimate of total overhead costs for that month? _____

c) What is the explanatory power of this regression model? _____

d) How confident are you that the true intercept and slope are not zero? Explain.

_____

_____

e) Compare the total fixed costs and variable costs per unit that you estimated using the high-low method to the regression model's estimates. After looking at the scatter plot you drew in exercise #1, can you explain the differences?

_____

_____

_____

_____

_____

_____

3. Trudy's Tables just designed a new granite-topped table with a center for condiments that spins. The first table took Trudy's craftsmen 60 hours to produce. Trudy believes that the percent of learning will be 78%.

   a) Plot the points on the learning curve for the first eight tables produced. Use the table below the graph for your computations.

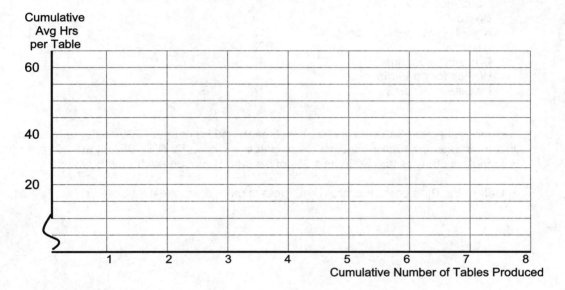

Computations:

X	r	X^r	$Y=\alpha X^r$
1			
2			
3			
4			
5			
6			
7			
8			

   b) Suppose Trudy's craftsmen make $25 per hour. Predict the total direct labor costs for

   producing 8 tables. _____

4. Bill's BBQ Beef sells sandwiches in a stall in the local commuter train station. Bill is interested in planning for the future and would like to estimate a cost function for his business. He has done some preliminary work trying to determine his costs, and he gives you the following information about his costs last month:

Beef	$360
Condiments	36
Bread	54
Napkin/plasticware packages	18
Rent	920
Carry-out containers	45
Wages for part time help	700
I ♥ Bill's BBQ pins	14
	$2,147

Last month he sold 300 sandwiches for $8 each and he counted 200 customers. Each customer gets one napkin/plasticware package and one "I ♥ Bill's BBQ" lapel pin per order. His landlord charges him $800 plus 5% of his sales revenue each month.

a) Determine Bill's cost function. (Hint: there is more than one cost driver.)

Total costs = _____

b) Discuss the types of uncertainties that could be in the data Bill gave you and how you might go about trying to reduce the uncertainty.

_____

_____

_____

_____

_____

_____

_____

_____

SOLUTION TO PROBLEM SET A

<u>Exercises</u>:
1.   α = 80 and percent of learning = 85%.
     r = ln(% learning)/ln(2) = -0.16252/0.693147 = -0.23447
     Y = cumulative average hours = 80 x (50)$^{-0.23447}$ = 31.9699 hours per playground. If X = 50,
          the total number of hours to produce 50 playgrounds = 50 x 31.9699 = 1,598.5 hours

2.   Matching graphs and cost descriptions

     1. G
     2. B
     3. C
     4. A
     5. E
     6. D
     7. F
     8. H

<u>Matching</u>:

     1. C   L is a good choice here as well. The bold highlights the computation of the
              cost, so C is even better.
     2. A   This is the definition of cost behavior.
     3. B   The highlight indicates a measure of activity, not a cost.
     4. O   Of course I is also correct here but the bold highlights indicate that we are
              interested in an indirect cost within a factory. H is also correct here but not
              the best answer because the highlighting of "cost object" indicates we are
              interested in how a cost is assigned to a cost object more than the cost
              behavior.
     5. I   I is the best answer because it refers to an indirect cost that is not a
              manufacturing cost. Again, H is also correct but the "cost object" highlighting
              shows that we are more interested in how a cost is assigned to a cost object
              than the cost behavior.
     6. E   The highlighting of "cost object" indicates that we are interested in how a
              cost is assigned to a cost object.
     7. L   L is a good choice here, especially since a measure of activity (# of meals
              eaten in the cafeteria) is mentioned.
     8. K   This is the definition of marginal cost.
     9. J   This is the definition of a learning curve.
     10. T   The highlighted portion of the description draws your attention to the fact
              that there are ranges of the cost driver, and the cost description states that
              the cost is fixed at different levels for these ranges.

Solutions to matching questions continued on next page

11. S The highlighted section of the description shows that the fixed cost behavior is only valid within a range of the cost driver, and the cost description portion is not highlighted.

12. G This is basically the definition of economies of scale.

13. D A cost object is anything for which you wish to determine total costs.

14. Q The highlighted portion draws your attention to a variable cost per unit that is constant for one range of the cost driver and is constant at a different level for another range of the cost driver.

15. F You didn't have to spend the $9 on the movie, did you?

16. M So it seems the movie really cost you $49, didn't it? Hope it was a good one!

17. U The bold word shows that the expenditure was in the past.

18. P This is the definition for percent of learning.

19. R This is the definition of the rate of learning index. Sure cost accounting would be easier a second time, but with good study habits you can make it through the first time!

20. V You may think the answer is F, because you think that of all expenditures on your sister's wedding. But the highlighted portion of the description indicates a cost that is constant per person (apparently no matter how many people are invited).

21. H This expenditure is constant at $4,000, no matter how many people are invited, within reason (i.e. within the relevant range).

SOLUTION TO PROBLEM SET B

True-False:

1. T

2. T

3. F No, a scatter plot shows the actual past cost for various levels of actual past activity.

4. F The fact that only 2 data points are used is a disadvantage of a two-point method.

5. F No, there is only one dependent variable (the Y) no matter how many X variables are used.

6. T

7. T The account analysis method helps determine cost behavior and then another method is used to separate mixed costs into their fixed and variable components.

8. T Yes, by definition the high-low method is using observations at the extreme ends of the range for the cost driver.

9. F There are more types of uncertainty than whether past cost behavior will mimic future cost behavior.

10. T A *p*-value of 92% indicates that there's a 92% probability that the true intercept is actually zero.

Matching:

1. D
2. H
3. F
4. K
5. I
6. C
7. J
8. G
9. A
10. L
11. N
12. B
13. E
14. M

END OF CHAPTER EXERCISES

Multiple Choice:

1. A
2. B
3. B   The engineered estimate of cost method analyzes the activities in a process and it is more likely to be used to estimate the direct costs of producing a product.
4. D   Even your sister's wedding!
5. C   There are some costs that could never be considered direct costs, no matter how detailed the bookkeeping system.
6. D
7. C
8. C
9. A
10. D
11. B   Firm B workers learn faster because each unit only takes 80% of the time it took to produce the prior unit.
12. A   85% times 200 hours
13. C   A high adjusted *R*-square does not indicate the linear relationship is "probably correct".
14. D   A *p*-value of 1% on the intercept means that there is a 1% probability that the true intercept is zero.
15. D   A *p*-value of 89% on the slope coefficient means that there is an 89% probability that the true slope is zero.
16. C
17. D   Total costs = $178,024 + ($12.30/units) x (1,000 units sold)

Exercises:

1. a)

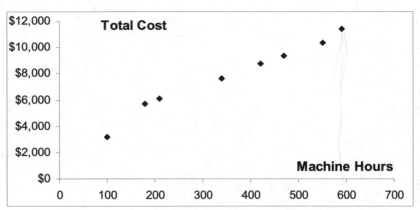

b) The high observation is the total cost at 590 machine hours and the low observation is the total cost at 100 machine hours.

First estimate the variable cost per machine hour, using the formula for the slope of a linear equation:
Slope = rise/run = increase in total costs/increase in activity
= [$11,400 - $3,210]/[590 machine hours – 100 machine hours]
= $8,190/490 machine hours
= $16.71/machine hour = variable cost per machine hour.

Next, use either of the two data points to determine the total fixed costs, using a linear cost function:
Total costs = total fixed costs + [variable cost per machine hour] x [# machine hours]
$3,210 = total fixed costs + [$16.71/machine hour] x [100 machine hours]
$3,210 = total fixed costs + $1,671
$1,539 = total fixed costs.

c) Total costs = $1,539 + [16.71/machine hour] x [600 machine hours] = $11,565

2. a) Total costs = $2,515 + [$14.78/machine hour] x [# machine hours]

b) Total costs = $2,515 + [$14.78/machine hour] x [600 machine hours] = $11,383

c) The adjusted *R*-square is 97.12%.

d) The *p*-value on the slope and intercept coefficients are very low, much lower than 5%, so I am extremely confident that the true intercept and slope are not zero.

e) The high low method computed a lower intercept and a higher slope than the regression method because it uses only the two extreme points for machine hours. The regression method uses all that data points to estimate the line. In this case the costs associated with the low volume for machine hours were a bit low compared to the line that we might draw through the data points, and the costs associated with the high volume for machine hours were a bit high compared to the line that we might draw. This brought the intercept for the high-low method down and the slope up. It explains why the estimated fixed costs and variable costs per machine hour are different and why the estimated total costs per period are different.

3.   a)

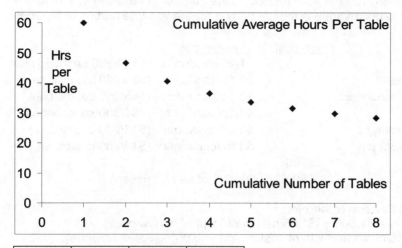

X	r	X^r	$Y=\alpha X^r$
1	-0.3585	1.000	60.00
2	-0.3585	0.780	46.80
3	-0.3585	0.674	40.47
4	-0.3585	0.608	36.50
5	-0.3585	0.562	33.70
6	-0.3585	0.526	31.57
7	-0.3585	0.498	29.87
8	-0.3585	0.475	28.47

b) Total time for making 8 tables = 28.47/table times 8 tables = 227.8 hours. At $25/hr, the predicted direct labor cost for 8 tables = $25/hour x 227.8 hours = $5,695.

4.   a) The beef, condiments, buns, and containers are variable with respect to the number of sandwiches prepared and sold. The napkin/plasticware packages and the "I ♥ Bill's BBQ" pins are variable with respect to the number of customers. The rent is a mixed cost, and sales revenue is the cost driver for the variable portion of the rent.

	Fixed cost	Variable cost	
Beef		$1.20/sandwich	($360/300 sandwiches)
Condiments		$0.12/sandwich	($36/300 sandwiches)
Carry-out containers		$0.15/sandwich	($45/300 sandwiches)
Bread		$0.18/sandwich	($54/300 sandwiches)
Napkin packages		$0.09/customer	($18/200 customers)
I ♥ Bill's BBQ pin		$0.07/customer	($14/200 customers)
Salaries	$700		
Rent	$800	$0.05/$ of sales	(given)

Bill's cost function is therefore:
Total costs = $1,500 + [$1.65/sandwich] x [# of sandwiches]
   + [$0.16/customer] x [# of customers] + [0.05] x [Sales revenue].

Of course, you may have determined that the variable portion of the rent is 5% x $8/sandwich, or $0.40/sandwich. This is perfectly fine. In this case you would have written your cost function as:

Total costs = $1,500 + [$1.87/sandwich] x [# of sandwiches]
   + [$0.16/customer] x [# of customers].

   b) It seems pretty clear that Bill has some fixed costs, some costs that vary with respect to the number of customers, and some costs that vary with respect to the number of sandwiches served. It may seem as if the only uncertainty is whether the costs will remain the same. However, there are other additional uncertainties, many of which involve the way the data was collected. To resolve these uncertainties, you should ask Bill the following questions:
   - Was last month a typical month?
   - Are the salaries really fixed or does he use hourly workers according to how busy the sandwich shop is?
   - Do any of the sandwich ingredients spoil, and, if so, was the spoilage last month about in proportion to the number of sandwiches served in other months?
   - Is he sure that only one pin and only one napkin/plasticware package is given to each customer?
   - Does Bill or any of his employees eat sandwiches while working at the shop?
   - Does he only serve one type of sandwich? If not, can he determine costs by type of sandwich and the number of each type of sandwich served?
   - Will the proportions of good and beverages remain the same as weather and seasons change?

Chapter 3

Cost-Volume-Profit Analysis

√ **Study Checklist – Monitor your progress**

☐ 1. Read the chapter in the text
☐ 2. Review the learning objectives below
☐ 3. Read the overview of the chapter
☐ 4. Read the chapter review for learning objectives 1, 2 & 4
☐ 5. Do Problem Set A and check your answers
☐ 6. Read the chapter review for learning objective 3
☐ 7. Do Problem Set B and check your answers
☐ 8. Read the chapter review for learning objectives 5 & 6
☐ 9. Do Problem Set C and check your answers
☐ 10. Do the End of Chapter Exercises in this study guide
☐ 11. Do the homework assigned by your instructor

CHAPTER LEARNING OBJECTIVES

After studying this chapter, you should be able to answer the following questions:

Q1. What is cost-volume-profit (CVP) analysis, and how is it used for decision making?
Q2. How are CVP calculations performed for a single product?
Q3. How are CVP calculations performed for multiple products?
Q4. What is the breakeven point?
Q5. What assumptions and limitations should managers consider when using CVP analysis?
Q6. How are the margin of safety and operating leverage used to assess operational risk?

OVERVIEW OF CHAPTER

Future revenues, expenses, and profits are estimated so that managers can plan and monitor operations. CVP analysis is used to help plan operations and evaluate decisions such as possible changes in selling prices or cost structure. Additionally, CVP analysis can be used to help assess operational risk. This chapter relies heavily on the cost behavior concepts learned in Chapter 2.

CHAPTER REVIEW: Learning Objectives 1, 2 & 4

Q1&4: What is CVP analysis and how is it used for decision making? What is the breakeven point?

- *CVP analysis* helps determine the effects on profit of changes in sales volumes, selling prices, fixed costs, and variable costs.

- A *CVP graph* has dollars on the y-axis and a measure of activity (usually units sold) on the x-axis. There are two lines shown on a CVP graph: a total revenue line and a total cost line.

- The *breakeven point* is the level of activity where revenues equal costs and profits are zero.

- The *contribution margin* is total revenues less total variable costs.

- *Profit* is total revenues less total costs, or contribution margin less total fixed costs. The text uses the term profit to mean pretax profit.

- The *contribution margin per unit* is selling price per unit less variable costs per unit. The contribution margin per unit shows how much of a unit's selling price is left (after variable costs per unit are covered) to contribute to fixed costs if a company is operating before the breakeven point. If a company is operating past the breakeven point, the contribution margin per unit shows how much of a unit's selling price contributes to profit after variable costs per unit are covered.

- The *contribution margin ratio* is contribution margin over total revenues. It can also be computed as contribution margin per unit over selling price per unit. The contribution margin ratio shows the percentage of a unit's selling price that contributes to covering fixed costs (or to profits, if a company is operating past the breakeven point).

- CVP analysis can be used to:

    o determine the sales levels, both in units and dollars, that are required to break even or achieve other targeted profit levels.

    o compare alternative cost structures or selling prices.

    o assess the feasibility of planned operations.

    o determine the effect on profit of changes in activity, costs, or selling prices.

    o assess the risk associated with alternatives.

- The *indifference point* between two alternatives is the level of activity where the profits of the two alternatives are equal.

Q2: How are CVP calculations performed for a single product?

The following abbreviations are used in the CVP analysis formulas:

- F = total fixed costs
- P = selling price per unit
- V = variable cost per unit
- CM = contribution margin
- CMR = contribution margin ratio
- Q = the number of units required to achieve target
- BEP = breakeven point

To determine the number of units required to achieve a targeted pretax profit level, use the following formula:

$$Q = \frac{F + \text{Profit}}{CM \text{ per unit}}, \text{ where CM per unit} = P - V.$$

To determine the revenues needed to achieve a targeted pretax profit level, use the following formula:

$$Q = \frac{F + \text{Profit}}{CMR}, \text{ where } CMR = \frac{P - V}{P} = \frac{CM}{\text{Total revenue}} = \frac{\text{Total revenue - Total variable costs}}{\text{Total revenue}}$$

To locate the breakeven point in either units or revenues, use the appropriate formula and set the target pretax profit to zero. If the desired target profit is stated as an after-tax profit, simply convert the after-tax profit to a pretax profit using the formula below:

$$\text{Pretax profit} = \frac{\text{After-tax profit}}{(1 - \text{Tax rate})}.$$

Demonstration problem-CVP analysis and graph

Ted's Toy Trucks makes an electric pick-up that is meant to be driven by toddlers. Ted's total fixed costs are \$124,000 and the variable costs per unit are \$60. The trucks sell for \$100.

a) Compute the number of units required to break even.

b) Compute the revenues required to break even.

c) Compute the number of units required to achieve a \$35,000 pretax profit.

d) Compute the revenues required to achieve a \$35,000 after-tax profit if the tax rate is 30%.

e) If Ted plans on operating at his full capacity of 5,000 units and desires a pretax profit of \$150,000, what is the highest amount that variable costs per unit can be so that he can still meet his goal?

f) Draw a CVP graph, making sure to label each line, each axis, and each value where a line intersects an axis. Circle the breakeven point on the graph, and note the BEP in revenues and units on the axes.

g) Suppose that Ted has an opportunity to invest in a high-technology production process. If he does, total fixed costs will be \$200,000 and variable costs per unit will drop to \$44. Compute the indifference point between these two alternatives.

Solution to demonstration problem

a) First, compute the CM per unit. CM per unit = $100 - $60 = $40. Then,

$$\text{the BEP in units} = Q = \frac{\$124,000 + \$0}{\$40} = 3,100 \text{ units.}$$

b) First, compute the CMR. CMR = $40/$100 = 40%. Then,

$$\text{the BEP in revenues} = \frac{\$124,000 + \$0}{40\%} = \$310,000.$$

> *(Note that this is equal to the BEP in units times the selling price per unit. However, you should still know the BEP in revenue formula because sometimes the given information is structured so that you cannot compute the BEP in units.)*

c) The # of units required to achieve target pretax profit = $Q = \dfrac{\$124,000 + \$35,000}{\$40} = 3,975 \text{ units.}$

d) First, compute the pretax profit required to achieve the after-tax profit.

Pretax profit = $35,000/(1 – 0.3) = $50,000. Then,

$$\text{The revenues required to achieve target pretax profit} = Q = \frac{\$124,000 + \$50,000}{40\%} = \$435,000.$$

e) To solve this, you can use the CVP formula in units, set Q = 5,000 and solve for V:

$$Q = 5,000 \text{ units} = \frac{\$124,000 + \$150,000}{\$100 - V} ; \$100 - V = \frac{\$274,000}{5,000 \text{ units}} = \$54.80/\text{unit}; V = \$45.20/\text{unit}$$

Ted must find a way to decrease variable cost per unit to $45.20 in order to achieve his goal.

f)

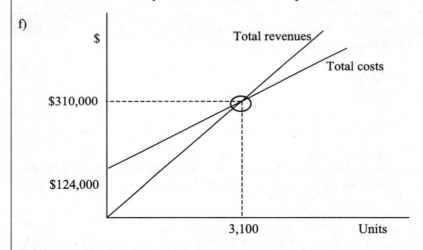

g) Recall that profit can be computed as the contribution margin per unit times the number of units sold less total fixed costs. The current alternative has a profit function = $40Q - $124,000, where Q is the number of units produced and sold. The proposed, high-technology alternative has a profit function = $56Q - $200,000. To determine the indifference point in unit, set the two profit equations equal and solve for Q.

$$\$40Q - \$124,000 = \$56Q - \$200,000$$
$$\$16Q = \$76,000$$
$$Q = 4,750 \text{ units.}$$

PROBLEM SET A (Learning Objectives 1, 2 & 4) Before answering the questions in this problem set, review the terms listed in Guide Your Learning (GYL) 3.1 in the text.

Matching: Match each term with the **most appropriate** definition or example by writing the appropriate letter in the space provided. You may use each term more than once.

A. Cost-volume-profit analysis	E. Breakeven point
B. Contribution margin	F. Cost-volume-profit graph
C. Contribution margin per unit	G. Profit
D. Contribution margin ratio	H. Total fixed costs

_____ 1. This equals the contribution margin at the breakeven point.

_____ 2. This equals zero at the breakeven point.

_____ 3. This can be used to plan operations and compare alternatives.

_____ 4. This shows the total revenue and total costs over a range of activity.

_____ 5. This shows the percentage of a unit's selling price that contributes to covering fixed costs if a company is operating before the breakeven point.

_____ 6. This equals total revenue less total costs.

_____ 7. This can be computed in terms of units or total revenue.

_____ 8. This equals total revenue less total variable costs.

_____ 9. This equals contribution margin over total revenue.

_____ 10. This equals profits plus total fixed costs.

_____ 11. This equals selling price per unit less variable cost per unit.

Multiple choice: Write the letter that represents the best choice in the space provided.

_____ 1. Stuart, Inc. produces one item, which sells for $2.40 and costs $1.40 per unit make. All manufacturing costs are variable. If fixed selling and administrative expenses total $140,000, how many units must be sold in order to break even?
  a. 100,000
  b. 140,000
  c. 58,333
  d. none of the above

_____ 2. The Jean Company expects sales of $500,000 and total variable costs of $200,000 in 2005. Total budgeted fixed costs are $180,000. What is the breakeven volume in sales dollars?
  a. $450,000
  b. $300,000
  c. $360,000
  d. none of the above

_____ 3. MacDonald Oil Co. expects sales of $1,000,000 and total variable costs of $600,000 for 2005. Total budgeted fixed costs are $200,000. What is the dollar amount of sales necessary to achieve pretax profits of $400,000?
   a. $2,000,000
   b. $1,200,000
   c. $1,500,000
   d. $1,000,000

_____ 4. The Martinez Game Co. produces and sells parlor games. In 2005 sales were $400,000, total variable costs were $200,000, and total fixed costs were $150,000. What is the total revenue required to <u>increase</u> pretax profits by $40,000 and to cover an expected increase of $20,000 in fixed costs?
   a. $300,000
   b. $400,000
   c. $480,000
   d. $520,000

_____ 5. The breakeven sales volume of the Patin Co. is $800,000. If the variable cost per unit increases next year, then the new breakeven point will be
   a. the same
   b. higher
   c. lower
   d. unable to determine from the given information

_____ 6. The breakeven sales volume of the Tuck Co. is 800,000 units. If the variable cost per unit increases by $1.50 and the selling price per unit increases by $2.00 next year, then the new breakeven point will be
   a. the same
   b. higher
   c. lower
   d. unable to determine from the given information

_____ 7. The contribution margin ratio of Yoshi enterprises is 60%. If total fixed costs are $200,000, then what is the total cost of producing and selling $1,000,000 of Yoshi's product?
   a. $600,000
   b. $400,000
   c. $900,000
   d. none of the above

_____ 8. The breakeven point occurs when
   a. sales equal fixed costs plus contribution margin
   b. total variable costs equal total contribution margin
   c. fixed costs plus profit equals sales
   d. total costs equal total revenue

_____ 9. If the selling price per unit and the variable cost per unit both increase by 5%, what is the effect on the contribution margin per unit and on the contribution margin ratio?

	Contribution margin per unit	Contribution margin ratio
a.	increase	increase
b.	increase	no effect
c.	decrease	no effect
d.	decrease	increase

_____ 10. Harvey Enterprises expects sales of $1,000,000 and total variable costs of $250,000 for 2005. Total budgeted fixed costs are $200,000. What is the dollar amount of sales necessary to achieve after-tax profits of $700,000 if the tax rate is 30%?
- a. $1,200,000
- b. $1,600,000
- c. $3,377,333
- d. $4,800,000

_____ 11. Once a firm reaches the breakeven point, the next unit sold will increase profit by an amount equal to
- a. the selling price per unit
- b. the variable cost per unit
- c. the contribution margin per unit
- d. the difference between contribution margin and fixed costs

_____ 12. Harmel, Inc. incurs the following costs each period:

Variable manufacturing costs per unit	$10
Variable selling costs per unit	$2
Total fixed manufacturing costs	$18,530
Total fixed selling costs	$41,370

If the company sells 6,000 units, what price must be charged to earn a pretax profit of $25,000?
- a. $26.15
- b. $13.20
- c. $17.25
- d. $24.15

<u>Use the graph below to answer questions 13-15</u>.

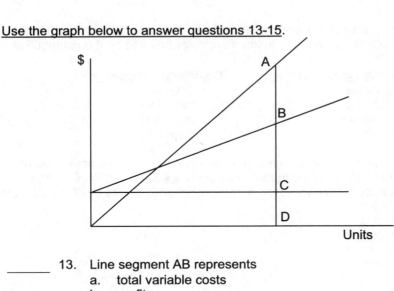

_____ 13. Line segment AB represents
   a. total variable costs
   b. profit
   c. contribution margin
   d. total fixed costs
   e. none of the above

_____ 14. Line segment AC represents
   a. total variable costs
   b. profit
   c. contribution margin
   d. total fixed costs
   e. none of the above

_____ 15. Line segment BC represents
   a. total variable costs
   b. profit
   c. contribution margin
   d. total fixed costs
   e. none of the above

<u>Exercise:</u>
Suppose that a company is trying to decide between two advertising campaigns. The first includes minimal advertising and a selling price per unit of $20. Total fixed advertising costs under this alternative are $480,000. The second advertising campaign is broader and the planned selling price under this alternative is $25. The total fixed advertising costs under the broad advertising campaign alternative are $600,000. Compute the indifference point, in units, between these two alternatives.

Indifference point _____

CHAPTER REVIEW: Learning Objective 3

Q3: How are CVP calculations performed for multiple products?

- When a company sells more than one product, the *sales mix* must be taken into consideration in the CVP analysis formulas. The sales mix refers to the ratio of each product sold to the total units sold. It can be computed in terms of relative numbers of the units sold or relative sales dollars for each product. These two approaches to stating the sales mix will not be the same unless the products all have the same selling price per unit.

  - Suppose a company sells 3 products, A, B & C. In 2005, the company budgeted sales in units for each of the products as 100, 100, and 800, respectively. The planned sales mix in terms of units for 2005 is 10%:10%:80% for A:B:C.

  - If the 3 products A, B & C sell for $10, $2, and $1, then the revenues budgeted for each product are $1000, $200, and $800, respectively. The sales mix in terms of revenues is 50%:10%:40%.

  - Note that the sales mix in revenues differs substantially from the sales mix in units. Each sales mix has a different purpose.

- To compute the breakeven point in units, we first compute the *weighted average contribution margin per unit (WACM).*

  $$WACM = \sum_{i=1}^{n} \lambda_i CM_i$$ where $*_i$ is product i's proportion of total sales in terms of units (from the sales mix in units), CM_i is product i's contribution margin in units, and n= the number of products.

  or, $WACM = \dfrac{\text{Total contribution margin}}{\text{Total number of units}}$

  Then use the CVP formula for the BEP in units, and Q will be the total number of units required. Finally, determine the number of units of each product that must be sold by multiplying the product's relative weight ($*_i$) times the total number of units required.

- To compute the breakeven point in sales dollars, we first compute the *weighted average contribution margin ratio (WACMR).*

  $$WACMR = \sum_{i=1}^{n} \alpha_i CMR_i$$ where α_i is product i's proportion of total sales in terms of revenues, CMR_i is product i's contribution margin ratio, and n= the number of products..

  or, $WACMR = \dfrac{\text{Total contribution margin}}{\text{Total revenue}}$

Then use the CVP formula for the BEP in sales dollars, and the result will be the total sales dollars required. Finally, determine the revenue required from each product by multiplying the product's relative weight (α_i) times the total revenue required.

Demonstration problem-Multiple product CVP analysis

Jean's Jumpsuits makes three types of coveralls: loose-fitting ones for working outdoors, fitted ones for casual wear, and designer one-piece outfits for business women. The following information comes from the budget for 2006:

	Loose	Fitted	Designer
Expected sales in units	3,000	1,200	800
Selling price per unit	$12	$25	$45
Variable cost per unit	$5	$10	$18

Total fixed costs are budgeted at $50,180 for 2006.

a) Compute the number of each type of jumpsuit that is required to break even.
b) Compute the revenues from each type of jumpsuit required to break even.
c) Compute the number of each type of jumpsuit that is required to achieve a $16,480 pretax profit.
d) Compute the revenues from each type of jumpsuit required to achieve a $13,524 after-tax profit if the tax rate is 40%.
e) If the sales mix changes to a higher proportion of designer jumpsuits, will the breakeven point increase or decrease? Explain.

Solution to demonstration problem

The easiest way to approach this problem is to first compute the total expected revenues and the total expected variable costs.

	Loose	Fitted	Designer	Total
Expected sales in units	3,000	1,200	800	5,000
Total expected revenue	$36,000	$30,000	$36,000	$102,000
Total expected variable costs	$15,000	$12,000	$14,400	$41,400
Total expected contribution margin	$21,000	$18,000	$21,600	$60,600
Contribution margin ratio	58.333%	60.000%	60.000%	59.412%
Sales mix in units	60.000%	24.000%	16.000%	100.000%
Sales mix in revenues	35.294%	29.412%	35.294%	100.000%

a) First, compute the WACM: WACM = 60%($12 - $5) + 24%($25 - $10) + 16%($45 - $18) = $12.12
     Note that WACM can also be computed as $60,600/5,000 units = $12.12.
   Next, compute the BEP in total units = $50,180/$12.12 = 4,140 units. But this is not useful information because details about the sales mix are lost. The BEP in the terms of the number of each product follows:

Loose	60% x	4,140 =	2,484
Fitted	24% x	4,140 =	994
Designer	16% x	4,140 =	662
			4,140

solution continues on next page →

Solution to demonstration problem continued

b) First, compute the WACMR. Since the WACMR = Total contribution margin/Total revenue, WACMR = 59.412% per the analysis done earlier. Note that the WACMR is also the weighted sum of the CMRs of the individual products, where the weights are the sales mix in terms of revenues:

WACMR = 35.294% x 58.333% + 29.412% x 60.000% + 35.295% x 60.000% = 59.412%.

Next, compute the BEP in total revenues = $50,180/59.412% = $84,461. But this is not useful information because details about the sales mix are lost. The BEP in the terms of the revenue required from each unit follows:

Loose	35.294%	x	$84,461	= $29,810
Fitted	29.412%	x	$84,461	= $24,841
Designer	35.294%	x	$84,461	= $29,810
				$84,461

The above answer contains a $13 rounding error. The exact sales dollars required to break even can be calculated as the number of each type of jumpsuit required to break even times its selling price: $12 x 2,484 + $25 x 994 + $45 x 662 = $84,448.

c) The # of units required to achieve target pretax profit = $Q = \dfrac{\$50,180 + \$16,480}{\$12.12} = 5,500$ units.

The BEP in terms of the number units of each type of product follows:

Loose	60%	x	5,500	= 3,300
Fitted	24%	x	5,500	= 1,320
Designer	16%	x	5,500	= 880
				5,500

d) First, compute the pretax profit required to achieve the after-tax profit.
Pretax profit = $13,524/(1 – 0.4) = $22,540. Then,

The revenues required to achieve target pretax profit = $Q = \dfrac{\$50,180 + \$22,540}{59.412\%} = \$122,400$.

The BEP in terms of revenues required from each type of product follows:

Loose	35.294%	x	$122,400	= $43,200
Fitted	29.412%	x	$122,400	= $36,000
Designer	35.294%	x	$122,400	= $43,200
				$122,400

e) The breakeven point will decrease because the product with the higher contribution margin becomes a larger portion of the sales mix.

PROBLEM SET B (Learning Objective 3)

<u>True-False</u>: Indicate whether each of the following is true (T) or false (F) in the space provided.

_____ 1. The weighted average contribution margin is the total expected contribution margin over the total expected revenue.

_____ 2. The sales mix in terms of units shows the relative proportion of revenue brought in by each product.

_____ 3. The weights used in computing the weighted average contribution margin are the sales mix in terms of revenues percentages.

_____ 4. The product with the highest contribution margin is weighted the most heavily in the computation of the weighted average contribution margin.

_____ 5. A company sells three products A, B & C that sell for $3, $4, and $2, respectively. Each product has a variable cost per unit of $1, and the products sell in a ratio of 3:2:1. The sales mix in terms of units is 50%:33%:17%.

_____ 6. A company sells three products A, B & C that sell for $3, $4, and $2, respectively. Each product has a variable cost per unit of $1, and the products sell in a ratio of 3:2:1. The sales mix in terms of revenues is 33%:44%:22%.

_____ 7. A company sells three products A, B & C that sell for $3, $4, and $2, respectively. Each product has a variable cost per unit of $1, and the products sell in a ratio of 3:2:1. The weighted average contribution margin $6.

_____ 8. A company sells three products A, B & C that sell for $3, $4, and $2, respectively. Each product has a variable cost per unit of $1, and the products sell in a ratio of 3:2:1. The weighted average contribution margin ratio is 68.4%.

_____ 9. A company sells three products A, B & C. The sum of the number of units of each product that must be sold to break even always equals total fixed costs over the weighted average contribution margin.

_____ 10. A company sells two products X & Y. Total fixed costs over the contribution margin ratio of X, added to total fixed costs over the contribution margin ratio of Y, equals the total revenues required to break even.

Exercises: Use the following information for Exercises 1 – 7. Write your answer in the space provided.

Garments-for-Babes, Inc. sells shirts for ladies and children. Next year's fixed costs are budgeted at $222,000 and the company plans sales of 30,000 ladies' shirts and 15,000 children's shirts. The selling prices and variable costs for each product are as follows:

	LADIES'	CHILDREN'S
Selling price	$12.00	$10.00
Variable cost	4.07	7.34

1. Compute the sales mix in terms of units. _____

2. Compute the sales mix in terms of revenues. _____

3. Compute the weighted average contribution margin. _____

4. Compute the weighted average contribution margin ratio. _____

5. Compute the number of each type of shirt required to break even

    Ladies'_____

    Children's_____

6. Compute the revenues required from each product to earn an $82,000 after-tax profit if the tax rate is 30%.

    Ladies' shirts _____

    Children's_____

7. If sales total $600,000, what dollar amount of this is attributable to ladies' shirts? _____

CHAPTER REVIEW: Learning Objectives 5 & 6

Q5: What assumptions and limitations should managers consider when using CVP analysis?
- CVP analysis assumes that costs and revenues are linear within a relevant range of activity. This linearity assumption implies that, within the relevant range:

  o selling prices per unit are constant.

  o variable costs per unit are constant.

  o total fixed costs are constant.

- For multiple product companies, the results of the CVP analysis hold only if the sales mix remains as predicted.

- There are many examples of cost and revenue behavior that violate these assumptions, including:

  o offering volume discounts to customers.

  o receiving volume discounts from suppliers.

  o productivity of workers that varies as the activity level changes.

- When CVP analysis is used for planning, managers must remember that the results of the CVP analysis only hold if the costs and selling prices remain as predicted.

- All results of CVP analysis should be evaluated to see if they are in the relevant range where the cost and revenue behavior assumptions hold.

- As in all uses of predicted information, managers must determine the quality of the data used for CVP analysis.

  o Questions that managers might consider for data that came from the accounting information system include:
    - Did the accounting information system aggregate the data in a manner appropriate for CVP analysis?
    - Is past revenue and cost information valid for predicting future costs and revenues?
    - Are there any important uncertainties that need to be incorporated into the data to better predict future costs and revenues?

  o Questions that managers might consider for information that came from outside the accounting information system include:
    - Is the source of the information is reliable?
    - How likely is it that this information might change during the planning horizon?

Q6: How are the margin of safety and operating leverage used to assess operational risk?

- The *margin of safety* measures how far away a company's actual or planned operations are from the breakeven point. The larger the margin of safety, the lower the risk of operating losses. It can be measured three different ways:

(1) Margin of safety in units = Actual or estimated units of activity - Units at breakeven

(2) Margin of safety in revenues = Actual or estimated revenue - Revenue at breakeven point

(3) Margin of safety % = $\dfrac{\text{Margin of safety in units}}{\text{Actual or estimated units}} = \dfrac{\text{Margin of safety in revenues}}{\text{Actual or estimated revenue}}$

- The *degree of operating leverage* is a measure of the level of fixed costs in the cost function. This is important when assessing the risk of operating losses because firms with relatively more fixed costs:

  - risk larger operating losses when activity is below the breakeven point.

  - benefit from higher contributions to profits when activity is past the breakeven point.

- The degree of operating leverage can be computed 3 ways:

Degree of operating leverage = $\dfrac{\text{Contribution margin}}{\text{Profit}} = \dfrac{\text{Total fixed costs}}{\text{Profit}} + 1 = \dfrac{1}{\text{Margin of safety \%}}$

- Notice that the degree of operating leverage is dependent upon the level of actual or estimated activity.

- The degree of operating leverage is useful in measuring the sensitivity of profits to changes in sales:

% change in profit = % change in sales x degree of operating leverage

Demonstration problem-Margin of safety and operating leverage

Ted's Toy Trucks makes an electric pick-up that is meant to be driven by toddlers. Ted's total fixed costs are $124,000 and the variable costs per unit are $60. The trucks sell for $100. In an earlier demonstration problem we computed that Ted's breakeven point was 3,100 units, or $310,000. Suppose Ted plans for 4,000 units of sales next year.

a) Compute the margin of safety in units.
b) Compute the margin of safety in revenues.
c) Compute the margin of safety percentage.
d) Compute the pretax profit at 4,000 units.
e) Compute the degree of operating leverage.
f) Suppose Ted's sales manager reports that next year's budget should be changed to 4,800 due to unexpected demand for the toy trucks from the west coast. Use the degree of operating leverage to compute the profits expected if Ted's sales manager is correct.

Solution to demonstration problem

a) The margin of safety in units is 4,000 units – 3,100 units to breakeven = 900 units.

b) The margin of safety in revenues is $100 x 4,000 - $310,000 revenue at breakeven = $90,000. Notice that this is also equal to the margin of safety in units times the selling price per unit.

c) The margin of safety % = 900 units/4,000 units = $90,000/$400,000 = 22.5%.

d) Pretax profit at 4,000 units = $40 contribution margin per unit x 4,000 units - $124,000 fixed costs
= $160,000 - $124,000 = $36,000.

e) The degree of operating leverage = $160,000/$36,000 = 4.44. Notice that this can also be computed as ($124,000/$36,000) + 1 = 3.44 + 1 = 4.44, or as 1/22.5% = 4.44.

f) An increase of 800 units from expected sales is a 20% increase. Therefore, profits will increase by 20% x 4.44 = 88.8%. The new profit level at 4,800 units is then = 1.888 x $36,000 = $67,968 (or $68,000, depending on the number of decimals to which you rounded the degree of operating leverage).

PROBLEM SET C (Learning Objectives 5 & 6)

<u>True-False</u>: Indicate whether each of the following is true (T) or false (F) in the space provided.

_____ 1. A company with a high margin of safely has less risk of operating losses than a company with a low margin of safety.

_____ 2. The margin of safety percentage is equal to the margin of safety in revenues divided by the margin of safety in units.

_____ 3. The margin of safety in revenues divided by the margin of safety in units is equal to the selling price per unit.

_____ 4. As the margin of safety increases, the degree of operating leverage increases.

_____ 5. A 10% increase in sales will result in a 10% increase in profits only when the degree of operating leverage is equal to 1.

_____ 6. A company should know its degree of operating leverage before it determines the planned level of activity for the next period.

_____ 7. As activity levels increase, the degree of operating leverage decreases.

_____ 8. As activity levels increase, the margin of safety percentage decreases.

_____ 9. A company that is operating below breakeven will have a negative degree of operating leverage.

_____ 10. If a company's actual operating activity is less than the planned operating activity, the actual degree of operating leverage is less than the planned degree of operating leverage.

_____ 11. Tilly's Tech Products has total fixed costs of $100,000 and profits last year were $75,000. The degree of operating leverage was 4.0.

_____ 12. Billy's Beauty Products expects a contribution margin of $320,000 and total fixed costs of $220,000 next year. The expected degree of operating leverage is 3.2.

_____ 13. Lloyd's Horse Care plans on a margin of safety percentage of 25% next year. If sales are 10% higher than expected, then profits will be 25% higher than expected.

_____ 14. For a company operating at the breakeven point, the degree of operating leverage is zero.

_____ 15. Tina's Trinkets has no fixed costs. Tina's degree of operating leverage is 1.0 regardless of the level of activity.

END OF CHAPTER EXERCISES

Multiple choice: Write the letter that represents the best choice in the space provided.

_____ 1. Bultena Enterprises projects the following for next year:

Sales	$300,000
Fixed costs	$100,000
After-tax profit	$12,000
Tax rate	40%

What is the firm's margin of safety in revenue?
   a. $200,000
   b. $20,000
   c. $188,000
   d. $50,000

Use the following information for questions 2 & 3:
Old MacDonald had a farm with expected fixed costs for next year of $91,000. The projected selling price per bushel is $12, with variable costs of $5 per bushel.

_____ 2. How many bushels past the breakeven point does MacDonald have to sell to realize a pretax profit of $37,100?
   a. 18,300
   b. 5,300
   c. 7,420
   d. 13,000

_____ 3. How much revenue past the breakeven point does MacDonald have to earn to realize a pretax profit of $36,000 if variable costs drop to $3 per bushel?
   a. $61,718
   b. $169,333
   c. $48,000
   d. $54,000

_____ 4. Wierschem, Inc. projects the following for next year:

Selling price per unit	$30
Variable manufacturing costs per unit	$16
Fixed manufacturing costs	$74,000
Variable selling costs per unit	$2
Fixed administrative costs	$24,480
After-tax profit	$48,000
Tax rate	40%

How many units will Wierschem have to sell to realize the projected after-tax profit?
   a. 12,833
   b. 12,207
   c. 12,749
   d. 14,873

_____ 5. The Patterson Company is subject to income taxes of 20% on income through
            $25,000 and 40% on income in excess of $25,000. Projected information for
            next year follows:

Selling price per unit	$40
Variable costs per unit	$15
Fixed costs	$400,000
Sales in units	20,000

What is Patterson's projected after-tax profit?
            a. $65,000
            b. $60,000
            c. $70,000
            d. $75,000

_____ 6. Tilker Manufacturing sells its product for $40 per unit. Last year variable costs
            per unit were $15, and fixed costs were $400,000. How many units must be
            sold this year to earn a pretax profit of $45,000 if variable costs increase by
            10%?
            a. 27,813
            b. 18,936
            c. 17,021
            d. 19,778

_____ 7. Which of the following is not an assumption of CVP analysis?
            a. The selling price per unit is constant.
            b. Total variable costs vary in proportion with changes in activity levels.
            c. The sales mix varies in proportion with changes in activity levels.
            d. Employee productivity is constant across all activity levels.

_____ 8. After a company exceeds the breakeven point,
            a. the total contribution margin increases.
            b. the profit per unit equals the contribution margin ratio.
            c. fixed costs become zero.
            d. the contribution margin ratio increases.

_____ 9. Before a company reaches the breakeven point,
            a. the total contribution margin is negative.
            b. the contribution margin per unit is less than the fixed costs per unit.
            c. total fixed costs are increasing.
            d. the contribution margin ratio is negative.

_____ 10. Bauer Company's sales increased but its pretax profits did not change. If the
            increase was within the relevant range, which of the following statements is
            true?
            a. Bauer's total fixed costs equal zero.
            b. Bauer's contribution margin is zero throughout the relevant range.
            c. Bauer's tax rate must have changed.
            d. None of the above; this could not have happened.

_____ 11. Lincoln Log Kits makes kits for pool cabanas. Currently, the company does not advertise and has a low selling price for its kits compared to competitors. Next year, the company plans to increase the selling price and begin a wide advertising campaign. Which of the following statements is true?
a.   Lincoln's breakeven point will be lower next year.
b.   There is not enough information to determine whether next year's profits will be higher or lower than this year's profits.
c.   Lincoln's profits will be higher next year.
d.   Lincoln's margin of safety will be lower next year.

_____ 12. Bhuyan Company's budgeted profit for next year is lower than this year's actual profit. The selling price, variable cost per unit, and total fixed costs did not change. Which of the following is false?
a.   Bhuyan's margin of safety next year will be lower than this year.
b.   Bhuyan's breakeven point is the same last year as this year.
c.   Bhuyan's degree of operating leverage will be higher this year than last.
d.   Bhuyan's contribution margin ratio this year will be lower than last year.

_____ 13. Mike Manager prefers alternatives that lower the degree of operating leverage. Which of the following statements about Mike is probably true?
a.   Mike loves to gamble in Las Vegas.
b.   Mike is a pessimist.
c.   Mike likes to avoid risk.
d.   Both (b) and (c) are likely to be true.

_____ 14. Melissa Manager expects next year's degree of operating leverage to increase. Which of the following statements is consistent with Melissa's expectations?
a.   Next year's activity level is budgeted to be lower than this year's.
b.   Next year's total fixed costs are expected to be lower than this year's.
c.   Next year's selling price is expected to increase.
d.   Next year's variable costs per unit are expected to decrease.

Use the following information for questions 15 & 16:
The Harris Co. sells three products in a ratio of 3:2:6. The contribution margins for the units are $10, $25, and $30, respectively. Total fixed costs are $119,600.

_____ 15. What is the breakeven point in total number of units?
a.   20,420
b.   10,120
c.   15,180
d.   5,060

_____ 16. How many of each product must be sold to realize a pretax profit of $39,000?
a.   450;   300;   900
b.   1,830;   1,220;   3,660
c.   1,380;   920;   2,760
d.   7,320;   4,880; 14,640

_____ 17. Johnston Co. has total variable costs equal to 40% of sales. Fixed costs are $120,000. What is the breakeven point in revenues?
  a. $300,000
  b. $200,000
  c. $120,000
  d. not enough information given to determine the answer

_____ 18. Ramser Co. has total variable costs equal to 40% of sales. Fixed costs are $120,000. What is the breakeven point in units?
  a. 300,000
  b. 200,000
  c. 480,000
  d. not enough information given to determine the answer

Use the following information for questions 19 & 20:
Blackmon Co. is deciding between two compensation plans. In Plan A, salaries are $100,000 and the commission is $2 per unit. In Plan B, salaries are $40,000 and the commission is $4 per unit.

_____ 19. At what level of sales, in units, is Blackmon indifferent between the two compensation plans?
  a. 30,000
  b. 20,000
  c. 10,000
  d. not enough information given to determine the answer

_____ 20. Which of the following statements is true?
  a. If expected sales are lower than the indifference point, Blackmon would prefer Plan A
  b. Plan A has a lower breakeven point than Plan B.
  c. If Plan B is adopted, the degree of operating leverage will decrease.
  d. The margin of safety will be larger if Plan A is adopted.

Exercises: Write your answer in the space provided.
1. Shauna's Shawls has total fixed costs of $240,000. The variable costs per shawl are $6, and planned sales next year are 30,000 shawls. If the tax rate is 40%, what selling price should Shauna set for her shawls if she desires an after-tax profit of $36,000?

_____

2. Gail Brown's Buns sells cinnamon rolls for $5 each. The variable costs per roll are $2 and total fixed costs are $24,000. The tax rate is 35%. Compute the following:

    a) The breakeven point in number of rolls _____

    b) The revenue required to earn a pretax profit of $40,000 _____

    c) The number of rolls required to earn an after-tax profit of $65,000 _____

    d) The margin of safety in units if Gail sells 10,000 rolls _____

    e) The margin of safety in revenues if Gail's revenues are $82,000 _____

    f) The degree of operating leverage if Gail's revenues are $82,000 _____

    g) The increase in profits if revenues increase from $82,000 to $90,200 _____

3. Taylor Industries sells 3 products, J, K, and L, with the following characteristics:

	J	K	L
Selling price per unit	$30	$36	$44
Variable costs per unit	$26	$34	$41

Taylor expects to sell 10,000 Js, 10,000 Ks, and 20,000 Ls next year, and fixed costs are expected to be $1,800,000.

a) Compute the break-even point in units of J, K, and L.

J _____

K _____

L _____

b) Draw a CVP graph, making sure to label all your axes and all lines on the chart. Label the value whenever a line hits an axis. Circle the breakeven point.

c) Compute the revenues required from J, K, and L in order to achieve a $300,000 pretax profit.

J _____

K _____

L _____

d) If sales total $30,000,000, what dollar amount of this revenue is from Product L?_____

4. Commander Riker is trying to decide whether to convert his company's sales staff's pay to a pure commission basis instead of the fixed salaries the company currently pays. Riker currently has the following cost and revenue structure:

Current <u>total</u> fixed costs	$130,000
Fixed salaries of sales staff (included in above total)	$42,000
Selling price per unit	$100
Variable costs per unit	$35

If he decides to compensate his sales staff with commission only, he will pay them zero salary plus a commission of 25% of sales dollars they bring in.

a) Compute the break-even point in units if Riker pays salary only _____

b) Compute the break-even point in units if Riker pays commission only _____

c) Compute the indifference point, in units, between the alternatives "salary" and

"commission". _____

d) Draw a CVP graph that includes a total cost line for both of the alternatives. Be sure to label each axis and the cost lines for each alternative. Draw a circle around the indifference point, and identify the value at the intersections of lines and axes.

5. Refer to Commander Riker's decision in Exercise 4, and answer the following questions.

a) What assumptions is Riker making if he uses the results of the CVP analysis in his decision making?

_____

_____

_____

_____

_____

_____

_____

b) What uncertainties does Riker face in this decision? Which information is the most reliable? Explain.

_____

_____

_____

_____

_____

_____

_____

c) Discuss the pros and cons of each alternative. Which one would you recommend? Why?

_____

_____

_____

_____

_____

_____

SOLUTION TO PROBLEM SET A

<u>Matching</u>:

1.	H	Contribution margin less total fixed costs = 0 at breakeven
2.	G	By definition of breakeven
3.	A	A is a better answer than F because F is just a tool of CVP analysis
4.	F	By definition of CVP graph
5.	D	By definition of CMR
6.	G	By definition of profit
7.	E	In learning objective 2, we learned to compute BEP in units and in $
8.	B	By definition of contribution margin
9.	D	By definition of CMR-remember that it can be computed 2 ways
10.	B	Contribution margin less total fixed costs = profit
11.	C	By definition of contribution margin per unit

<u>Multiple choice</u>:

1.	B	The CM/unit is $1; $140,000/$1 = 140,000 units
2.	B	CM = $300,000, so CMR = 60%; $180,000/60% = $300,000
3.	C	CM = $400,000, so CMR = 40%; ($200,000+$400,000)/40% = $1.5 million
4.	D	Note the CMR = 50%. Since the problem asks what is required to cover increases in profits and fixed costs, ($40,000 + $20,000)/50% = $120,000 required increase. Add this to the sales of 2005.
5.	B	If you increase the variable cost per unit, the CM per unit will decrease. Therefore, the BEP will increase.
6.	C	Here the CM/unit increases by $0.50. This will decrease the BEP.
7.	A	If the CMR is 60%, then variable costs are 40% of sales. Yoshi's total costs = 40% x $1,000,000 variable costs + $200,000 fixed costs = $600,000
8.	D	This is the definition of the breakeven point. A is wrong because sales = fixed costs + total variable costs at the BEP. B just says that the CMR is 50%. C is wrong because fixed costs plus profit = contribution margin.
9.	B	The CM per unit will increase because a 5% increase in the selling price will be larger than a 5% increase in the variable cost per unit. The CMR will not change because the new numerator = $1.05P - 1.05V$ and the new denominator = $1.05P$. The 1.05 cancels out.
10.	B	The CM is $750,000 and the CMR = 75%. To achieve after-tax profits of $700,000 you need pretax profits of $700,000/(1 – 0.3) = $1,000,000. The revenue needed is ($200,000 + $1,000,000)/75% = $1,600,000.
11.	C	This is the definition of CM per unit.
12.	A	6,000 units = ($59,900 + $25,000)/($P$ - $12). Solve for P = $26.15
13.	B	Revenue less total cost = profit
14.	E	This is just revenue less fixed cost, which is the same as profit + total variable cost, which doesn't match any of the answer choices. (Yes, sometimes the answer IS none of the above!)
15.	A	Total costs less total fixed costs is total variable costs.

Exercise:

The first advertising campaign has total fixed costs of $480,000 and a selling price of $20. The second has total fixed costs of $600,000 and a selling price $25. Certainly there must be other variable costs and other fixed costs that we are not told about, but this doesn't matter. To show you this, let F = the other fixed costs (that are the same between the 2 alternatives) and let V = the other variable costs per unit (that are the same between the alternatives). Let Q = the indifference point.

    The profit of the first alternative is ($20 – V)Q – ($480,000 +F).
    The profit of the second alternative is ($25 – V)Q – ($600,000 +F).
Set the two profit equations equal and solve for Q:
    ($20 – V)Q – ($480,000 +F) = ($25 – V)Q – ($600,000 +F)
    $20Q –VQ - $480,000 –F = $25Q – VQ - $600,000 – F
    $5Q = $120,000
    Q = 24,000 units.
Notice that F and V cancel out.

SOLUTION TO PROBLEM SET B

True-False:

1.	T	This is one of the ways to compute the WACM
2.	F	The sales mix in <u>revenues</u> shows this
3.	T	This is one of the ways to compute the WACMR
4.	F	This is not true because it doesn't take into account the sales mix. The product with the higher <u>relative revenue</u> will receive the greatest weight.
5.	F	If the products sell in a ratio of 3:2:1, imagine a bin with 6 products in it. Three of them are As, 2 of them are Bs and 1 of them is a C. The sales mix in units is 50%:20%:10%.
6.	F	If only 6 items were sold, the revenues brought in by A are 3 x $3 = $9; for B it is 2 x $4 = $8; for C it is 1 x $2 = $2. The total revenue for the 6 items is $19. The sales mix is 9/19:8/19:2/19, or 47.4%:42.1%:10.5%. If you answered "true" then you forgot to weight the selling prices by the sales mix.
7.	F	The CM per unit for the 3 products are $2, $3, and $1, respectively. This sums to $6, but this is not the WACM. The WACM = $2 x 3 units + $3 x 2 units + $1 x 1 unit = $13/(6 units needed to achieve a total CM of $13) = $2.17.
8.	T	The selling price for 6 units = $3 x 3 units + $4 x 2 units + $2 x 1 unit = $19. The contribution margin for 6 units is $13, as computed in #7 above. The WACMR is $13/$19 = 68.4%.
9.	T	The BEP in total units for a multiple product company is total fixed costs over the WACM.
10.	F	This is incorrect because the BEP in units of X is computed as if X is the only product sold. The same thing is done for the BEP in units of Y. But X and Y are sold together, in some sales mix. The company does not just sell either X or either Y.

Exercises:

First compute the revenue and variable costs for the planned level of activity:

	Ladies'	Children's	Total
Planned sales in units	30,000	15,000	45,000
Expected total revenue	$360,000	$150,000	$510,000
Expected total variable costs	122,100	110,100	232,200
Expected contribution margin	$237,900	$39,900	$277,800
Expected CM per unit	$7.93	$2.66	$6.173
Expected CMR	66.083%	26.600%	54.470%

1. The sales mix in units is 30/45 ladies' to 15/45 children's, or 66.667%:33.333%.

2. The sales mix in revenues is 360/510 ladies' to 150/510 children's, or 70.588%:29.412%.

3. The WACM is $277,800/45,000 units = $6.173. Alternatively, the WACM = 66.667%($7.93) + 33.333%($2.66) = $6.173.

4. The WACMR is $277,800/$510,000 = 54.47%. Alternatively, the WACMR = 70.588%(66.083%) + 29.412%(26.6%) = 54.47%.

5. The total number of shirts required to break even is $222,000/$6.173 = 35,963. This is 66.667%(35,963) = 23,975, and 33.333%(35,963) = 11,988 children's shirts.

6. The pretax revenues required to earn $82,000 after-tax = $82,000/(1 − 0.3) = $117,143. The revenues required to achieve this = ($222,000 + $117,143)/54.47% = $622,623. The portion of this attributable to ladies' shirts = 70.588% x $622,623 = $439,497. The portion of this attributable to children's shirts = 29.412% x $622,623 = $183,126.

7. $600,000 x 70.588% = $423,528.

SOLUTION TO PROBLEM SET C

<u>True-False:</u>

1. T   True, because the margin of safety measures how far away from breakeven a company is operating.
2. F   The margin of safety in revenues divided by the margin of safety in units is not even a percentage. The label on this ratio is $/unit. In fact, it is equal to the selling price per unit.
3. T   True, see the comments for #2 above.
4. F   Since the degree of operating leverage is the reciprocal of the margin of safety percentage, the two are inversely related. When one increases, the other decreases and vice versa.
5. T   The % change in profits = the % change in sales x degree of operating leverage.
6. F   The degree of operating leverage is dependent upon the actual or planned activity level, so it cannot be determined before the planning takes place.
7. T   As activity levels increase beyond the breakeven point, the margin of safety increases. Therefore, the degree of operating leverage decreases. Also, remember that the degree of operating leverage shows the extent to which costs are fixed. As activity levels increase, total variable costs increase, which decreases the proportion of the total costs that are fixed.
8. F   As activity levels increase beyond the breakeven point all 3 measures of the margin of safety increase.
9. T   Since the degree of operating leverage is contribution margin over profit, it is negative when profit is negative.
10. F   This is like #7. Operating leverage increases as activity levels decrease.
11. F   Degree of operating leverage = 1 + total fixed costs over profit = 1 + $100,000/($75,000) = 1 + 1.33 = 2.33.
12. T   Degree of operating leverage = 1 + total fixed costs over profit = 1 + $100,000/($320,000 - $100,000) = 1 + 2.2 = 3.2.
13. F   If the margin of safety percentage is 25%, then the degree of operating leverage = 1/25% = 4.0. If sales are 10% higher than planned, then profits will be 40% higher than planned.
14. F   The degree of operating leverage = contribution margin over profit, so at breakeven the degree of operating leverage = 1/0 = undefined.
15. T   Degree of operating leverage = 1 + total fixed costs over profit = 1.0 for all activity levels when fixed costs are zero.

SOLUTION TO END OF CHAPTER EXERCISES

Multiple choice:

1. D Bultena projects after-tax profits of $12,000, which is $12,000/(1 – 0.4) = $20,000 pretax. Since CM – fixed costs = pretax profit, CM - $100,000 = $20,000, so we know CM = $120,000. Then CMR = $120,000/$300,000 = 40%. The BEP in revenue = $100,000 over the 40% CMR = $250,000. Projected revenues are past this level by $50,000.

2. B Since the problem only asks about what units past breakeven are required to cover the pretax profit, then past breakeven Bultena needs only to cover the pretax profit. The additional units required past breakeven = $37,100/CM per unit = $37,100/$7 = 5,300 additional units.

3. C The new CM per unit = $12 - $3 = $9/unit, and the new CMR = $9/$12 = 75%. The additional revenues required to cover the pretax profit are $36,000/75% = $48,000.

4. D Variable costs per unit = $16 + $2 = $18, so CM/unit = $3. Total fixed costs = $74,000 + $24,480 = $98,480. The pretax profit required = $48,000/(1 – 0.4) = $80,000. The units required to cover the target profit = ($98,480 + $80,000)/$12 = 14,873.

5. A The CM/unit = $40 - $15 = $35. Pretax profit is projected as $25 x 20,000 - $400,000 = $100,000.
   Taxes on this amount are 20% x $25,000 + 40% x ($100,000 - $25,000) = $35,000. After-tax projected profit = $100,000 - $35,000 = $65,000.

6. B This year's variable cost = $15 x 1.1 = $16.50. This year's CM/unit = $40 - $16.50 = $23.50. The units required = ($400,000 + $45,000)/$23.50 = 18,936.

7. C The sales mix must remain constant over the relevant range under CVP assumptions.

8. A B can't be right – the contribution margin per unit is not even a percentage. C can't be right – our CVP assumptions are that fixed costs don't change over the relevant range. D can't be right – the contribution margin ratio is constant over the relevant range. As activity levels increase, the contribution margin increases, whether or not the company is past the breakeven point, so A is right.

9. B A can't be right – hopefully a company's contribution margin is never negative! C can't be right – the CVP assumptions are that fixed costs don't change over the relevant range. D isn't right either – the contribution margin ratio can NEVER be negative unless the company sells its products for less than the variable cost of the product. Before breakeven, the contribution margin is less than total fixed costs, so this must be true on a per unit basis also.

10. B A can't be right – if fixed costs are zero, then an increase in sales would increase profits, unless the selling price per unit was less than the variable cost per unit. C can't be right – the tax rate isn't relevant at all because the problem states that pretax profits did not change. But B is right – if the selling price equals the variable costs per unit, then the contribution margin is zero and profits will always equal negative total fixed costs, regardless of activity level.

11. B   Currently the company's fixed costs for advertising are lower than they will be next year, and its contribution margin per unit will be higher than it will be next year. However, A can't be right because we don't know how much higher the fixed costs and the contribution margin per unit will be, so we can't compare the breakeven point next year to the breakeven point this year. C and D can't be right either because we don't know the level of activity next year.

12. D   A is true because the BEP for both years is the same and next year's lower expected profits can only be due to a lower expected activity level. B is true because variable cost per unit, total fixed costs, and the selling price per unit haven't changed. C is true because operating leverage increases as activity decreases, and lower profits when costs and selling prices haven't changed can only be due to lower activity. D is false because the contribution margin ratio is constant over the relevant range.

13. D   A lower degree of operating leverage indicates less risk of operating losses. If Mike always chooses alternatives with this characteristic, then Mike probably is risk averse and doesn't like to gamble. Risk aversion is often related to pessimism because the decision maker is more concerned about the worst outcome than the best outcome.

14. A   B can't be right because a decrease in fixed costs lowers the degree of operating leverage. C & D can't be right because an increase in the selling price or a decrease in variable costs per unit (all else held constant) would increase profits and decrease the degree of operating leverage. A is right because the degree of operating leverage increases as activity decreases.

15. D   Suppose that Harris only sold 11 units. Then the CM from those 11 units would equal $3 \times \$10 + 2 \times \$25 + 6 \times \$30 = \$260$. The WACM = $\$260/11 = \$23.637$. The BEP in total units = $\$119,600/\$23.637 = 5,060$ units.

16. B   The total number of units required = $(\$119,600 + \$39,000)/\$23.637 = 6,710$. This 6,710 units is allocated to the 3 products according to the sales mix in units of 3/11:2/11:6/11.

17. B   If variable costs are 40% of revenue then the CMR = 60%. The BEP in revenues = $\$120,000/60\% = \$200,000$.

18. D   This is just like #17, in a way. We know from #17 that the BEP in revenues is $\$200,000$. However, we don't know the contribution margin per unit or the selling price per unit so we have no way of converting this to the BEP in units.

19. A   We don't have any revenue information, but the only difference between the two plans is costs, so we can determine the indifference point by setting the 2 cost functions equal and solving for Q:
$2Q + 100,000 = 4Q + 40,000$; $2Q = 60,000$; $Q = 30,000$

20. A   C & D can't be right because the margin of safety and the degree of operating leverage are dependent upon the level of activity, which we don't know. B is only right if the selling price less other variable costs is less than $\$5.33$ (see if you can figure out this number for yourself – it's a good exercise!). A is right because the total costs of Plan A exceed the total costs of Plan B for all activity levels up to the indifference point. (Draw a quick graph to prove this to yourself.)

Exercises:

1. The pretax profit required to earn $36,000 after taxes = $36,000/(1 − 0.4) = $60,000. Use the CVP formula for the units required but set Q = 30,000 and solve for P:

$$Q = 30,000 = \frac{\$240,000 + \$60,000}{P - \$6}; \quad P - \$6 = \frac{\$300,000}{30,000} = \$10; \quad P = \$16$$

2. First note that the CM per unit is $3 and the CMR = $3/$5 = 60%.
   a) Q = $24,000/$3 = 8,000 rolls.

   b) Revenue required = ($24,000 + $40,000)/60% = $106,667.

   c) The pretax profit required for $65,000 after taxes = $65,000/(1 − 0.35) = $100,000. The units required to achieve this = ($24,000 + $100,000)/$3 = 41,333.

   d) The margin of safety if Gail sells 10,000 rolls = 10,000 − 8,000 = 2,000 rolls.

   e) The BEP in revenue = $24,000/60% = $40,000, so the margin of safety = $82,000 − $40,000 = $42,000.

   f) If revenue = $82,000, the margin of safety percentage = $42,000/$82,000 = 51.22%. The degree of operating leverage = 1/0.5122 = 1.95.

   g) This is a 10% increase in sales, so profits will increase by 1.95 x 10% = 19.5%. The profits when revenues are $82,000 = $82,000 x 60%CMR - $24,000 = $25,200. Therefore, the increase in profits is $25,200 x 19.5% = $4,914.

3. First compute the revenue and variable costs for the planned level of activity:

	J	K	L	Total
Planned sales in units	10,000	10,000	20,000	40,000
Expected total revenue	$300,000	$360,000	$880,000	$1,540,000
Expected total variable costs	260,000	340,000	820,000	1,420,000
Expected contribution margin	$40,000	$20,000	$60,000	$120,000
Expected CM per unit	$4	$2	$3	$3
Expected CMR	13.333%	5.556%	6.818%	7.792%

   a) The WACM = $120,000/40,000 = $3. (Of course, the WACM also can be computed summing the weighted CMs/unit of the 3 products, where the weights are the sales mix in units: (10/40) x $4+(10/40) x $2+(20/40) x $3 = $3.) The BEP in total units = $1,800,000/$3 = 600,000 units. This is (10/40) x 600,000 Js, (10/40) x 600,000 Ks, and (20/40) x 600,000 Ls, or 150,000 Js, 150,000 Ks, and 300,000 Ls.

b).

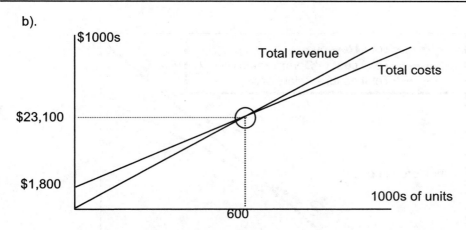

c). The WACMR = $120,000/$1,540,000 = 7.792%. (Of course, the WACMR also can be computed summing the weighted CMRs of the 3 products, where the weights are the sales mix in revenues: (300/1540) x 13.33%+(360/1540) x 5.556%+(880/1540) x 6.818% = 7.792%.) The revenue required = ($1,800,000 + $300,000)/7.792% = $26,950,719. This is (300/1540) x $26,950,719 from J, (360/1540) x $26,950,719 from K, and (880/1540) x $26,950,719 from L, or $5,250,140 from J, $6,300,168 from K, and $15,400,411 from L.

d) $30,000,000 x (880/1540) = $17,142,857.

4. The current plan has total fixed costs of $130,000, variable costs per unit of $35, and a contribution margin per unit of $100 - $35 = $65. The proposed commission-only plan has total fixed costs of $130,000 - $42,000 = $88,000, variable costs per unit of $35 + 25% x $100 = $60, and a contribution margin per unit of $100 - $60 = $40.

a) The BEP in units for the current plan is $130,000/$65 = 2,000 units.

b) The BEP in units for the proposed commission-only plan is $88,000/$40 = 2,200 units.

c) Determine the indifference point by setting the 2 profit functions equal and solving for Q:
   $65Q - 130,000 = 40Q - 88,000$; $25Q = 42,000$; $Q = 1,680$ units

d) see graph on next page

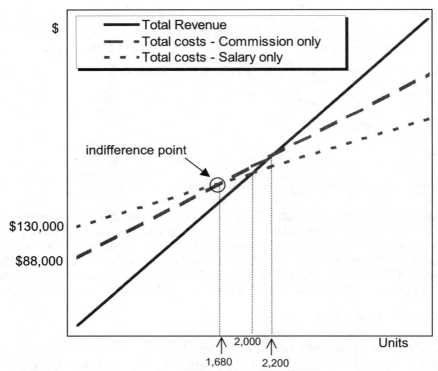

5. a) Riker is assuming that the selling price will be $100 over the relevant range, a range he needs to define. He is also assuming that the total fixed costs of each alternative will remain constant over this range and that the variable costs per unit, excluding commissions, will be $35 per unit under each plan. He does not need to assume that the $25 per unit commission in the commission-only plan will remain constant over the relevant range because he has control over this cost.

   b) Riker doesn't know the level of activity that will be achieved next year under either plan. He may be able to alleviate some of this uncertainty by investigating the detailed sales estimates made by his salespersons. There may be some customers that have a commitment for a certain number of units per month, or at least a history that shows a purchasing pattern. Most likely he expects that sales under the commission-only plan will be higher than under the salary-only plan, but he can't be certain of that.

   Since the selling price and cost information are merely estimates of future costs and revenues, he can't be sure that the actual selling price and costs will be near these estimates. The most reliable estimate is the amount of the commission because Riker has control over that amount.

   If Riker looks into the details as to how the total fixed cost information was compiled, he can determine how reliable this estimate is. Some elements of predicted total fixed costs are probably extremely reliable. For example, salaries of employees that are not likely to quit, rent if Riker has a signed long-term lease contract, and depreciation most likely contain very little uncertainty. Similarly, some elements of the variable cost per unit may be very reliable. If Riker has a long-term commitment from a supplier for materials, or a wage agreement with a union, then these prices are predictable. He still can't be certain about the efficiency of the use of material and labor resources, however, which could still affect his variable costs per unit.

c) The salary-only plan has the advantage of larger profits than the commission-only plan if sales exceed the breakeven point and the disadvantage of larger fixed costs that must be covered if sales are less than the breakeven point. The commission-only plan is less risky if sales are less than the breakeven point, but this reduced risk comes at the expense of lower profits when sales exceed breakeven. However, it could be that the commission-only plan will yield higher sales levels than the salary-only plan, so the two plans cannot necessarily be compared for the same activity level. Which plan is optimal depends on Riker's feelings about risk. If Riker feels that there is a high probability that sales will exceed 1680 units, then the total costs of the salary-only plan are lower than the total costs of the commission-only plan. However, the incremental expected contribution margin from increased activity due to the use of the commission-only plan would need to be taken into account. If this is substantial, then the commission-only plan would be optimal.

Chapter 4

Relevant Costs for
Nonroutine Operating Decisions

√ Study Checklist – Monitor your progress

1. Read the chapter in the text
2. Review the learning objectives below
3. Read the overview of the chapter
4. Read the chapter review for learning objectives 1 - 4
5. Do Problem Set A and check your answers
6. Read the chapter review for learning objectives 5 - 7
7. Do Problem Set B and check your answers
8. Do the End of Chapter Exercises in this study guide
9. Do the homework assigned by your instructor

CHAPTER LEARNING OBJECTIVES

After studying this chapter, you should be able to answer the following questions:

Q1. What is the process for making nonroutine operating decisions?
Q2. How are decisions made to accept, reject, and price special orders?
Q3. How are decisions made to keep or drop products, segments, or whole businesses?
Q4. How are decisions made to insource or outsource an activity (make or buy)?
Q5. How are decisions made for product emphasis and constrained resources?
Q6. What qualitative factors are important to nonroutine operating decisions?
Q7. What limitations and uncertainties should be considered when making nonroutine operating decisions?

OVERVIEW OF CHAPTER

Managers rely on management accountants for assistance in making nonroutine operating decisions such as whether to accept a customer's special order, or whether to keep or eliminate a seemingly unprofitable business segment. Other examples of nonroutine operating decisions include whether or not to outsource a business activity (or the manufacture of a subcomponent) and how to allocate scarce resources to products. There are quantitative decision rules to use for these types of decisions, but the quality of the information used must be considered, as must any relevant qualitative factors, before a final decision is made.

CHAPTER REVIEW: Learning Objectives 1 - 4

Q1: What is the process for making nonroutine operating decisions?

The general rule is to choose the alternative that maximizes profits (subject to qualitative considerations). This general rule can be made more specific once the nature of the decision at hand is identified. The process for making nonroutine operating decisions is:

- Identify the type of decision to be made
- Identify the relevant quantitative analysis technique(s)
- Apply the relevant quantitative analysis technique(s)
    - Identify the variables that are required as input, and which of these are known versus unknown
    - Estimate the unknown input variables
    - Apply the general rule for this type of decision
    - Interpret the results, taking the quality of information into consideration
- Identify and analyze the qualitative factors
- Consider the quantitative and qualitative information and make a decision

Q2: How are decisions made to accept, reject, and price special orders?

The general decision rule for special order decisions depends on whether or not there is sufficient idle capacity to produce the order. If there is enough capacity, then the special order should be accepted when the price exceeds the relevant costs. The decision may include determining the price for the order, so the price must at least exceed these relevant costs. Quite often (but not always) variable costs are relevant and fixed costs are not relevant. The demonstration problem below includes examples of exceptions to this.

When there is not enough idle capacity to produce the order, and it can be accepted only by replacing regular business, then the opportunity cost of accepting the special order must be included as part of the relevant costs. The opportunity cost of a lost unit of regular business is the contribution margin per unit that this regular business would have provided.

Demonstration problem-Special order decisions

Lanam Co. has been producing and selling 10,000 units per month, with the following total costs:

Direct materials...	$20,000
Direct labor..	35,000
Manufacturing overhead: Variable.................	15,000
Fixed	24,000
Selling expenses: Variable............................	10,000
Fixed...................................	13,000

The normal selling price is $15 per unit. The company has received an offer from a special customer who would like to buy <u>exactly</u> 5,000 units of product for $9 per unit. This special order would incur none of the usual variable selling expenses. Additional administrative expenses specifically related to this special order would be $1,500.

Required:
a) Suppose plant capacity is 18,000 units. Should Lanam accept this special order?
b) Suppose plant capacity is 13,000 units. Should Lanam accept this special order?

<u>Solution to demonstration problem</u>

Note the variable costs are $8 per unit.

Direct materials $2.00
Direct labor 3.50
Manufacturing overhead: Variable............. 1.50
Selling expenses: Variable .... <u>1.00</u>
                                                $<u>8.00</u>

> In this case, not all variable costs are relevant because this special order will incur no variable selling expenses.

a) Here there is sufficient capacity to accept this order without replacing regular business because regular business of 10,000 units plus the special order of 5,000 units is less than capacity of 18,000 units.

Incremental revenue if accept (5,000 units @ $9)	$45,000
Relevant variable costs (5,000 units @ $7)	(35,000)
Relevant fixed costs (additional admin costs)	(1,500)
Increase in profit if accept special order	$8,500

Here the quantitative analysis shows that the order should be accepted.

b) In this case, there is not sufficient capacity to accept this order without replacing regular business because regular business of 10,000 units plus the special order of 5,000 units exceeds capacity of 13,000 units. The order can only be accepted only if it replaces 2,000 units of regular business. The analysis for part (a) only needs to be changed to include the opportunity cost of accepting the order.

Increase in profit if accept special order when there was idle capacity	$8,500
Less: opportunity cost: lost contribution margin on 2,000 units of regular business ($15 - $8) x 2,000 units	14,000
Effect on profit if accept special order	$(5,500)

Here the quantitative analysis shows that the order should not be accepted.

Q3: How are decisions made to keep or drop products, segments, or whole businesses?

The general decision rule for keep or drop decisions is that the segment should be dropped if its contribution margin is less than the sum of the relevant fixed costs plus the opportunity costs of keeping the segment. The only fixed costs that are relevant are those that can be avoided if the business segment is dropped. The opportunity costs are the benefits forgone when the decision is made to keep the segment; these benefits stem from the opportunity to use the released capacity for other purposes.

Demonstration problem-Keep or drop decisions
Mikkee Corporation has three departments. Data for the most recent year is presented below. There are $20 in corporate headquarters fixed costs that are not traceable to individual departments.

	A	B	C	Total
Sales	$400	$200	$80	$680
Variable costs	128	52	34	214
Contribution margin	272	148	46	466
Department fixed costs:				
Unavoidable	96	52	12	160
Avoidable	60	104	54	218
Allocated fixed costs	12	6	2	20
Operating income	$104	$(14)	$(22)	$68

Required:
a) Should any department(s) be dropped? Which one(s) and why? What is the effect on operating income if your advice is followed?
b) Without regard to your answer for (a) above, suppose that Departments B and C are both eliminated. What is the new operating income for the Mikkee Corporation?
c) Suppose that a decision to drop Department B will free up capacity that can be used by Department A, and will save Mikkee $49 per year. Should Mikkee drop Department B in this case?

Solution to demonstration problem
a) First compute each department's contribution margin less avoidable fixed costs:

	A	B	C	Total
Contribution margin	$272	$148	$ 46	$466
Avoidable fixed costs	60	104	54	218
Effect on profit if keep	$212	$44	$(8)	$248

Department C is the only department that should be dropped. Operating income will increase by $8 if it is dropped.

b) Dropping Department C will increase income by $8 and dropping Department B will decrease income by $44, so dropping both departments will decrease income by $44 - $8 = $32.

c) The opportunity cost of keeping Department B is $49.

Contribution margin	$148
Avoidable fixed costs	104
	44
Opportunity cost of keeping Department B	49
Effect on profit if keep	$(5)

In this case, Department B should be dropped (subject to qualitative considerations) because it will increase income by $5.

Q4: How are decisions made to insource or outsource an activity (make or buy)?
The general decision rule for make or buy decisions is to outsource (buy) if the acquisition cost is less than or equal to the sum of variable costs plus relevant fixed costs, minus opportunity costs. The only relevant fixed costs are those that will be avoided when the decision is made to buy. The opportunity costs are the benefits forgone when the decision is made to insource, or make, the subcomponent. As in Q3, these benefits stem from the opportunity to use the released capacity for other purposes.

Demonstration problem-Make (insource) or buy (outsource) decisions
Gibson, Inc. manufactures a subcomponent that it needs for the production of its main product. Gibson currently makes, and uses, 100,000 of these subcomponents per year. The per-unit production costs of the subcomponent follow:

Direct materials	$2.60
Direct labor	1.00
Manufacturing overhead: Variable	1.20
Fixed	1.60
Total cost per unit	$6.40

Quaid, Inc. has offered to sell Gibson all 100,000 units it will need during the coming year for $6.00 per unit. If Gibson accepts the offer from Quaid, the facilities used to manufacture the subcomponent could be used elsewhere in production. This change would save Gibson $90,000 in the fixed costs of producing its main product. In addition, a $50,000 cost item included in fixed factory overhead which is specifically related to producing this subcomponent (rental of special equipment not usable in the manufacture of other products) would be eliminated.

Required:
Determine whether Gibson should make the component or buy it from Quaid. What is the effect on operating income if your advice is followed?

Solution to demonstration problem
Note that the variable costs per unit of the subcomponent are $4.80, and the total fixed costs associated with producing the subcomponent are $1.60 x 100,000 = $160,000. This $160,000 includes $50,000 of avoidable fixed costs. This $50,000 is relevant but the remaining $110,000 is not relevant because it cannot be avoided, regardless of the decision.

The relevant cost to make the subcomponent is computed as follows:

Incremental variable costs ($4.80 x 100,000)	$480,000
Incremental (or avoidable, or relevant) fixed cost	50,000
Opportunity cost of making subcomponent (benefits forgone)	90,000
	$620,000

The relevant cost to buy is $6.00 x 100,000 =	$600,000

Gibson should buy, not make, the subcomponent because income will increase by $20,000.

PROBLEM SET A (Learning Objectives 1 - 4)

<u>True-False</u>: Indicate whether each of the following is true (T) or false (F) in the space provided.

_____   1. Fixed costs are always irrelevant in nonroutine decision making.

_____   2. Avoidable costs are always relevant in nonroutine decisions.

_____   3. When a company is operating at capacity, the minimum acceptable price for a customer's special order is equal to the relevant variable and fixed costs associated with producing the order.

_____   4. In a make or buy decision, the relevant cost to make the subcomponent is the sum of the variable and fixed costs that will be avoided if the component is purchased, plus the opportunity costs associated with not releasing the capacity for other uses.

_____   5. Any business segment that has a negative contribution margin should be dropped.

_____   6. Any business segment that has a negative operating income should be dropped.

_____   7. Opportunity costs are always relevant in nonroutine decision making.

_____   8. For a company with sufficient excess capacity to produce a customer's special order, the opportunity cost of accepting the special order is zero.

_____   9. For a company without sufficient excess capacity to produce a customer's special order, the opportunity cost of the special order is equal to the contribution margin per unit of regular business times the number of units of regular business that will be replaced.

_____   10. Variable costs are always relevant when making nonroutine decisions.

<u>Multiple choice</u>: Write the letter that represents the best choice in the space provided.

_____   1. Each year Wright's Widgets buys 10,000 subcomponents that it needs in the production of its widgets from an outside supplier for $15 each. If Wright instead used its existing idle capacity to produce it in-house, the variable production costs would be $8 per unit and $3 of fixed production overhead would be allocated to each unit. Additionally, Wright would need to hire one quality control technician for $28,000 per year. The excess capacity that would be required is currently leased to another company for $25,000 per year. What is the advantage or disadvantage if Wright continues to buy the subcomponent from the outside supplier?
     a. $13,000 advantage
     b. $17,000 disadvantage
     c. $37,000 advantage
     d. $3,000 disadvantage

<u>Use the following information for questions 2 - 4:</u>
Taylor Enterprises sells its product for $40 per unit. Production costs per unit for regular sales are:

Direct materials	$6
Direct labor	14
Manufacturing overhead (2/3 variable)	12

Taylor recently received a special order from a customer for 20,000 units.

_____ 2. Suppose the special order price is $600,000 for all 20,000 units, and assume that Taylor has sufficient capacity to fill the special order. Should it be accepted?
a. Yes, because profits will increase by $120,000
b. No, because profits will decrease by $200,000
c. No, because profits will decrease by $40,000
d. Yes, because profits will increase by $40,000

_____ 3. Suppose that Taylor would like to earn $50,000 on this order and assume that there is sufficient capacity to fill the special order. What price per unit should Taylor charge for the special order?
a. $34.50
b. $42.50
c. $30.50
d. $26.50

_____ 4. Suppose that the special order price is $600,000 for all 20,000 units, but there is not sufficient capacity to fill the order; 8,000 units of regular business will be replaced by the special order if it is accepted. Should Taylor accept the special order?
a. No, because profits will decrease by $56,000
b. Yes, because profits will increase by $40,000
c. No, because profits will decrease by $24,000
d. No, because profits will decrease by $280,000

_____ 5. Moore Manufacturing has two major product lines, Gidgets and Gadgets. Income statements for the two product lines follow:

	Gidgets	Gadgets
Revenues	$400,000	$400,000
Variable expenses	225,000	150,000
Product line fixed expenses	130,000	100,000
Allocated corporate fixed expenses	120,000	90,000
Net operating income (loss)	$(75,000)	$60,000

If the Gidget product line were dropped, all of its product line fixed expenses could be avoided. Should the Gidget product line be dropped?
a. Yes, because profits will increase by $75,000
b. No, because profits will decrease by $45,000
c. No, because profits will decrease by $55,000
d. No, because profits will decrease by $175,000

Use the following information for questions 6 - 8:
Solo Co. made and sold 100,000 of its only product in 2004. Solo's income statement for 2004 follows:

Sales	$1,000,000
Direct materials	300,000
Direct labor	150,000
Variable manufacturing overhead	50,000
Fixed manufacturing overhead	100,000
Gross margin	400,000
Variable selling & administrative expenses	75,000
Fixed selling & administrative expenses	60,000
Operating income	$265,000

In 2005, Solo expects to produce and sell 80,000 units, and the selling price and variable costs per unit will remain unchanged. One third of the direct materials costs are for a subcomponent that Solo purchases from an outside supplier. In 2005, Solo will be producing the component internally for $0.75 per unit.

_____ 6. Compute the contribution margin per unit in 2005.
     a. $5.25
     b. $4.50
     c. $2.81
     d. $0.81

_____ 7. Compute the 2005 expected operating income.
     a. $232,000
     b. $90,000
     c. $200,000
     d. $105,000

_____ 8. What is the effect on 2005 profits of Solo's decision to produce the component internally?
     a.   The decision will increase 2005 profits by $25,000
     b.   The decision will increase 2005 profits by $20,000
     c.   The decision will decrease 2005 profits by $65,000
     d.   The decision will decrease 2005 profits by $33,000

_____ 9. Relevant costs in a special order decision include all of the following except:
     a.   direct materials costs of $3 per unit
     b.   a fixed cost of $1500 for rental of a machine needed to produce the order
     c.   the contribution margin per unit of regular sales when there is sufficient capacity to produce the order
     d.   unusual shipping charges of $4 per unit for the special order

Use the following information for questions 10 - 12:
Loso Co. made and sold 100,000 of its only product in 2004 for $15 each. Loso's costs per unit for 2004 follow:

Direct materials	$5.00
Direct labor	2.00
Variable manufacturing overhead	1.00
Fixed manufacturing overhead	1.50
Variable selling & administrative expenses	0.80
Fixed selling & administrative expenses	0.50
	$10.80

In 2005, Loso expects to produce and sell 80,000 units. The selling price and variable costs per unit will remain unchanged, as will total fixed costs. Early in 2005, a new customer approaches Loso and requests a one-time special order for 30,000 units.

_____ 10. What are total budgeted fixed costs for 2005?
  a. $160,000
  b. $150,000
  c. $120,000
  d. $200,000

_____ 11. Suppose the special order will incur only half the regular variable selling & administrative expenses and will require the rental of a special grinding machine for $15,000. Assume the capacity of Loso is 120,000 units per year. What is the minimum price per unit for the special order that Loso should accept?
  a. $9.00
  b. $8.90
  c. $11.00
  d. $10.90

_____ 12. Suppose the special order will incur only half the regular variable selling & administrative expenses and will require the rental of a special grinding machine for $15,000. Assume the capacity of Loso is 100,000 units per year. What is the minimum price per unit for the special order that Loso should accept?
  a. $10.97
  b. $15.10
  c. $11.10
  d. $15.50

Use the following information for questions 13 - 15:
Ricardo Company has three products, A, B, and C. The following information is available:

	Product A	Product B	Product C
Sales	$30,000	$70,000	$34,000
Variable costs	18,000	27,000	18,000
Contribution margin	12,000	43,000	16,000
Fixed costs:			
Avoidable	4,500	12,000	12,000
Unavoidable	3,000	10,000	6,200
Operating income	$4,500	$21,000	$ (2,200)

_____ 13. If Ricardo drops Product C, then
    a. operating income will increase by $2,200
    b. operating income will decrease by $16,000
    c. operating income will decrease by $4,000
    d. operating income will decrease by $9,800

_____ 14. Suppose that eliminating Product C will free up warehouse space for Product A's use, and will reduce the avoidable fixed costs of Product A by $1,500. If Ricardo drops Product C, then
    a. operating income will increase by $3,700
    b. operating income will decrease by $14,500
    c. operating income will decrease by $8,300
    d. operating income will decrease by $2,500

_____ 15. Suppose that eliminating Product C will reduce sales of Product B by 10%. If Ricardo drops Product C, then
    a. operating income will decrease by $11,000
    b. operating income will decrease by $6,100
    c. operating income will decrease by $4,300
    d. operating income will decrease by $8,300

CHAPTER REVIEW: Learning Objectives 5 - 7

Q5: How are decisions made for product emphasis and constrained resources?
Companies must determine how to allocate limited resources to their various products. When there is not enough of a resource (e.g. materials, labor hours, or machine hours), then this is known as a *constraint*, and the resource is known as a constrained, or scarce, resource. Any constrained resource that involves time is called a *bottleneck*.

Only one constrained resource, multiple products, unlimited customer demand
If there is only one constrained resource and customer demand for all products is unlimited, then it will be optimal to produce only one of the products. The general rule is to produce the product with the highest contribution margin per unit of the constrained resource.

- Note that this general rule is not "make the product with the highest contribution margin per unit".

- The contribution margin per unit of the constrained resource is the product's contribution margin per unit divided by the number of units of the scarce resource required to produce a unit of the product.

  - For example, suppose the constrained resource is machine hours. If the contribution margin per unit of Product A is $35, and it takes 2 machine hours to produce one Product A, then the contribution margin per unit of the constrained resource (machine hours) is $35/2 machine hours = $17.50/machine hour.

  - The *shadow price* shows how much (above the normal cost) that a company would be willing to pay in order to obtain one more unit of the scarce resource (assuming that it has not yet satisfied customer demand for the scarce resource). It is equal to the contribution margin per unit of the scarce resource for the product that the company is producing when the scarce resource is fully consumed.

Only one constrained resource, multiple products, limited customer demand
If there is a limit on customer demand for one or more of the products, the general rule is very similar to the above case with unlimited customer demand. First compute the contribution margin per unit of constrained resource for each product, then rank the products. The company should first make the product with the highest contribution margin per unit of the constrained resource, until customer demand for that product is satisfied. Then it should produce the product with the next-highest contribution margin per unit of the constrained resource, until customer demand for that product is satisfied, and so on.

- The shadow price for the constrained resource is the contribution margin per unit of the constrained resource for the product the company is producing when it runs out of the resource. Suppose a company sells 3 products, A, B & C and the contribution margin per machine hour for each of them is $12/hour, $15/hour, and $10/hour, respectively. The company should first produce B until customer demand is satisfied, then A ,and then C. If the company runs out of machine hours while it is producing Cs, for example, the shadow price is $10/hour. The company would be willing to pay up to $10 (in addition to the normal cost of a machine hour) for each additional machine hour it could acquire.

Demonstration problem-Constrained resource decisions (multiple products; 1 scarce resource)
Bobshi Productions makes 3 products, X, Y, and Z. The only constrained resource is labor hours; there are only 100,000 labor hours available each year. You are given the following per-unit information:

	X	Y	Z
Selling price	$9.00	$10.00	$33.00
Variable costs	1.00	6.00	17.00
Contribution margin	$8.00	$4.00	$16.00
Labor hrs required	1.25	0.80	20.00

Required:
a) Suppose there is unlimited customer demand for each product. Which product(s), and how many of each, should Bobshi produce? What is the total contribution margin if Bobshi follows your advice? What amount, above the normal cost for a labor hour, would Bobshi be willing to pay to acquire one more labor hour?
b) Suppose customer demand for X, Y, and Z is 40,000, 50,000, and 70,000 units, respectively. Which product(s), and how many of each, should Bobshi produce? What is the total contribution margin if Bobshi follows your advice? What amount, above the normal cost for a labor hour, would Bobshi be willing to pay to acquire one more labor hour?

Solution to demonstration problem
a) First compute the contribution margin per labor hour for each product:

	X	Y	Z
Contribution margin per unit	$8.00	$4.00	$16.00
Labor hrs required	1.25	0.80	20.00
Contribution margin/hr	$6.40	$5.00	$0.80

With one scarce resource and unlimited customer demand, it will always be optimal to produce only one product. Since X has the highest contribution margin per labor hour, Bobshi should produce all Xs. Each X requires 1.25 labor hours, and 100,000 hours are available, so Bobshi can make 100,000/1.25 = 80,000 Xs. Total contribution margin is the $8.00 contribution margin per X times 80,000 Xs, or $640,000. The shadow price is the contribution margin per labor hour for the product that Bobshi is producing when it runs out of hours, which is of course, product X. Bobshi would be willing to pay up to $6.40 above the normal cost of a labor hour to acquire one more hour.

b) Use the contribution margin per direct labor hour for each product computed in part (a). Bobshi should produce Xs first, then Ys, and finally Zs until it runs out of direct labor hours. To produce the 40,000 units of X demanded by customers will use 40,000 units x 1.25 hrs/unit = 50,000 hours. To produce the 50,000 units of Y demanded by customers will use 50,000 units x 0.80 hrs/unit = 40,000 hours. This leaves 10,000 available hours to produce Z. The number of units of Z that can be produced with 10,000 hours is 10,000 hrs/20 hrs per unit, or 500 Zs, which is less than customer demand. Bobshi should make 40,000 Xs, 50,000 Ys, and 500 Zs.

Total contribution margin is 40,000 Xs times $8 + 50,000 Ys times $4 + 500 Zs times $16 = $528,000. Since Bobshi was making Zs when it ran out of labor hours, the shadow price is $0.80 per hour. Bobshi would be willing to pay up to $0.80 above the normal cost to acquire one more labor hour.

<u>Multiple constrained resources, two products, limited or unlimited customer demand</u>
When there are only two products, and multiple constrained resources, there is a solution technique that is useful in building your intuition for these types of problems, which are called *linear programming problems*. When there are two products the problem can be viewed graphically. If customer demand for any of the products is limited, it can be included as one of the constraints.

- With multiple products and multiple constraints, the problem is easier if you organize the information. A linear programming formulation is a method of organizing the data and includes an algebraic description of the *objective function* and of the constraints.

  o The objective function states what you are trying to achieve. In the product emphasis/constrained resource problems in this chapter, we are trying to maximize total contribution margin. The objective function for a company with two products, A and B, would be written as:

  $$\underset{A,B}{\text{Max}}\ CM_A A + CM_B B,$$

    where A, B represent the number of units of products A and B produced and CM_i is the contribution margin per unit of product i. If you were to read this aloud, you would say, "Max over your choice of A and B the total contribution margin from A and B".

  o Each constraint is written as an inequality. If a company has two constrained resources, α and β, there would be two constraints:

  $$\alpha_A A + \alpha_B B \leq \text{Total amount of resource } \alpha \text{ available, and}$$
  $$\beta_A A + \beta_B B \leq \text{Total amount of resource } \beta \text{ available, where}$$

    α_i is the amount of resource α it takes to make one unit of i, and β_i is the amount of resource β it takes to make one unit of product i.

- In this solution technique, draw a graph and label the axes as A and B. Then graph the constraint inequalities, remembering that graphing an inequality includes shading the area where the inequality is true. The area where all constraints are true (shaded) is the *feasible set*, and the optimal production of A and B will be at one of the corners of the set. An example is shown below:

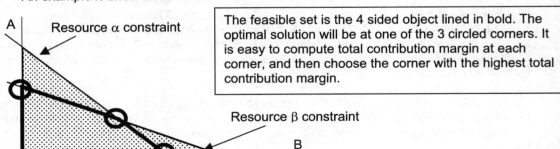

The feasible set is the 4 sided object lined in bold. The optimal solution will be at one of the 3 circled corners. It is easy to compute total contribution margin at each corner, and then choose the corner with the highest total contribution margin.

Demonstration problem-Product emphasis/constrained resource decisions (2 products; 2 scarce resources)
Joseph's Jewelry produces two products, silver rings (SR) and gold bracelets (GB). Production and
contribution margin information is given below:

	SR	GB
Contribution margin per unit	$40	$70
Direct labor hours required per unit	12	18
Machine hours required per unit	5	10

Required:
a) Suppose DL hours are limited to 180 hours a week, but machine hours are unlimited. How many of each
   product should the company make? What is the total contribution margin for this production plan? What
   is the shadow price for direct labor hours? for machine hours?
b) Suppose machine hours are limited to 90 hours a week, but DL hours are unlimited. How many of each
   product should the company make? What is the total contribution margin for this production plan? What
   is the shadow price for direct labor hours? for machine hours?
c) Suppose that DL hours are limited to 180 hours a week *and* machine hours are limited to 90 hours a
   week. Formulate this as a linear programming problem. Draw a graph of the trade-offs between SR and
   GB, putting SR on the y axis. Put both constraints on the graph, labeling them and the values where they
   intersect the GB or SR axis. How many of each product should the company make? What is the total
   contribution margin for this production plan?

Solution to demonstration problem
First compute the contribution margin per direct labor hour and the contribution margin per machine hour
for each product, because parts (a) and (b) are actually problems with only one scarce resource.

	SR	GB
Contribution margin per direct labor hour	$3.33	$3.89
Contribution margin per machine hour	8.00	7.00

a) Since direct labor hours is the only constrained resource, Joseph will make only the product with the
   highest contribution margin per direct labor hour, which is GB. If there are 180 direct labor hours
   available each week, Joseph can make 180 hours/18 hours per GB = 10 GB per week. The total
   contribution margin per week is 10 GB times $70/GB = $700. Since Joseph has unlimited machine
   hours, he would be willing to pay $0 for an extra machine hour. However, he'd be willing to pay up to
   $3.89 over his normal cost of a direct labor hour to acquire one more direct labor hour.

b) Since machine hours is the only constrained resource, Joseph will make only the product with the highest
   contribution margin per machine hour, which is SR. If there are 90 machine hours available each week,
   Joseph can make 90 hours/5 hours per SR = 18 SR per week. The total contribution margin per week is
   18 SR times $40/SR = $720. Since Joseph has unlimited direct labor hours, he would be willing to pay
   $0 for an extra direct labor hour. However, he'd be willing to pay up to $8 over his normal cost of a
   machine hour to acquire one more machine hour.

solution continues on next page →

Solution to demonstration problem continued

c) The linear programming formulation is:

$$\underset{SR,GB}{\text{Max}} \quad 40SR + 70GB \text{ , subject to:}$$

$$12SR + 18GB \le 180 \quad \text{direct labor hour constraint}$$
$$5SR + 10GB \le 90 \quad \text{machine hour constraint}$$

The graph for this problem is:

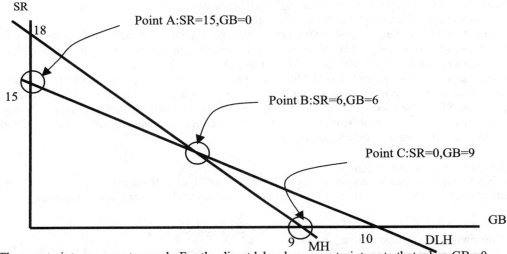

The constraints are easy to graph. For the direct labor hour constraint, note that when GB =0, SR=180/12=15 and when SR=0, GB=180/18=10. For the machine hour constraint, note that when GB =0, SR=90/5=18 and when SR=0, GB=90/10=9.

To find the number of SR and GB where the constraints intersect, either use substitution (solve the first constraint as an equality for SR, substitute this into the second constraint and solve for GB) or "cleverly" subtract one constraint from the other, like this:

12SR + 18GB = 180	12SR + 18GB = 180
5SR + 10GB = 90 multiply both sides of this by 1.8 to get	9SR + 18GB = 162
Subtract the second equality from the first	3SR + 0GB = 18, or SR = 6.

If SR = 6, then 12SR + 18GB = 180, or 12 x 6 + 18GB = 180, or 18GB= 180 – 72 = 108, or GB = 6.

Now, what is the total contribution margin (TCM) at each of the 3 corners?
  Point A: TCM = 15($40) + 0($70) = $600
  Point B: TCM = 6($40) + 6($70) = $660
  Point C: TCM = 0($40) + 9($70) = $630
Point B is optimal. Joseph should produce 6 SR and 6 GB each week to earn a TCM of $660 per week.

Multiple constrained resources, multiple products, limited or unlimited customer demand
When there are two products and more than two constraints, you can still use the graphing
solution approach shown above; there will just be more corners of the feasible set that could be
optimal solutions. However, when there are more than two products, the graphing approach will
not work. The problem can still be solved mathematically, but it is tedious. There are several
software packages that can solve linear programming problems quickly, and the output from the
software packages provides useful information beyond just the optimal production plan.

The text and this study guide discuss how to use an Excel add-in called Excel Solver to solve
linear programming problems. The demonstration problem below shows how to interpret the Excel
Solver output, and Exhibit 4A.2 of the text, shows how to put data into the Excel dialog boxes.
The output provides information about which constraints are *binding* (i.e. all of the resource is
consumed), and which constraints are *not binding*, or *slack* (i.e. there are resources remaining
after the production of the optimal plan).

The output shown in this study guide is from Excel 2000, version 9.0. The output may appear
slightly different under different versions of Excel.

Demonstration problem-Constrained resource decisions & Excel Solver (3 products; 2 scarce resources)
Misha Manufacturing makes 3 products, A, B, and C. Each year, Misha has 6,000 direct labor hours and
10,000 machine hours available. Production and contribution margin information is given below:

	A	B	C
Contribution margin per unit	$100	$8	$40
Direct labor hours required per unit	10	10	8
Machine hours required per unit	20	10	4

Required:
a) Use Excel Solver to find the optimal number of each product that Misha should make. In the Solver
   Results dialog box, request the answer and sensitivity reports. Interpret the answer report.
b) Use the Sensitivity Report to determine and interpret the shadow prices for the direct labor and machine
   hour constraints. What does the shadow price on the nonnegativity of Product C mean?

Solution to demonstration problem
The formulas entered into the Excel worksheet are the objective function in cell C7 and the left hand sides
(LHS) of the constraints in cells B10 and B11. The right hand side (RHS) of the constraints are entered into
cells C10 and C11. After Solver is run, the optimal production plan will appear in cells B6, C6 and D6. The
nonnegativity constraints are needed for most problems so that Excel Solver doesn't allow a negative
quantity of As, Bs, or Cs to be chosen. The formulas are shown on the next page.

solution continues on next page →

Solution to demonstration problem continued

	A	B	C	D
1			Misha Manufacturing	
2				
3			Product Mix	
4		A	B	C
5	Changing Cells:			
6				
7	Target Cell:		=100*B5+80*C5+40*D5	
8				
9	Constraints:	Used	Maximum	
10	Direct labor hours	=10*B5+10*C5+8*D5	6000	
11	Machine hours	=20*B5+10*C5+4*D5	10000	
12				
13	Nonnegativity constraints:		Minimum	
14	A	=B5	0	
15	B	=C5	0	
16	C	=D5	0	

a) The Excel Solver Answer Report is shown below:

Microsoft Excel 9.0 Answer Report

Target Cell (Max)

Cell	Name	Original Value	Final Value
$C$7	Target Cell: B	0	$56,000

Adjustable Cells

Cell	Name	Original Value	Final Value
$B$5	Changing Cells: A	0	400
$C$5	Changing Cells: B	0	200
$D$5	Changing Cells: C	0	0

Constraints

Cell	Name	Cell Value	Formula	Status	Slack
$B$10	Direct labor hours Used	6000	$B$10<=$C$10	Binding	0
$B$11	Machine hours Used	10000	$B$11<=$C$11	Binding	0
$B$14	A Used	400	$B$14>=$C$14	Not Binding	400
$B$15	B Used	200	$B$15>=$C$15	Not Binding	200
$B$16	C Used	0	$B$16>=$C$16	Binding	0

solution continues on next page →

Solution to demonstration problem continued
The optimal production plan is to produce 400 As, 200 Bs, and zero Cs. This will yield a total contribution margin of $56,000. All of the direct labor hours and all of the machine hours are consumed by this production plan; these constraints are binding. The nonnegativity constraints for products B and C are not binding because the optimal plan includes a positive quantity of these products. Since the optimal plan includes zero product C, the nonnegativity constraint for product C is binding.

b) The Excel Solver Sensitivity Report is shown below:

Microsoft Excel 9.0 Sensitivity Report

Adjustable Cells

Cell	Name	Final Value	Reduced Gradient
$B$5	Changing Cells: A	400	0
$C$5	Changing Cells: B	200	0
$D$5	Changing Cells: C	0	0

Constraints

Cell	Name	Final Value	Shadow Price
$B$10	Direct labor hours Used	6000	6
$B$11	Machine hours Used	10000	2
$B$14	A Used	400	0
$B$15	B Used	200	0
$B$16	C Used	0	-15.99995565

This report provides information about the shadow prices for the constraints. Misha would be willing to pay up to $6 above the normal cost of a direct labor hour to obtain one more direct labor hour.

Misha would be willing to pay up to $2 above the normal cost of a machine hour to obtain one more machine hour.

The optimal plan includes no units of Product C. Misha would have to be *given* nearly $16 in order to produce one unit of C because the production of a unit of C uses resources that are more profitably used to produce Products A and B.

Q6: What qualitative factors are important to nonroutine operating decisions?
Qualitative information is information that cannot be expressed quantitatively. Examples include the effects of decisions on employee morale or the company's reputation, and the quality of products or services obtained from suppliers. Qualitative information can sometimes have more effect on a decision than quantitative information. Examples of qualitative concerns (for which a company might attempt to gather qualitative information) for the types of nonroutine operating decisions covered in this chapter follow.

- Special order decisions
  - Will regular customers have concerns about the company selling products to their competitors at a lower price?
  - Will accepting the special order forge a valuable relationship with a new customer?
  - If the special order replaces regular business, what is the effect on the company's reputation when regular orders are not filled in a timely fashion?

- Keep or drop decisions
    - What will be the effect on the morale of remaining employees if a business segment is dropped?
    - What is the effect of on the company's reputation of dropping (or keeping) the business segment?
    - Will dropping the business segment increase or decrease sales of the remaining business segments?

- Insource or outsource (make or buy) decisions
    - Will the supplier be able to provide sufficient quantities of satisfactory quality of the item? (make or buy)
    - Is the business activity one of the core competencies of the company? (insource or outsource)

- Product emphasis/constrained resource decisions
    - Is the quantitative analysis' optimal production plan in agreement with the company's long-term strategic plans?
    - Will relaxing a labor hour or machine hour constraint affect product quality?
    - How would customers respond to a price change?
    - Can a constraint on the availability of materials be relaxed by changing suppliers, without reducing product quality?

Q7: What limitations and uncertainties should be considered when making nonroutine operating decisions?

In all decision making, the quality of the quantitative and qualitative information available should be considered. This is especially true for nonroutine operating decisions, because a company may have less experience gathering this type of information than it does for routine decisions.

- There are always uncertainties accompanying the information; suppliers may change their prices, future market forces may require a change in the product's price, or competitors may introduce a product that makes the company's product obsolete.

- The quality of the information may be lower if the information is not up-to-date or if the accounting system is not aggregating and summarizing cost and revenue information in an appropriate way.

- The information used in making the decision is only useful input to a quantitative analysis technique if the assumptions of the technique are not violated. Companies need to consider whether linear cost and revenue assumptions hold for any range of activity. If the assumptions do hold for some relevant range of activity, then companies need to make sure they plan to operate within this relevant range.

The quality of the decision-making process must also be taken into consideration.

- Companies must watch for decision-maker bias. Decision-makers may have a stake in a decision. A product line manager most likely does not want his product discontinued, and a supervisor of a particular business process will not want this activity outsourced. Since these individuals are so close to the necessary information, they frequently cannot be removed from the decision-making process.

- The decision-making process can be improved by performing sensitivity analyses, which show how the decision might change if the input data changes.

- The decision-making process should include the consideration of the company's long-term strategic plans. Even if the analysis shows that a particular business segment should be eliminated, for example, keeping the segment may be more in line with the company's goals.

PROBLEM SET B (Learning Objectives 5 - 7)

<u>True-False</u>: Indicate whether each of the following is true (T) or false (F) in the space provided.

_____ 1. The qualitative information in a decision may override the quantitative analysis.

_____ 2. The shadow price is the same thing as the contribution margin per unit of the constrained resource.

_____ 3. The shadow price for a resource that has a slack constraint is zero.

_____ 4. In all product emphasis/constrained resource decisions the company should make the product with the highest contribution margin per unit.

_____ 5. In a product emphasis/constrained resource decision with unlimited customer demand and one constrained resource, it will always be optimal to produce only one product.

_____ 6. In a product emphasis/constrained resource decision with limited customer demand and one constrained resource, it will always be optimal to produce more than one product.

_____ 7. In a product emphasis/constrained resource decision with two products and four constrained resources, the problem can be solved by graphing the constraints.

_____ 8. The quality of information used for nonroutine decisions is most likely higher than the quality of information used for routine decisions.

_____ 9. Sensitivity analysis is used to see how the changes in the input data for a decision might change the results of the quantitative analysis.

_____ 10. Since the quality of the decision-making process is reduced by decision-maker bias, all persons with a stake in the decision should be removed from the process.

Multiple choice: Write the letter that represents the best choice in the space provided.

Use the following information for questions 1 - 3:
Clark, Inc. makes 3 products, B, C, and D. Clark only has 110 machine hours available each week. Contribution margin, machine hour requirements, and weekly customer demand information is as follows:

	B	C	D
Contribution margin per unit	$8	$4	$7
Machine hours required per unit	0.6	0.4	0.2
Weekly customer demand	200	600	100

     1. In what order should the products be produced?
- a. B, C, D
- b. C, D, B
- c. D, B, C
- d. B, D, C

     2. Determine the number of units of each product that should be produced.
- a. 200 Bs, 0 Cs, and 100 Ds
- b. 150 Bs, 0 Cs, and 100 Ds
- c. 0 Bs, 600 Cs, and 0 Ds
- d. 200 Bs, 100 Cs, and 100 Ds

     3. Determine the maximum amount that Clark would be willing to pay, above the normal cost, for one more machine hour per week.
- a. $10.00
- b. $13.33
- c. $35.00
- d. $0.00

     4. Quantitative factors in a nonroutine operating decision
- a. include nonfinancial information
- b. could never include product quality considerations
- c. are always relevant to a nonroutine operating decision
- d. are of a higher quality than qualitative factors

     5. Qualitative information used in a make or buy decision is least likely to include
- a. the reliability of the supplier
- b. the quality of the supplier's product
- c. the effect of purchasing a component on the company's long-term strategic plan
- d. all of the above are good examples of qualitative factors that may be considered in a make or buy decision

Use the following information for questions 6 - 8:
Karl, Inc. makes 2 products, W and X. Karl only has 100 machine hours and 400 labor hours available each week. Customer demand for both products is unlimited. Contribution margin and machine and direct labor hour requirements are as follows:

	W	X
Contribution margin per unit	$12	$28
Machine hours required per unit	1.2	2.2
Labor hours required per unit	2.4	4.4

_____ 6. Which of the following statements is true?
    a. The machine hour constraint is slack.
    b. The labor hour constraint is binding.
    c. Karl should only produce one product.
    d. This problem cannot be solved without using software or tedious mathematical computations not covered in this chapter.

_____ 7. What is the optimal production plan?
    a. Produce 83 Ws and no units of X.
    b. Produce 45 Xs and no units of W.
    c. Produce 83 Ws and 45 Xs.
    d. This problem cannot be solved without using software or tedious mathematical computations not covered in this chapter.

_____ 8. How much would Karl be willing to pay, above the normal cost, to obtain one more machine hour and one more labor hour, respectively?
    a. $12.73 and $6.36
    b. $12.73 and $0
    c. $10.00 and $0
    d. This problem cannot be solved without using software or tedious mathematical computations not covered in this chapter.

_____ 9. Which of the following is considered a bottleneck in a product emphasis/constrained resource decision?
    a. Suppliers can only provide 1,000 pounds of direct material each month.
    b. The company's 12 machines can only operate 18 hours per day.
    c. Customer demand for product A is limited to 1200 units per month.
    d. All of the above are considered bottlenecks.

_____ 10. Which of the following is true?
    a. In a product emphasis/constrained resource decision with 2 products and 2 constraints, it will always be optimal to make both products.
    b. In a product emphasis/constrained resource decision with 2 products and 1 constraint, it will always be optimal to make only one product.
    c. Product emphasis/constrained resource decisions with more than 2 products and more than 2 constraints cannot be solved without software.
    d. All of the above are true.

END OF CHAPTER EXERCISES

Exercises: Write your answer in the space provided.

1. The Maxwell Company, your client, has asked for your assistance in analyzing the mix of their board game sales. Their objective is to increase profits without expanding capacity. The company gathered the following data for your use:

Game	Estimated customer demand	Selling price per unit	Materials cost per unit	Labor costs per unit
Oligopoly	100,000	$6.00	$2.00	$1.50
War of the Moons	60,000	4.75	0.50	1.20
Money	70,000	3.25	1.25	0.50
Risky	80,000	2.50	0.25	0.50

The above information is based on a labor rate of $5.00 per hour. The factory has an annual capacity of 35,000 labor hours. Fixed costs average $10,000 per month. Variable administrative costs are estimated at 50% of the labor cost.

a) Determine the order that the games should be produced.

Produce first _____

Produce second _____

Produce third _____

Produce fourth _____

b) Determine the quantity of each game that should be produced.

Oligopoly _____

War of the Moons _____

Money _____

Risky _____

c) What is the shadow price for labor? _____

2. Gamma Company is considering the feasibility of purchasing from a nearby supplier a subcomponent that it currently makes. Gamma produces and uses 10,000 of the subcomponents each year. The supplier will furnish the subcomponent for $4.50 per unit, including shipping costs. Currently, Gamma incurs materials costs of $1.06/unit when producing the subcomponent. Other costs assigned to the production of the subcomponent are direct labor costs of $3/unit and fixed manufacturing overhead of $2/unit. The machine used to produce the subcomponent is on a month-to-month lease for $100/month.

    Determine whether Gamma should make or buy the subcomponent. What is the advantage of your chosen alternative over the other one?

    Make   or   Buy   (Circle one)   Advantage _____

3. Beta Company expects to produce 30,000 units next year, which is 50% of its capacity. The selling price of each unit is $20. The variable costs per unit are $6.50, and fixed manufacturing overhead of $0.60 will be assigned to each unit. Another company asks Beta for a one-time special order of 10,000 units at a selling price of $8 per unit.

    a) Should Beta accept or reject the special order? What is the effect on profit if Beta follows your advice?

    Accept or   Reject   (Circle one)   Advantage _____

    b) Assume instead that 30,000 units is 80% of capacity. In this case what is the effect on profit if Beta follows accepts the special order?

    Effect on profit _____

4. Foix Industries has 3 divisions. Income statements for last year are shown below. Since no changes in revenues or expenses are expected this year, Foix is considering the elimination of South Division. In the South Division, 40% of its division fixed costs are unavoidable. If South is eliminated, the North Division will lose the volume discounts from a supplier to both divisions; this lost amount is estimated at $60,000 per year. However, this elimination would allow West Division to save $80,000 per year in travel expenses for its salespersons because they could use the abandoned offices of South Division. Since South and West produce related products, the elimination of South means that West would lose approximately $100,000 of sales revenue.

	South	North	West	Total
Revenues	$220,000	$600,000	$320,000	$1,140,000
Variable costs	140,000	285,000	160,000	585,000
Contribution margin	80,000	315,000	160,000	555,000
Division fixed costs	100,000	115,000	85,000	300,000
Allocated corporate fixed costs	40,000	100,000	65,000	205,000
Operating income	($60,000)	$100,000	$10,000	$50,000

a) What is the effect on profit if the South Division is dropped? _____

b) List some of the concerns that Foix might have about uncertainties and the quality of the information it is using to make this decision.

_____

_____

_____

_____

c) List some examples of the qualitative factors that Foix might have to consider in this decision.

_____

_____

_____

_____

5. Anderson Enterprises manufactures 2 products that require both machine processing and labor operations. There is unlimited demand for both products. Unit prices, cost data, and processing requirements are shown below. There are only 160,000 machine hours and 780,000 DL hours available.

	Product A	Product M
Unit selling price	$80	$220
Unit variable costs	$40	$90
Machine hours per unit	0.4	1.4
DL hours per unit	2.0	6.0

a) Formulate this as a linear programming problem.

b) Draw a graph with M on the y axis and A on the x axis.

c) Find the optimal production plan, and determine the total contribution margin for that plan.

Number of units of M _____

Number of units of A _____

Total contribution margin _____

6. Cowboy Hats, Inc. sells custom felt cowboy hats in 3 sizes: 2 gallon hats, 5 gallon hats, and 10 gallon hats for the real rancher who rides the range for days and uses his hat for a wash basin. There are 3 resource constraints; Cowboy can only obtain a limited quantity of the special compressed, waterproof felt it requires, and the cutting and steaming machines have a limited number of hours available. There is limited customer demand for all 3 products. The contribution margin and constraint data for all 9 constraints (3 scarce resources, 3 customer demand limits, and 3 nonnegativity) were entered into Excel Solver. The answer and sensitivity reports are shown below this text. Use this output to answer the questions on the next page. It's acceptable to report the production of partial units because partial units of this period can be completed next period.

Microsoft Excel 9.0 Answer Report

Target Cell (Max)

Cell	Name	Original Value	Final Value
$C$7	Target Cell: 5 Gallon	$0	$31,147

Adjustable Cells

Cell	Name	Original Value	Final Value
$B$5	Changing Cells: 2 Gallon	0	125.3333333
$C$5	Changing Cells: 5 Gallon	0	400
$D$5	Changing Cells: 10 Gallon	0	26.66666667

Constraints

Cell	Name	Cell Value	Formula	Status	Slack
$B$10	Felt Used	773	$B$10<=$C$10	Not Binding	26.66666667
$B$11	Cutting hours Used	600	$B$11<=$C$11	Binding	0
$B$12	Steaming hours Used	400	$B$12<=$C$12	Binding	0
$B$13	Demand for 2 Gallon Used	125	$B$13<=$C$13	Not Binding	374.6666667
$B$14	Demand for 5 Gallon Used	400	$B$14<=$C$14	Binding	0
$B$15	Demand for 10 Gallon Used	27	$B$15<=$C$15	Not Binding	23.33333333
$B$18	2 Gallon Used	125.3333333	$B$18>=$C$18	Not Binding	125.3333333
$B$19	5 Gallon Used	400	$B$19>=$C$19	Not Binding	400
$B$20	10 Gallon Used	26.66666667	$B$20>=$C$20	Not Binding	26.66666667

Microsoft Excel 9.0 Sensitivity Report

Adjustable Cells

Cell	Name	Final Value	Reduced Gradient
$B$5	Changing Cells: 2 Gallon	125.3333333	0
$C$5	Changing Cells: 5 Gallon	400	0
$D$5	Changing Cells: 10 Gallon	26.66666667	0

Constraints

Cell	Name	Final Value	Shadow Price
$B$10	Felt Used	773	0
$B$11	Cutting hours Used	600	21
$B$12	Steaming hours Used	400	37
$B$13	Demand for 2 Gallon Used	125	0
$B$14	Demand for 5 Gallon Used	400	9
$B$15	Demand for 10 Gallon Used	27	0
$B$18	2 Gallon Used	125.3333333	0
$B$19	5 Gallon Used	400	0
$B$20	10 Gallon Used	26.66666667	0

a) What is the optimal production plan? Round your answers to the nearest whole hat.

2 Gallon _____   5 Gallon _____   10 Gallon _____

b) What is the RHS of each of the 3 resource constraints?

Felt _____   Cutting hours _____   Steaming hours _____

c) What is the RHS of each of the 3 customer demand constraints?

2 Gallon _____   5 Gallon _____   10 Gallon _____

d) The supplier of the felt told Cowboy that it could obtain more felt than it currently purchases if Cowboy would be willing to pay only 3% more for the additional square yards of felt. Should Cowboy consider this? Why or why not?

_____

_____

e) Cowboy recently located a steaming machine that it could rent for $30 per hour. Should Cowboy consider renting this machine? Why or why not? What is the effect on profit if Cowboy rented this machine for an additional 20 hours per period?

_____

_____

f) Cowboy recently located a cutting machine that it could rent for $30 per hour. Should Cowboy consider renting this machine? Why or why not? What is the effect on profit if Cowboy rented this machine for an additional 20 hours per period?

_____

_____

g) Cowboy's sales manager is considering a special advertising campaign targeted at increasing customer demand for 10 gallon hats. The campaign will cost $800 and is expected to increase demand for the 10 gallon hats by 100 hats. Should Cowboy consider this campaign? Why or why not? What is the effect on profit if Cowboy begins this campaign?

_____

_____

h) Cowboy's sales manager is considering a special advertising campaign targeted at increasing customer demand for 5 gallon hats. The campaign will cost $800 and is expected to increase demand for the 5 gallon hats by 100 hats. Should Cowboy consider this campaign? Why or why not? What is the effect on profit if Cowboy begins this campaign?

_____

_____

SOLUTION TO PROBLEM SET A

<u>True-False:</u>

1. F   Although fixed costs are often irrelevant, any fixed cost that differs across the alternatives is relevant.
2. T   Some people use the terms relevant, avoidable and incremental cost interchangeably.
3. F   This is false because the opportunity cost of the regular business replaced by the special order was not included.
4. T
5. T   The general rule is to drop the segment if contribution margin less avoidable fixed costs is negative. If contribution margin is negative, then contribution margin less avoidable fixed costs will also be negative.
6. F   This is false; see the statement about the general rule for keep or drop decisions in #5 above.
7. T   Opportunity costs are the benefits forgone when one alternative is chosen over another. By definition, then, this differs across the alternatives and is hence relevant.
8. T   The opportunity cost of accepting a special order includes the lost contribution margin on regular business when that business is replaced. If the company has idle capacity, no regular business is replaced.
9. T   This is true; see the discussion for #8 above.
10. F   Although variable costs are often relevant, any variable cost that does not differ across the alternatives is irrelevant.

<u>Multiple choice:</u>

1. B   The variable costs per unit if Wright makes the subcomponent are $8/unit, or $80,000 annually. Add to this cost the $28,000 salary for the technician that is required when the subcomponent is produced and the $25,000 opportunity cost of not leasing out the released capacity to arrive at a relevant cost to make of $133,000. The cost to buy is $15 x 10,000 = $150,000. The cost to buy exceeds the relevant cost to make by $17,000, so Wright should really be making the subcomponent.

     If you chose A, then you used the cost to make the product of $11/unit ($8/unit variable cost + $3/unit fixed cost). This is incorrect – fixed costs are not relevant in this decision.

2. D   The manufacturing overhead cost per unit is $8 variable and $4 fixed, and the $4 is not relevant. The total variable costs to produce a unit are $6 + $14 + $8 = $28. This exceeds the special order price of $30/unit ($600,000/20,000 units) by $2 per unit. The special order will increase profits by $40,000.

   If you chose A, then you computed the incremental cost of producing the special order as $6 + $14 + $4; you used fixed manufacturing overhead as an incremental cost instead of variable manufacturing overhead.

   If you chose B, then you used the difference in the regular and special order prices of $10 ($40 - $30) times 20,000 units. This ignores relevant costs of producing the special order.

   If you chose C, then you used the total manufacturing cost per unit of $32 ($6 + $14 + $12) and compared it to the special order price of $30. This is not correct because the $32 cost includes irrelevant fixed costs.

   If you got this question wrong, then you got the next one wrong. Stop now, go back and re-do #3 and #4. Then come back and check your answers.

3. C   Taylor would like a profit of $50,000, which is $50,000/20,000 units = $2.50 per unit. The minimum price per unit must cover variable costs of $28 plus the required profit of $2.50.

   If you chose A then you added the $32 total production cost per unit to the required profit per unit of $2.50. The $32 includes irrelevant fixed costs.

   If you chose B then you added the required profit of $2.50 to the selling price of a regular unit, which makes no sense at all (sorry!).

   If you chose D, then you took the correct incremental (relevant) production cost of $28 and subtracted the required profit per unit on the special order. It may seem that costs and profit are "opposites", but in this case you add them; you want the special order price to cover costs and the required profit.

4. A   The opportunity cost of accepting the order is the lost contribution margin on the 8,000 units of replaced regular business, or ($40 - $28) x 8,000 = $96,000. The increase in profit under idle capacity was $40,000; $40,000 - $96,000 = a $56,000 decrease in profits if the order is accepted.

   If you chose B, you forgot the opportunity cost for the lost regular business.

   If you chose C, you included the opportunity cost but you incorrectly computed the opportunity cost as $40 - $32 production cost. The $32 includes irrelevant fixed costs.

   If you chose D, then you included the opportunity cost but incorrectly computed it as the $40 of lost revenue. When Taylor loses a unit of regular business, it does not lose the $40 in revenue, it loses the contribution margin of $12 ($40 - $28).

5. B   Gidget's contribution margin is $400,000 = $225,000 = $175,000. Contribution margin less avoidable fixed costs = $175,000 - $130,000 = $45,000 increase in profit if Moore keeps the Gidget product line, or a $45,000 decrease if it drops the Gidget product line.

If you chose A or D then you forgot the general rule for keep or drop decisions.

If you chose C, you subtracted allocated corporate fixed expenses from the contribution margin, instead of avoidable fixed expenses.

6. B   This problem is really here to remind you that contribution margin per unit is selling price per unit less all variable costs per unit, not just production variable costs. The selling price is $10/unit, and the per unit variable costs are $2.75 for direct materials (because in 2005 Solo will make a subcomponent for $0.75 per unit, and in 2004 it purchased the subcomponent for $1.00), $1.50 for direct labor, $0.50 for variable manufacturing overhead, and $0.75 for variable selling & admin. expenses, or $5.50 total. The contribution margin/unit is $10.00 - $5.50 = $4.50.

If you chose A then you forgot to include the variable selling & administrative expenses.

If you chose C then you took the total variable costs from 2004, adjusted for the decrease in materials costs for 2005, then divided this by 80,000 units of production in 2005. Remember that the total variable costs shown for 2004 are based on 100,000 units of production.

If you chose D then your error was similar to the one described for answer choice C but you compounded the error by including fixed costs in the numerator.

If you got this one wrong, you probably got #7 and #8 wrong. Go back and re-do your answers for #7 and #8. Then come back and check your answers.

7. C   The contribution margin per unit in 2005 is $4.50, so the total contribution margin is $4.50 x 80,000 units = $360,000. Fixed costs in 2005 will be the same as 2004: $100,000 + $60,000 = $160,000. Therefore, expected operating income in 2005 = $360,000 - $160,000 = $200,000.

If you chose A then you incorrectly assumed that the fixed costs in 2005 would be 80% times the fixed costs in 2004 because 2005 activity was only 80% of 2004 activity. Remember that total fixed costs don't change as activity within the relevant range changes.

If you chose B you used correct 2005 revenue, but you used 2004 cost information and updated it for the decrease in materials costs but not for the change in activity level.

If you chose D then you were just guessing!

8. B   To answer this, you cannot compare the income of 2004 to the income of 2005 because of the difference in volume. Instead, note that the subcomponent cost $1 in 2004 but only $0.75 in 2005. This $0.25 savings times 80,000 units = an increase of $20,000.

   If you chose A then you were on the right track but you multiplied the $0.25 savings times 100,000 units instead of 80,000 units.

   If you chose C you compared the 2004 income to the 2005 income. The difference between these two figures is attributable to the volume difference as well as the decision to produce the component internally.

   If you chose D, then you chose A for #7, and carried the error through to #8.

9. C   Answers A, B and D are all relevant to a special order decision. The contribution margin per unit of regular business is only relevant if some regular business needs to be replaced.

10. D   This question is here to remind you to beware of per-unit fixed costs. The fixed cost per unit of $2 ($1.50 + $0.50) is only valid for 100,000 units of activity. Total fixed costs do not change as activity changes.

   If you chose A then you multiplied the $2/unit fixed cost times the new level of activity of 80,000 units.

   If you chose B then you correctly used the 100,000 units of activity but included only fixed manufacturing overhead and forgot fixed selling & administrative expenses.

   If you chose C then you used only the fixed manufacturing overhead, ignoring fixed selling & administrative overhead, and multiplied it by the 80,000 units of activity for 2005.

11. B   The capacity of Loso is sufficient to produce the special order without replacing regular business. Variable costs for the special order are $5 for materials, $2 for labor, $1 for variable manufacturing overhead, plus $0.40 (50% x $0.80) for variable selling & administrative expenses, or $8.40 total. If a special machine is rented for the special order at a cost of $15,000, this is an extra $0.50 ($15,000/30,000 units) that must be covered by the special order price. The minimum acceptable price is $8.40 + $0.50 = $8.90.

   If you chose A then you incorrectly computed the variable selling & administrative expenses associated with the special order.

   If you chose C then you computed the variable costs incorrectly. You first multiplied the given per-unit information by the 100,000 units of activity in 2004, adjusted for the change in variable selling & administrative expenses, and then divided by 80,000 units of activity in 2005.

   If you chose D then you included irrelevant fixed costs in your computation of the relevant cost of producing the special order.

12. A   The order can only be accepted if 10,000 units of regular business are replaced (80,000 regular units + 30,000 special order units = 110,000, which exceeds capacity by 10,000 units). The contribution margin per unit of regular business is $15.00 – variable costs per unit of $8.80 = $6.20. The opportunity cost of accepting the order is $6.20 x 10,000 replaced regular units = $62,000. Each unit is the special order must cover the $8.90 discussed in #11 plus its share of this opportunity cost. $8.90 + $62,000/30,000 units = $10.97.

   If you chose B then you added the contribution margin of a regular unit to the $8.90. This would be correct if every special order unit replaced a regular unit (i.e. if 30,000 units of regular business were replaced).

   If you chose C then you were close, but you incorrectly computed the contribution margin per unit on regular units to be $6.60. You did this by assuming that regular units had 50% of the variable selling & administrative expenses listed in the given information.

   If you chose D then you made both of the mistakes mentioned in B and C.

13. C   The general rule is to keep the segment if the contribution margin exceeds the avoidable fixed cost. $16,000 - $12,000 = $4,000, so Product C should not be dropped. If it is, this $4,000 will be lost.

   If you chose A then you included irrelevant unavoidable fixed costs.

   If you chose B then you forgot the general rule for keep or drop decisions.

   If you chose D then you were confused about the general rule and used unavoidable fixed costs instead of avoidable fixed costs.

   If you got this one wrong, you probably got #14 and #15 wrong. Stop now and go back to re-do your answers for #14 and #15. Then come back and check your answers.

14. D   In #13 we determined that profit will decrease by $4,000 if Product C is dropped. Now, dropping Product C will save $1,500, so the net effect on profit is a decrease of $4,000 less this $1,500 savings.

   If you chose A then you included irrelevant unavoidable fixed costs (and you chose A for #13).

   If you chose B then you chose B for #13 and carried the error to #14.

   If you chose C then you chose C for #13 and carried the error to #14.

15. D   If Product B's sales decrease by 10%, then Product B loses 10% of its contribution margin (it loses 10% of its revenue but saves 10% of its variable costs). This amounts to $43,000 x 10% = $4,300. In # 13 we determined that profit will decrease by $4,000 if Product C is dropped. Now we add the lost contribution margin from the effect on Product B's sales to get a decrease in profit of $4,000 + $4,300 = $8,300.

   If you chose A then you thought that a 10% loss of Product B's sales would be 10% x $70,000 = $7,000.

   If you chose B then you thought that a 10% loss of Product B's sales would be a 10% loss of B's income: 10% x $21,000 = $2,100.

   If you chose C then you made the same error as B but also did not use the $4,000 decrease in income if C is dropped. You must have chosen A for #13. That's why you were supposed to stop after your error in #13 and re-do your answers to #14 and #15!

SOLUTION TO PROBLEM SET B

<u>True-False:</u>

1. T
2. F   This is not always true. We can compute the contribution margin per unit of scarce resource, but the shadow price will be $0 if the optimal production plan does not consume all of the resource. Why would a company pay extra to obtain something if it can't even use what it has available?
3. T   This is true for the same reason that #2 is false.
4. F   No, this is never the general rule, regardless of the number of constraints.
5. T   If you got this wrong, re-read page 4-11.
6. F   It *may* be optimal to produce more than one product, but not always.
7. T   You can always use the graphing approach when there are 2 products.
8. F   The information gathering process for routine decisions is likely to be more reliable than for nonroutine decisions because of the frequency of routine decisions.
9. T
10. F   Persons with a stake in the decision are likely to have much of the necessary information so they most likely cannot be removed from the process.

<u>Multiple choice:</u>

1. C   Produce the products in the order of the highest contribution margin per machine hour:
   Product B: $8.00/0.6 hrs = $13.33/hr
   Product C: $4.00/0.4 hrs = $10.00/hr
   Product D: $7.00/0.2 hrs = $35.00/hr
   The order to produce is Product D first, then Product B, then Product C.
       If you got this wrong, you probably got #2 and #3 wrong. Go back and re-do your answers for #2 and #3, then come back and check your answers.
2. B   First Clark should produce all the Ds it can sell. This is 100 Ds, and this uses 100 x 0.2 hr/unit, or 20 hours. There are 90 hours remaining. Next produce all the Bs that can be sold, if there are enough hours. Customer demand for Bs is 200 units, which requires 200 x 0.6 hrs, or 120 hours. There were only 90 hours available after Ds were produced, so customer demand for Bs won't be fully satisfied. With the remaining 90 hours, Clark can produce 90/0.6 hrs = 150 Bs. There are no hours left to make any Cs.
3. B   Since Clark was producing Bs when it ran out of machine hours, the shadow price is $13.33.
4. A   Answer B isn't right because product quality could be measured quantitatively (e.g. tensile strength measures). Answer C ignores that the quantitative information may include irrelevant cost information. Answer D is silly – just because information is stated numerically does not mean that it is somehow better than information that is not stated in quantitative terms.
5. D

6. C   Since there are only two products, we can graph the constraints.
        The machine hour constraint is 1.2W + 2.2X ≤ 100.
        The labor hour constraint is 2.4W + 4.4X ≤ 400.

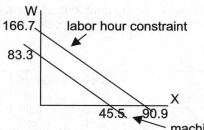

        When there is only one binding constraint, it is always true that it will be
        optimal to produce only one product.

7. B   The contribution margin per machine hour for a W is $12/1.2 hrs = $10/hr.
        The contribution margin per machine hour for an X is $28/2.2 hrs =
        $12.73/hr. Karl should produce all Xs. There are 100 machine hours
        available, so Karl can produce 100/2.2 hrs per unit = 45.5 Xs.

8. B   Karl would pay $0 for a labor hour because he already has labor hours
        available that he can't use because machine hours are constrained. He
        would pay $12.73 for a machine hour, the contribution margin per machine
        hour for an X.

9. B   A bottleneck is a constraint that involves time.

10. B   A is not correct because it won't *always* be optimal to make both products.
        C is not correct because there are mathematical methods for solving these
        problems, even though we didn't cover them in this text or this study guide.

SOLUTION TO END OF CHAPTER EXERCISES

<u>Exercises:</u>

1. First compute the contribution margin per unit and the contribution margin per hour. The hours required per unit is computed as the labor costs per unit divided by $5/hour. Don't forget the variable administrative costs!

Game	Estimated customer demand	Selling price per unit	Materials cost per unit	Labor costs per unit	Variable admin costs per unit	Contrib- ution margin per unit	Hours required per unit	Contrib- ution margin per hour
Oligopoly	100,000	$6.00	$2.00	$1.50	$0.75	$1.75	0.30	$5.83
War of the Moons	60,000	4.75	0.5	1.2	0.60	2.45	0.24	$10.21
Money	70,000	3.25	1.25	0.5	0.25	1.25	0.10	$12.50
Risky	80,000	2.5	0.25	0.5	0.25	1.50	0.10	$15.00

a) The games are produced in the order of the highest contribution margin per hour: Risky first, then Money, then War of the Moons, then Oligopoly.

b) Risky is produced first. It takes 80,000 x 0.10 = 8,000 hours to satisfy customer demand, leaving 35,000 – 8,000 = 27,000 hours for remaining products.

Money is produced next. It takes 70,000 x 0.10 = 7,000 hours to satisfy customer demand, leaving 27,000 – 7,000 = 20,000 hours for remaining products.

War of the Moons is produced next. It takes 60,000 x 0.24 = 14,400 hours to satisfy customer demand, leaving 20,000 – 14,400 = 5,600 hours for Oligopoly.

Oligopoly is produced last. There are only 5,600 hours remaining. These 5,600 hours can produce 5,600/0.3 hours per unit = 18,667 units of Oligopoly.

Maxwell should produce 18,667 units of Oligopoly, 60,000 units of War of the Moons, 70,000 units of Money, and 80,000 units of Risky.

c) The shadow price is $5.83, since Maxwell ran out of labor hours while it was producing Oligopoly.

2. The variable costs associated with making the subcomponent are $1.06 materials + $3.00 labor = $4.06 per unit.

   The incremental cost of producing the subcomponent is $4.06 x 10,000 plus $1,200 for renting the required machine (for 12 months) = $40,600 + $1,200 = $41,800. The cost to buy is $4.50 x 10,000 = $45,000. The advantage of the make alternative over the buy alternative is $45,000 - $41,800 = $3,200.

3. a) If the variable costs of producing the unit are $6.50 and the special order price is $8, the special order will increase profit by $1.50 per unit. There is sufficient capacity to produce the units for the special order without losing regular business, so Gamma should accept the special order. It will increase profit by $1.50 x 10,000 = $15,000.

   b) If 30,000 units is 80% of Gamma's capacity, then Gamma's capacity is 30,000/0.8 = 37,500 units. In order to accept the special order, Gamma will lose 2,500 regular units. The opportunity cost of accepting then is 2,500 x ($20.00 - $6.50) = $33,750. The increase in profit before considering a capacity constraint was $15,000, so the effect on profit of accepting the order, including the opportunity cost, is a $15,000 increase less $33,750, or an $18,750 decrease if Gamma accepts the special order.

4. a) The effect on profits if South is eliminated is the $80,000 contribution margin less the avoidable fixed costs of 60% x $100,000, or $20,000, before the effects on the other Divisions are considered. The net effect on profits if South Division is dropped is this $20,000 increase less the $60,000 lost volume discounts for North Division plus the $80,000 travel expense savings of West Division, less the lost contribution margin for West Division of $50,000, or a net increase in profits of $10,000 if South Division is dropped. [Note that the West Division has a 50% contribution margin ration ($320,000/$160,000 = 50%). A loss of $100,000 in West Division revenue is a loss of $50,000 of West Division contribution margin.]

   b) Foix cannot be sure that the revenue and cost information from last year will hold for the upcoming year. The 40%/60% split between unavoidable and avoidable fixed costs for the South Division is probably just an estimate. Foix should investigate the reliability of this estimate. Also, the lost volume discounts for North Division is probably just an estimate. However, this estimate is likely to be more reliable than the estimated travel expense savings and the lost revenue for West Division. Foix can look into the details of these estimates; some are probably more reliable than others.

   c) Examples of qualitative factors that Foix should consider include:
      • employee morale for the North and West Divisions
      • the company's reputation in the regions where the South Division operates
      • whether elimination of South Division is in line with Foix's long-term strategic plans
      • the effect on the elimination of South Division on the reputation of the company in the regions in which it operates the North and West divisions

5. a) First note that the contribution margin per unit of A is $80 - $40 = $40, and the contribution margin per unit of B is $220 - $90 = $130. The linear programming formulation is:

$$\underset{A,B}{\text{Max}} \quad 40A + 130B, \text{ subject to: } 0.4A + 1.4M \leq 160{,}000 \text{ (machine hour constraint)}$$

$$2A + 6M \leq 780{,}000 \text{ (DL hour constraint)}$$

b&c) The graph of this problem is shown below:

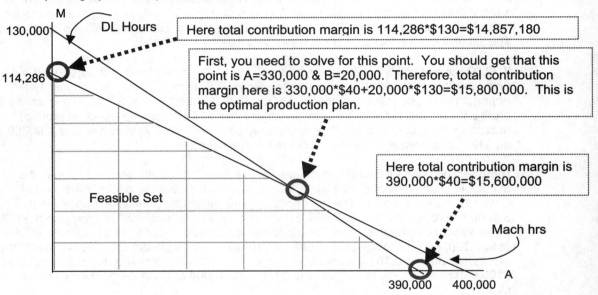

M

130,000   DL Hours

Here total contribution margin is 114,286*$130=$14,857,180

114,286

First, you need to solve for this point. You should get that this point is A=330,000 & B=20,000. Therefore, total contribution margin here is 330,000*$40+20,000*$130=$15,800,000. This is the optimal production plan.

Feasible Set

Here total contribution margin is 390,000*$40=$15,600,000

Mach hrs

390,000   400,000   A

The optimal production plan is A=330,000 and M=20,000. The total contribution margin at this point is $15,800,000.

6. a) The optimal production plan is 125 2 Gallons hats, 400 5 Gallon hats, and 27 10 Gallon hats. This is rounded from 125.3 2 Gallon hats and 26.7 10 Gallon hats.

b) The RHS of the felt constraint is the 773 used plus the 27 slack, or 800. The RHS of the cutting hours constraint is the 600 used plus the 0 slack, or 600. The RHS of the steaming hour constraint is the 400 used plus the 0 slack, or 400.

c) The RHS of the 2 Gallon hat customer demand constraint is the 125.3 used plus the 374.7 slack, or 500. The RHS of the 5 Gallon hat customer demand constraint is the 400 used plus the 0 slack, or 400. The RHS of the 10 Gallon hat customer demand constraint is the 26.7 used plus the 23.3 slack, or 50.

d) No, Cowboy should not increase its purchases of felt, because the felt constraint is slack.

e) If Cowboy rents the machine for 20 hours, the increase in profit is 20 x ($37 shadow price, or per-hour value of increasing the resource - $30 per hour cost of the resource) = $140 increase in profits. Cowboy should rent the steaming machine.

f) If Cowboy rents the machine for 20 hours, the decrease in profit is 20 x ($21 shadow price, or per-hour value of the increasing the resource - $30 per hour cost of the resource) = $180 decrease in profits. Cowboy should not rent the cutting machine.

g) Cowboy should not consider an advertising campaign to increase sales of 10 Gallon hats, because the customer demand constraint for 10 Gallon hats is slack. If Cowboy does begin this campaign, then profits will decrease by $800, the cost of the campaign.

h) The campaign costs Cowboy $800/100 hats, or $8 per hat. The shadow price shows that it is worth $9/hat to increase customer demand for the 5 Gallon hats. The $8 cost is lower than this value by $1 per hat. Cowboy should begin this advertising campaign; it will increase profits by $1 x 100 hats, or $100.

Chapter 5

Job
Costing

√ **Study Checklist – Monitor your progress**

1. Read the chapter in the text
2. Review the learning objectives below
3. Read the overview of the chapter
4. Read the chapter review for learning objectives 1 - 3
5. Do Problem Set A and check your answers
6. Read the chapter review for learning objectives 4 - 6
7. Do Problem Set B and check your answers
8. Do the End of Chapter Exercises in this study guide
9. Do the homework assigned by your instructor

CHAPTER LEARNING OBJECTIVES

After studying this chapter, you should be able to answer the following questions:

Q1. How are costs assigned to customized goods and services?
Q2. How is overhead allocated to individual jobs?
Q3. What is the difference between actual costing and normal costing?
Q4. What are the uses and limitations of job cost information?
Q5. How are spoilage, rework, and scrap handled in job costing?
Q6. What are the quality and behavioral implications of spoilage?

OVERVIEW OF CHAPTER

Managers need to assign costs to customized products and services for financial reporting purposes, pricing, and other decision-making purposes. Cost assignment involves tracing direct costs to jobs and allocating indirect costs to individual jobs. When defects occur, the costs of these defective units must be assigned to the good units produced or to expense accounts.

CHAPTER REVIEW: Learning Objectives 1 - 3

Q1: How are costs assigned to customized goods and services?

Companies need to assign *product costs* to the goods or services they produce in order to value inventories for balance sheet reporting, and to cost of goods sold for income statement reporting. Product (or *inventoriable*) costs include the direct and indirect costs of producing the goods or services. Recall from Chapter 2 that direct costs are easily traced to a cost object and indirect costs must be allocated to a cost object.

- When the goods or services are homogenous and mass produced (for example aspirin or drywall), it is easiest to assign costs to the processing departments and then average all processing costs over the units produced to determine the production cost of a unit. This type of costing is known as *process costing*, and is covered in detail in Chapter 6. In process costing the cost objects are the processing departments. The costs of the processing departments are then averaged over the units produced.

- If all goods or services are not the same (i.e. yachts designed to customer specifications or individual consulting services performed for clients), it doesn't make sense to average costs over all goods or services performed because each good or service will consume different quantities of resources. For customized production, we use *job costing*. In job costing, the cost object is the individual job, or batch or production.

- Some processing is a combination of these two extremes, where portions of the goods or services provided are similar and portions of the processing are customized. In these instances, a hybrid costing system can be used.

Job costing for manufactured goods is easiest to understand when you first understand the flow of costs in manufacturing. Manufacturers purchase raw materials to be used in production. The costs of these raw materials are kept in an asset account, *Raw materials inventory*. Raw materials include materials that are considered direct costs as well as indirect materials. The costs of producing units that are not yet complete are maintained in another asset account, *Work in process inventory*. When the units are completed, their costs are transferred to F*inished goods inventory.* Finally, the costs of units sold to customers are transferred out of finished goods inventory and into the expense account *Cost of goods sold*.

In job costing we maintain only one work in process inventory account, with a subsidiary ledger for each job in process. If all materials are direct, then the flow of costs is shown in Exhibit 5.1.

Exhibit 5.1: Flow of costs in job costing when all raw materials are direct

Raw Materials Inventory		Work in Process Inventory		Finished Goods Inventory	
Beg Inv		Beg Inv		Beg Inv	
RM Purchased	RM Used →	RM Used Direct Labor Overhead Applied	Cost of Goods Manufact-ured →	Cost of Goods Manufact-ured	To Cost of Goods Sold Account
End Inv		End Inv		End Inv	

Under generally accepted accounting principles (GAAP), product costs debited to work in process inventory are the three manufacturing costs described in Chapter 2: direct materials, direct labor, and manufacturing overhead (or just "overhead"). These are product costs for financial reporting purposes, and are also known as *inventoriable costs.*

- Manufacturers incur other costs that are not placed into inventory accounts. For example, the salaries of office workers or gasoline for salespersons' cars are expensed in the period they are incurred. These types of costs are known as *period costs.* Note that under GAAP, all manufacturing costs are inventoriable.

- All manufacturing costs, including factory rent and depreciation on machines increase work in process, and are not expensed until the goods are sold.

  - On the income statement, this expense is called cost of goods sold. On any income statement of a manufacturer that is prepared under GAAP, there will never appear any expenses such as "wages of factory workers" or "depreciation on factory machines" because these amounts are included in cost of goods sold.

Demonstration problem-Cost flows in job costing

You are given the following information for calendar year 2005 for Park Manufacturing Company:

Sales	$177,000
Raw material purchases	$35,000
Factory rent	$20,000
Office rent	$13,000
Direct material used	equals 40% of prime costs*
Beginning raw materials inventory	$20,000
Ending raw materials inventory	$25,000
Beginning work in process inventory	$8,000
Ending work in process inventory	$6,000
Beginning finished goods inventory	$5,000
Ending finished goods inventory	$10,000

   * prime costs are direct materials (DM) plus direct labor (DL)

All raw materials are direct materials.

Required:

a) Use t-accounts to compute the cost of goods manufactured and the cost of goods sold for 2005.

b) Prepare a formal schedule of cost of goods manufactured for 2005.

c) Prepare an income statement 2005.

solution begins on next page →

Solution to demonstration problem

a) Amounts in t-accounts are in $1000s

Raw Materials Inventory				Work in Process Inventory				Finished Goods Inventory		
BI	20			BI	8			BI	5	
DM				DM				Cost of		Cost of
purch.		DM		used	40	122 Cost of		good		117 goods
ased	35	40 used		Over-		goods		manuf'd		sold
				head*	20	manuf'd			122	
				DL**	60					
El	15			El	6			El	10	

*Factory rent is the only manufacturing overhead item listed.
**If DM used of $40,000 equals 40% of prime costs, then prime costs must equal $100,000. Since prime costs are the DM and DL costs incurred on the factory floor, then DL must be $60,000.

b) A schedule of cost of goods manufactured is simply a formatted version of the first two t-accounts shown above:

Park Manufacturing Company
Schedule of Cost of Goods Manufactured
Year ended December 31, 2005

Beginning work in process inventory			$8,000
Manufacturing costs added this period:			
Direct materials used:			
Begininning direct materials inventory	$20,000		
Direct material purchases	35,000		
Cost of materials available for use	55,000		
Less ending direct materials inventory	15,000	$40,000	
Direct labor		60,000	
Manufactuing overhead		20,000	120,000
			128,000
Less ending work in process inventory			6,000
Cost of goods manufactured			$122,000

solution continues on next page →

Solution to demonstration problem continued

c)

Park Manufacturing Company
Income Statement
Year ended December 31, 2005

Sales		$177,000
Less cost of goods sold:		
Begininning finished goods inventory	$5,000	
Cost of goods manufactured	122,000	
Cost of goods available for sale	127,000	
Less ending finished goods inventory	10,000	117,000
Gross margin		60,000
Nonmanufacturing expenses		13,000
Operating income		$47,000

The work in process subsidiary ledger keeps track of the costs assigned to the individual jobs in process. Each job has a *job cost record* that accumulates the direct materials and direct labor costs traced to the job as well as the overhead costs allocated (or applied) to the job.

- Direct materials and direct labor costs are traced to the job cost records via *source documents*.

  o When direct materials are taken from raw materials inventory and brought to the factory floor, a *materials requisition form* (manual or electronic) will be completed showing for which job the materials are to be used.

  o Direct labor employees keep track of which jobs they are working on by using *time records*.

- Indirect production costs (overhead) are allocated to jobs. This is covered in detail in learning objective 2.

The journal entries to account for direct manufacturing costs are shown in Exhibit 5.2 on the next page.

Exhibit 5.2: Journal entries for direct production costs

Direct materials are purchased on account:

Raw materials inventory	XX	
Accounts payable		XX

Direct materials are requisitioned to the factory floor: ⎫ This information comes from
Work in process inventory	XX	
Raw materials inventory		XX

materials requisitions. After this
entry, job cost records are
updated.

Direct labor costs are accrued (or paid):   ⎫ This information comes from
Work in process inventory	XX	
Accrued payroll (or Cash)		XX

time records. After this entry,
job cost records are updated.

Q2: How is overhead allocated to individual jobs?

Overhead is allocated to jobs by using an overhead allocation rate, which equals overhead costs divided by an *allocation base* such as direct labor hours, machine hours, or some other measure of activity.

- If the numerator is the year's actual overhead costs and the denominator is the actual quantity of the allocation base then the allocation rate is known as the *actual allocation rate*.

- When the numerator and denominator are the budgeted or estimated quantities of overhead costs and allocation base, then the allocation rate is known as the *estimated allocation rate*.

The allocation base used should be a cost driver for the overhead costs in the numerator, if possible. Manufacturing overhead includes costs such as indirect labor, indirect materials, factory rent, depreciation on factory machines, etc.

- These costs most likely have different cost drivers, so companies often aggregate overhead costs into *cost pools*.

- For overhead allocation purposes, the costs in a cost pool should have similar cost behavior. Each overhead cost pool can then use a different allocation base.

The overhead costs assigned to jobs in work in process inventory will be the overhead rate times the actual quantity of the allocation base that the job consumed. For example, if the allocation rate is $12/direct labor hour, and Job #123 used 100 direct labor hours this period, then the overhead allocated to Job #123 this period would be $1,200.

Q3: What is the difference between actual costing and normal costing?

When companies use the actual allocation rate to assign overhead to work in process, this is called *actual costing*. If the estimated allocation rate is used, this is called *normal costing*. Under both actual and normal costing, actual direct materials and direct labor costs are traced to jobs in process through materials requisitions and time records. The only difference between actual and normal costing is the allocation rate used to assign overhead to jobs in process.

- Under actual costing, a job cost record will show the actual direct materials and direct labor costs plus allocated overhead, where allocated overhead will be the actual allocation rate times the actual quantity of the allocation base the job consumed.

- Under normal costing, a job cost record will show the actual direct materials and direct labor costs plus allocated overhead, where allocated overhead will be the estimated allocation rate times the actual quantity of the allocation base the job consumed.

The actual allocation rate cannot be computed until the end of the period because neither the numerator (actual overhead costs), nor the denominator (actual quantity of allocation base for the year) are known until the end of the year.

- Actual costing does not allow a company to cost its jobs until the end of the year.

- Normal costing is used so that job costs can be computed as the year progresses.

Under normal costing, the actual overhead costs incurred are not debited to work in process. Instead, a temporary account called Overhead control is debited for actual overhead costs. If a company has several cost pools for overhead, it may use several different overhead contol accounts. Periodically, estimated overhead is debited to work in process. In this entry the Overhead control account is credited.

At the end of the year, the sum of the debits made to the Overhead control account is the actual overhead for the year. The sum of the credits made to Overhead control is the total overhead allocated to work in process during the year.

- If the net balance is a debit, then actual overhead exceeded the allocated overhead. This is known as *underallocated* overhead.

- If the net balance is a credit, then actual overhead was less than allocated overhead. This is known as *overallocated* overhead.

At the end of the year, the overhead control account is closed.

- If overhead was underallocated, then the amount of overhead credited to work in process during the year was too low. The entry to close the overhead control account will credit overhead control and debit work in process, finished goods, and cost of goods sold. The debits go to all three accounts because this underallocation of overhead affects jobs still in process, jobs that were in process during the year but are not yet sold, as well as jobs that were in process during the year but have been sold to customers.

- If overhead was overallocated, the entry to close overhead control will debit overhead control and credit work in process, finished goods, and cost of goods sold.

- The debits (or credits) to work in process, finished goods, and cost of goods sold will be prorated to the three accounts. A common method of determining this proration is based upon the ratio of the ending balances (before this entry) for the three accounts.

  o If the amount of under- or overallocated is immaterial, then some accountants will forgo this proration and put the entire debit or credit into cost of goods sold.

  o The text uses a rule-of-thumb for determining materiality: if the under- or overallocated overhead is less than 10% of actual overhead costs, then the amount is considered immaterial.

The journal entries to account for overhead, completed jobs, and the sale of jobs to customers are shown in Exhibit 5.3 below.

Exhibit 5.3: Journal entries to account for overhead, completed jobs, and sold jobs

Actual overhead costs are incurred:			Examples of accounts credited are Accrued payroll for indirect labor, or Cash if factory rent is paid.
Overhead control	XX		
Various accounts		XX	

Overhead costs are allocated to work in process:			The amount of this entry is the estimated allocation rate times the actual quantity of the allocation base used by jobs this period.
Work in process inventory	XX		
Overhead control		XX	

A job is completed:			The amount of this entry is the total costs on the job cost records for completed jobs.
Finished goods inventory	XX		
Work in process inventory		XX	

A job is sold on account:			The cost of the jobs comes from the job cost records for the jobs sold.
Accounts receivable	XX		
Cost of goods sold	XX		
Sales		XX	
Finished goods inventory		XX	

The overhead control account is closed:			This entry assumes overhead was overallocated. If overhead is underallocated, reverse the debits and credits.
Overhead control	XX		
Cost of goods sold		XX	
Finished goods inventory		XX	
Work in process inventory		XX	

Demonstration problem-Journal entries in job costing
The Greg White Corporation manufactures a custom product according to customer specifications. White uses a job costing system.. Factory overhead is allocated to work in process based on direct labor hours. On January 1, 2005, White budgeted $520,000 of factory overhead and 52,000 direct labor hours.

Required:
Prepare journal entries for the following selected 2005 transactions.
a) Purchased production materials on account for $20,000. Of this amount, $16,000 was for direct materials and $4,000 was for indirect materials.
b) Paid the rent of $100,000. This is 60% factory and 40% office rent.
c) Materials were issued to production: $13,000 direct materials and $6,000 indirect materials.
d) Accrued the weekly factory payroll: (ignore payroll taxes)

Direct labor	$4,000 (600 hours)
Indirect labor	$2,000 (350 hours)

e) Allocated overhead to work in process inventory for the weekly payroll mentioned in (d) above.
f) Job #621 with a total cost of $3,500 was completed.
g) Job #621 was shipped to the customer and invoiced at $5,000.
h) Prepare the most correct December 31 adjusting journal entry to close Overhead control. Actual 2005 factory overhead was $560,000 and actual 2005 direct labor hours were 49,000. The balances for work in process inventory, finished goods inventory, and cost of goods sold at 12/31/05, before this adjustment, were $200,000, $300,000, and $500,000, respectively.

Solution to demonstration problem
First note that the estimated allocation rate is $520,000/52,000 hours = $10/hour.

a)	Raw materials inventory	20,000		Note that all raw materials, direct and
	Accounts Payable		20,000	indirect, are debited to Raw materials.
b)	Overhead control	60,000		The factory rent is an inventoriable
	Office rent expense	40,000		cost, and is debited to Overhead
	Cash		100,000	control under normal costing. The
				office rent is a period cost.
c)	Work in process inventory	13,000		
	Overhead control	6,000		Notice in these two entries that the
	Raw materials inventory		19,000	direct costs are debited to Work in
				process and the indirect costs are
d)	Work in process inventory	4,000		debited to Overhead control.
	Overhead control	2,000		
	Accrued payroll		6,000	
e)	Work in process inventory	6,000		
	Overhead control		6,000	(600 hrs @ $10/hr)
f)	Finished goods inventory	3,500		
	Work in process inventory		3,500	

solution continues on next page →

Solution to demonstration problem continued

g)	Accounts receivable	5,000			Job costing uses the perpetual
	Cost of goods sold	3,500			inventory method, so cost of goods
	Sales			5,000	sold is recorded at time of sale.
	Finished goods inventory			3,500	
					Actual direct labor hours were 49,000,
h)	Work in process inventory*	14,000			so credits to Overhead control were
	Finished goods inventory*	21,000			$490,000 ($10/hr x 49,000 hours).
	Cost of goods sold*	35,000			Debits to overhead control = actual
	Overhead control			70,000	overhead of $560,000.

*Overhead control has a debit balance of $70,000 at the end of the year, so a $70,000 credit (overhead is underapplied by $70,000) is required to close the account. This $70,000 is material because it is larger than 10% of actual overhead of $560,000, so it is debited to work in process, finished good, and cost of goods sold in a ratio of the ending balances of these accounts before this adjustment.

Work in process	$200,000	20%
Finished goods	300,000	30%
Cost of goods sold	500,000	50%
	$1,000,000	100%

PROBLEM SET A (Learning Objectives 1 - 3)

<u>Matching</u>: Match each term with the best definition or example by writing the appropriate letter in the space provided. Use each term only once.

List of terms

A. Actual costing	I. Direct cost	R. Actual allocation rate
B. Normal costing	J. Indirect cost	S. Estimated allocation rate
C. Cost of goods manufact'd	K. Period cost	T. Work in process inventory
D. Job costing	L. Job cost record	U. Finished goods inventory
E. Process costing	M. Inventoriable cost	V. Raw materials inventory
F. Overallocated overhead	O. Prime costs	W. Time record
G. Underallocated overhead	P. Cost pool	X. Material requisition form
H. Manufacturing overhead	Q. Allocation base	Y. Source documents

_____ 1. All indirect manufacturing costs

_____ 2. All direct manufacturing costs

_____ 3. A cost that is easily traceable to the cost object

_____ 4. Accumulates direct and indirect production cost for a specific job

_____ 5. Actual overhead over the actual quantity of the allocation base

_____ 6. The denominator in the allocation rate computation

_____ 7. Used to trace direct production costs to jobs

_____ 8. Expensed in the period incurred

_____ 9. Manufacturing costs incurred, plus or minus the change in work in process

_____ 10. Used to trace direct labor costs to jobs

_____ 11. A cost that is not easily traceable to the cost object

_____ 12. Costs that are not expensed until the product is sold

_____ 13. An accounting system where the product's cost is an average of all costs for the period

_____ 14. An accounting system where each product may have a different cost

_____ 15. The production costs for all jobs in process

_____ 16. An accounting system where overhead is allocated using the actual allocation rate

_____ 17. Actual overhead exceeds allocated overhead

_____ 18. The cost of all direct and indirect materials available for use in production

_____ 19. An accounting system where overhead is allocated using the estimated allocation rate

_____ 20. Used to trace direct materials costs to jobs

_____ 21. An aggregation of costs that have something in common

_____ 22. Allocated overhead exceeds actual overhead

_____ 23. Estimated overhead over the estimated quantity of the allocation base

_____ 24. The production costs for completed but unsold jobs

Exercises: Write your answer in the space provided.
1. Determine whether the listed costs are inventoriable (product) costs or period costs by placing an X in the appropriate column. For the inventoriable costs, determine if the cost is direct or indirect when the cost object is the job.

Cost description	Inventoriable or period cost?		If inventoriable, is it direct or indirect?	
	Inventoriable	Period	Direct	Indirect
Indirect labor				
Factory depreciation				
Indirect materials				
Insurance on the office				
Sales commissions				
Factory property taxes				
Rent on the administrative offices				
Direct labor				
Salaries of administrative workers				
Direct materials				
Depreciation of office equipment				
Factory utilities				

2. Last year Geodgi Company experienced the following: direct materials used $50,000, direct labor $80,000, overhead (60% fixed) $120,000, selling costs (30% variable) $90,000. There were no beginning or ending work in process inventories and 40% of everything produced was sold. Determine the following amounts:

a) Total inventoriable (product) costs _____

b) Total indirect manufacturing costs _____

c) Total fixed costs _____

d) Total period costs _____

e) Total prime costs _____

f) Total variable costs _____

g) Total expenses _____

3. The Lonnie Corporation manufactures widgets to customer specifications. It uses a job order cost system. On January 1, Lonnie budgeted manufacturing overhead of $100,000 and expected direct labor hours for the year to be 50,000. Factory overhead is allocated to work in process inventory based on direct labor hours.

    a) Compute the estimated overhead allocation rate. _____

    b) Prepare the summary journal entries for the selected transactions described below:

    (i) Purchased direct and indirect materials for $30,000 on account.

    (ii) Direct materials of $4,500 and indirect materials of $7,000 were issued to work in process inventory.

    (iii) Direct labor of $18,000 (which was for 1,000 direct labor hours) and indirect labor of $6,000 was accrued.

    (iv) Overhead was allocated to work in process inventory for the 1,000 direct labor hours mentioned above.

    c) Suppose that actual overhead for the year was $121,000 and that actual direct labor hours were 48,000 for the year. Prepare the December 31 journal entry to close the overhead control account. Assume that the misallocated overhead is considered material, and that work in process inventory and finished goods inventory had identical balances at December 31, and that the cost of goods sold balance was 3 times as large as the balance in work in process inventory at December 31.

4. You are given the following information for Peg's Products for 2005. Assume that all raw materials are direct materials, and that Peg uses actual costing.

	1/1/05	12/31/05
Direct materials inventory	$20,000	$30,000
Work in process inventory	10,000	5,000
Finished goods inventory	25,000	40,000
Direct material purchases		50,000
Factory depreciation		12,000
Rent on office space		20,000
Factory utilities		5,000
Indirect labor		25,000
Depreciation on factory machines		8,000
Direct labor		47,000
Rent on factory		40,000

a) Use t-accounts to compute the following:

Direct mat-
erials used _____

Cost of goods
manufactured _____

Cost of
goods sold _____

Direct Materials Inventory

Work in Process Inventory

Finished Goods Inventory

b) Prepare a schedule of cost of goods manufactured in good form in the space below.

5. You are given the following information for Wanda's Widget Company for 2005. Assume that all raw materials are direct materials.

Direct material purchases	$4,000
Factory equipment depreciation	2,000
Direct material used	3,500
Beginning work in process inventory	3,000
Ending work in process inventory	?
Beginning finished goods inventory	4,000
Ending finished goods inventory	3,000
Direct labor	6,000
Indirect labor	1,000
Cost of goods sold	12,500
Sales	25,000

a) Prepare the journal entry for the purchase of direct materials on account.

b) Prepare the journal entry for the use of direct materials.

c) Prepare the journal entry to accrue direct and indirect labor costs.

d) Prepare the journal entry to record factory depreciation.

e) Prepare the journal entry to allocate overhead of $3,000 to work in process.

f) Prepare the journal entry to transfer the costs of completed jobs to finished goods.

g) Prepare the journal entry to record the sale of completed jobs.

CHAPTER REVIEW: Learning Objectives 4 - 6

Q4: What are the uses and limitations of job cost information?

Job cost information is used to prepare financial statements and tax returns, but it is also useful to managers in other ways. Bids for potential jobs use job cost information, and managers must use job cost information to monitor jobs in process.

Other short-term or long-term decisions can be made using job cost information, but the fixed overhead allocated to jobs is not relevant for most short-term decisions, as we saw in Chapter 4.

There is minimal uncertainty about the direct costs traced to jobs, but the overhead allocated to a job is only an estimate of the job's share of the period's indirect manufacturing costs. Overhead allocation estimates can be improved if the allocation base used is a cost driver for the overhead cost pool.

Q5: How are spoilage, rework, and scrap handled in job costing?

When defective units are produced or partially produced, this is known as *spoilage*.

- Most manufacturers consider some part of spoilage as part of regular operations. This is called *normal spoilage*.

- Excessive spoilage that occurs for whatever reason is called *abnormal spoilage*.

- Some spoiled units can be repaired and sold at regular prices as good units or at reduced prices as flawed units; this is known as *rework*.

- *Scrap* is the portion of raw materials that is left over from the normal production process. Scrap is either discarded or sold at a minimal price.

Normal spoilage is an inventoriable, or product, cost. The costs of normal spoilage are estimated at the beginning of the period as part of estimated overhead, so all units absorb estimated normal spoilage costs when overhead is allocated to jobs. Abnormal spoilage is a period cost and its costs are debited to a loss account.

In job costing, there are three possible scenarios for spoilage costs.

- The spoilage is considered normal and it is not attributable to the specifications of the job in which the spoilage occurred. In this case, the costs of the defective units are removed from Work in process inventory (and from the job cost record for the job) and debited to Overhead control as an actual overhead cost.

- The spoilage is considered abnormal. In this case, the costs of the defective units are removed from Work in process inventory (and from the job cost record for the job) and debited to Loss from abnormal spoilage.

- The spoilage occurred only because of the demanding specifications of the job. In this case, the costs remain in Work in process inventory and on the job cost record.

Demonstration problem-Journal entries for spoilage in job costing
Positronics makes robot brains to customers' specifications. The brains are tested for defects just before transfer to finished goods inventory. Job #23HK is for 100 brains, and its job cost record shows total manufacturing costs of $100,000. Upon completion of production, an inspection reveals that 5 brains are defective.

Required:
a) Suppose the spoilage is not due to the demanding specifications of the job, and that the spoilage is considered normal. The brains cannot be reworked and must be destroyed. Prepare the journal entry to account for the spoilage and the entry to transfer the job's cost to finished goods. What is the cost per unit of the brains in Job #23HK?
b) Suppose the spoilage is not due to the demanding specifications of the job, and that the spoilage is considered normal. The brains cannot be reworked, but the silicone in the brains can be salvaged and sold as scrap for a total of $3,000. Prepare the journal entry to account for the spoilage and the sale of scrap, and the entry to transfer the job's cost to finished goods. What is the cost per unit of the brains in Job #23HK?
c) Suppose the spoilage is considered abnormal, and the brains cannot be reworked or sold for scrap. Prepare the entry to account for the spoilage and the entry to transfer the job's cost to finished goods. What is the cost per unit of the brains in Job #23HK?
d) Suppose the spoilage occurred only because of the customer's unusual specifications for this job, and that the brains cannot be reworked or sold as scrap. Prepare the entry to account for the spoilage and the entry to transfer the job's cost to finished goods. What is the cost per unit of the brains in Job #23HK?

Solution to demonstration problem
Note that the production cost of a brain, before any adjustment for scrap, is $100,000/100 brains or $1,000 per brain.

a) Overhead control   5,000
        Work in process inventory   5,000

    Finished goods inventory   95,000
        Work in process inventory   95,000

> After the entry to remove the costs of normal spoilage, the job cost record for Job #23HK shows totals costs of $95,000. Since the job is for 95 non-defective brains, the cost/brain is $1,000.

b) Overhead control   2,000
    Cash   3,000
        Work in process inventory   5,000

    Finished goods inventory   95,000
        Work in process inventory   95,000

> After the entry to remove the costs of normal spoilage, the job cost record for Job #23HK shows totals costs of $95,000. Again, the cost/brain is $1,000.

c) Loss from abnormal spoilage   5,000
        Work in process inventory   5,000

    Finished goods inventory   95,000
        Work in process inventory   95,000

> Again, the job cost record shows $95,000 of total costs and the cost per brain is $1,000.

solution continues on next page →

Solution to demonstration problem continued

d)   There is no entry to remove costs from work in process | In this case the job cost record shows $100,000 of total costs. The cost per brain is $100,000/95 brains = $1,053 per brain.

      Finished goods inventory   100,000
        Work in process inventory   100,000

Q6: What are the quality and behavioral implications of spoilage?

When a company spends time producing defective units that cannot be sold at regular prices, it loses the contribution margin it could have made if the units were not defective. Spoiled units can also potentially affect the company's reputation. These are the opportunity costs of spoilage.

Manager's may invest in product quality by adopting performance benchmarks that include ever-decreasing limits for acceptable spoilage. The benefits and costs of these practices are hard to measure because many factors are qualitative (e.g. company reputation), rather than quantitative.

Whenever managers are compensated using accounting information, the information used will affect the managers' behavior. Some accounting procedures may not provide incentives for managers to control spoilage, including:

- the failure of the accounting system to capture any information about spoilage.

- overestimating normal spoilage so that costs of defects are considered part of expected overhead costs.

- the failure to track rework costs separately from other production costs.

PROBLEM SET B (Learning Objectives 4 - 6)

<u>True-False</u>: Indicate whether each of the following is true (T) or false (F) in the space provided.

_____ 1. All units produced absorb some costs of normal spoilage.

_____ 2. The costs of abnormal spoilage reduce reported income.

_____ 3. After inspection, 10% of Job 245's units were found to be defective. This was considered abnormal spoilage. The cost per non-defective unit of the items in Job 245 is unchanged by this spoilage.

_____ 4. After inspection, 10% of Job 245's units were found to be defective. This was considered normal spoilage, but it is not due to any unusual aspects of Job 245. The cost per non-defective unit of the items in Job 245 is unchanged by this spoilage.

_____ 5. After inspection, 10% of Job 245's units were found to be defective. This spoilage occurred because of unusual customer demands on Job 245. The cost per unit of the items in Job 245 is unchanged by this spoilage.

_____ 6. Scrap is leftover raw materials that must be discarded.

_____ 7. If defective units can be repaired and sold at regular prices, the cost of this repair is known as rework.

_____ 8. One way to focus management attention on the costs of spoilage is to set the acceptable level for normal spoilage at zero.

_____ 9. On a job cost record, the quality of the direct cost information is higher than the quality of the indirect cost information.

_____ 10. A job cost system can be used to estimate costs of potential jobs.

_____ 11. Normal spoilage arises under efficient operating practices.

_____ 12. There may be costs associated with reducing the number of defective units, but it will always be worth it in order to preserve a company's reputation for quality products.

_____ 13. Having an inspection point in the middle of the production process, rather than at the end, can reduce the costs of spoilage.

_____ 14. At the inspection point, 3% of Job 678's units were found to be defective, because the customer's requests for this job were hard to fulfill. The defective units are discarded. There is no journal entry to record this spoilage.

_____ 15. At the inspection point, 3% of Job 678's units were found to be defective, because the customer's requests for this job were hard to fulfill. The defective units are sold for $180. There is no journal entry to record this spoilage.

<u>Multiple choice</u>: Write the letter that represents the best choice in the space provided.

_____   1. The cost of poor quality products includes
    a.   the company's loss of reputation
    b.   the lost contribution margin from sales of high quality products
    c.   the potential loss of future market share
    d.   all of the above

_____   2. Abnormal spoilage costs appear
    a.   on the balance sheet as part of work in process
    b.   on the income statement as part of cost of goods manufactured
    c.   on the balance sheet as part of finished goods
    d.   on the income statement as a loss

_____   3. If spoiled goods have a positive disposal value
    a.   the disposal value increases the debit to Overhead control if the spoilage is normal
    b.   the disposal value decreases the job's cost per unit if the spoilage is directly attributable to the job
    c.   the disposal value increases the job's cost per unit if the spoilage is normal
    d.   the disposal value decreases the debit to Overhead control if the spoilage is abnormal

_____   4. Mike's Bikes makes gears for mountain bikes. It is considered normal for 3% of the good gears in a batch to be defective. The spoilage costs of a defective gear are $20, but a defective gear can be sold for $5 as scrap. Batch #248 contains 103 gears, and 3 are defective. Which of the following is the correct entry to record the costs of spoilage and the sale of the scrap?
    a.   Cash   15
         Loss from abnormal spoilage   45
              Work in process inventory   60
    b.   Work in process inventory   45
         Cash   15
              Overhead control   60
    c.   Cash   15
         Overhead control   45
              Work in process inventory   60
    d.   Cash   15
         Finished goods inventory   45
              Work in process inventory   60

_____ 5. Gloria's Garments makes house dresses. Defective units have their labels removed and are sold as "seconds". This is an example of
  a. scrap
  b. rework
  c. abnormal spoilage
  d. fashion suicide

_____ 6. Pete's Plastic Products makes plastic toys and car parts. The injection molding machines leave behind plastic that can be sold to a plastic supplier. This is an example of
  a. scrap
  b. rework
  c. abnormal spoilage
  d. normal spoilage

_____ 7. Upon inspection, Joe's Jumpsuits found that all of the jumpsuits in Batch #987 had the sleeves sewn in backwards. One of the new seamstresses had not been properly trained, which is highly unusual. The jumpsuits had to be thrown away. This is an example of
  a. scrap
  b. rework
  c. abnormal spoilage
  d. both (a) and (c)

_____ 8. Patsy's Products recently moved the inspection point for spoilage to an earlier point in the production process. The most likely effect of this is
  a. to reduce the costs associated with normal spoilage
  b. to reduce the costs associated with abnormal spoilage
  c. to eliminate abnormal spoilage
  d. both (a) and (b)

_____ 9. Pete's Plastic Products makes plastic toys and car parts. The injection molding machines leave behind plastic that can be ground up and used again in the next batch of production. The entry to record this includes
  a. a credit to Work in process inventory
  b. a credit to Overhead control
  c. a debit to Raw materials inventory
  d. both (a) and (c)

_____ 10. For Fiona Company, defective units of 2% of the good units completed is considered normal. Job #456 included some unusual specifications. Because of these, 5% of the units in Job #456 were defective. Which of the following is true?
  a. The cost of producing 3% of the units in Job #456 is abnormal spoilage.
  b. The cost of producing 2% of the units in Job #456 is part of overhead.
  c. The cost of producing 5% of the units in Job #456 is part of overhead.
  d. None of the above are true.

END OF CHAPTER EXERCISES

<u>Multiple choice</u>: Write the letter that represents the best choice in the space provided.

_____ 1. The basic difference between product and period costs is that
    a. period costs are expensed in the period the product is sold
    b. period costs are initially inventoried, then expensed
    c. product costs are expensed as the product is produced
    d. product costs are expensed in the period the product is sold

_____ 2. Prime costs are $72,000 for the period and overhead is 40% of the period's total manufacturing costs. If beginning work in process was $12,500 and ending work in process is $10,000, what is the cost of goods manufactured?
    a. $122,500
    b. $120,000
    c. $74,500
    d. $182,500

_____ 3. The cost credited to work in process and debited to finished goods is known as
    a. total manufacturing costs
    b. cost of goods sold
    c. cost of goods manufactured
    d. cost of goods available for sale

_____ 4. Cost of goods available for sale on the statement of cost of goods manufactured is equal to
    a. beginning finished goods plus cost of goods manufactured
    b. beginning work in process plus total manufacturing costs minus ending work in process
    c. direct materials used plus direct labor plus overhead
    d. cost of goods manufactured plus or minus the change in the balance in finished goods inventory

_____ 5. In job costing, the allocation of overhead results in a debit to
    a. Overhead control
    b. Work in process inventory
    c. Finished goods inventory
    d. Cost of goods sold

_____ 6. Accounting for overhead involves averaging in

	Job order costing	Process costing
a.	yes	no
b.	yes	yes
c.	no	yes
d.	no	no

_____ 7. When developing an estimated overhead allocation rate, which of the following is used in the numerator?
   a. actual annual overhead cost
   b. estimated output in units
   c. estimated annual overhead cost
   d. estimated direct labor hours

Use the following information for questions 8 & 9:
Tulalip uses a job costing system that allocates overhead as a percentage of direct labor costs. The budget for this year was: direct materials $60,000; direct labor $30,000; overhead $45,000. Actual costs for this year were: direct materials $50,000; direct labor $35,000; overhead $45,000.

_____ 8. What is the estimated overhead allocation rate?
   a. 50% of direct labor costs
   b. 129% of direct labor costs
   c. 150% of direct labor costs
   d. 67% of direct labor costs

_____ 9. What is the over- or underallocated overhead for this year?
   a. $0
   b. $150 overallocated
   c. $21,550 underallocated
   d. $7,500 overallocated

Use the following information for questions 10 - 12:
Bothell Company uses a job costing system that allocates estimated overhead as 40% of prime costs. The full normal cost of its products are 80% of the products' billed prices to customers.

_____ 10. What is the cost of a job that required direct materials of $2,000 and direct labor of $5,200?
   a. $9,280
   b. $10,080
   c. $7,200
   d. $8,000

_____ 11. Assume total revenue for the month is $1,750,000 and that all units produced were sold. There were no beginning or ending work in process inventories. How much overhead was allocated this period?
   a. $560,000
   b. $600,000
   c. $875,000
   d. $400,000

_____ 12. Assume the full cost of Job #392 was $12,000. What was the price billed?
   a. $15,000
   b. $14,400
   c. $16,000
   d. $16,500

<u>Exercises</u>: Write your answer in the space provided.
1. The Brier Company is a small printing company that uses a job costing system. Overhead is allocated at the rate of 200% times direct labor costs. Direct labor costs are $12 per hour.

Actual overhead costs for the current period were $2,900. Jobs #201, #202, and #204 were completed. Jobs #201 and #202 were sold on account for $4,000 total (not $4,000 each). Job #203 was still in process at the end of the period. The following is a partial summary of the costs associated with the jobs worked on during this period:

	201	202	203	204	Total
Costs in beginning work in process inventory	$688	$0	$0	$0	$688
Current period costs:					
Direct materials	20	600	2,000	3,000	5,620
Direct labor	96	120	480	600	1,296

a) Determine the total cost of each job.

Job 201 _____   Job 202 _____   Job 203 _____   Job 204 _____

b) Prepare the journal entry to record the cost of direct materials used this period.

c) Prepare the journal entry to record the direct labor costs incurred this period.

d) Prepare the journal entry to allocate overhead to work in process for the period.

e) Prepare the journal entry to record the costs of jobs completed this period.

f) Prepare the journal entry to record the sale of Job #201 and Job #202.

g) Prepare the journal entry to close the Overhead control account. Assume the misallocated overhead is considered immaterial.

2. Yakutsk Company manufactures special tools for the airline industry and uses job costing to account for production costs. Its direct labor cost is $12 per hour and overhead is allocated to work in process at the rate of $15 per direct labor hour. There were no units in beginning Finished goods inventory. Jobs #128 and #129 were completed this month, and Job #129 was sold for $110,000. Other data for the month include:

a) Prepare a statement of cost of goods manufactured for the current month.

| | Job # | | | |
	128	129	130	Total
Costs in beginning work in process inventory	$107,500	$0	$0	$107,500
Current period costs:				
Direct materials	60,000	40,000	30,000	130,000
Direct labor	60,000	18,000	12,000	90,000

b) Prepare an income statement for the current month, and assume that total selling and administrative expenses for the month were $31,000.

3. Yarrow Company's estimated overhead for this year was $120,000 plus $1.25/machine hour. At the beginning of the year, Yarrow expected to produce 16,000 units and use 80,000 machine hours. During the year, Yarrow actually produced 17,000 units and used 84,500 machine hours. Actual overhead costs for the year were $120,000 for fixed overhead and $106,600 for variable overhead.

   a) Assume that Yarrow uses actual costing. Determine the amount of overhead allocated to work in process this year and the amount of over- or underallocated overhead this year.

   Allocated overhead _____   Misllocated overhead _____

      under   over   (circle one)

   b) Assume that Yarrow uses normal costing. Determine the amount of overhead allocated to work in process this year and the amount of over- or underallocated overhead this year.

   Allocated overhead _____   Misllocated overhead _____

      under   over   (circle one)

4. Scott & Sam is an architectural firm specializing in home remodeling. Its job costing system has a single direct cost pool, professional labor costs, and a single indirect cost pool, office support costs. The office support costs are allocated to remodeling projects based on number of blueprints. You are given the following information for 2005:

	Budgeted	Actual
Professional labor costs	$720,000	$825,000
Office support costs (indirect costs)	$240,000	$323,000
Professional labor hours	10,000 hours	11,000 hours
Number of blueprints	800 blueprints	850 blueprints

   a) Compute the actual and estimated indirect cost allocation rates for indirect costs.

   Actual indirect cost allocation rate _____   Estimated indirect cost allocation rate _____

   b) The Willis family room project took place in 2005. This project was budgeted to use 60 professional labor hours and 2 blueprints, but actually used 55 hours and 3 blueprints. Compute the total cost (direct plus indirect) of this project using actual costing and normal costing.

   Actual costing _____   Normal costing _____

5. Laska Company makes hats with the customer's logo embroidered on them. The hats are inspected for quality just before transfer to finished goods inventory. Job #209 is for 1,000 hats, and its job cost record shows total manufacturing costs of $1,500. Upon completion of production, an inspection reveals that 25 of the hats are defective.

   a) Suppose the spoilage is not due to the demanding specifications of the job, and that the spoilage is considered normal. The hats cannot be reworked and must be destroyed. Prepare the journal entry to account for the spoilage and the entry to transfer the job's cost to finished goods. What is the cost per unit of the hats in Job #209?

   b) Suppose the spoilage is considered abnormal, and the hats cannot be reworked or sold for scrap. Prepare the entry to account for the spoilage and the entry to transfer the job's cost to finished goods. What is the cost per unit of the hats in Job #209?

   c) Suppose the spoilage occurred only because of the customer's unusual specifications for the logo design, and that the hats cannot be reworked or sold as scrap. Prepare the entry to account for the spoilage and the entry to transfer the job's cost to finished goods. What is the cost per unit of the hats in Job #209?

SOLUTION TO PROBLEM SET A

<u>Matching</u>:

1.	H	Indirect manufacturing costs is synonymous with manufacturing overhead
2.	O	Direct labor and direct materials are the only direct manufacturing costs
3.	I	By definition of direct cost (from Chapter 2)
4.	L	
5.	R	
6.	Q	
7.	Y	
8.	K	
9.	C	If work in process decreased during the period, then cost of goods manufactured equals total manufacturing costs incurred plus this decrease. If work in process increased during the period, then cost of goods manufactured equals total manufacturing costs incurred minus this change.
10.	W	
11.	J	By definition of indirect cost (from Chapter 2)
12.	M	
13.	E	
14.	D	
15.	T	
16.	A	
17.	G	
18.	V	
19.	B	
20.	X	
21.	P	
22.	F	
23.	S	
24.	U	

Exercises:

1.

Cost description	Inventoriable or period cost?		If inventoriable, is it direct or indirect?	
	Inventoriable	Period	Direct	Indirect
Indirect labor	X			X
Factory depreciation	X			X
Indirect materials	X			X
Insurance on the office		X		
Sales commissions		X		
Factory property taxes	X			X
Rent on the administrative offices		X		
Direct labor	X		X	
Salaries of administrative workers		X		
Direct materials	X		X	
Depreciation of office equipment		X		
Factory utilities	X			X

2. a) Total inventoriable (product) costs = $250,000
    direct materials $50,000 + direct labor $80,000 + overhead $120,000

b) Total indirect manufacturing costs = $120,000
    indirect manufacturing costs is synonymous with manufacturing overhead

c) Total fixed costs = $135,000
    fixed overhead $120,000 x 60% + fixed selling $90,000 x 70% = $72,000 + $63,000

d) Total period costs = $90,000
    selling costs is the only period cost listed

e) Total prime costs = $130,000
    direct materials $50,000 + direct labor $80,000

f) Total variable costs = $205,000
    direct materials $50,000 + direct labor $80,000 + variable overhead $120,000 x 40%
    + variable selling $90,000 x 30% = $50,000 + $80,000 + $48,000 + $27,000

g) Total expenses = $190,000
    cost of goods sold $250,000 x 40% sold + selling $90,000 = $100,000 + $90,000

3. a) Estimated overhead allocation rate = $100,000/50,000 hours = $2/hour

   b) The journal entries for the selected transactions are:

   i) Raw materials inventory   30,000   ⎤ All raw materials, direct and
         Accounts Payable   30,000 ⎦ indirect are debited to Raw
                                                            materials

   ii) Overhead control   7,000   ⎤ Indirect materials used are an
       Work in process inventory   4,500   ⎬ actual overhead cost and go to
         Raw materials inventory   11,500 ⎦ Overhead control in normal costing

   iii) Overhead control   6,000   ⎤ Notice the similarity between the
        Work in process inventory   18,000   ⎬ above entry and this one.
          Accrued payroll   24,000 ⎦

   iv) Work in process inventory   2,000   ⎤
         Overhead control   2,000 ⎬ (1,000 hrs @ $2/hr)

   c) The amount of overhead allocated this year must have been 48,000 hours x $2/hour = $96,000, so there were credits of $96,000 to Overhead control this year. The debits to Overhead control totals the actual overhead of $121,000. At the end of the year, then, Overhead control as a debit balance of $25,000 ($121,000 - $96,000). The entry will credit Overhead control and have 3 debits to Work in process, Finished goods, and Cost of goods sold. If the balance in Work in process before adjustment is denoted as X, then the sum of the balances in all 3 accounts is X + X + 3X = 5X. Work in process and Finished goods will each take 1/5 (20%) of the $25,000 and Cost of goods sold will take 3/5 (60%) of the $25,000.

       Work in process inventory   5,000
       Finished goods inventory   5,000
       Cost of goods sold   15,000
         Overhead control   25,000

4. a) Direct materials used = $40,000, Cost of goods manufactured = $182,000, and Cost of goods sold = $167,000, as shown in the t-accounts below.

Direct Materials Inventory		Work in Process Inventory		Finished Goods Inventory	
20,000		10,000		25,000	
50,000	40,000	DM 40,000	182,000	182,000	167,000
		DL 47,000	CGM	CGM	CGS
		MO* 90,000			
30,000		5,000		40,000	

* Manufacturing overhead = $12,000 + $5,000 + $25,000 + $8,000 + $40,000; the rent on office space is not part of manufacturing overhead.

Peg's Products
Schedule of Cost of Goods Manufactured
Year ended December 31, 2005

Beginning work in process inventory			$10,000
Manufacturing costs added this period:			
Direct materials used:			
Begininning direct materials inventory	$20,000		
Direct material purchases	50,000		
Cost of materials available for use	70,000		
Less ending direct materials inventory	30,000	$40,000	
Direct labor		47,000	
Manufacturing overhead		90,000	177,000
			187,000
Less ending work in process inventory			5,000
Cost of goods manufactured			$182,000

4. b)
5.

a)

Raw materials inventory	4,000	
Accounts Payable		4,000

b)

Work in process inventory	3,500	
Raw materials inventory		3,500

}All raw materials are direct.

c)

Overhead control	1,000	
Work in process inventory	6,000	
Accrued payroll		7,000

d)

Overhead control	2,000	
Accumulated deprec'n		2,000

e)

Work in process inventory	3,000	
Overhead control		3,000

f)

Finished goods inventory	11,500	
Work in process inventory		11,500

}See note below for the computation of the $11,500.

h)

Accounts receivable	25,000	
Cost of goods sold	12,500	
Sales		25,000
Finished goods inventory		12,500

Note: If cost of goods sold is $12,500, and Finished goods inventory decreased by $1,000, then cost of goods manufactured must be $11,500 (draw a t-account for Finished goods inventory).

SOLUTION TO PROBLEM SET B

<u>True-False:</u>

1. T   Normal spoilage is estimated as part of overhead at the beginning of the year, so the estimated overhead allocation rate includes the estimated costs of normal spoilage.
2. T   True, because theses costs go to a loss account.
3. T   The costs will be removed from the job cost record, so the cost per unit of Job 245 will be the lower total costs divided by the reduced number of units.
4. T   In this case, the costs will also be removed from the job cost record, so again the cost per unit is unchanged.
5. F   Here the costs will not be removed from the job cost record. This cost will be divided by a reduced number of units to calculate cost per unit of the job and the cost per unit will be increased.
6. F   Scrap may be discarded but sometimes it can be sold for a minimal amount.
7. T
8. T   If normal spoilage limits are zero, all spoilage is considered abnormal and will appear on the income statement as a loss, which should focus attention on the spoilage.
9. T   The indirect costs on a job cost record are just estimates, but source documents back up the direct cost information.
10. T
11. T   By definition of normal spoilage.
12. F   It is not necessarily true that any cost is worth a company's reputation for quality products. In fact, some companies do not have product quality as a main goal.
13. T   The earlier in the process that the spoiled units are recognized, the sooner processing of those units can cease.
14. T   The costs remain on the job cost record – there is no journal entry to remove costs.
15. F   The $180 would be removed from the job cost record. When the defective units are sold the entry would be a debit to Cash for $180 and a credit to Work in process.

<u>Multiple choice:</u>

1. D   Refer to the chapter summary for learning objective 6.
2. D   Refer to the chapter summary for learning objective 5.
3. B   When the spoilage is attributable to the demanding specifications of a job, the costs remain on the job cost record and hence affect the per unit cost of the job. However, these spoilage costs are reduced by the disposal value of the defective units. A is not correct because the disposal value decreases the debit to Overhead control in the entry to record normal spoilage. C is not right-normal spoilage costs are removed from the job cost record so the job's cost per unit is unchanged. D is not right-there is no debit to Overhead control if spoilage is abnormal.
4. C   Refer to the demonstration problem in the chapter review for learning objective 5.
5. B   This is the definition of rework.
6. A   This is the definition of scrap.

7. D   It is abnormal spoilage because it is highly unusual that a seamstress is not properly trained. It is also scrap that was discarded.
8. D   The earlier in the process that the spoiled units are recognized, the sooner processing of those units can cease whether the spoilage is considered normal or abnormal.
9. D   This wasn't specifically reviewed in this study guide, but hopefully you could figure this out. The ground up plastic leaves the factory floor (credit Work in process) and goes back to the materials storeroom (debit Raw materials).
10. D   Yes, sometimes "none of the above" IS the correct answer! The spoilage occurred because of the unusual specifications of the job. The spoilage is not abnormal, and it is not part of overhead.

SOLUTION TO END OF CHAPTER EXERCISES

Multiple choice:

1. D   By definition of product and period costs.
2. A   Overhead = 40% x (DM + DL + overhead) = 40% x (Prime costs + overhead) = 40% x ($72,000 + overhead). So, overhead = $28,800 + 40% x overhead; 60% x overhead = $28,800, or overhead = $48,000. Total manufacturing costs = Prime costs + overhead = $72,000 + $48,000 = $120,000. Beginning work in process $12,500 + $120,000 less ending work in process $10,000 = CGM $122,500.
3. C
4. A   Note that "cost of goods available for sale", as well as "cost of goods manufactured", are the names of subtotals on the statements of cost of goods sold and cost of goods manufactured, respectively. They are not general ledger account titles.
5. B   Overhead is allocated to work in process inventory.
6. B   In process costing, all manufacturing costs are averaged over the units produced. In job costing, overhead costs are averaged over the units produced.
7. C
8. C $45,000 estimated overhead over $30,000 estimated direct labor costs = 150% of direct labor cost overhead allocation rate.
9. D   Misallocated overhead is a comparison of actual overhead to allocated overhead. Allocated overhead is $35,000 actual direct labor costs times the estimated overhead allocation rate of 150% = $52,500. Allocated overhead exceeds actual overhead by $7,500.
10. B   Total prime cost of the job is $7,200, so overhead allocated is $7,200 times 40% = $2,880. Total cost of the job is $7,200 + $2,880 = $10,080.
11. D   CGS = 80% x $1,750,000 = $1,400,000. If all units produced were sold, then CGS = CGM. CGM = prime costs + 40% x prime costs = 1.4 x prime costs. Prime costs = $1,000,000; overhead = $400,000.
12. A   Cost = $12,000 = 80% x price; price = $15,000

Exercises:
1. a) The total cost of each job is computed below.

	201	202	203	204	Total
Costs in beginning work in process inventory	$688	$0	$0	$0	$688
Current period costs:					
Direct materials	20	600	2,000	3,000	5,620
Direct labor	96	120	480	600	1,296
Overhead	192	240	960	1,200	2,592
	$996	$960	$3,440	$4,800	$10,196

b) Work in process inventory   5,620
     Raw materials inventory   5,620

c) Work in process inventory   1,296
     Accrued payroll (or Cash)   1,296

d) Work in process inventory   2,592
     Overhead control   2,592 } 200% x $1,296

e) Finished goods inventory   6,756
     Work in process inventory   6,756 } $996 + $960 + $4,800

f) Accounts receivable   4,000
    Cost of goods sold   1,956
     Sales   4,000 } $996 + $960
     Finished goods inventory   1,956

g) Cost of goods sold   308   } $2,900 actual less $2,592 allocated
     Overhead control   308 } is $308 underallocated

2. a) Note you can compute the number of hours used by each job by dividing the direct labor costs by the $12/hour cost of direct labor. Allocated overhead is then $15/hour.

| | Job # | | | |
	128	129	130	Total
Direct labor hours used this period	5,000	1,500	1,000	7,500
Costs in beginning work in process inventory	$107,500	$0	$0	$107,500
Current period costs:				
Direct materials	60,000	40,000	30,000	130,000
Direct labor	60,000	18,000	12,000	90,000
Overhead allocated	75,000	22,500	15,000	112,500
	$302,500	$80,500	$57,000	$440,000
Job status	completed, not sold	completed and sold	not yet completed	

b)

Yakutsk Company
Schedule of Cost of Goods Manufactured

Beginning work in process inventory		$107,500
Manufacturing costs added this period:		
Direct materials used	$130,000	
Direct labor	90,000	
Manufactuing overhead	112,500	332,500
		440,000
Less ending work in process inventory		57,000
Cost of goods manufactured		$383,000

c)

Yakutsk Company
Income Statement

Sales	$110,000
Less cost of goods sold (job #129)	80,500
Gross margin	29,500
Selling & administrative expenses	31,000
Operating income	($1,500)

3. a) The overhead allocated to work in process under actual costing is just the actual overhead = $120,000 + $106,600 = $226,600. The is never any misallocated overhead in actual costing because misallocated factory overhead is the difference between actual overhead and allocated overhead.

   b) The estimated overhead rate is total estimated overhead/estimated machine hours = [$120,000 fixed + $1.25/hour x 80,000 hours]/80,000 hrs = $220,000/80,000 hrs = $2.75/hour. As an aside, note that we could break this down into two pieces: the fixed overhead rate is $2.00/hour and the variable overhead rate is $1.25/hour.

   Allocated overhead is $2.75/hour x 84,500 machine hours = $232,375.
   Overallocated overhead = $232,375 allocated - $226,600 actual = $5,775.

4. a) Actual indirect cost allocation rate = $323,000/850 blueprints = $380/bluprint.
      Estimated indirect cost allocation rate = $240,000/800 blueprints = $300/blueprint.

   b) Note that the information about the budgeted 60 professional labor hours and the estimated 2 blueprints is totally irrelevant to this computation because both actual and normal costing are based on the actual consumption of resources, not on the budgeted consumption of resources.

   Also note that the actual cost of a professional labor hour is $825,000/11,000 hours = $75/hour, so the direct costs of this project are 55 professional labor hours x $75/hour = $4,125.

Under actual costing the project cost is $4,125 direct costs + indirect costs of $380/blueprint x 3 blueprints = $4,125 + $1,140 = $5,265.	Under normal costing the project cost is $4,125 direct costs + indirect costs of $300/blueprint x 3 blueprints = $4,125 + $900 = $5,025.

5. First note that the processing cost per hat before any adjustments is $1,500/1,000 hats = $1.50/hat.

   a)   Overhead control   37.50
            Work in process inventory   37.50   Cost/hat =
                                                                                         $1,462.50/975 hats =
            Finished goods inventory   1,462.50 $1.50/hat.
            Work in process inventory   1,462.50

   b)   Loss from abnormal spoilage   37.50
            Work in process inventory   37.50   Cost/hat =
                                                                                         $1,462.50/975 hats =
            Finished goods inventory   1,462.50 $1.50/hat.
            Work in process inventory   1,462.50

   c)   There is no entry to remove costs from work in process   Cost/hat =
                                                                                         $1,500/975 hats =
            Finished goods inventory   1,500.00 $1.538/hat.
            Work in process inventory   1,500.00

Chapter 6

Process Costing

√ **Study Checklist – Monitor your progress**

1. Read the chapter in the text
2. Review the learning objectives below
3. Read the overview of the chapter
4. Read the chapter review for learning objectives 1 – 4
5. Do Problem Set A and check your answers
6. Read the chapter review for learning objectives 5 - 8
7. Do Problem Set B and check your answers
8. Do the End of Chapter Exercises in this study guide
9. Do the homework assigned by your instructor

CHAPTER LEARNING OBJECTIVES

After studying this chapter, you should be able to answer the following questions:

Q1. How are costs assigned to mass produced units?
Q2. What are equivalent units and how do they relate to the production process?
Q3. How is the weighted average method used in process costing?
Q4. How is the FIFO method used in process costing?
Q5. What alternative methods are used for mass production?
Q6. How is process costing performed for multiple production departments?
Q7. How are spoilage costs handled in process costing?
Q8. What are the uses and limitations of process cost information?

OVERVIEW OF CHAPTER

Process costing is a procedure that assigns costs to services provided or units produced. It is used when the units produced or services provided are identical and it is appropriate for each unit or service to be assigned the same cost. For example, in the pharmaceutical industry, it is appropriate for each aspirin to be assigned the same manufacturing cost. In banking, it would be appropriate to assign the same transaction cost to each cancelled check. This differs from job costing (Chapter 5) where the accounting procedures are designed to capture costs for units or jobs that are dissimilar. In job costing the cost object is the job, but in process costing the initial cost object is the processing department.

CHAPTER REVIEW: Learning Objectives 1 - 3

Q1: How are costs assigned to mass produced units?

In process costing, a separate general ledger work in process (WIP) inventory account is maintained for each of the sequential processing departments. When all raw materials are considered direct, the flow of costs in process costing for a two department production process is shown in Exhibit 6.1 below.

Exhibit 6.1: Flow of costs in process costing when all raw materials are direct

Raw Materials Inv		WIP Inv, Dep't 1		WIP Inv, Dep't 2		FG Inventory	
Beg Inv		Beg Inv		Beg Inv		Beg Inv	
RM	RM Used	RM Used	Cost of	RM Used	Cost of	Cost of	Cost of
Purch'd	RM Used	CC	Goods	CC	Goods → Goods	Goods	Goods
			Transf'd Out → TI Costs		Manuf'd	Manuf'd	Sold
End Inv		End Inv		End Inv		End Inv	

Compare this to Exhibit 5.1 on page 5-2 of this study guide. They may look quite similar but they represent quite different processes for aggregating costs. In process costing, we usually combine direct labor and overhead into one cost category called conversion costs (CC). Costs that are considered direct costs are direct to the department, not to the product being produced. Any materials requisitioned by Department 1 are direct to Department 1 and the wages of an individual who works solely for Department 1 are also direct to Department 1. Even depreciation on a machine used solely by Department 1 is a direct cost to Department 1. Therefore, conversion costs includes direct labor, overhead costs that are traced as direct costs to Department 1, and factory-wide overhead costs that are allocated to Department 1.

Since we have a separate account for the WIP inventory of each processing department, the second (and third, and fourth, etc.) departments have an additional cost category called transferred-in costs (TI). The transferred-in costs that a second or third processing department must account for include the cumulative direct materials and conversion costs from all prior departments.

Q2: What are equivalent units and how do they relate to the production process?

Process costing is an easy matter when beginning and ending work in process inventories are zero. Suppose we use a t-account to summarize the physical flow of production as we often do to summarize the accumulation of costs. Then Exhibit 6.2 on the next page shows a department that had no units in process at the beginning or end of the time period, started working on 10,000 units, and completed all 10,000 of them. There were, of course, no dollars attached to beginning or ending inventory in this department, and the production costs for this period totaled $30,000.

Exhibit 6.2: Summarizing the flow of units and costs; no beginning or ending inventories

WIP Inventory - Units		
Beg Inv 0		
Units Started	Units Com-	
10,000	pleted 10,000	
End Inv 0		

WIP Inventory - $		
Beg Inv $0		
DM $11,000	Cost of units trans-	
CC $19,000	ferred out $30,000	
End Inv $0		

The average manufacturing cost is clearly $3/unit for this scenario, and the $30,000 of production costs are all assigned to the units completed and transferred out. But what if the department had only completed 6,000 units, leaving 4,000 units in ending WIP inventory? How much of $30,000 should be assigned to the units transferred out and how much should be assigned to the units in ending inventory? Your first guess might be to assign 60% of the costs to the units transferred out and 40% to ending inventory. This would preserve the unit cost at $3/unit because [60%*$30,000]/6,000 units completed = $3/unit. Similarly, [40%*$30,000]/4,000 units in ending WIP inventory = $3/unit. But this is inaccurate because it assigns the same $3/unit cost to the completed units as it does to the unfinished units that remain in WIP inventory. This approach doesn't work because it treats unfinished units as if they are the same as completed units.

In order to compute unit cost we need a procedure that recognizes the difference between completed units and the units still in process at the end of the period. The key to understanding process costing is the concept of equivalent units of production (EUP). The calculation of EUP translates units into a measure of equivalent whole units. For example, 10,000 completed units are equivalent to 10,000 whole units, but 10,000 units that are only 60% complete are equivalent to 6,000 whole units because (theoretically) we could have made 6,000 units with the same resources that we used to take 10,000 units to the 60% stage of completion. In fact, process costing is all about keeping track of when work on units was completed and when costs were incurred.

Imagine a company with sequential operations (such as an assembly line). During any given month, a processing department will first expend resources to complete the beginning inventory units that were unfinished at the start of the month. Then it will start some new units that actually get completed during the month. We call these "started and completed" (S&C) units. Then, before the month ends, the department will begin work on some units that will not be finished in the department by the end of the month and will remain in ending WIP inventory. To simplify our discussion, suppose that a unit never takes more than 30 days to complete. Therefore, there are three categories of units:

BI: Units in the department's beginning WIP inventory. These units have work performed on them in the current month as well as in the prior month. Therefore, some costs that were incurred this month and in the prior month should be attached to these units.

S&C: Units that the department started and completed in the current month. These units should have only current month costs attached to them.

EI: Units in the department's ending WIP inventory. These units have work performed on them in the current month, and as of the end of the month should have only current month costs attached to them. They will, of course, be the beginning WIP inventory for the next month, and will then absorb some of next month's costs.

<u>Q3&4: How are the weighted average and FIFO method useds in process costing?</u>
There are two methods of process costing covered in this text, and the only difference between them is the definition of the time frame for the question of how much work was performed. The first-in, first-out (FIFO) method defines the time frame as the current month, but the weighted average (WA) method defines the time frame as the current and prior month combined. That is, when calculating EUP for the 3 categories of units (BI, S&C and EI), FIFO makes a distinction between work performed this month and the prior month. The WA method does not.

<u>Demonstration problem-Summarizing the flow of units and simple EUP calculations</u>
The Grinding Department is the first processing department of Stashu Manufacturing. All units are processed in under 30 days so that no unit is ever in both beginning and ending WIP inventory of a given month. For April the department had 10,000 units in beginning work in process inventory, it started processing 70,000 units, and it had 30,000 units in ending work in process inventory. In the Grinding Department, all costs are incurred evenly throughout production so that a unit that is 30% complete has incurred 30% of its production costs. Compute the April equivalent units of production under both the WA and FIFO methods for the Grinding Department. Suppose the BI units were 20% complete and the EI units were 30% complete.

<u>Required:</u>
a) Use t-accounts to determine the number of units started and completed and to summarize the physical flow of the units.
b) Compute the EUP under both the weighted average and FIFO methods.

<u>Solution to demonstration problem</u>
a)

Grinding Department WIP Inventory - Units

Beg Inv	10,000		
Units Started	70,000	Units Completed	50,000
End Inv	30,000		

This was not given, but it was easy to "plug" the t-account to compute the units completed

BI	10,000
S&C	40,000
	50,000

Once we determined that the department had completed 50,000 units, it was an easy matter to compute that the department must have started and completed 40,000 units. If 50,000 units were completed and transferred out, then the first 10,000 of them must have been the BI units that were completed this month. Only 40,000 of the 50,000 completed units were started this month.

b) To compute total EUP for the month, we need to compute the EUP for each category of unit and then add them up. We can make a schedule of EUP to organize these computations.

	Physical Units	WA EUP	FIFO EUP	
BI	10,000	10,000	8,000	100% credit for WA, 80% credit for FIFO
S&C	40,000	40,000	40,000	100% credit for both methods
EI	30,000	9,000	9,000	30% credit for both methods
Total		59,000	57,000	

solution continues on next page →

Solution to demonstration problem continued

The WA method calculates total EUP for April to be 59,000 and FIFO calculates total EUP to be 57,000. The WA method "gives credit" for work done in the prior month and the current month, so the EUP for the 10,000 BI units is 10,000. In fact, the WA method always gives 100% credit for BI units. FIFO only gives credit for the last 80% of production on these BI units, because 20% of the work was performed on these units last month. Both methods always give 100% credit for the S&C units because all work on them is done in the current month, by definition of S&C. Since the EI units were 30% complete, both methods give 30% credit for the work done on these units. The only difference between WA and FIFO is how they handle the BI units, because WA gives credit for prior work and FIFO does not.

Because the calculations for process costing can be complex, this study guide chapter incorporates practice exercises for you to work on specific parts of the material before you try the problem sets. Work Practice Exercise 1 below and review the solutions before continuing your review of this study guide.

Practice Exercise 1

Before we move on to more complicated matters, you need to make sure you can compute EUP for simple scenarios. Use the spaces below to solve this exercise and then check your answers before you continue forward. Don't look at the solution to Practice Exercise 1 until you are done with your work.

Department 1 is the first processing department of Scott Manufacturing. All units are processed in under 30 days so that no unit is ever in both beginning and ending WIP inventory. For December the department had 15,000 units in beginning WIP inventory. During December, it started processing 100,000 units, and there were 20,000 units in ending WIP inventory. In Department 1, all costs are incurred evenly throughout production. Compute the December EUP under both the WA and FIFO methods for the Department 1, assuming that the BI units were 40% complete and the EI units were 10% complete.

First summarize the physical flow of the units using the t-account below. Don't forget to also compute the number of units started and completed.

Department 1 WIP Inventory - Units

Next, compute the equivalent units of production.

	Physical Units	**WA EUP**	**FIFO EUP**
BI			
S&C			
EI			
Total			

Now check your answers and figure out your error if you didn't get it all right.

Solution to Practice Exercise 1

First summarize the physical flow of the units.

Department 1 WIP Inventory - Units

Beg Inv	15,000			
Units Started	100,000	Units Com-pleted 95,000	BI	15,000
			S&C	80,000
End Inv	20,000			95,000

Next, compute the total EUP.

	Physical Units	WA EUP	FIFO EUP
BI	15,000	15,000	9,000
S&C	80,000	80,000	80,000
EI	20,000	2,000	2,000
Total		97,000	91,000

Equivalent Units Computations When Costs Are Not Incurred Evenly

In the last section we assumed that production costs were incurred evenly throughout the process, which made the calculations for EUP relatively simple. In fact, we usually do assume for instruction purposes that conversion costs are incurred evenly throughout production, so what we learned in the last section holds for the computation of EUP for conversion costs. However, materials costs are rarely incurred evenly throughout production. An example of evenly-incurred materials costs is a department that spray paints automobile body parts. In other instances, materials costs are incurred at the beginning of production. Imagine a brewery, where the first department mixes the water, hops, yeast and sugar. These materials are added when the production process begins. In this case, ending inventory units have incurred all of their materials costs in the current period whether the units are 10%, 20% or 80% complete at the end of the period. With respect to materials, then, these units are complete and should absorb all materials costs incurred to start these units.

Materials costs may be incurred in ways that differ from evenly throughout production or at the beginning of production. For example, consider a department that assembles tables. Some materials costs are incurred when the department requisitions the wood for the table tops. Then the table tops may have to be sanded or otherwise worked on before the department requisitions the materials for the table legs. However, we will leave these types of calculations for the next section.

Demonstration problem-Summarizing the flow of units and EUP calculations for separate cost categories

Department 1 is the first processing department of Samantha Enterprises. All units are processed in under 30 days so that no unit is ever in both the beginning and ending WIP inventories of a given month. For March the department had 8,000 units in beginning work in process inventory, it started processing 60,000 units, and it had 12,000 units in ending work in process inventory. In the Assembly Department, conversion costs are incurred evenly throughout production and materials costs are incurred the moment the units are begun. Compute the March equivalent units of production under both the WA and FIFO methods for the Assembly Department. Suppose the BI units were 25% complete and the EI units were 40% complete.

Required:
a) Use t-accounts to determine the number of units started and completed and to summarize the physical flow of the units.
b) Compute the EUP for DM & CC under both the weighted average and FIFO methods.

solution begins on next page →

Solution to demonstration problem

a) We first need to summarize the physical flow of the units in Department 1 for March.

Department 1 WIP Inventory - Units

Beg Inv	8,000			This was not given, but it was easy to "plug" the t-account to compute the units completed
Units Started	60,000	Units Completed	56,000	BI 8,000
				S&C 48,000
				56,000
End Inv	12,000			

b) Now that we are doing separate EUP calculations for the two cost categories, DM & CC, we need separate columns in our schedule of equivalent units of production.

	Physical Units	Wtd Avg		FIFO		
		DM	CC	DM	CC	
BI	8,000	8,000	8,000	0	6,000	100% credit for DM & CC under WA, 75% credit for CC under FIFO, no credit for DM under FIFO
S&C	48,000	48,000	48,000	48,000	48,000	100% credit under both methods
EI	12,000	12,000	4,800	12,000	4,800	100% credit for DM under both methods, 40% credit for CC under both methods
Total		68,000	60,800	60,000	58,800	

For the BI units, FIFO gives 75% credit for CC because CC are incurred evenly and the BI units were 25% complete at the start of the month. But for DM, the FIFO method gives no credit. This is because FIFO only gives credit for work done in the current month. For the BI units, all DM costs are incurred the moment the units are begun, which was last month. As always, FIFO and WA agree on the EI calculations. DM is given 100% credit because the EI units were started this month, and all DM costs were incurred at that time. The EI was 40% complete, so 40% of the CC should attach to these units.

The t-account approach is useful for intuition building, but by the end of this chapter we will be preparing formal process cost reports.

In Exhibit 6.3 on the next page, the data from the recent demonstration problem is used to show a section of a process cost report. This section of the process cost report replaces the t-account and EUP schedule above. It is a more formal presentation of the information.

Exhibit 6.3: Summarizing the flow of units and equivalent units section of process cost report

Here is the t-account summary of the physical flow of the units, and below that is a section of the production cost report.

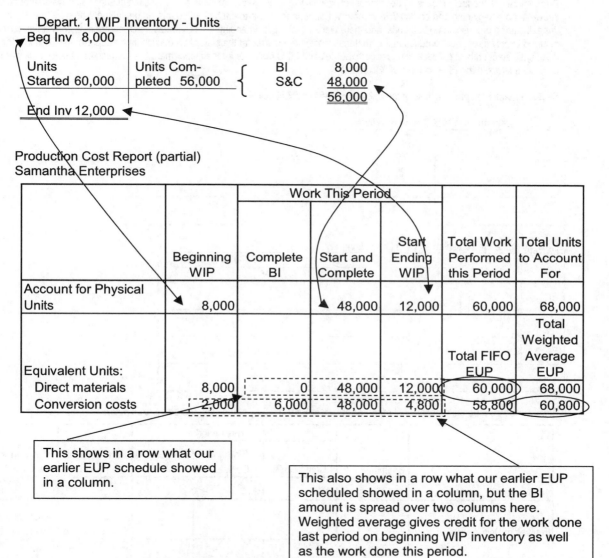

Depart. 1 WIP Inventory - Units

Beg Inv 8,000	
Units Started 60,000	Units Completed 56,000
End Inv 12,000	

BI	8,000
S&C	48,000
	56,000

Production Cost Report (partial)
Samantha Enterprises

		Work This Period				
	Beginning WIP	Complete BI	Start and Complete	Start Ending WIP	Total Work Performed this Period	Total Units to Account For
Account for Physical Units	8,000		48,000	12,000	60,000	68,000
					Total FIFO EUP	Total Weighted Average EUP
Equivalent Units: Direct materials	8,000	0	48,000	12,000	60,000	68,000
Conversion costs	2,000	6,000	48,000	4,800	58,800	60,800

This shows in a row what our earlier EUP schedule showed in a column.

This also shows in a row what our earlier EUP scheduled showed in a column, but the BI amount is spread over two columns here. Weighted average gives credit for the work done last period on beginning WIP inventory as well as the work done this period.

Practice Exercise 2
Let's see if you can compute EUP when not all costs are incurred evenly throughout processing. Use the spaces below to solve this problem and then check your answers before you continue forward.

Department 1 is the first processing department of Philip's Productions, Inc. All units are processed in under 30 days so that no unit is ever in both beginning and ending WIP inventory. For June the department had 9,000 units in beginning WIP inventory. During June, it started processing 80,000 units, and there were 10,000 units in ending WIP inventory. In Department 2, conversion costs are incurred evenly throughout production, but materials costs are incurred at the start of production in the department. Compute the June equivalent units of production under both the WA and FIFO methods for the Department 1, assuming that the BI units were 30% complete and the EI units were 90% complete.

First summarize the physical flow of the units using the t-account below.

Department 1 WIP Inventory - Units

Next, compute the equivalent units of production.

	Physical Units	WA EUP		FIFO EUP	
		DM	CC	DM	CC
BI					
S&C					
EI					
Total					

Finally, prepare a partial process cost report as shown in Exhibit 6.3 by completing the gray boxes below.

			Work This Period		Total Work	
	Beginning WIP	Complete BI	Start and Complete	Start Ending WIP	Performed this Period	Total Units to Account For
Account for Physical Units						
Equivalent Units:					Total FIFO EUP	Total Weighted Average EUP
Direct materials						
Conversion costs						

Now check your answers and figure out your error if you didn't get it all right.

Solution to Practice Exercise 2
First summarize the physical flow of the units.

Department 1 WIP Inventory - Units				
Beg Inv	9,000			
Units Started	80,000	Units Completed 79,000	BI	9,000
			S&C	70,000
End Inv	10,000			79,000

Next compute the equivalent units of production.

	Physical Units	WA EUP		FIFO EUP	
		DM	CC	DM	CC
BI	9,000	9,000	9,000	0	6,300
S&C	70,000	70,000	70,000	70,000	70,000
EI	10,000	10,000	9,000	10,000	9,000
Total		89,000	88,000	80,000	85,300

Finally, prepare a partial process cost report as shown in Exhibit 6.3.

		Work This Period			Total Work	
			Start and	Start Ending	Performed this	Total Units to
	Beginning WIP	Complete BI	Complete	WIP	Period	Account For
Account for Physical Units	9,000		70,000	10,000	80,000	89,000
						Total Weighted
Equivalent Units:					Total FIFO EUP	Average EUP
Direct materials	9,000	0	70,000	10,000	80,000	89,000
Conversion costs	2,700	6,300	70,000	9,000	85,300	88,000

EUP Computations For Materials Costs Incurred After Production Begins

We assume for the purposes of this study guide that conversion costs are incurred smoothly throughout production. In the prior sections, we learned to summarize the physical flow of production and then to convert this information into equivalent units when materials were added evenly throughout production as well as when materials were added at the beginning of production. However, materials costs may be incurred in discrete ways other than at the start of processing. For example, an assembly department may incur a portion of the materials costs when assembly begins and incur additional materials costs at the 70% stage of completion when an expensive component is added to the units. In cases like this, the stage of completion percentages are not directly used to compute the equivalent units of production for materials. Rather, they serve as indicators as to whether the stage of processing has passed the time when the additional materials were added.

Demonstration problem-EUP calculations when DM are added after production begins
The Assembly Department is the third and final department for processing at Kenny's Toy Cars. The painted car bodies are transferred in from the prior department and assemblers immediately requisition the decals from materials inventory. The decals represent 20% of the materials costs in the Assembly Department. Assemblers are done with the decals when the cars are at the 30% stage of production. At that time, the rest of the materials (wheels, axles, etc.) are requisitioned and the assembly is completed.

In August, the Assembly Department received 3,000 car bodies from the prior department. The department had 1,200 cars in beginning work in process that were 27% complete. At the end of August, there were 1,000 cars in the Assembly Department's WIP inventory that were 18% complete. Compute the EUP for direct materials for August.

Required:
a) Use t-accounts to determine the number of units started and completed and to summarize the physical flow of the units.
b) Compute the EUP for DM under both the weighted average and FIFO methods.

Solution to demonstration problem
a) First, summarize the physical flow of the units.

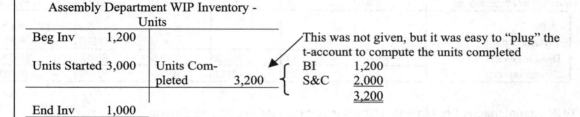

Assembly Department WIP Inventory - Units

Beg Inv	1,200		
Units Started	3,000	Units Completed	3,200
End Inv	1,000		

This was not given, but it was easy to "plug" the t-account to compute the units completed

BI	1,200
S&C	2,000
	3,200

solution continues on next page →

Solution to demonstration problem continued

In order to compute the equivalent units of production for materials, it is helpful to organize the information about how materials costs are incurred.

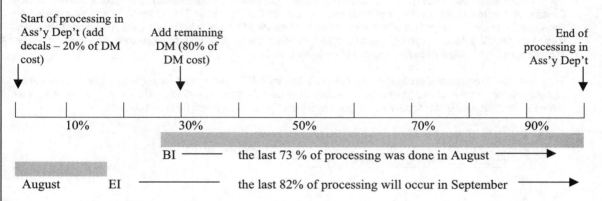

The gray areas represent work done in the current month. In August, the wheels and other parts were added to the BI units, so 80% of the DM costs were incurred in August to complete those units. Only the decals were added to the EI units in August, which represents 20% of the DM costs.

The DM columns of the schedule of EUP are shown below.

	Physical Units	WA EUP DM	FIFO EUP DM	
BI	1,200	1,200	960	100% credit under WA, 80% credit under FIFO because the wheels and other parts were added this month
S&C	2,000	2,000	2,000	100% credit under both methods
EI	1,000	200	200	20% credit under both methods, because only the decals were added this month
Total		3,400	3,160	

Notice that the 27% stage of completion of the BI units was not directly used in the computation of EUP for BI. In fact, if the stage of completion of the BI units was anything between 1% and 29%, the FIFO EUP for BI units would still be 960. Can you determine the BI EUP under FIFO if the stage of completion of BI was anything between 31% and 99%?[1]

Similarly, notice that the 18% stage of completion of the EI units was not directly used in the computation of EUP for EI. If the stage of completion for EI units was anywhere between 1% and 29%, the EUP for EI would still be 200 because only the decals would have been added during August. Can you determine the EI EUP if the stage of completion was anything between 31% and 99%?[2]

---

[1] The answer is zero, because no materials would have been added during August.
[2] The answer is 1,000 because both the decals and all the other materials would have been added in August.

Practice Exercise 3
Let's see if you can compute EUP for materials when materials costs are incurred in discrete portions throughout production. Use the spaces below to solve this problem and then check your answers before you continue forward.

Mike's Magic Mud produces face cream that diminishes wrinkles. Department 2 requires a total of 10 hours to process the cream. In Department 2, no materials are added to the cream as it ferments for 4 hours in a vat. Then at the 40% stage of completion in Department 2, magic ingredient #1 is added to the cream. It is then stirred for 3 more hours and at the 70% stage of completion magic ingredient #2 is added. Magic ingredient #1 represents 35% of the materials costs for Department 2 and magic ingredient #2 accounts for the remaining 65% of the department's materials costs.

There were 10,000 gallons of Magic Mud in Department 2's January 1 WIP inventory that were 80% complete. The department started processing another 90,000 gallons during January. At January 31, there were 12,000 gallons in WIP inventory that were 30% complete. Compute the EUP for direct materials using both the weighted average and FIFO methods.

First summarize the physical flow of the units using the t-account below.

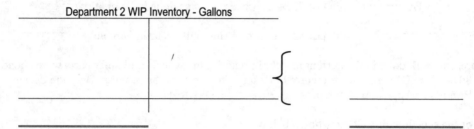

Department 2 WIP Inventory - Gallons

Next, compute the equivalent units of production for direct materials

	Physical Units	WA EUP DM	FIFO EUP DM
BI			
S&C			
EI			
Total			

Now check your answers and find you error if you didn't get it all right.

Solution to Practice Exercise 3
First summarize the physical flow of the units.

Department 2 WIP Inventory - Gallons

Beg Inv	10,000			
Units Started	90,000	Units Completed	88,000	
				BI	10,000
				S&C	78,000
End Inv	12,000			88,000

Solution to Practice Exercise 3 continues on next page →

Solution to Practice Exercise 3 continued
Next, compute the total EUP.

	Physical Units	WA EUP - DM	FIFO EUP - DM
BI	10,000	10,000	0
S&C	78,000	78,000	78,000
EI	12,000	0	0
Total		88,000	78,000

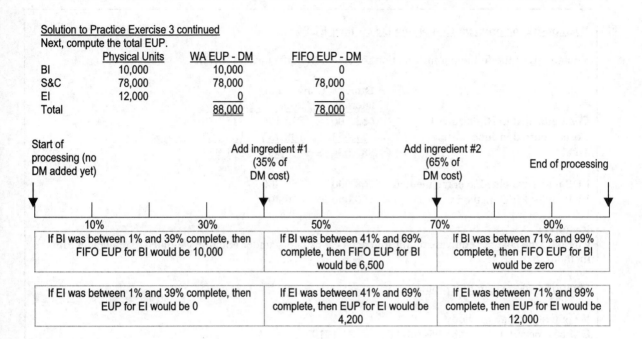

Start of processing (no DM added yet) — Add ingredient #1 (35% of DM cost) — Add ingredient #2 (65% of DM cost) — End of processing

10%   30%   50%   70%   90%

If BI was between 1% and 39% complete, then FIFO EUP for BI would be 10,000	If BI was between 41% and 69% complete, then FIFO EUP for BI would be 6,500	If BI was between 71% and 99% complete, then FIFO EUP for BI would be zero
If EI was between 1% and 39% complete, then EUP for EI would be 0	If EI was between 41% and 69% complete, then EUP for EI would be 4,200	If EI was between 71% and 99% complete, then EUP for EI would be 12,000

Computing The Costs Per Equivalent Unit

If a company is using standard costs in its process costing system then this is unnecessary. The standard costs per equivalent unit will be given for all cost categories. If a company is not using standard costs, then all costs per EUP must be calculated. In the prior section of this study guide we concentrated on the computation of EUP for materials and conversion costs. These figures are used as the denominators in the cost per EUP calculation.

The cost per EUP computations are relatively simple. For example, materials costs divided by EUP for DM equals DM cost per EUP. However, the weighted average and FIFO methods differ on the amount of costs included in the numerator. Under FIFO, the numerator includes only the costs incurred in the current month. This makes sense because the denominator under FIFO includes only work done in the current period. The weighted average method, on the other hand, calculates EUP by "giving credit" for work done in the prior month on the BI units. It should also seem intuitive, then, that the numerator in the weighted average calculation of cost per EUP includes current costs as well as the costs that were attached to the BI units at the start of the month. The weighted average method averages prior month costs incurred on the beginning inventory units with the current costs incurred to complete the beginning inventory units. It computes the cost per EUP as a two-month moving weighted average cost.

Demonstration problem-Computing the cost per EUP

You are given the following information for Helch Manufacturing for June:

	Direct Materials	Conversion Costs	Total
Costs attached to BI on June 1	$3,400	$12,170	$15,570
Costs incurred in June	77,654	108,733	186,387
Total	$81,054	$120,903	$201,957
EUP under weighted average method	68,000	60,800	
EUP under FIFO method	60,000	60,300	

Required:
Compute the cost per equivalent unit for each cost category under both the weighted average and FIFO methods.

Solution to demonstration problem

Weighted average method:
DM cost per EUP = $81,054/68,000 = $1.19197
CC per EUP = $120,903/60,800 =   1.98854
        Total processing cost per EUP $3.18051

FIFO method:
DM cost per EUP = $77,654/60,000 = $1.29423
CC per EUP = $108,733/60,300 =   1.80320
        Total processing cost per EUP $3.09743

Assigning Costs To Ending Inventory Units

Once we have computed the costs per equivalent unit of production for all cost categories, we are ready to attach the costs to the units in ending inventory. To do this we use the EUP figures from the ending inventory row of the schedule of EUP. The procedure is the same for both the weighted average and FIFO methods. For the first processing department, we need to compute only the DM and CC per EUP.

DM EUP for EI x DM cost per EUP =   Total DM costs attached to EI
CC EUP for EI x CC cost per EUP =   Total CC costs attached to EI
                                          Total costs attached to EI

Assigning Costs To Units Transferred Out; Journal Entry

This is a simple calculation under the weighted average method because you don't have to treat costs incurred in prior periods differently than costs incurred in the current period.

Total costs attached to units transferred out under the weighted average method
= Number of units transferred out x Total processing cost per EUP

The FIFO method is much more complicated because only current costs may be assigned to work done in the current period. Consider the following information.

WIP Inventory - Units

Beg Inv	10,000				
Units Started	90,000	Units Completed	86,000	BI	10,000
				S&C	76,000
					86,000
End Inv	14,000				

If the weighted average total cost per equivalent unit was $2, then the weighted average method would assign $172,000 ($2/unit times 86,000 units) to the units transferred out. But the FIFO method treats the S&C units differently from the BI units and costs are assigned to these units separately. The costs assigned to the 76,000 S&C units would be 76,000 times the FIFO current cost per EUP. The costs assigned to the 10,000 BI units that were completed this month would be the current costs that were expended to complete the BI plus the costs attached to BI at the start of the month.

The journal entry is the same for both methods; it is only the dollar amount of the journal entry that is different. WIP-Department 2 is debited and WIP-Department 1 is credited to transfer costs out of Department 1 and in to Department 2. When transferring costs out of the last processing department, the debit is to Finished goods inventory.

Demonstration problem-Assigning costs to ending inventory units and units transferred out
You are given the following November schedule of equivalent units of production and costs per EUP for K Company's Department 1:

	Physical Units	WA EUP		FIFO EUP			Costs per EUP	
		DM	CC	DM	CC		WA	FIFO
BI	5,000	5,000	5,000	3,000	2,500	DM	$1.80	$1.45
S&C	24,000	24,000	24,000	24,000	24,000	CC	2.00	2.10
EI	6,000	4,000	4,800	4,000	4,800	Total	$3.80	$3.55
Total		33,000	33,800	31,000	31,300			

Required:
Compute the costs assigned to the units in ending inventory and the costs assigned to the units transferred out using both the weighted average and FIFO methods. Assume that BI cost was $16,320.

solution begins on next page →

Solution to demonstration problem

Weighted average method:
Costs assigned to units transferred out = 29,000 x $3.80 = $110,200

Costs assigned to units in ending inventory:
  DM costs = 4,000 x $1.80 = $7,200
  CC = 4,800 x $2.00 =   <u>9,600</u>   <u>16,800</u>
                         $<u>127,000</u>

FIFO method:
Costs assigned to units transferred out:
  Cost to complete BI:
  DM added = 3,000 x $1.45 = $4,350
  CC added = 2,500 x $2.10 =   <u>5,250</u>
                    9,600
  Add costs attached to BI   <u>16,320</u>
  Total costs assigned to the 5,000 BI units   25,920
  Cost of processing the S&C units = 24,000 x $3.55 =   <u>85,200</u> $111,120

Costs assigned to units in ending inventory:
  DM costs = 4,000 x $1.45 = $5,800
  CC = 4,800 x $2.10 =   <u>10,080</u>   <u>15,880</u>
                         $<u>127,000</u>

Notice that the costs assigned to EI plus the costs assigned to units transferred out sum to $127,000 under each method. This is called total costs to account for. After preparing a schedule such as the one shown above (a process cost report), the accountant makes a journal entry to transfer the costs out of WIP Inventory-Department 1 and into WIP Inventory-Department 2. For example, if the company used the weighted average method, then the accountant would prepare this journal entry after the process cost report was completed:

    WIP Inventory-Department 2 $110,200
      WIP Inventory-Department 1 $110,200
    To transfer costs to Department 2

After the journal entry is posted, the balance in the general ledger account WIP Inventory-Department 2 will be $16,800, exactly the balance in ending inventory as computed in the process cost report.

We now have learned all the pieces of cost assignment in process costing and should be ready to prepare a full process cost report.

Demonstration problem-Preparing a process cost report

Regina's Rugs manufactures throw rugs in a one-process cycle. All materials are added at the start of processing. There were 5,000 rugs in beginning inventory that were 40% complete, and 20,000 rugs were started in May. The ending inventory of 6,000 rugs was 70% complete. An analysis of the costs for May follows:

	Direct Materials	Conversion Costs	Total
Work in process, May 1	$4,170	$3,384	$7,554
Costs added in May	41,280	18,656	59,936
Total	$45,450	$22,040	$67,490

Required:

Prepare a formal process cost report using both the weighted average and FIFO methods. Also prepare the journal entry to transfer costs out of work in process inventory and into finished goods inventory using the FIFO method's figure.

Solution to demonstration problem:

The first section of the process cost report summarizes the physical and equivalent units.

Summarize Physical and Equivalent Units:

		Work This Period				
	Beginning WIP	Complete BI	Start and Complete	Start Ending WIP	Total Work Performed this Period	Total Units to Account For
Account for Physical Units	5,000		14,000	6,000	20,000	25,000
Equivalent Units:					Total FIFO EUP	Total Weighted Average EUP
Direct materials	5,000	0	14,000	6,000	20,000	25,000
Conversion costs	2,000	3,000	14,000	4,200	21,200	23,200

The second section of the process cost report computes the costs per EUP.

Calculate Cost per EUP:

	Cost	EUP	Cost/EUP
FIFO:			
Direct materials	$41,280	20,000	$2.0640
Conversion costs	$18,656	21,200	0.8800
			$2.9440
Weighted average:			
Direct materials	$45,450	25,000	$1.8180
Conversion costs	$22,040	23,200	0.9500
			$2.7680

solution continues on next page →

Solution to demonstration problem continued

The third and final section summarizes the cost assignment.

Process Cost Report Cost Assignment:

	FIFO			Weighted Average		
	Computation	Units	Costs	Computation	Units	Costs
Beginning WIP		5,000	$7,554			
Cost to complete beginning WIP:						
Direct materials	(0 x $2.064)		0			
Conversion costs	(3,000 x $0.88)		2,640			
Total costs added this period			2,640			
Total cost of beginning WIP			10,194			
Started, completed, & transferred out	(14,000 x $2.944)	14,000	41,216			
Total completed & transferred out		19,000	51,410	(19,000 x $2.768)	19,000	$52,592
Ending WIP:		6,000			6,000	
Direct materials	(6,000 x $2.064)		12,384	(6,000 x $1.818)		10,908
Conversion costs	(4,200 x $0.88)		3,696	(4,200 x $0.95)		3,990
Total ending WIP cost			16,080			14,898
Total accounted for		25,000	$67,490		25,000	$67,490

The journal entry under FIFO is:

Finished goods inventory   51,410
     Work in process inventory   51,410

PROBLEM SET A (Learning Objectives 1 - 4)

True-False: Indicate whether each of the following is true (T) or false (F) in the space provided.

_____ 1. When computing the direct materials cost per equivalent unit under the weighted average method, the direct materials costs attached to beginning work in process inventory are not included.

_____ 2. The weighted average method averages prior month costs incurred on the beginning inventory units with the current costs incurred to complete the beginning inventory units.

_____ 3. One advantage of the FIFO method is that it provides information about how processing costs fluctuate from month to month.

_____ 4. When direct materials costs are incurred in discrete portions during the production process, the weighted average and FIFO methods will never compute the same equivalent units for ending inventory units.

_____ 5. The equivalent units of production for the direct materials in ending inventory will be the same under the weighted average and FIFO methods no matter how materials costs are incurred during production.

_____ 6. Suppose that all materials are added at the 50% stage of processing and that ending inventory units are 40% complete. Then the equivalent units of production for the direct materials in ending inventory equals zero.

_____ 7. Suppose that all materials are added at the 50% stage of processing and that beginning inventory units are 40% complete. Then the equivalent units of production for the direct materials in beginning inventory equals zero under the weighted average method.

_____ 8. Suppose that all materials are added at the 50% stage of processing and that beginning inventory units are 40% complete. Then the equivalent units of production for the direct materials in beginning inventory equals zero under the FIFO method.

_____ 9. Suppose that all materials are added at the 50% stage of processing and that ending inventory units are 60% complete. Then the equivalent units of production for the direct materials in ending inventory equals zero.

_____ 10. Suppose that all materials are added at the 50% stage of processing and that beginning inventory units are 60% complete. Then the equivalent units of production for the direct materials in beginning inventory equals zero under the FIFO method.

Multiple choice: Write the letter that represents the best choice in the space provided.

_____ 1. Process costing is most likely to be used by which of the following companies?
a.   a construction company that builds custom homes
b.   a shipyard
c.   a manufacturer of metal folding chairs
d.   a producer of special order furniture

_____ 2. Equivalent units of production are
a.   the number of units a company produced during a specified time period
b.   the number of units a company worked on during a specified time period
c.   the same as the number of units started and completed during a specified time period
d.   the number of whole units a company could have produced during a specified time period if it would have produced only whole units

_____ 3. The difference between the weighted average and FIFO methods of computing equivalent units of production is
a.   the manner in which the equivalent units for beginning inventory is computed
b.   the manner in which the number of units started and completed is computed
c.   the manner in which the equivalent units for ending inventory is computed
d.   the manner in which the number of units completed and transferred out is computed

_____ 4. Which of the following statements about the weighted average and FIFO methods is true?
a.   Equivalent units of production cannot be the same under the two methods.
b.   Equivalent units of production under FIFO is always greater than or equal to equivalent units of production under the weighted average method.
c.   Equivalent units of production under FIFO will equal equivalent units of production under the weighted average method only when there are no units in ending inventory.
d.   Equivalent units of production for ending inventory units is the same under the two methods.

_____   5. Suppose that a company adds material at the beginning of production and
            that conversion costs are incurred evenly throughout production. In May, the
            beginning work in process inventory was 20% complete and the ending work
            in process inventory was 30% complete. Under the FIFO method, the number
            of equivalent units of production for direct materials for May is equal to
            a.   the number of units started in May
            b.   the number of units started and completed in May plus 30% times the
                 number of units in ending inventory for May
            c.   the number of units started and completed in May plus 20% times the
                 number of units in beginning inventory plus 30% times the number of
                 units in ending inventory for May
            d.   the number of units started and completed in May plus 80% times the
                 number of units in beginning inventory plus 30% times the number of
                 units in ending inventory for May

_____   6. Suppose that a company adds material at the beginning of production and
            that conversion costs are incurred evenly throughout production. In May, the
            beginning work in process inventory was 20% complete and the ending work
            in process inventory was 30% complete. Under the weighted average method,
            the number of equivalent units of production for direct materials for May is
            equal to
            a.   the number of units started in May plus the number of units in beginning
                 inventory for May
            b.   the number of units started and completed in May plus 30% times the
                 number of units in ending inventory for May
            c.   the number of units started and completed in May plus 20% times the
                 number of units in beginning inventory plus 30% times the number of
                 units in ending inventory for May
            d.   the number of units started and completed in May plus 80% times the
                 number of units in beginning inventory plus 30% times the number of
                 units in ending inventory for May

_____   7. Suppose that a company adds material at the beginning of production and
            that conversion costs are incurred evenly throughout production. In May, the
            beginning work in process inventory was 20% complete and the ending work
            in process inventory was 30% complete. Under the FIFO method, the number
            of equivalent units of production for conversion costs for May is equal to
            a.   the number of units started in May
            b.   the number of units started and completed in May plus 30% times the
                 number of units in ending inventory for May
            c.   the number of units started and completed in May plus 20% times the
                 number of units in beginning inventory plus 30% times the number of
                 units in ending inventory for May
            d.   the number of units started and completed in May plus 80% times the
                 number of units in beginning inventory plus 30% times the number of
                 units in ending inventory for May

8. Suppose that a company adds material at the beginning of production and that conversion costs are incurred evenly throughout production. In May, the beginning work in process inventory was 20% complete and the ending work in process inventory was 30% complete. Under the weighted average method, the number of equivalent units of production for conversion costs for May is equal to
   a. the number of units completed in May plus 30% times the number of units in ending inventory for May
   b. the number of units started and completed in May plus 30% times the number of units in ending inventory for May
   c. the number of units started and completed in May plus 20% times the number of units in beginning inventory plus 30% times the number of units in ending inventory for May
   d. the number of units started and completed in May plus 80% times the number of units in beginning inventory plus 30% times the number of units in ending inventory for May

9. When will both the weighted average and FIFO methods compute the same dollar amount for the costs to be transferred to the next department?
   a. when there are no units in ending inventory
   b. when there are no units in beginning inventory
   c. when the number of units in beginning inventory equals the number of units in ending inventory
   d. when beginning and ending inventory were at the same stage of completion

10. Which of the following is the correct journal entry to transfer costs out of the Finishing Department, which is the last processing department?
    a. debit Work in Process Inventory – Finishing Department and credit Finished Goods Inventory
    b. debit Cost of Goods Sold and credit Finished Goods Inventory
    c. debit Cost of Goods Sold and credit Work in Process Inventory – Finishing Department
    d. debit Finished Goods Inventory and credit Work in Process Inventory – Finishing Department

11. Under the weighted average method of process costing, the costs attached to the units in beginning work in process inventory are
    a. not included in the computation of cost per equivalent unit
    b. handled the same way as they are in FIFO process costing
    c. included with the current costs when cost per equivalent unit is calculated
    d. included with the costs attached to the units in ending work in process inventory

_____   12. Which of the following statements is false?
- a. Under the FIFO method, beginning inventory costs are kept separate from the current period's costs.
- b. Under the weighted average method, beginning inventory costs are combined with the current period's costs.
- c. The weighted average and FIFO methods will assign the same amount of costs to the ending inventory units under a standard cost system.
- d. The weighted average method is superior to the FIFO method for the purposes of controlling costs.

_____   13. Sundae's Sundries uses the weighted average method of process costing. The company's ending work in process inventory consisted of 8,000 units that were 80% complete. Materials are added at the beginning of processing. The direct materials cost per EUP was $3.20 and the conversion cost per EUP was $1.80. What is the amount of cost Sundae would assign to ending work in process inventory?
- a. $28,480
- b. $37,120
- c. $32,000
- d. $40,000

_____   14. Mikey's Mugs uses the FIFO method of process costing. The company's ending work in process inventory consisted of 12,000 units that were 40% complete and had incurred 80% of the materials costs. The direct materials cost per EUP was $2.40 and the conversion cost per EUP was $3.30. What is the amount of cost Mikey would assign to ending work in process inventory?
- a. $27,360
- b. $38,880
- c. $46,800
- d. $68,400

_____   15. Schachte Corporation uses the weighted average method of process costing. The company had 7,000 units in ending work in process inventory and it started 70,000 units this month. There were 12,000 units in beginning work in process inventory. If the total processing cost per EUP is $3, what is the amount of cost transferred out of work in process this month?
- a. $189,000
- b. $210,000
- c. $225,000
- d. $231,000

Exercises: Write your answer in the space provided.

1. Graham Manufacturing uses process costing to account for its operations. For the month of February, beginning work in process inventory consisted of 10,000 units that were 75% complete. The company began production of 60,000 units in February, and had 12,000 units in February's ending work in process inventory that were 20% complete. Compute the number of units completed and transferred out, using the t-account below to organize your computations.

WIP Inventory - Units	

The number of units completed and transferred out equals _____

2. Stanley Tools uses process costing to account for its operations. Stanley began the month of June with 27,000 units in beginning work in process inventory that were 30% complete. The company completed 120,000 units in June and transferred them to finished goods inventory. At June 30, there were 18,000 units in ending work in process inventory that were 80% complete. Compute the number of units that Stanley started in June, using the t-account below to organize your computations.

WIP Inventory - Units	

The number of units started equals _____

3. Wanda's Widgets uses process costing for all of its production departments. During March, Wanda began the production of 100,000 widgets in Department 1. The March 1 work in process inventory for Department 1 was 14,000 units that were 15% complete. Department 1 completed and transferred out 92,000 units during March. Department 1's ending work in process inventory consisted of widgets that were 71% complete. Compute the number of widgets in Department 1's ending work in process inventory for March, as well as the number of units that were started and completed in March. Use the t-account below to organize your computations.

Department 1 WIP Inventory - Units

The number of units in EI equals _____

The number of units S&C equals _____

4. Don's Droids makes robots and uses process costing to account for production costs. In Department 4, the robots are assembled. Components arrive from Department 3 and the 5 hour assembly operation begins. After 1 hour (the 20% stage of completion), the positronic brain is requisitioned from materials inventory. The brains account for 2/3 of the materials costs in Department 4. Next, the software is downloaded to the robot, which takes 3 hours. At this time (the 80% stage of completion), the remaining materials are requisitioned and attached to the robot.

For the month of March, Department 4 had 120 robots in beginning work in process inventory that were 15% complete. Another 600 robots were started during March and the 150 robots in ending work in process inventory were 50% complete. Compute the equivalent units of production for materials using both the weighted average and FIFO methods.

EUP for materials under the weighted average method equals _____

EUP for materials under the FIFO method equals _____

5. Redo exercise 4 assuming instead that the units in beginning inventory were 70% complete and the units in ending inventory were 10% complete.

   EUP for materials under the weighted average method equals _____

   EUP for materials under the FIFO method equals _____

6. Helen's Hats uses process costing for its only production department. Felt is requisitioned from materials inventory as soon as production begins. Felt accounts for 80% of the materials costs. At the 75% stage of production, the hats' decorations are added which accounts for the remaining 20% of materials costs. During May, Helen began the production of 1,000 hats. The May 1 work in process inventory was 130 units that were 30% complete. There were 900 hats completed and transferred to finished goods inventory in May. The hats in May's ending work in process inventory were 80% complete. Prepare the first section of the process cost report that summarizes physical and equivalent units, using both methods.

| | Beginning WIP | Work This Period | | | Total Work Performed this Period | Total Units to Account For |
		Complete BI	Start and Complete	Start Ending WIP		
Account for Physical Units						
Equivalent Units:					Total FIFO EUP	Total Weighted Average EUP
Direct materials						
Conversion costs						

7. Samscott Herbals manufactures a dietary supplement in a one-process cycle. Direct materials are added at the beginning of processing. There were 30,000 units in beginning inventory that were 20% complete, and 50,000 units were started in May. The ending inventory of 10,000 units was 70% complete. An analysis of the costs for May follows:

	DM	CC	Total
Work in process, May 1	$13,400	$7,840	$21,240
Costs added in May	96,600	33,920	130,520
Total	$110,000	$41,760	$151,760

Prepare a process cost report for May, using both methods. Also prepare the June 30 journal entry to transfer costs out of work in process using the FIFO method's figure.

Summarize Physical and Equivalent Units:

		Work This Period				
	Beginning WIP	Complete BI	Start and Complete	Start Ending WIP	Total Work Performed this Period	Total Units to Account For
Account for Physical Units						
Equivalent Units:					Total FIFO EUP	Total Wtd Avg EUP
DM						
CC						

Calculate Cost per EUP:

	Cost	EUP	Cost/EUP
FIFO:			
DM			
CC			
Weighted average:			
DM			
CC			

Process Cost Report Cost Assignment:

	FIFO			Weighted Average		
	Computation	Units	Costs	Computation	Units	Costs
Beginning WIP						
Cost to complete beginning WIP:						
Direct materials						
Conversion costs						
Total costs added this period						
Total cost of beginning WIP						
Started, completed, & transferred out						
Total completed & transferred out						
Ending WIP:						
Direct materials						
Conversion costs						
Total ending WIP cost						
Total accounted for						

Journal entry:

CHAPTER REVIEW: Learning Objectives 5 - 8

Q5: What alternative methods are used for mass production?

There are alternative methods that a company can use to account for the costs of its mass produced units.

- Standard process costing is a costing system where predetermined costs per EUP are used to assign production costs to ending inventory and to units transferred out of a processing department. A process cost report for this costing method looks identical to the one we prepared in the prior section, except that it is not necessary to compute the costs per equivalent unit.

- Some companies use just-in-time (JIT) production, where raw materials are delivered from suppliers as they are needed in production and products are not produced until needed by customers. These companies generally have very low inventory levels, so costs per EUP are really just production costs averaged over units produced.

- Some production processes are such that accounting for costs is best done with a costing system that uses some of the characteristics of job costing and some of the characteristics of process costing. These costing systems are known as *hybrid costing systems*.

  - *Operation costing* is a type of hybrid costing system used for companies that produce batches of identical products, even though each batch is different.

Q6: How is process costing performed for multiple production departments?

The extension of the process costing we learned so far to multiple production departments is not difficult. In this case there are 3 cost categories: DM, DL and TI, where TI stands for transferred-in costs. Every processing department except the first one must account for TI costs. TI costs are just the accumulated DM and DL costs from prior departments. TI costs are incurred the moment the units are transferred in from the prior processing department, so the calculation of the EUP for the TI cost category is identical to the calculation of EUP for DM when materials are added at the beginning of processing. TI cost are assigned to ending inventory units and to the units completed and transferred out of the department in the same fashion as DM and DL costs are assigned.

Demonstration problem-Process cost report with transferred-in costs

Flip's Pharmaceuticals manufactures a synthetic drug to help people recover from cost accounting burn out. It is called Itzoversune and is made in a two-process cycle. In Department 2, direct materials are added as follows: no materials are added at the beginning of processing, one-fourth of materials costs are added at the 30% stage of processing, and three-fourths of materials costs are added at the 70% stage of processing. There were 6,000 units in Department 2's beginning inventory that were 40% complete, and Department 2 completed and transferred out 30,000 units in June. Department 2's ending inventory of 4,000 units was 20% complete. An analysis of the Department 2 costs for June follows:

	DM	CC	TI	Total
Work in process, June 1	$12,000	$2,040	$39,800	$53,840
Costs added in June	114,000	53,400	154,000	321,400
Total	$126,000	$55,440	$193,800	$375,240

Required:

Prepare a process cost report for June using both the weighted average and FIFO methods.

Solution to demonstration problem:

Summarize Physical and Equivalent Units:

		Work This Period				
		Complete	Start and	Start Ending	Total Work Performed	Total Units to Account
	Beginning WIP	BI	Complete	WIP	this Period	For
Account for Physical Units	6,000		24,000	4,000	28,000	34,000

					Total FIFO EUP	Total Wtd Avg EUP
Equivalent Units:						
DM	1,500	4,500	24,000	0	28,500	30,000
CC	2,400	3,600	24,000	800	28,400	30,800
TI	6,000	0	24,000	4,000	28,000	34,000

Calculate Cost per EUP:

	Cost	EUP	Cost/EUP
FIFO:			
DM	$114,000	28,500	$4.0000
CC	$53,400	28,400	1.8803
TI	$154,000	28,000	5.5000
			$11.3803
Weighted average:			
DM	$126,000	30,000	$4.2000
CC	$55,440	30,800	1.8000
TI	$193,800	34,000	5.7000
			$11.7000

Process Cost Report Cost Assignment:

	FIFO			Weighted Average		
	Computation	Units	Costs	Computation	Units	Costs
Beginning WIP		6,000	$53,840			
Cost to complete beginning WIP:						
DM	(4,500 x $4.000)		18,000			
CC	(3,600 x $1.8803)		6,769			
TI	(0 x $5.5000)		0			
Total costs added this period			24,769			
Total cost of beginning WIP			78,609			
Started, completed, & transferred out	(24,000 x $11.3803)	24,000	273,127			
Total completed & transferred out		30,000	351,736	(30,000 x $11.70)	30,000	$351,000
Ending WIP:		4,000			4,000	
DM	(0 x $4.000)		0	(0 x $4.2000)		0
CC	(800 x $1.8803)		1,504	(800 x $1.8000)		1,440
TI	(4,000 x $5.5000)		22,000	(4,000 x $5.7000)		22,800
Total ending WIP cost			23,504			24,240
Total accounted for		34,000	$375,240		34,000	$375,240

Q7: How are spoilage costs handled in process costing?

In most manufacturing companies, it is considered a normal part of operations for some units to spoil. This is called *normal spoilage*, and the costs of normal spoilage are included in the costs of processing the good units transferred out of a production department. Sometimes a quantity of units will spoil that exceeds normal expectations. For example, a broken machine or a batch of poor quality inputs from a supplier may result in an unexpected amount of spoiled units. This is called *abnormal spoilage* and the costs associated with abnormal spoilage are written off as a loss in the period incurred.

Accounting for spoilage begins by accounting for the spoiled units when the physical flow of production is summarized. The spoiled units will also be accounted for in the computation of equivalent units of production, depending on when the inspection for spoilage occurs. To ease computations, the text and this study guide assume that spoilage occurs just before inspection (so that there were no spoiled units in beginning work in process inventory) and that the inspection for spoiled units occurs at the end of processing.

Demonstration problem-Accounting for spoilage in process costing

Samantha's Plastics makes kits for model cars. In Department 1, there were 12,000 kits in beginning work in process inventory that were 40% complete. The ending inventory of 8,000 kits was 30% complete. During June, Samantha began working on 60,000 kits, and 62,000 good kits were transferred to the next department. There is an inspection for spoilage at the end of processing in Department 1, and all materials are added at the beginning of processing. Spoilage is considered normal if it is less than or equal to 2% times the number of good units transferred out to Department 2.

You are given the following information about the costs for June:

	Direct Materials	Conversion Costs	Total
Work in process, June 1	$41,800	$34,200	$76,000
Costs added in June	422,200	189,440	611,640
Total	$464,000	$223,640	$687,640

Required:

Prepare a process cost report and the FIFO method's journal entry to transfer costs out of WIP-Department 1 and record spoilage costs.

solution begins on next page →

Solution to demonstration problem:

Summarize Physical and Equivalent Units:

		Work This Period					
	Beginning WIP	Complete BI	Start and Complete	Start Ending WIP	Total Work Performed this Period	Total Units to Account For	Spoiled Units
Account for Physical Units	12,000		52,000	8,000	60,000	72,000	(2,000)
					Total FIFO EUP	Total Wtd Avg EUP	
Equivalent Units:							
DM	12,000	0	52,000	8,000	60,000	72,000	(2,000)
CC	4,800	7,200	52,000	2,400	61,600	66,400	(2,000)
Total spoilage							2,000
Less: Normal Spoilage							1,240
Abnormal Spoilage							760

Calculate Cost per EUP:

	Cost	EUP	Cost/EUP
FIFO:			
DM	$422,200	60,000	$7.0367
CC	$189,440	61,600	3.0753
			$10.1120
Weighted average:			
DM	$464,000	72,000	$6.4444
CC	$223,640	66,400	3.3681
			$9.8125

The journal under FIFO entry is:
Work in process inventory-Dep't 2   616,281
Loss from abnormal spoilage   7,685
    Work in process inventory-Dep't 1   618,575

Process Cost Report Cost Assignment:

	FIFO			Weighted Average		
	Computation	Units	Costs	Computation	Units	Costs
Beginning WIP		12,000	$76,000			
Cost to complete beginning WIP:						
DM	(0 x $7.0367)		0			
CC	(7,200 x $3.0753)		22,142			
Total costs added this period			22,142			
Total cost of beginning WIP			98,142			
Normal spoilage	(1,240 x $10.112)	1,240	12,539		1,240	$12,168
Good units started, completed, & tr'd out	(50,000 x $10.112)	50,000	505,600			
Good Units				(62,000 x $9.8125)	62,000	608,376
Total completed & transf'd out (incl spoilage)		63,240	616,281		63,240	620,544
Abnormal spoilage	(760 x $10.112)	760	7,685	(760 x $9.8125)	760	7,458
Ending WIP:		8,000			8,000	
DM	(8,000 x $7.0367)		56,293	(8,000 x $6.4444)		51,556
CC	(2,400 x $3.0753)		7,381	(2,400 x $3.3681)		8,083
Total ending WIP cost			63,674			59,639
Total accounted for		72,000	$687,640		72,000	$687,640

Q8: What are the uses and limitations of process cost information?

Information from the process costing system is required for the preparation of financial statements and tax returns. Additionally, process cost information helps managers monitor the quality of products and the cost of operations. However, there are several limitations of process cost information.

- Process cost information is generally not useful for many short-term decisions because unavoidable fixed costs are allocated to the products.

- Estimates as to the stage of processing when direct materials, or even conversion costs, are incurred may be inaccurate.

- All units in beginning and ending WIP inventories are most likely not at the same stages of completion at the beginning and end of the periods. The percentage of completion used in the calculation of EUP is just an estimate.

PROBLEM SET B (Learning Objectives 4 - 8)

Multiple choice: Write the letter that represents the best choice in the space provided.

_____   1.   Which of the following statements is true?
a.   Transferred-in costs are the materials costs from the prior department.
b.   Transferred-in costs are the costs from all prior departments.
c.   Transferred-in costs are the costs from the prior period.
d.   All transferred-in costs will be assigned to the units completed and transferred out during the period.

_____   2.   Maka Manufacturing uses the weighted average method of process costing. You are given the following information for Department 2 for February:

		Percent
	Units	Complete
Beginning work in process inventory	2,200	30%
Transferred in from the prior department during February	70,000	
Ending work in process inventory	4,500	20%

Suppose the conversion cost per equivalent unit is $2.10. How much conversion costs were transferred to the next department during February?
a. $137,550
b. $142,170
c. $147,000
d. $151,620

_____   3.   Normal spoilage is
a.   unacceptable units of production that occur because of an unexpected event
b.   spoilage that exceeds expectations
c.   unacceptable units of production that occur because of poor quality inputs
d.   unacceptable units of production that are considered part of normal manufacturing operations

_____   4.   Abnormal spoilage is
a.   debited to Cost of Goods Sold
b.   spoilage that exceeds expectations
c.   considered a product cost
d.   unacceptable units of production that are considered part of normal manufacturing operations

_____   5.   The costs of normal spoilage
a.   are debited to a loss account
b.   are included with the costs of the good units transferred out
c.   decrease the per unit processing cost for the good units transferred out
d.   do not affect the per unit processing cost for the good units transferred out

_____ 6. The costs of abnormal spoilage
    a. are debited to a Finished Goods Inventory
    b. are included with the costs of the good units transferred out
    c. decrease the per unit processing cost for the good units transferred out
    d. do not affect the per unit processing cost for the good units transferred out

_____ 7. You are given the following information for Joseph Manufacturing:

BI units	1,000
EI units	5,000
Units started	24,000
Good units completed	17,000

Suppose that a 4% defect rate (based on the number of good units completed) is considered normal. Compute the number of units of normal spoilage and the number of units of abnormal spoilage, respectively, assuming that the inspection for spoiled units occurs at the end of processing.
    a. 960 and 2,040
    b. 800 and 2,200
    c. 1,160and 1,840
    d. 680 and 2,320

The following information should be used for questions 8 – 12:
You are given the following information for the SJK Company for January:

BI units	2,000
EI units	1,000
Units started	28,000
Good units completed	27,000

The total processing cost per equivalent unit was $15 in January. SJK considers spoilage equal to 5% of the good units transferred out to finished goods to be normal. SJK uses the weighted average method of process costing for its sole production department, and inspection for spoiled units occurs at the end of processing.

_____   8. The costs attached to normal spoilage total
        a. $35,250
        b. $30,000
        c. $20,250
        d. $9,750

_____   9. The costs attached to abnormal spoilage total
        a. $35,250
        b. $30,000
        c. $20,250
        d. $9,750

_____   10. The costs attached to good units completed and transferred out total
        a. $375,000
        b. $405,000
        c. $425,250
        d. $435,000

_____   11. The per unit cost of the good units transferred out equals
        a. $13.89
        b. $15.00
        c. $15.75
        d. $16.11

_____   12. The entry to transfer costs out of work in process and into finished goods and a loss from abnormal spoilage account includes a credit to Work in Process Inventory for
        a. $384,750
        b. $414,750
        c. $425,250
        d. $435,000

_____ 13. In April, the beginning work in process inventory for Department 2 was 40% complete and the ending work in process inventory was 90% complete. Under the FIFO method, the number of equivalent units of production for transferred-in costs for April is equal to
a. the number of units started and completed in April plus 90% times the number of units in ending inventory for April
b. the number of units started and completed in April plus 40% times the number of units in beginning inventory plus 90% times the number of units in ending inventory for April
c. the number of units started and completed in April plus 40% times the number of units in beginning inventory plus 90% times the number of units in ending inventory for April
d. the number of units started in April

_____ 14. In April, the beginning work in process inventory for Department 2 was 40% complete and the ending work in process inventory was 90% complete. Under the weighted average method, the number of equivalent units of production for transferred-in costs for April is equal to
a. the number of units started and completed in April plus 90% times the number of units in ending inventory for April
b. the number of units started and completed in April plus 40% times the number of units in beginning inventory plus 90% times the number of units in ending inventory for April
c. the number of units started and completed in April plus 40% times the number of units in beginning inventory plus 90% times the number of units in ending inventory for April
d. the number of units started in April plus the number of units in beginning inventory for April

Exercises: Write your answer in the space provided.
1. The accountant for McGowan Manufacturing fell asleep before completing the July process cost report for Department 2. Help her out by completing the section of the process cost report that summarizes physical and equivalent units. Since you don't know whether McGowan uses the weighted average or FIFO method of process costing, you had better do both methods to be sure. You found a note on the accountant's desk that states the Department 2 beginning work in process inventory was 20% complete and the ending work in process inventory was 45% complete. You know that all materials are added at the beginning of production in Department 2. There were 12,000 units in beginning WIP, 10,000 units in ending WIP, and 89,000 units were completed and transferred out.

Summarize Physical and Equivalent Units:

		Work This Period			Total Work Performed this Period	Total Units to Account For
	Beginning WIP	Complete BI	Start and Complete	Start Ending WIP		
Account for Physical Units						
Equivalent Units:					Total FIFO EUP	Total Wtd Avg EUP
DM						
CC						
TI						

2. You are given the information below for Babs Manufacturing for June. Compute the total cost per equivalent unit of production using both the weighted average and FIFO methods.

	Direct Materials	Conversion Costs	Transferred-in Costs	Total
Costs attached to BI on June 1	$34,800	$6,890	$12,450	$54,140
Costs incurred in June	97,840	27,040	42,900	167,780
Total	$132,640	$33,930	$55,350	$221,920
EUP under WA method	32,000	29,800	34,000	
EUP under FIFO method	28,000	24,120	30,000	

Total cost per EUP under the weighted average method equals _____

Total cost per EUP under the FIFO method equals _____

3. Scott's Scary Foods makes chocolate candies in the shape of bugs to be used on a reality television program. In Department 1, all materials are added at the beginning of processing. There were 14,000 units in beginning WIP, 10,000 units in ending WIP, and 71,000 good units were completed. Scott started 70,000 units in March. You are given the following information about costs of Department 1 and the units produced for the month of March:

	Direct Materials	Conversion Costs	Total
WIP, March 1	$65,200	$42,700	$107,900
Costs added in March	590,000	290,000	880,000
Total	$655,200	$332,700	$987,900

The beginning inventory units were 20% complete and the ending inventory units were 70% complete. It is considered normal for 3% of the good units completed and transferred to Department 2 to spoil. The inspection for spoilage occurs at the end of processing in Department 1. Prepare a process costing report and the required March 31 journal entry to transfer costs out of Department 1's work in process inventory using both methods.

Summarize Physical and Equivalent Units:

	Beginning WIP	Work This Period			Total Work Performed this Period	Total Units to Account For	Spoiled Units
		Complete BI	Start and Complete	Start Ending WIP			
Account for Physical Units							
Equivalent Units:					Total FIFO EUP	Total Wtd Avg EUP	
DM							
CC							
Total spoilage Less: Normal Spoilage Abnormal Spoilage							

solution space for exercise #3 continues on next page →

3. solution space continued

Calculate Cost per EUP (go to four decimals):

	Cost	EUP	Cost/EUP
FIFO:			
DM			
CC			
Weighted average:			
DM			
CC			

Process Cost Report Cost Assignment:

	FIFO			Weighted Average		
	Computation	Units	Costs	Computation	Units	Costs
Beginning WIP						
Cost to complete beginning WIP:						
DM						
CC						
Total costs added this period						
Total cost of beginning WIP						
Normal spoilage						
Good units started, completed, & tr'd out						
Good Units Completed & tr'd out						
Total completed & transferred out						
Abnormal spoilage						
Ending WIP:						
DM						
CC						
Total ending WIP cost						
Total accounted for						

END OF CHAPTER EXERCISES

<u>Completion – Fill in the blank space with the appropriate word or phrase.</u>

1. _____ costing is most useful when a company produces unique, custom-ordered products.

2. The _____ method of process costing does not distinguish between work performed in prior months and work performed in the current month.

3. _____ costing is a method of averaging costs over similar units.

4. The number of units completed and transferred out minus the number of units in beginning inventory is known as _____.

5. Costs that are incurred in Department 1 are called _____ when the units arrive in Department 2 for processing.

6. The only difference between the equivalent units computations under the weighted average and FIFO methods of process costing is the treatment of _____.

7. Under the weighted average method, the equivalent units for beginning inventory will always be equal to _____.

8. Under the FIFO method, the equivalent units for the transferred-in costs for beginning inventory will always be equal to _____.

9. When there is no spoilage, the number of units in beginning work in process inventory plus the number of units started minus the number of units in ending work in process inventory is equal to _____.

10. When there is no spoilage, the number of units in ending work in process inventory plus the number of units transferred out minus the number of units in beginning work in process inventory is equal to _____.

Exercises: Write your answer in the space provided.
1. Stella's Starships makes wind chimes for science fiction fans in a two process operation. In the molding department, plastic shapes are created in injection molding machines. All materials are added at the beginning of this process in the molding department. After cooling, the shapes are transferred to the painting department, where all materials are added evenly throughout production. There is no spoilage in either department. You are given the following information for Stella's operations for the month of September:

	Molding	Painting
Number of units in beginning WIP inventory	1,200	2,100
Number of units in ending WIP inventory	2,700	1,000
Number of units started during the month	17,000	?
Stage of completion of beginning WIP inventory	20%	40%
Stage of completion of ending WIP inventory	70%	25%

Prepare the section of the process cost report that summarizes physical and equivalent units for September for each department using both the weighted average and FIFO methods. Hint: the number of units started in the painting department in September is equal to the number of units transferred out of the molding department in September.

Molding Department

		Work This Period				
	Beginning WIP	Complete BI	Start and Complete	Start Ending WIP	Total Work Performed this Period	Total Units to Account For
Account for Physical Units						
					Total FIFO EUP	Total Weighted Average EUP
Equivalent Units:						
Direct materials						
Conversion costs						

Painting Department

		Work This Period			Total Work Performed this Period	Total Units to Account For
	Beginning WIP	Complete BI	Start and Complete	Start Ending WIP		
Account for Physical Units						
					Total FIFO EUP	Total Wtd Avg EUP
Equivalent Units:						
DM						
CC						
TI						

2. Phil's Fun Products makes gag gifts for 50th birthday parties. Phil considers spoilage equal to 2% of the good units transferred out to finished goods to be normal. Inspection for spoiled units occurs at the end of processing. Prepare a process cost report for October using both methods and the October 31 journal entry to transfer costs out of Department 1 under both methods. You are given the following information for Department 1 for October. Direct materials are added at the beginning of processing. The BI units were 15% complete and the EI units were 35% complete.

	Direct Materials	Conversion Costs	Total
WIP, October 1	$21,200	$17,400	$38,600
Costs added in October	218,300	98,220	316,520
Total	$239,500	$115,620	$355,120

BI units	2,000
EI units	1,000
Units started	28,000
Good units completed	27,000

Summarize Physical and Equivalent Units:

		Work This Period					
	Beginning WIP	Complete BI	Start and Complete	Start Ending WIP	Total Work Performed this Period	Total Units to Account For	Spoiled Units
Account for Physical Units							
Equivalent Units:					Total FIFO EUP	Total Wtd Avg EUP	
DM							
CC							
Total spoilage Less: Normal Spoilage Abnormal Spoilage							

solution space for exercise #2 continues on next page →

2. solution space continued

Calculate Cost per EUP (go to four decimals):

	Cost	EUP	Cost/EUP
FIFO:			
DM			
CC			
Weighted average:			
DM			
CC			

Process Cost Report Cost Assignment:

	FIFO			Weighted Average		
	Computation	Units	Costs	Computation	Units	Costs
Beginning WIP						
Cost to complete beginning WIP:						
DM						
CC						
Total costs added this period						
Total cost of beginning WIP						
Normal spoilage						
Good units started, completed, & tr'd out						
Good Units Completed & tr'd out						
Total completed & transferred out						
Abnormal spoilage						
Ending WIP:						
DM						
CC						
Total ending WIP cost						
Total accounted for						

SOLUTION TO PROBLEM SET A

<u>True-False:</u>

1. F   The numerator in the WA method's cost per EUP computation includes costs of BI – it is the numerator under the FIFO method that excludes these costs.
2. T   The cost per equivalent unit calculation under the WA method includes current costs and the costs attached to BI units in the numerator.
3. T   The FIFO method computes only the current cost per EUP – it doesn't average past month's costs with the current costs like the WA method does.
4. F   The two methods always compute the same EUP for EI units.
5. T   See the explanation for question 4 above.
6. T   The ending inventory units had no materials added during the period.
7. F   The WA method always gives full credit to BI units.
8. F   All materials were added to BI units in the current month. The FIFO method would give full credit to BI units, not zero.
9. F   All materials were added to EI units in the current month. Both methods would give full credit to EI units.
10. T   No materials were added to BI units in the current month.

<u>Multiple choice:</u>

1. C   All the other choices do not involve the production of identical units.
2. D   by definition of EUP
3. A   Notice that B & D don't even involve the computation of EUP, only summarizing the physical flow of units. For C, the WA and FIFO methods always agree on the computation of EUP for EI.
4. D   A is false because WA and FIFO will compute the same EUP when BI=0. B would be correct if it said "less than or equal to". C would true if it said "beginning inventory" instead of "ending inventory".
5. A   B is wrong because it didn't give 100% credit to the EI units and DM is added at the beginning of processing. C is wrong for the same reason and also because it gave some credit to BI when DM is added at the beginning. D would be right if we were computing the EUP for CC instead of DM. The EUP for DM in this case is S&C units + 0%*BI units + 100%*EI units. But S&C + EI equals the number of units started. Draw a physical flow t-account to prove this to yourself.
6. A   B, C & D can be dismissed because they didn't give 100% credit to the BI units and the WA method always does. The EUP for DM in this case is S&C units + 100%*BI units + 100%*EI units. But S&C + EI equals the number of units started.
7. D   A & B can be dismissed because they didn't give any credit for completing the BI units this month. C would be right if it said "80% times the BI units" instead of 20%.
8. A   B, C & D can be dismissed because they didn't give 100% credit to the BI units and the WA method always does. Note that the number of units completed equals beginning inventory plus started & completed units.

9. B   In this instance the two methods will yield the same EUP and cost per EUP figures. (If BI units equal zero, then the costs attached to BI equal zero also.) All the other choices are just silly.

10. D   B & C can be dismissed because the units were finished, they were not yet sold. A is incorrect because it decreases FG Inventory when we are transferring units *into* FG Inventory.

11. C   The WA method includes the prior month's costs in the numerator because the denominator, EUP, is computed by giving credit for the prior month's work.

12. D   D is the false statement because the WA method averages costs across the prior period and the current period. FIFO does not do this, so a change in the processing costs of this month is more likely to stand out under the FIFO method. C is a correct statement because the WA and FIFO use the same computation for computing costs attached to EI units, and the two methods agree on the EUP for all cost categories. If a company is using standard costs, then the two methods would arrive at the same cost for EI.

13. B   The EUP for the DM costs in EI is 8,000 because materials are added at the beginning of processing. The DM costs assigned to EI is 8,000 x $3.20 = $25,600. The EUP for the CC in EI is 80% x 8,000=6,400. The CC assigned to EI is 6,400 x $1.80 = $11,520. Therefore, the total costs assigned to EI are $25,600 + $11,520 = $37,120.

14. B   The EUP for the DM costs in EI is 80% x 12,000 = 9,600. The DM costs assigned to EI is 9,600 x $2.40 = $23,040. The EUP for the CC in EI is 40% x 12,000=4,800. The CC assigned to EI is 4,800 x $3.30 = $15,840. Therefore, the total costs assigned to EI are $23,040 + $15,840 = $38,880.

15. C   Use a t-account to determine the number of units transferred out. You should get 75,000 units. Then 75,000 x $3 = $225,000.

Exercises:

1. Notice that you didn't need any of the information about stage of completion because you were only asked to summarize physical flow of units, not to compute EUP.

WIP Inventory - Units			
Beg Inv	10,000		
Units		Units Com-	
Started	60,000	pleted	**58,000**
End Inv	30,000		

2. Again, you didn't need any of the information about stage of completion to answer this question.

WIP Inventory - Units			
Beg Inv	27,000		
Units		Units Com-	
Started	**111,000**	pleted	120,000
End Inv	18,000		

3. Again, you didn't need any of the information about stage of completion to answer this question.

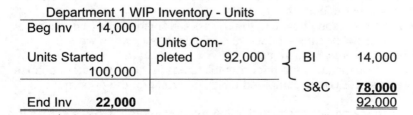

Department 1 WIP Inventory - Units					
Beg Inv	14,000	Units Com-			
Units Started		pleted	92,000	BI	14,000
	100,000				
				S&C	**78,000**
End Inv	**22,000**				92,000

4. First summarize the physical flow of the units

Department 4 WIP Inventory - Units					
Beg Inv	120	Units Com-			
Units Started	600	pleted	570	BI	120
				S&C	450
End Inv	150				570

Next, compute the total EUP.

	Physical Units	WA EUP - DM	FIFO EUP - DM
BI	120	120	120
S&C	450	450	450
EI	150	100	100
Total		**670**	**670**

5.

	Physical Units	WA EUP - DM	FIFO EUP - DM
BI	120	120	40
S&C	450	450	450
EI	150	0	0
Total		**570**	**490**

6.

		Work This Period				
	Beginning WIP	Complete BI	Start and Complete	Start Ending WIP	Total Work Performed this Period	Total Units to Account For
Account for Physical Units	130		770	230	1,000	1,130
Equivalent Units:					Total FIFO EUP	Total Weighted Average EUP
Direct materials	104	26	770	230	1,026	1,130
Conversion costs	39	91	770	184	1,045	1,084

Note how this relates to the t-account summary of the physical flow:

```
                WIP Inventory - Units
Beg Inv          130  |
                      | Units Com-
Units Started  1,000  | pleted        900  ⎧ BI    130
                      |                    ⎨ S&C   770
End Inv          230  |                    ⎩       900
```

The DM EUP for BI under FIFO is 20% x 130 units = 26, because the BI already had 80% of its DM costs attached when the month began. The CC EUP under FIFO is 70% x 130 units = 91 because the BI units were 30% complete and the last 70% of production (and the incurrence of CC) occurred during March.

The DM EUP for EI under both methods is 100% x 230 units = 230 because the EI units had passed both stages of production where materials were added (and hence had all their DM costs in them) before the month ended. The CC EUP for EI under both methods is 80% x 230 units = 184 units because the EI units had 80% of their work done before the month ended.

7. **Summarize Physical and Equivalent Units:**

		Work This Period			Total Work Performed this Period	Total Units to Account For
	Beginning WIP	Complete BI	Start and Complete	Start Ending WIP		
Account for Physical Units	30,000		40,000	10,000	50,000	80,000

					Total FIFO EUP	Total Wtd Avg EUP
Equivalent Units:						
DM	30,000	0	40,000	10,000	50,000	80,000
CC	6,000	24,000	40,000	7,000	71,000	77,000

Calculate Cost per EUP:

	Cost	EUP	Cost/EUP
FIFO:			
DM	$96,600	50,000	$1.93200
CC	$33,920	71,000	$0.47775
Total			$2.40975
Weighted average:			
DM	$110,000	80,000	$1.37500
CC	$41,760	77,000	$0.54234
Total			$1.91734

The journal entry under FIFO is:
Finished goods inventory   129,096
   Work in process inventory   129,096

Process Cost Report Cost Assignment:

	FIFO			Weighted Average		
	Computation	Units	Costs	Computation	Units	Costs
Beginning WIP		30,000	$21,240			
Cost to complete beginning WIP:						
Direct materials	(0 x $1.932)		$0			
Conversion costs	(24,000 x $0.47775)		11,466			
Total costs added this period			11,466			
Total cost of beginning WIP			32,706			
Started, compl'd, & tr'd out	(40,000 x $2.40975)	40,000	96,390			
Total completed & transferred out			129,096	(70,000 x $1.91734)	70,000	$134,214
Ending WIP:		10,000			10,000	
Direct materials	(10,000 x $1.932)		19,320	(10,000 x $1.375)		13,750
Conversion costs	(7,000 x $0.47775)		3,344	(7,000 x $0.54234)		3,796
Total ending WIP cost			22,664			17,546
Total accounted for		80,000	$151,760		80,000	$151,760

SOLUTION TO PROBLEM SET B

<u>Multiple choice:</u>

1. B   Transferred-in costs are cumulative as the units move through the processing departments.
2. B   Use a t-account to determine the number of units transferred out. You should get 67,700 units. Then 67,700 x $2.10 = $142,170.
3. D   by definition of normal spoilage
4. B   by definition of abnormal spoilage
5. B   The costs of normal spoilage are attached to the goods units transferred out of the department because normal spoilage is considered part of everyday manufacturing operations. The costs of normal spoilage actually increase the processing cost of the good units.
6. D   A is wrong because the costs of abnormal spoilage are debited to a loss account. Because these costs are not included with the transferred out with the good units, abnormal spoilage costs do not affect the processing cost per unit of the good units.
7. D   First summarize the physical flow to determine total spoilage and then break this down between normal and abnormal spoilage

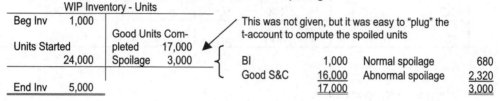

WIP Inventory - Units

Beg Inv	1,000			This was not given, but it was easy to "plug" the t-account to compute the spoiled units			
Units Started		Good Units Com-pleted	17,000				
	24,000	Spoilage	3,000	BI	1,000	Normal spoilage	680
				Good S&C	16,000	Abnormal spoilage	2,320
End Inv	5,000				17,000		3,000

For questions 8-12, first summarize the physical flow to determine total spoilage and then break this down between normal and abnormal spoilage.

WIP Inventory - Units

Beg Inv	2,			This was not given, but it was easy to "plug" the t-account to compute the spoiled units			
Units Started	28,	Good Units Com-pleted	27,000				
		Spoilage	2,000	BI	2,000	Normal spoilage	1,350
				Good S&C	25,000	Abnormal spoilage	650
End Inv	1,				27,000		2,000

8. C   The costs attached to normal spoilage are $15 x 1,350 = $20,250
9. D   The costs attached to abnormal spoilage are $15 x 650 = $9,750
10. C   The costs attached to goods completed and transferred out equals the cost of processing the good units transferred out plus the costs of normal spoilage = $15 x 27,000 + $20,250 = $425,250.
11. C   The cost/unit for the good units completed & transferred out = $425,250 over the number of good units transferred out = $425,250/27,000 = $15.75.
12. D   The entry to transfer costs out of work in process and into finished goods is

FG Inventory $425,250
Loss from Abnormal Spoilage $9,750
    WIP Inventory $435,000

13. D   TI costs are treated the same as DM added at the beginning of processing.
14. D   TI costs are treated the same as DM added at the beginning of processing.

Exercises:
1.

Summarize Physical and Equivalent Units:

		Work This Period			Total Work Performed this Period	Total Units to Account For
	Beginning WIP	Complete BI	Start and Complete	Start Ending WIP		
Account for Physical Units	12,000		77,000	10,000	87,000	99,000
Equivalent Units:					Total FIFO EUP	Total Wtd Avg EUP
DM	12,000	0	77,000	10,000	87,000	99,000
CC	2,400	9,600	77,000	4,500	91,100	93,500
TI	12,000	0	77,000	10,000	87,000	99,000

2.

Weighted average method:
DM cost per EUP =	$132,640/32,000 =	$4.14500
CC per EUP =	$33,930/29,800 =	1.13859
TI cost per EUP =	$55,350/34,000 =	1.62794
Total processing cost per EUP		$6.91153

FIFO method:
DM cost per EUP =	$97,840/28,000 =	$3.49429
CC per EUP =	$27,040/24,120 =	1.12106
TI cost per EUP =	$42,900/30,000 =	1.43000
Total processing cost per EUP		$6.04535

3.

Summarize Physical and Equivalent Units:

		Work This Period					
	Beginning WIP	Complete BI	Start and Complete	Start Ending WIP	Total Work Performed this Period	Total Units to Account For	Spoiled Units
Account for Physical Units	14,000		60,000	10,000	70,000	84,000	(3,000)
					Total FIFO EUP	Total Wtd Avg EUP	
Equivalent Units:							
DM	14,000	0	60,000	10,000	70,000	84,000	(3,000)
CC	2,800	11,200	60,000	7,000	78,200	81,000	(3,000)
Total spoilage							3,000
Less: Normal Spoilage							2,130
Abnormal Spoilage							870

How did we know spoiled units totaled 3,000? See the t-account summary below:

```
      Department 1 WIP Inventory - Units
Beg Inv          14,000
                         Good Units                This was not given, but it was easy to "plug" the
Units Started    70,000  Completed     71,000      t-account to compute the spoiled units
                         Spoilage       3,000   {  BI          14,000   Normal spoilage    2,130
                                                   Good S&C    57,000   Abnormal spoilage    870
End Inv           8,000                                        62,000                      3,000
```

The rest of the process
cost report is to the right
and on the next page.

Calculate Cost per EUP:

	Cost	EUP	Cost/EUP
FIFO:			
DM	$590,000	70,000	$8.42857
CC	$290,000	78,200	3.70844
			$12.13701
Weighted average:			
DM	$655,200	84,000	$7.80000
CC	$332,700	81,000	4.10741
			$11.90741

3. solution continued

Process Cost Report Cost Assignment:

	FIFO			Weighted Average		
	Computation	Units	Costs	Computation	Units	Costs
Beginning WIP		14,000	$107,900			
Cost to complete beginning WIP:						
DM	(0 x $8.42857)		0			
CC	(11,200 x $3.70844)		41,535			
Total costs added this period			41,535			
Total cost of beginning WIP			149,435			
Normal spoilage	(2,130 x $12.13701)	2,130	25,852	(2,130 x $11.90741)	2,130	$25,363
Good units started, completed, & tr'd out	(57,000 x $12.13701)	57,000	691,810			
Good Units Completed & tr'd				(71,000 x $11.90741)	71,000	845,426
Total completed & transferred out (incl spoilage)		73,130	867,096		73,130	870,789
Abnormal spoilage	(870 x $12.13701)	870	10,559	(870 x $11.90741)	870	10,359
Ending WIP:		10,000			10,000	
DM	(10,000 x $8.42857)		84,286	(10,000 x $7.80)		78,000
CC	(7,000 x $3.70844)		25,959	(7,000 x $4.10741)		28,752
Total ending WIP cost			110,245			106,752
Total accounted for		84,000	$987,900		84,000	$987,900

The required journal entry under the weighted average method is:

Finished goods inventory	870,789	
Loss from abnormal spoilage	10,359	
Work in process inventory		881,148

To transfer costs of completed units to Finished goods & record the loss from abnormal spoilage.

The required journal entry under the FIFO method is:

Finished goods inventory	867,096	
Loss from abnormal spoilage	10,559	
Work in process inventory		877,655

To transfer costs of completed units to Finished Goods & record the loss from abnormal spoilage.

SOLUTION TO END OF CHAPTER EXERCISES

Completion:

1. Job (or job order)
2. weighted average
3. Process
4. started & completed units
5. transferred-in costs
6. beginning inventory units
7. the number of units in beginning inventory
8. zero
9. the number of units transferred out
10. the number of units started

Exercises:

1. Molding Department

	Beginning WIP	Work This Period Complete BI	Work This Period Start and Complete	Work This Period Start Ending WIP	Total Work Performed this Period	Total Units to Account For
Account for Physical Units	1,200		14,300	2,700	17,000	18,200
Equivalent Units:					Total FIFO EUP	Total Weighted Average EUP
Direct materials	1,200	0	14,300	2,700	17,000	18,200
Conversion costs	240	960	14,300	1,890	17,150	17,390

Painting Department

	Beginning WIP	Work This Period Complete BI	Work This Period Start and Complete	Work This Period Start Ending WIP	Total Work Performed this Period	Total Units to Account For
Account for Physical Units	2,100		14,500	1,000	15,500	17,600
Equivalent Units:					Total FIFO EUP	Total Wtd Avg EUP
DM	840	1,260	14,500	250	16,010	16,850
CC	840	1,260	14,500	250	16,010	16,850
TI	2,100	0	14,500	1,000	15,500	17,600

2.

Summarize Physical and Equivalent Units:

	Beginning WIP	Complete BI	Start and Complete	Start Ending WIP	Total Work Performed this Period	Total Units to Account For	Spoiled Units
			Work This Period				
Account for Physical Units	2,000		27,000	1,000	28,000	30,000	(2,000)
Equivalent Units:					Total FIFO EUP	Total Wtd Avg EUP	
DM	2,000	0	27,000	1,000	28,000	30,000	(2,000)
CC	300	1,700	27,000	350	29,050	29,350	(2,000)
Total spoilage							2,000
Less: Normal Spoilage							540
Abnormal Spoilage							1,460

Calculate Cost per EUP:

	Cost	EUP	Cost/EUP
FIFO:			
DM	$218,300	28,000	$7.7964
CC	$98,220	29,050	3.3811
			$11.1775
Weighted average:			
DM	$239,500	30,000	$7.9833
CC	$115,620	29,350	3.9394
			$11.9227

solution continued on next page →

2. solution continued

Process Cost Report Cost Assignment:

	FIFO			Weighted Average		
	Computation	Units	Costs	Computation	Units	Costs
Beginning WIP		2,000	$38,600			
Cost to complete beginning WIP:						
DM	(0 x $7.7964)		0			
CC	(1,700 x $3.3811)		5,748			
Total costs added this period			5,748			
Total cost of beginning WIP			44,348			
Normal spoilage	(540 x $11.1775)	540	6,036	(540 x $11.9227)	540	6,438
Good units started, completed, & tr'd out	(25,000 x $11.1775)	25,000	279,437			
Good Units Completed & tr'd out				(27,000 x $11.9227)	27,000	321,913
Total completed & tr'd out (incl spoilage)		27,540	329,821		27,540	328,351
Abnormal spoilage	(1,460 x $11.1775)	1,460	16,319	(1,460 x $11.9227)	1,460	17,407
Ending WIP:		1,000			1,000	
DM	(1,000 x $7.7964)		7,796	(1,000 x $7.9833)		7,983
CC	(350 x $3.3811)		1,183	(350 x $3.9394)		1,379
Total ending WIP cost			8,980			9,362
Total accounted for		30,000	$355,120		30,000	$355,120

The required journal entry under the FIFO method is:

Finished goods inventory	329,821	
Loss from abnormal spoilage	16,319	
Work in process inventory		346,140

To transfer costs of completed units to Finished goods & record the loss from abnormal spoilage.

The required journal entry under the weighted average method is:

Finished goods inventory	328,351	
Loss from abnormal spoilage	17,407	
Work in process inventory		345,758

To transfer costs of completed units to Finished Goods & record the loss from abnormal spoilage.

Chapter 7

Activity-Based Costing and Management

√ **Study Checklist – Monitor your progress**

1. Read the chapter in the text
2. Review the learning objectives below
3. Read the overview of the chapter
4. Read the chapter review for learning objectives 1 - 4
5. Do Problem Set A and check your answers
6. Read the chapter review for learning objectives 5 - 6
7. Do Problem Set B and check your answers
8. Do the End of Chapter Exercises in this study guide
9. Do the homework assigned by your instructor

CHAPTER LEARNING OBJECTIVES

After studying this chapter, you should be able to answer the following questions:

Q1. How is activity-based costing (ABC) different from traditional costing?
Q2. What are activities and how are they identified?
Q3. What process is used to assign costs in an ABC system?
Q4. How are cost drivers selected for activities?
Q5. What is activity-based management (ABM)?
Q6. What are the benefits, costs, and limitations of ABC and ABM?

OVERVIEW OF CHAPTER

In Chapter 5 we learned a method for assigning costs to unique jobs and in Chapter 6 we learned to assign costs to mass-produced products. Activity-based costing (ABC) is a costing system that assigns costs in two stages: costs are first assigned to cost pools for similar activities and then from these cost pools to jobs or to processing departments. ABC is a refinement of traditional job costing or traditional process costing. When used for product costing, ABC is most useful when the products or services consume resources in different proportions. Using ABC information to improve operations is known as activity-based management (ABM).

CHAPTER REVIEW: Learning Objectives 1 - 4

Q1: How is activity-based costing (ABC) different from traditional costing?

When the cost object is the product, a traditional costing system traces direct product costs and allocates indirect costs from a minimal number of cost pools, whereas ABC uses a two-stage process for the allocation of indirect product costs. Costs are first traced and allocated to activity cost pools. Then each pool of activity costs is allocated to the product using an allocation base that is the cost driver for that activity. For product costing, ABC is most useful when a company provides services or produces products that consume resources in different ways.

Q2: What are activities and how are they identified?

Activities are tasks or functions performed by a business. To help identify an organization's activities, accountants use a cost hierarchy that categorizes costs based on the level of the organization that the costs sustain. The ABC hierarchy includes the following categories:

- *Organization-sustaining activities* are those that occur to support the whole business. Examples of organization-sustaining activities include the oversight of corporate borrowing and the accounts payable function. A good deal of the costs associated with organization-sustaining activities are fixed costs and are not allocated to the activities performed at lower levels of the organization.

- *Facility-sustaining activities* are those that support the various facilities of an organization. The costs of these activities may be variable at the organization level, but are often fixed for lower levels of the organization. For example, if each factory needs one plant supervisor, then Supervisors' Salaries is a fixed cost at the facility level, but variable at the organization level because it will increase as the business adds more factories.

- *Customer-sustaining activities* support past, current, and future customers. Some of the costs of these activities will be fixed at this level (e.g. rent on an office building dedicated to customer service) and some of these will vary with the number of customers (e.g. the wages for the customer service representatives that work in the building).

- *Product-sustaining activities* are tasks or functions that support the production and distribution of a single product or product line. The depreciation on a fleet of distribution trucks is an example of a fixed cost (within the relevant range) for this activity and the commissions of the salespersons for this product line is an example of a product-sustaining activity cost that is variable with respect to the sales volume of the product.

- *Batch-level activities* are tasks performed for a collection of goods or services. Suppose a garment manufacturer dyes its own yard goods and the dying vat must have one laborer to oversee the process regardless of the quantity of fabric in the vat. This cost is variable with respect to the number of batches the manufacturer dyes, not with respect to the number of bolts of fabric dyed.

- *Unit-level activities* are those that are performed for every unit produced or service provided, within the product line category under consideration. For example, if it takes 3 carpenter's labor hours to produce one unit of output, then this is a variable cost of a unit-level activity.

Demonstration problem-Identifying and categorizing activities
You are the accountant for Pete's Perfect Pizza, Inc. Pete has 5 pizza parlors in the Dallas-Fort Worth area. Pete has corporate offices in Fort Worth, and a manager for each restaurant. Three of the restaurants serve only pizza, but two of them serve pizza and a few pasta dishes. At each restaurant, pizzas are made individually, although the dough is made in batches that can make 20 pizzas. At the 2 restaurants that serve pasta, the sauce is made and the pasta is boiled in batches. You successfully convinced Pete that an activity-based costing system would help him better manage his organization. One of the first steps in setting up an ABC system is the identification of the business activities. After interviewing employees at the corporate office and employees at all 5 restaurants, you arrived at a list of activities, which is reproduced below:

Partial list of activities performed by employees of Pete's Perfect Pizza:
1. Manage accounts payable to suppliers
2. Answer the phones for customer complaints
3. Chop ingredients for the pizzas
4. Prepare corporate tax returns
5. Create weekly schedules for each employee in the restaurant
6. Handle special customer requests for catering
7. Take customer orders in person and on the phone
8. Make dough
9. Complete corporate tax returns
10. Prepare advertisements for pizza
11. Prepare advertisements for pasta dishes
12. Negotiate rental agreement for corporate headquarters
13. Negotiate purchase price for pizza machines
14. Box individual pizzas for customer pick up
15. Prepare individual pizzas for customers orders

Required:
For each of the above activities, identify the category of the ABC hierarchy to which it belongs.

solution begins on next page →

Solution to demonstration problem

		ABC hierarchy	Comments
1.	Manage accounts payable to suppliers	Organization-sustaining	Most likely accounts payable functions are handled at the corporate offices. If they are instead handled at the restaurant level, then this would be a facility-sustaining activity.
2.	Answer the phones for customer complaints	Customer-sustaining	
3.	Chop ingredients for the pizzas	Batch-level	Most likely each of Pete's restaurants chops enough ingredients at one time to make several pizzas.
4.	Prepare corporate tax returns	Organization-sustaining	If there is only one corporate entity, it will prepare consolidated tax returns for all of its locations.
5.	Create weekly schedules for each employee in the restaurant	Facility-sustaining	Whether this is done at the corporate office or by each individual restaurant's manager, this activity supports the individual restaurant.
6.	Handle special customer requests for catering	Customer-sustaining	
7.	Take customer orders in person and on the phone	Unit-level	This cost increases as more orders are placed.
8.	Make dough	Batch-level	Each batch makes 20 pizzas.
9.	Prepare advertisements for restaurants	Facility-sustaining	This cost supports each restaurant.
10.	Prepare advertisements for pizza	Product-sustaining	This cost supports the pizza product line.
11.	Prepare advertisements for pasta dishes	Product-sustaining	This cost supports the pasta product line.
12.	Negotiate rental agreement for corporate headquarters	Organization-sustaining	
13.	Negotiate purchase price for pizza ovens	Facility-sustaining	Each restaurant needs at least one oven.
14.	Box individual pizzas for customer pick up	Unit-level	
15.	Prepare individual pizzas for customers orders	Unit-level	

Q3: What process is used to assign costs in an ABC system?

- Identify the relevant cost object. The final cost object in the two-stage cost assignment could be the end product or service, or it could be a department or other business segment.

- Identify activities, and group *homogeneous activities*. Homogenous activities are related in some logical manner and consume resources in similar ways.

- Assign costs to the activity cost pools. Some costs will be direct costs to the activity cost pools and can be traced to the activity. Other costs will be indirect costs that need to be allocated across the activity cost pools.

- Choose a cost driver for each activity cost pool. This is covered in learning objective 4 below.

- Calculate an allocation rate for each activity cost pool. The estimated allocation rate is estimated total activity costs divided by the estimated total quantity for the allocation base. When estimating the total quantity for the allocation base, some measure of volume for the year must be assumed. If the estimated volume for the year is assumed to be the maximum volume that can be achieved, allowing for normal downtime, the allocation base is said to be a measure of *practical capacity*. When a practical capacity measure is used to estimate the quantity of the allocation base, the resultant activity-based costs provide an estimate of the cost of supplying production capacity (and the costs of not using the capacity available).

- Allocate activity costs to the final cost object. Direct costs are traced to the final cost object and the indirect activity costs are allocated to the final cost object.

Q4: How are cost drivers selected for activities?

Indirect cost allocation is always an estimate, by definition of indirect costs. This estimate is a better estimate when the cost allocation base is also a cost driver for the activity costs. Recall from Chapter 2 that cost drivers are measures of volume that have a cause and effect relationship with the costs. Chapter 2 also covered methods (such as regression) for locating good cost drivers for a pool of costs.

Some costs do not have a good cost driver. For example, rent on the factory is fixed and there is no measure of activity that we could choose so that rent would increase when the cost driver increased. This is why we use the term "allocation base" instead of cost driver. Unfortunately, in the ABC literature, the term "cost driver" has become predominant in place of "allocation base". The text and this study guide uses this generally accepted ABC terminology, even though some "cost drivers" chosen to allocate activity costs to the final cost objects are allocation bases and not cost drivers.

Demonstration problem-Choosing cost drivers for activities

After listing the activities for Pete's Perfect Pizza, grouping like activities, and classifying them into the ABC hierarchy, you arrived at the list below. Supposes you determined that the final cost object is an individual pizza or pasta dinner.

	Activity group	ABC hierarchy
1.	Manage budgets, bookkeeping, prepare financial statements and tax returns, negotiate lease, rental, and purchase agreements for restaurants	Organization-sustaining
2.	Hire and fire employees, oversee restaurant operations	Facility-sustaining
3.	Prepare weekly work schedules, prepare payroll	Facility-sustaining
4.	Customer service activities, which mostly includes bidding for and managing catering jobs	Customer-sustaining
5.	Prepare advertisements for all five restaurants	Organization-sustaining
6.	Chop ingredients for the pizzas, make dough, make pizza sauce	Batch-level
7.	Prepare pasta sauce and pasta	Batch-level
8.	Take customer orders in person and on the phone	Batch-level
9.	Service customers at tables	Batch-level
10.	Clean tables and dishes	Batch-level
11.	Prepare pizzas	Unit-level
12.	Prepare individual pasta dish orders	Unit-level

Required:

Choose a cost driver for each activity cost pool and discuss how the costs would be allocated to the final cost object, the individual pizza or pasta dish.

Solution to demonstration problem

1   Manage budgets, bookkeeping, prepare financial statements and tax returns, negotiate lease, rental, and purchase agreements for restaurants

For determining the selling price of pizzas and pasta dishes, these costs could be allocated to the final products because selling prices must cover all costs in the long run if the company is to be profitable. These costs could be allocated to the catering jobs, if this is a significant part of operations. If catering is not a significant part of operations, then it may not be necessary to allocate these costs to catering jobs, and allow for the pricing of catering jobs to be based on incremental costs of the job (i.e. catering jobs could be priced like special orders were in Chapter 4). These costs should definitely not be allocated to the final product for determining the profitability of the individual restaurants if this information will be used to assess the performance of the restaurant's manager, because the managers do not have any control over these costs.

If these costs are allocated to the final product, then a good cost driver would be total revenue. The cost allocation rate would then be a percentage, which could be applied to the selling price of each individual pizza or pasta dish. When total revenue is used as a cost allocation base, products absorb costs in proportion to the revenues they bring in.

solution continues on next page →

Solution to demonstration problem continued

2   Hire and fire employees, oversee restaurant operations - If this is done at the restaurant level, these costs could be allocated based on the number of pizzas plus pasta dishes (i.e. the denominator in the allocation rate computation could be total items served). Then each pasta dish and each pizza would be allocated the same amount of these costs.

3   Prepare weekly work schedules, prepare payroll - These costs are probably at least partly variable with respect to the number of employees or the number of labor hours. Total labor hours could be used as the cost driver, and the cost per hour used to allocate costs to pizzas and pasta dishes. If it takes longer to prepare a pizza than a pasta dish, then a pizza would absorb more of these costs than would a pasta dish.

4   Customer service activities, which mostly includes bidding for and managing catering jobs - These costs could be allocated based on the number of hours the customer service representative spends managing the catering job. If this is done, then none of these costs will be allocated to pizza or pasta dishes prepared for regular customers. Based on the description of these activities, this is probably appropriate.

5   Prepare advertisements for all five restaurants - Hopefully there is a cause and effect relationship between advertising and revenues, so total revenue would be a good cost driver. Then each pizza or pasta dish would absorb these costs based on a percentage of its selling price.

6   Chop ingredients for the pizzas, make dough, make pizza sauce - The total number of pizzas that can be made from the batch should be used as the cost driver. Then each pizza will be allocated the same amount of these costs. If some pizzas use more ingredients than others (e.g. stuffed pizzas), then Pete would need to estimate how much more time it takes to chop ingredients for stuffed pizzas. For example, if it takes twice as long to chop ingredients for stuffed pizzas, then the cost driver could be total number of regular pizzas plus 2 x the total number of stuffed pizzas. Then costs would be allocated to the pizzas so that each regular pizza was allocated the same cost and each stuffed pizza was allocated twice the cost of a regular pizza. If desired, more sophisticated cost drivers could be developed based on the number of ingredients on a pizza.

7   Prepare pasta sauce and pasta - The total number of pasta dishes that can be made from the batch should be used as the cost driver so that each pasta dish is allocated the same cost.

8   Take customer orders in person and on the phone

9   Service customers at tables

10 Clean tables and dishes

For activity groups 8, 9, and 10, the total number of pizzas plus the total number of pasta dishes could be used as a cost driver so that each item is allocated the same amount of cost.

11 Prepare pizzas - The cost driver should be the number of individual pizzas prepared so that each pizza is allocated the same cost. If some pizzas require more preparation time than others (e.g. stuffed pizzas) then an estimate as to how much more time it takes to prepare a stuffed pizza compared to a regular pizza should be made.

12 Prepare individual pasta dish orders - The cost driver should be the number of individual pasta dishes prepared so that each pasta dish is allocated the same cost. This assumes that the preparation of each individual pasta dish uses the same amount of resources

ABC is a better estimate of product cost because it tracks resource consumption more carefully than does traditional costing. This is shown in the next demonstration problem.

Demonstration problem-Traditional costing versus ABC

Cecilia's Ceramics makes two types of coffee mugs, plain and designer. She produces and sells them in equal quantities. Cecilia herself shapes the mugs on a spinning wheel. The direct costs per mug are:

	Plain	Designer
Clay @ $3/lb	$0.75	$1.50
Paint	0.10	0.50
Glaze	0.10	0.15
Labor costs of Cecilia @ $10/hour	2.00	2.00
	$2.95	$4.15

Cecilia's estimated annual production overhead for the year is listed below by type of cost.

Rent on the studio	$6,000
Wages for kiln helpers	8,000
Wages for assistant artists	7,500
Utilities in the studio	1,200
Kiln supplies	800
Cleaning supplies	500
Depreciation on the kiln	1,000
	$25,000

Cecilia estimates that she spends 1,250 hours at the spinning wheel each year. She uses her spinning hours as the cost allocation base for overhead. The estimated allocation rate is $25,000/1,250 spinning hour = $20/spinning hour. Each mug uses 12 spinning minutes (1/5 of an hour).

Using traditional costing, Cecilia computed the production cost per mug as follows:

	Plain	Designer
Direct costs	$2.95	$4.15
Overhead allocated: 1/5 of a spinning hour @ $20/spinning hour	4.00	4.00
	$6.95	$8.15

Cecilia took a cost accounting class at the local community college and asked for your help implementing an ABC system. Since you already took cost accounting, you realize that the designer mugs probably consume more resources and should be allocated more overhead than plain mugs. You discuss the production process with Cecilia and learn the following:

- The kiln helpers watch the mugs as they are being fired and then remove them to the cooling area. Each time a mug is fired, it stays in the kiln 20 minutes. The plain mugs are only fired once, but the designer mugs are fired twice; first the undecorated mug is fired and then, after the artists add more clay so that the designer mug takes the shape of a person or an animal, it is fired again.
- The kiln area occupies 600 square feet of the studio; the art area occupies 400 square feet.
- The assistant artists are the ones who mold the cute faces on the designer mugs and do the painting and glazing of the designer mugs. They spend 10% of their time painting and glazing plain mugs and 90% of their time molding faces, painting, and glazing designer mugs. Assistant artists make $7.50/hour.
- Utilities in the studio are mostly electricity costs, and Cecilia estimates that 75% of the electricity is for running the kiln.
- The cleaning supplies are mostly for cleaning up the art area.

demonstration problem continues on the next page →

Demonstration problem continued
After your discussions with Cecilia, you decide that, in addition spinning the clay, the costs of which are direct to the mugs, there are really two activities in Cecilia's operation: kiln activities and art activities.

Required:
a) Choose a cost driver to use to allocate each of the overhead costs to the activities. If a cost is associated with only one of the activities then it is a direct cost to that activity and no cost driver needs to be chosen.
b) Compute the total costs assigned to the kiln activities and art activities cost pools.
c) Choose a cost driver for each activity. Compute the estimated cost allocation rate for each activity, and the costs allocated to each type of mug for the year.
d) Compute the cost per plain and designer mugs using ABC, and compare this to the cost under traditional costing.

Solution to demonstration problem
a)

	Possible Cost Driver
Rent on the studio	Square feet of space used by activity
Wages for kiln helpers	N/A – this is a direct cost to the kiln activity
Wages for assistant artists	N/A – this is a direct cost to the art activity
Utilities in the studio	75% to kiln activity; 25% to art activity based on Cecilia's estimates
Kiln supplies	N/A – this is a direct cost to the kiln activity
Cleaning supplies	N/A – this is a direct cost to the art activity
Depreciation on the kiln	N/A – this is a direct cost to the kiln activity

b)

	Kiln Activity	Art Activity	
Rent on the studio	$3,600	$2,400	(60% to kiln, 40% to art, based on square feet)
Wages for kiln helpers	8,000	0	
Wages for assistant artists	0	7,500	
Utilities in the studio	900	300	(75% to kiln, 25% to art, per Cecilia's estimate)
Kiln supplies	800	0	
Cleaning supplies	0	500	
Depreciation on the kiln	1,000	0	
	$14,300	$10,700	

c) Kiln activity: The most obvious cost driver to use to is kiln hours. To compute the number of kiln hours per year, note that Cecilia can spin 5 mugs per hour. 1,250 spinning hours x 5 mugs per hour = 6,250 mugs per year. Since she produces the same number of plain and designer mugs, she produces 3,125 of each type of mug per year. 3,125 plain mugs x 20 kiln minutes = 62,500 kiln minutes per year and 3,125 designer mugs x 40 kiln minutes = 125,000 kiln minutes per year, for a total of 187,500 kiln minutes, or 3,125 kiln hours. The estimated cost allocation rate is $14,300/3,125 kiln hours = $4.576/kiln hour.

Art activity: The most obvious cost driver to use is the quantity of assistant artists' hours. Since Cecilia estimates $7,500 for assistant artists wages, and they make $7.50/hour, there are 1,000 budgeted assistant artist hours. The estimated cost allocation rate is $10,700/1,000 assistant artist hours = $10.70/assistant artist hour.

solution continues on next page →

Solution to demonstration problem continued

Plain mugs are budgeted to use 3,125 mugs x 1/3 kiln hour/mug = 1,041.67 kiln hours, so plain mugs are allocated $4.576/kiln hour x 1,041.67 kiln hours = $4,767 of kiln activity costs.

Designer mugs are budgeted to use 3,125 mugs x 2/3 kiln hour/mug = 2,083.33 kiln hours, so designer mugs are allocated $4.576/kiln hour x 2,083.33 kiln hours = $9,533 of kiln activity costs.

Plain mugs are budgeted to use 1,000 assistant artists hours x 10% = 100 assistant artist hours, so plain mugs are allocated $10.70/assistant artist hour x 100 assistant artist hours = $1,070 of art activity costs.

Designer mugs are budgeted to use 1,000 assistant artists hours x 90% = 900 assistant artist hours, so designer mugs are allocated $10.70/assistant artist hour x 900 assistant artist hours = $9,630 of art activity costs.

d) Total overhead costs allocated to plain mugs = $4,767 + $1,070 = $5,837. This is $5,837/3,125 plain mugs = $1.87/plain mug. Total overhead costs allocated to designer mugs = $9,533 + $9,630 = $19,163. This is $19,163/3,125 designer mugs = $6.13/designer mug.

Using ABC, the production cost per mug as follows:

	Plain	Designer
Direct costs	$2.95	$4.15
Overhead allocated: as computed above	1.87	6.13
	$4.82	$10.28

Traditional costing assigned $6.95 and $8.15 of production costs to plain and designer mugs, respectively. The difference in the two traditional costing figures was only due to the difference in direct costs because traditional costing assigned $4 of overhead to each mug. ABC captures the additional resource consumption of the designer mugs, and the overhead allocated to a designer mug is over three times the overhead allocated to a plain mug.

PROBLEM SET A (Learning Objectives 1 - 4)

True-False: Indicate whether each of the following is true (T) or false (F) in the space provided.

_____ 1. An ABC system yields more accurate costs than a traditional costing system.

_____ 2. ABC is best used when the products are similar.

_____ 3. In a traditional costing system, if one product is allocated a cost that is too low compared to its resource consumption, then at least one other product is allocated a cost that is too high compared to its resource consumption.

_____ 4. ABC systems can be used in manufacturing and in service industries.

_____ 5. An ABC system has multiple cost pools for overhead whereas a traditional system has only one cost pool for overhead.

_____ 6. Costs associated with organization-level activities are often not allocated to the product in an ABC system.

_____ 7. An ABC system will usually have more overhead cost allocation rates than a traditional costing system.

_____ 8. An ABC system is more complex than a traditional costing system.

_____ 9. Unit-level costs are variable with respect to the number of units produced.

_____ 10. Batch-level costs are variable with respect to the number of units produced.

Matching: Maria's Mexican Food operates a chain of 12 fast food restaurants in Texas. Taco sauce is made and cheese grating occurs at one central location and is delivered to each restaurant. Match each cost with the most likely activity cost hierarchy level to which it relates. You may use each hierarchy level more than once.

Activity hierarchy level

A. Organization-sustaining   D. Product-sustaining

B. Facility-sustaining   E. Batch-level

C. Customer-sustaining   F. Unit-level

_____ 1. Costs of an advertisement for the new stuffed taco dish

_____ 2. Costs of tortillas

_____ 3. Cost of making taco sauce

_____ 4. Rent on corporate offices

_____ 5. Depreciation on microwaves

_____ 6. Cost of a market research study about customer preferences

_____ 7. Cost of a research study on the shelf life of the tortillas used in making tostadas

_____ 8. Costs of grating the cheese

_____ 9. Cost of taco meat

_____ 10. Cost of taco shells

Exercises: Write your answer in the space provided.
1. Maka Productions produces 40,000 units of Product A and 10,000 units of Product B each year. Each year, 4 machine tool changes are required. Product A is made with the regular machine tool, and the regular machine tool is in place at the beginning of the year. After producing 20,000 units of Product A, Maka changes the machine tool to the special machine tool needed for Product B, and 5,000 units of it are produced. Then the regular machine tool is replaced, and 10,000 units of Product A are made. Again the machine tool is changed and another 5,000 units of Product B are made. The final machine tool change for the year is made and 10,000 units of Product A are produced. Each machine tool change costs $800. What is the per-unit cost for machine tool changes that should be assigned to each product? Explain.

Product A _____   Product B _____

2. Galena Manufacturing makes two types of its products, Regular and Deluxe. The Regular and Deluxe models are budgeted to incur total direct material and labor costs of $120 and $220, respectively. Estimated manufacturing overhead for the year is $870,000, and estimated total direct labor hours for the year are 100,000. Each product uses 20 direct labor hours to produce.
   a) Calculate the total estimated cost per unit for each product using traditional costing, assuming that direct labor hours are used as the cost allocation base.

   Regular _____   Deluxe _____

   b) Suppose Galena is implementing an ABC system and identified three activities: materials handling, inspections, and shipping. The cost drivers for each activity cost pool are number of materials requisitions, number of inspections, and number of orders shipped, respectively. Galena has come up with the following estimates for the cost drivers and the costs in each activity cost pool:

Product	Materials Handling	Inspections	Shipping
Costs per pool	$420,000	$150,000	$300,000
Estimated annual use of cost driver:			
Regular	70	50	400
Deluxe	280	100	400

   Calculate the total estimated cost per unit for each product using ABC, assuming that Galena makes 4,000 units of Regular and 1,000 units of Deluxe each year. Compare to the traditional cost figures.

   Regular _____   Deluxe _____

CHAPTER REVIEW: Learning Objectives 5 - 6

Q5: What is activity-based management (ABM)?

In an ABC system, information about resource consumption is highlighted. Because of this, ABC provides information for managers to locate opportunities for improvements in quality, operational efficiency, and profitability. Using ABC information to this end is known as *activity-based management* (ABM). The text discusses five examples of ABM.

- Managing customer profitability. As the costs of customer-sustaining activities are allocated to customers, or categories of customers, managers learn which types of customers consume the most resources. For example, a hotel manager may categorize patrons as business or vacation patrons. ABC would allow her to assess which category of customer consumes the most staff resources. This information may allow for pricing differentials (within legal restrictions) or for changes in how the staff responds to customer requests.

- Managing product and process design. *Value-added activities* are those that enhance the final product or service from the viewpoint of the customer, and *non-value added activities* are those that do not. If inspections increase the quality of the product to the customer, then inspecting is a value-added activity. If materials are requisitioned to an assembly area, and labor hours are used to sort this material, this is a non-value added activity. The product's value to the customer is not improved by this sorting. If there is a way to reduce or eliminate this sorting, production efficiency will be increased.

- Managing environmental costs. ABC information allows managers to capture the costs of controlling pollution. Decisions that involve trade-offs between profitability and saving the environment can then be made with better information. Additionally, a company can publicly disclose its costs for environmental safety processes, which may enhance its "green" reputation.

- Managing quality. In highly competitive industries, companies often compete based on the quality of their products rather than on product price. ABC information can be used to capture the costs of maintaining quality products. Different categories of quality activities include

  - *Prevention activities.* Changes in the design of the product or the manufacturing process can sometimes reduce defects.

  - *Appraisal activities.* These activities are performed in order to identify defects or items of low quality.

  - *Production activities.* These activities are performed to repair or rework defective items or the machines that produce them.

  - *Postsales activities.* When a defective unit does make it through the inspection process and is delivered to the customer, postsales activities such as product recalls, warranty repairs, or replacements are required. The costs of postsales activities include the lost future revenues from unhappy customers.

- Managing constrained resources. In Chapter 4 we learned about maximizing profits when managers face resource constraints. ABC information allows managers to determine the costs of production or business processes, which can help identify constraints.

Q6: What are the benefits, costs, and limitations of ABC and ABM?

ABC provides more accurate product cost information than does traditional costing, but ABC's aggregation of costs by activities is sometimes even more useful than the improved product cost information. However, ABC systems are difficult to design and require that more information be captured, so that they are usually more expensive to maintain than traditional costing systems.

When the decision is made to implement an ABC system and begin using ABM, managers face various uncertainties.

- A great deal of judgment is involved in determining an organization's activities, the costs of each activity, and the cost driver to be used to allocate the costs to the final cost object.

- For each activity cost pool, the denominator level of the cost driver must be chosen before the upcoming year's volume is known.

- When making any type of change, managers cannot be sure how supervisors and employees will use the information. There may be resistance to change if employees feel the new system may yield unfair or even different performance evaluation information. Because of this resistance, the information gathered from employees when the ABC system is first being designed may not be accurate.

- Because ABC results in unitized product cost information, managers need to be sure to use the right information for the right decisions. As we learned in Chapter 4, per-unit information for fixed costs is not relevant for most short-term decision making. Most ABC software products allow users to classify costs assigned to activity cost pools as *flexible costs* or *committed costs*. Committed costs are fixed in the short term and are not relevant for most short-term decisions. Flexible costs vary with activity, and usually are relevant for most short-term decisions. ABC software allows for product costs to be computed that exclude the allocation of committed costs, and managers need to ascertain that they are using the correct data for the decision at hand.

PROBLEM SET B (Learning Objectives 1 - 4)

Matching: Sam's Seafood Shoppe is an expensive, high-quality, full-service seafood restaurant. Listed below are some of the activities that Sam undertakes to ensure the highest quality meals are served to his customers and that they receive outstanding service. Match each activity with its category of quality costs. You may use a category of quality cost more than once.

Cost of quality category	
A. Prevention activities	C. Production activities
B. Appraisal activities	D. Postsales activities

_____ 1. Customer reservations are keypunched to a database with all details as to customer preferences (smoking, non-smoking, table, booth, etc.)

_____ 2. All employees are trained that the customer is always right.

_____ 3. Upon receiving a customer complaint the waiter tells the customer that he or she is right and the complaint will be corrected immediately.

_____ 4. All new recipes are taste-tested by all employees.

_____ 5. Any customer unhappy with his meal is not charged for the meal, and apologies are offered.

_____ 6. All dishes prepared are inspected by Sam before served.

_____ 7. All waiters must have prior experience, good references, and receive 2 days of training.

_____ 8. Any dish not cooked to perfection is not served – instead the contents are saved to be made into soup then next day

_____ 9. Restrooms are inspected for cleanliness every hour.

_____ 10. Sam buys only the highest quality and freshest ingredients.

_____ 11. Dishes going into the clean dish cupboard are inspected for cracks or dried food.

_____ 12. Dishes coming from the clean dish cupboard are inspected for cracks or dried food

_____ 13. Sam's maitre d' watches the waiters to make sure they are properly serving customers.

_____ 14. Any rest room failing its inspection is cleaned immediately.

_____ 15. If a customer orders something on the menu and the kitchen has run out of the ingredients, the problem is explained to the customer, who is allowed to choose any other menu selection for half price.

<u>True-False</u>: Indicate whether each of the following is true (T) or false (F) in the space provided.

_____ 1. Committed costs do not change with activity levels.

_____ 2. Flexible costs do not change with activity levels.

_____ 3. Assembling the product is an example of a value-added activity.

_____ 4. Inspecting the product is an example of a value-added activity.

_____ 5. Storing the product before the customer purchases it is an example of a value-added activity.

_____ 6. Storing the raw materials before they are used in production is an example of a value-added activity.

_____ 7. Repairing defects is an example of a value-added activity.

_____ 8. Because there are more cost allocations in ABC, there is more chance of measurement errors.

_____ 9. The data that comes from an ABC system is only as good as the information that is input into the system.

_____ 10. ABC can help managers determine the most profitable type of customer.

_____ 11. Activity-based management refers to the process of assigning costs to activity cost pools.

_____ 12. In an ABC system, the final cost object is always the end product produced or service rendered.

_____ 13. The total costs associated with postsales activities include the opportunity costs of lost revenue from dissatisfied customers.

_____ 14. The prevention quality costs occur before production begins.

_____ 15. The production quality costs occur after a defect is discovered but before the defective unit is sold to the customer.

Exercise: Write your answer in the space provided.
Randy's Regalia makes Halloween costumes. Last year, Randy incurred the following costs related to quality control:

Repairs for costumes under warranty	$42,000
Seamstress training	1,800
Wages of part-time inspector of products	8,000
Cost of replacements given for defective costumes	21,000
Product liability insurance	9,000
Inspection of sewing machines as part of routine maintenance	1,200
Inspection of fabric and thread for defects	1,200
Repairing defective costumes prior to sale	7,000
	$91,200

a) Compute the total quality cost by category.

Prevention _____   Appraisal _____   Production _____   Postsales_____

b) Do you have any advice for Randy?

_____

_____

_____

_____

_____

_____

_____

_____

_____

_____

_____

_____

END OF CHAPTER EXERCISES

<u>Multiple choice</u>: Write the letter that represents the best choice in the space provided.

_____ 1. A cost system will be improved if
 a. as many costs as possible are classified as direct costs
 b. each indirect cost pool includes costs that have the same cost driver
 c. each indirect cost pool uses the same cost driver
 d. both (a) and (b) will improve a cost system

_____ 2. Which of the following is the best cost driver for the activity "distributing products" if the final cost object is the product?
 a. number of trucks in the fleet of delivery vehicles
 b. total pounds of product delivered
 c. direct labor hours used in producing the products
 d. the number of people who work in the distribution activity

_____ 3. ABC provides more accurate product costs than traditional costing because
 a. traditional costing uses fewer cost pools for indirect costs
 b. traditional costing is less likely to have indirect cost pools with similar cost behavior
 c. activities are measurable events, and activity counts often make good cost drivers in ABC because there is a better cause-and-effect relationship with costs
 d. all of the above are reasons that ABC provides more accurate product costs

_____ 4. Product costs under traditional costing will be the most different from product costs under ABC when
 a. the products consume different amounts of direct materials
 b. the products consume different amounts of direct labor
 c. the products are made at different times of the year
 d. the products require differing amounts of special services during production

Use the following information for questions 5 – 8:
Iowa Industries has two divisions, North and South. You are given the following information about the costs of 5 activities that occur at corporate headquarters:

Activity	Total Costs	Activity cost drivers
Managing accounts payable	$100,000	4,000 hours
Managing human resources	200,000	700 employees
Managing accounts receivable	150,000	3,000 hours
Managing computer network	250,000	500 computers
Total costs	$700,000	

The two divisions use the above activities as follows:

	North Division	South Division
Accounts payable hours	1,500 hours	2,500 hours
Number of employees	300 employees	400 employees
Accounts receivable hours	2,000 hours	1,000 hours
Number of computers	200 computers	300 computers

_____ 5. How much of the accounts payable cost will be allocated to North Division?
a. $262,500
b. $37,500
c. $62,500
d. $100,000

_____ 6. How much of the human resource cost will be allocated to South Division?
a. $28,571
b. $150,000
c. $85,714
d. $114,286

_____ 7. How much of the total activity costs will be allocated to South Division?
a. $323,214
b. $376,786
c. $341,463
d. $358,537

_____ 8. How much of the total activity costs will be allocated to North Division?
a. $323,214
b. $376,786
c. $341,463
d. $358,537

_____ 9. For which of the following is it more likely to be difficult to find a good cost driver?
   a. unit-level costs
   b. batch-level costs
   c. customer-sustaining costs
   d. organization-sustaining costs

_____ 10. Regarding the use of ABC product cost information for short-term decision making, which of the following is likely to be true?
   a. flexible costs should be excluded from the computation of product cost
   b. committed costs should be excluded from the computation of product cost
   c. ABC product cost information should not be used for most short-term decisions
   d. ABC product cost information cannot be used for decision making when there are constrained resources

_____ 11. In traditional costing, the cost allocation base used for overhead is most likely to be a
   a. unit-level cost driver
   b. batch-level cost driver
   c. customer-sustaining cost level driver
   d. facility-sustaining cost level driver

_____ 12. Ted's Manufacturing makes two products, B and C. They each take 2 direct labor hours and 2 machine hours to produce. A batch of Product B, however, uses twice the number of machine set-ups and requires 3 times as many materials requisitions as does Product C. Which of the following is most likely false?
   a. The product cost of Product C will be higher under ABC than under traditional costing.
   b. Traditional costing assigns a product cost that is too high to Product B.
   c. Traditional costing assigns a product cost that is too low to Product C.
   d. The product cost of Product B will be higher under ABC than under traditional costing.

_____ 13. What is the correct order for the steps in the process to implement an ABC system?
   A. Assign costs to the activity cost pools
   B. Choose a cost driver for each activity cost pool
   C. Calculate an allocation rate for each activity cost pool
   D. Allocate activity costs to the final cost object
   E. Identify activities
   F. Identify the relevant cost object
   a. F, B, A, C, D, E
   b. E, F, B, A, C, D
   c. E, F, A, B, C, D
   d. F, E, A, B, C, D

Exercises: Write your answer in the space provided.
1. Paula's Products makes two products, X and Y. Product X incurs $700 of direct costs and Product Y incurs $1,200 of direct costs. Paula makes 150 Xs and 100 Ys each year. You are given the following information about annual activities and costs:

Product	Number of Setups	Number of Material Requisitions	Number of DL Hours
X	22	8	375
Y	28	12	225
Overhead costs	$50,000	$20,000	

a) Compute the cost per unit for each product under traditional costing if overhead is allocated using DL hours.

Product X _____   Product Y_____

b) Compute the cost per unit for each product under ABC.

Product X _____   Product Y_____

2. Ann's Accounting and Tax Services provides basic bookkeeping and tax return preparation for clients. Monthly bookkeeping clients are assigned direct professional labor costs at the rate of $100/hour. Indirect costs are allocated at 120% of direct professional labor costs. Client A's bookkeeping requires 7 direct professional labor hours per month, as does Client B's bookkeeping. Client A is a small company with offices in her building. Client B is a two hour drive away and Ann must visit them once per month. Client B's manager is constantly calling Ann's office to have the secretary look something up for him or make additional financial statement copies and express mail them out. Can you suggest any improvements to Ann's costing system?

_____

_____

_____

_____

_____

3. Four people went out to dinner. You are given the following information about the costs incurred that evening.

Cost	Wino Wally	Fat Wanda	Veggie Victor	Healthy Heather	Totals	Average
Entreé	$18	$48	$22	$18	$106	$26.50
Martinis	46	24	6	0	76	19.00
Dessert	0	8	12	0	20	5.00
subtotal	$64	$80	$40	$18	$202	$50.50
Appetizers for table					48	12.00
subtotal					$250	$62.50
Tip					40	10.00
Totals					$290	$72.50

If they split the bill 4 ways, they will each pay $290/4 = $72.50. This method of sharing would be a cost system that treated all costs as indirect and used a cost allocation base (denominator) of # of people.

a) If they each paid $72.50, who is getting a good deal, and who is getting a bad deal? Why?

Name	Good deal or bad deal? Why?
Wally	
Wanda	
Victor	
Heather	

b) Suppose that Wanda ate most of the appetizers, but Heather ate none as she was on a diet. Victor only had a little since he doesn't eat meat products. Wally only ate the few items he could float in his martini. Can you think of a cost system that seems more fair than sharing the bill equally?

Cost	Direct or indirect cost?	Cost allocation base to be used for indirect costs
Entrée		
Martinis		
Dessert		
Appetizers for table		
Tip		

exercise continues on next page →

3. continued

c) Support your responses in the above table. For the items you determined should be direct costs, tell me why you they should be direct costs and how the information should be obtained. For the items you determined to be indirect costs, explain why. Explain why you chose the allocation base that you chose, and how this information could be obtained.

_____

_____

_____

_____

_____

d) Still considering the information mentioned above requirement (b) (about who ate the appetizers, etc.), design a cost system that minimizes Wally's cost. Fairness is NOT the objective when you design this cost system, the objective is ONLY to minimize Wally's cost.

Cost	Direct or indirect cost?	Cost allocation base to be used for indirect costs
Entrée		
Martinis		
Dessert		
Appetizers for table		
Tip		

e) Explain your choices for the designation of costs as direct or indirect and for the cost allocation bases.

_____

_____

_____

_____

_____

SOLUTION TO PROBLEM SET A

True-False:

1. T
2. F
3. T
4. T
5. F   A traditional costing system usually has fewer overhead cost pools than ABC, but not necessarily just one.
6. T
7. T
8. T
9. T
10. F   Batch-level costs are variable with respect to the number of batches. They would be variable with respect to the number of units produced only when the number of units in a batch is constant.

Matching:

1. D
2. F   If tortillas are bought in bulk, and some spoil without making it to the customer order, then this could be a batch-level cost.
3. E   Batch-level, most likely, but if all taco sauce is used in customer orders without any waste, then it could be unit-level.
4. A
5. B   Most likely the microwaves are used for several different products; if used for only one product then this would be product-sustaining.
6. C
7. D   This cost supports a particular product.
8. E   If all cheese is used in customer orders without any waste, then this could be a unit-level cost.
9. E   If all taco meat makes it to customer orders without any waste, then this could be considered a unit-level cost.
10. F   This is probably a unit-level cost, but if a significant number of the taco shells purchased are wasted, then it should be classified as a batch-level cost.

Exercises:

1. There are 4 machine tool changes per year at a cost of $800 each. This is $3200 that needs to be shared across Products A and B. There's not necessarily one correct answer here. Some would say that the products should share the cost equally, and the machine tool cost assigned to A and B in this case would be $3200/50,000 units = $0.064/unit. Others would say that Product A is the main product and Product B causes the machine tool changes. These people would probably assign all of the $3200 to Product B. In this case, the per unit cost assigned to Product A would be $0 and the per-unit cost assigned to Product B would be $3200/10,000 = $0.32/unit. Chapter 8 will cover these types of allocation decisions in more detail.

2. a) Under traditional costing, the estimated overhead allocation rate is $870,000/100,000 direct labor hours = $8.70/direct labor hour. Since each product takes 20 direct labor hours to complete, each product would be assigned 20 hours x $8.70/hour = $174 of overhead. The total cost per unit for Regular then would be $120 + $174 = $294. The total cost per unit for Deluxe would be $220 + $174 = $394.

    b) Under ABC, estimated overhead allocation rates are computed for each activity cost pool.

Product	Materials Handling	Inspections	Shipping
Costs per pool	$420,000	$150,000	$300,000
Estimated annual use of cost driver:			
Regular	70	50	400
Deluxe	280	100	400
Total	350	150	800
Estimated allocation rate	$1,200/use*	$1,000/use*	$375/use*

   *$420,000/350 uses = $1,200/use; $150,000/150 uses = $1,000/use; *$300,000/800 uses = $375/use

Costs allocated to products:	Regular*	Deluxe*	Total
Materials handling	$84,000	$336,000	$420,000
Inspections	50,000	100,000	150,000
Shipping	150,000	150,000	300,000
Total	$284,000	$586,000	$870,000
Overhead per unit	$71	$586	

   *Calculations: $1,200 x 70 = $84,000; $1,200 x 280 = $336,000
   $1,000 x 50 = $50,000; $1,000 x 100 = $100,000
   $375 x 400 = $150,000 for each product
   $284,000/4,000 units = $71/unit; $586,000/1,000 units = $586/unit

   The total cost per unit for Regular is $120 + $71 = $191. The total cost per unit for Deluxe is $220 + $586 = $806.

SOLUTION TO PROBLEM SET B

<u>Matching</u>: The solutions below define the "production" or service period as the period from the customer's entering the restaurant to leaving the restaurant.

1.	A	This occurs before customer arrives.
2.	A	This occurs before customer arrives
3.	D	If the customer has a complaint then there is already something wrong that needs to be fixed.
4.	A	This occurs before customer arrives.
5.	D	The customer has already been served an unsatisfactory meal.
6.	B	The customer is already in the restaurant, so it is not prevention.
7.	A	This occurs before customer arrives.
8.	C	The production of the meal already occurred but the customer did not yet receive the unsatisfactory meal.
9.	B	The customer is already in the restaurant, so it is not prevention.
10.	A	This occurs before customer arrives.
11.	A	This occurs before customer arrives.
12.	B	The customer is already in the restaurant.
13.	B	The customer is already in the restaurant.
14.	C	The customer is already in the restaurant and something occurred during this period that needed to be fixed.
15.	D	The customer has already had unsatisfactory service because the order was not available.

<u>True-False</u>:

1.	T	
2.	F	
3.	T	
4.	T	
5.	F	
6.	F	
7.	F	
8.	T	
9.	T	
10.	T	
11.	F	Assigning costs to activity pools is part of ABC not ABM
12.	F	The final cost object can be any business segment
13.	T	
14.	T	
15.	T	

Exercise:

Repairs for costumes under warranty	$42,000	Postsales
Seamstress training	1,800	Prevention
Wages of part-time inspector of products	8,000	Appraisal
Cost of replacements given for defective costumes	21,000	Postsales
Product liability insurance	9,000	Postsales
Inspection of sewing mach. as part of routine maintenance	1,200	Prevention
Inspection of fabric and thread for defects	1,200	Prevention
Repairing defective costumes prior to sale	7,000	Production
	$91,200	

a) The total prevention quality costs are $4,200.
   The total appraisal quality costs are $8,000.
   The total production quality costs are $7,000.
   The total postsales quality costs are $72,000.

b) Randy spends the least amount of money on prevention and a large amount repairing poor quality costumes. The most worrisome thing is that he spent almost all his quality costs on repairing costumes that already went to customers. There very likely could be additional opportunity costs associated with postsales quality issues because some customers may never return or may tell their friends not to buy Randy's poor quality costumes.

Randy should investigate how he can best prevent poor quality production. Perhaps additional training or an inspector for the raw materials that are delivered would help. If he looks into the reasons he has so many defective units, he will be better able to make this determination.

Randy should also try to determine how so many defects make it past his inspector. Perhaps he does not have a sufficient quantity of his units inspected, or maybe his inspector needs additional training (or replacement). Placing the inspection point at a different place in the production process, when defects are easier to locate could improve this deficiency.

SOLUTION TO END OF CHAPTER EXERCISES

Multiple choice:

1. D
2. B   This has the best cause-and-effect relationship with the costs.
3. D
4. D
5. B   (1500/4000) x $100,000 = $37,500
6. D   (400/700) x $200,000 = $114,286
7. A   For #7 & #8, here's how total activity costs are allocated to the 2 divisions:
8. B

	North	South
Accounts payable	$37,500	$62,500
Human resources	85,714	114,286
Accounts receivable	100,000	50,000
Comp. network	100,000	150,000
	$323,214	$376,786

9. D   Most of these costs are fixed with respect to activity level changes.
10. B   We learned in Chapter 4 that fixed costs per unit should not be used in short-term decision making.
11. A   Traditional costing frequently uses direct labor hours or direct labor cost or machine hours as the cost allocation base for overhead.
12. D   Product B is more difficult to produce, and ABC will capture this.
13. D

Exercises:

1. a) Under traditional costing, the estimated overhead allocation rate is $70,000/(375+225) direct labor hours = $116.67/direct labor hour. Product X would be allocated $116.67/hour x 375 hours = $43,751 of overhead, which is $43,751/150 units = $292/unit. Product Y would be allocated $116.67/hour x 225 hours = $26,251 of overhead, which is $26,251/100 units = $263/unit. The total cost per unit for Product X then would be $700 + $292 = $992. The total cost per unit for Product Y would be $1,200 + $263 = $1,463.

    b) Under ABC, estimated overhead allocation rates are computed for each activity cost pool.

Product	Machine Setups	Mat'ls Handling
Costs per pool	$50,000	$20,000
Estimated annual use of cost driver:		
Regular	22	8
Deluxe	28	12
Total	50	20
Estimated allocation rate	$1,000/set up*	$1,000/requis'n

*$50,000/50 setups = $1,000/set up; $20,000/20 requisitions = $1,000/requisition.

solution continues on next page→

1. continued

Costs allocated to products:	Product X*	Product Y*	Total
Machine setups	$22,000	$28,000	$50,000
Materials handling	8,000	12,000	20,000
Total	$30,000	$40,000	$70,000
Overhead per unit	$200	$400	

*Calculations: $1,000 x 22 = $22,000; $1,000 x 28 = $28,000
$1,000 x 8 = $8,000; $1,000 x 12 = $12,000
$30,000/150 units = $200/unit; $40,000/100 units = $400/unit

The total cost per unit for Product X is $700 + $200 = $900. The total cost per unit for Product Y is $1,200 + $400 = $1,600.

2. Anna should consider making some of the costs in her indirect cost pool direct costs. For example, telephone charges could be direct if Anna's phone company provides enough information on the bill. Copying costs could be direct if Anna's copy machine is capable of providing this information (e.g. if there is an input device on the machine that allows for the keypunching of a customer number). If these measures aren't possible, then Anna should increase the number of indirect cost pools. If the indirect cost pools are pools of activity costs, then this is ABC.

Anna could have a separate indirect cost pool for travel costs. The cost driver could be miles driven. Then Client A would be assigned zero travel and Client B would be assigned the appropriate travel costs. She could have another cost pool called "special secretarial support services" or something similar. The secretary could estimate what percentage of his or her time is spent performing special services for clients. This percentage of his or her salary could then be allocated to the special services cost pool, and the cost driver for that cost pool could be based on estimates that the secretary provides about the time spent providing special services to which clients.

3. This problem is more about refining cost systems in general than it is about ABC, but it is useful exercise here because ABC is one form of cost system refinement. In order to understand the cost sharing arrangements, you could compute the average cost for each cost item:

Expense	Wino Wally	Fat Wanda	Veggie Victor	Healthy Heather	Totals	Average
Entrée	$18	$48	$22	$18	$106	$26.50
Martinis	46	24	6	0	76	19.00
Dessert	0	8	12	0	20	5.00
subtotal	$64	$80	$40	$18	$202	$50.50
Appetizers for table*	12	12	12	12	48	12.00
Tip*	10	10	10	10	40	10.00
Totals	$86	$102	$62	$40	$290	$72.50

* If you assume equal sharing of these costs.

solution continued on next page →

3. continued

a)

Name	Good deal or bad deal?	Why?
Wally	Good deal	It seems clear that Wally and Wanda got a good deal and Victor and Heather got a bad deal. Since the given information lists the actual costs for the entrée, martinis, and dessert, these costs are eligible for consideration as direct costs. If you then assume an equal sharing of the remaining costs (appetizers and tip) then Wally and Wanda got a good deal by $13.50 and $29.50, respectively ($86-$72.50 and $102-$72.50). Similarly, Victor got a bad deal by $10.50 ($72.50-$62) and Heather got the worst deal by $32.50 ($72.50-$40).
Wanda	Good deal	
Victor	Bad deal	
Heather	Bad deal	

b)

Expense	Direct or indirect cost?	Cost allocation base to be used for indirect costs
Entrée	Direct	
Martinis	Direct	
Dessert	Direct	
Appetizers for table	Indirect	See discussion below for possible cost allocation bases
Tip	Indirect	Total DC+IC (before tip)

c) The idea that people should absorb their own costs is usually seen as "fair". Each person should pay for their own entrée, martini and dessert; in other words, these items should be considered direct costs. The thing that seems a bit unfair is the equal sharing of the cost of the appetizers and the tip. The appetizer cost (indirect cost) should be shared using a cost allocation base that most appropriately assigns the estimated cost to the largest consumers of the cost. One idea is to use "# of pieces of appetizers eaten". Another idea is to use the # of pounds of humans as the cost allocation base, as the skinny people ate fewer appetizers. But this would still assign a non-zero cost of appetizers to Heather, who ate none but weighs more than zero pounds, so "# pieces eaten" is probably a better cost driver. Another idea is that people keep the toothpicks that are stuck in the appetizers. Then the total # of toothpicks could be the cost allocation base.

The tip would definitely have to be an indirect cost. The tip amount is directly related to the bill's subtotal before tip. Therefore, the most reasonable cost allocation base is total cost (excluding tip). Since the tip was exactly 16% of this total ($40/$250=16%), then each person would add 16% to their total. For example, Heather's total would be $18*116%=$20.88 (assuming that the indirect cost allocation base used for appetizers gave her a zero cost for appetizers).

solution continued on next page →

3. continued

d) There is no one correct answer for this; lots of different answers are possible.

Expense	Direct or indirect cost?	Cost allocation base to be used for indirect costs
Entrée	Direct	
Martinis	Indirect	# people at the table
Dessert	Direct	
Appetizers for table	Indirect	# pieces eaten
Tip	Indirect	Total DC+IC (before tip)

e) The best answers are the ones that recognize that Wally always wants cost items to be direct if his actual cost is less than the average (e.g. Wally wants the entrée and the desserts to be direct costs). For the remaining items, he would like to think of a cost allocation base that minimized his share of the cost, or at least allocated less to him than he actually consumed. For example, he would like to share the cost of the martinis equally, but he would not want to share the appetizer cost equally as he consumed less than one-fourth of the appetizers. Instead, he would probably prefer "# pieces eaten" as a cost allocation base for the appetizers. Since this cost system was designed to minimize his cost, he would like to share the tip according to the subtotal before tip, so that each person paid 16% of his or her bill as a tip.

The most clever answer here is to say that all costs are indirect and the cost allocation base is $ spent on dessert. Note that Wally's costs are zero under this plan!

Chapter 8

Measuring and Assigning
Support Department Costs

√ **Study Checklist - Monitor your progress**

	1. Read the chapter in the text
	2. Review the learning objectives below
	3. Read the overview of the chapter
	4. Read the chapter review for learning objectives 1 - 5
	5. Do Problem Set A and check your answers
	6. Read the chapter review for learning objectives 6 - 7
	7. Do Problem Set B and check your answers
	8. Do the End of Chapter Exercises in this study guide
	9. Do the homework assigned by your instructor

CHAPTER LEARNING OBJECTIVES

After studying this chapter, you should be able to answer the following questions:

Q1. What are support departments, and why are their costs allocated to other departments?

Q2. What process is used to allocate support department costs?

Q3. How is the direct method used to allocate support costs to operating departments?

Q4. How is the step-down method used to allocate support costs to operating departments?

Q5. How is the reciprocal method used to allocate support costs to operating departments?

Q6. What is the difference between single- and dual-rate allocations?

Q7. What are the limitations of support cost allocation, and how can the quality of information be improved?

OVERVIEW OF CHAPTER

Organizations have operating departments that are responsible for producing goods or providing services to customers. However, these departments rely on services from the organization's support departments (such as accounting, human resources, marketing, and maintenance). To be profitable, managers must know the full costs of their goods and services and operating department costs as well as support department costs must be controlled. Support department costs may be allocated to other support departments and to operating departments for different purposes, including decisions on product or service pricing and support department cost management.

CHAPTER REVIEW: Learning Objectives 1 - 5

Q1: What are support departments, and why are their costs allocated to other departments?

Departments in an organization that are directly responsible for the production of goods and services are called *operating departments*. However, every operating department relies on some departments for providing services that it needs. These departments are called *support departments*. They incur costs in order to provide essential services to various operating departments; since more than one operating department uses these services, the support departments' costs are called *common costs*.

For financial statement purposes, support department costs are period costs, and allocating their costs to operating departments is not necessary. However, there are other valid reasons for allocating support department costs to operating departments.

- An organization that accepts government contracts frequently must disclose department level cost information. Some contracts (government and non-government) are "cost plus" contracts where the selling price of a product or service is based on a mark-up of the costs incurred.

- Allocating support department costs can be important for performance evaluation purposes and for motivating appropriate manager and employee behavior. If the manager of Operating Department A, for example, is not allocated any of the costs of the Maintenance Support Department, then she has no incentive to efficiently use the services of the Maintenance Department. In some cases, the purpose of the cost allocation is to incent managers of operating departments to use a support department, as may be the case with a newly created support department.

- Some types of decisions are better made after support department cost allocation. For example, long-term pricing decisions should be based on the full costs of producing the product or providing the service.

Q2: What process is used to allocate support department costs?

The steps in the process of allocating support department costs are:

1. Clarify the purpose of the allocation. This is the most important step. There are a myriad of ways to handle support department cost allocation and any method is useless unless it achieves the appropriate objectives. For example, if the objective is to provide an incentive for operating department managers to use a newly created support department, the decision may be made that no cost allocation is performed for the support department's first year. The cost to the operating department of using the new support department would be zero for the first year. Choosing an allocation scheme that is inappropriate can result in department managers behaving in a manner that is contrary to the well-being of the organization overall.

2. Identify the support and operating department cost pools. The number of cost pools must be determined, as must the types of costs that will be assigned to each cost pool.

3. Assign costs to cost pools. Before support department allocation can take place, the appropriate support department costs must be aggregated. Some costs will be direct costs to the support department and some indirect costs will need to be allocated to support departments. In other words, support departments may have some common costs among themselves that need to be shared.

4. For each support department cost pool, choose an appropriate allocation base. As we learned in prior chapters, the best allocation base is one that is a cost driver for the costs in the cost pool.

5. Choose and apply a method to allocate support department costs to operating departments. There are 3 general methods that can be used to allocate support department costs to operating departments: the direct, step-down, and reciprocal methods. Each have their pros and cons, and are covered in detail in learning objectives 3 through 5.

Q3: How is the direct method used to allocate support costs to operating departments?

Although it is common for support departments to use each other's services, the direct method ignores these cost allocations. Each service department allocates its costs only to operating departments, and not to other service departments. The advantage of the direct method is its simplicity, but it provides the least accurate cost allocation of the 3 methods covered in this text.

Demonstration problem-Allocating support department costs using the direct method

Phil's Phiner Phoods operates a chain of upscale grocery stores, and it separates its operating departments into 2 categories: Perishable Goods and Non-Perishable Goods. The company has 3 support departments: Accounting, Information Systems, and Vendor Relations. Phil wishes to allocate all support department costs to the 3 operating departments, because the purpose of the allocation is to allocate full costs for product pricing. Once all support department costs are allocated to the 2 operating departments, Phil will use another allocation procedure to allocate the operating department costs to each of the products within the operating departments (but this is not covered in this demonstration problem).

Phil spent a good deal of time with his chief accountant determining the best way to aggregate support department costs, as well as the assignment of costs (before support department cost allocation) to the operating departments. Phil has determined that the Accounting Department should be allocated based on the number of employees, since the largest cost of the Accounting Department involves payroll preparation. For Information Systems, the number of computers in each department was determined to be the most appropriate allocation base. Finally, for Vendor Relations costs, the number of vendors was determined to be the most appropriate allocation base. The schedule on the next page contains the data that Phil collected.

demonstration problem continues on next page →

Demonstration problem continued

| | Support Departments | | | Operating Departments | | |
	Acc-ounting	Information Systems	Vendor Relations	Perishable Goods	Non-perishable Goods	Total
Total department costs	$240,000	$176,000	$58,000	$422,000	$286,000	$1,182,000
Number of employees	3	5	4	18	15	45
Number of computers	4	7	4	3	3	21
Number of vendors	5	17	3	32	51	108

Required:
Use the direct method to allocate support department costs to the operating departments.

Solution to demonstration problem:
Under the direct method, there are no allocations of support department costs to other support departments. The direct method ignores the facts that all support departments use each other's services. In the solution below, the Perishable Goods Department is allocated 18/(18+15)=18/33 of the Accounting Department's costs, because it has 18 of the 33 employees that work in operating departments. The Non-Perishable Goods Department is allocated 15/33 of the Accounting Department's costs. Review the calculations for the Information Systems and Vendor Relations cost allocations to make sure you understand this method.

| | Support Departments | | | Operating Departments | | |
	Acc-ounting	Information Systems	Vendor Relations	Perishable Goods	Non-perishable Goods	Total
Total department costs	$240,000	$176,000	$58,000	$422,000	$286,000	$1,182,000
Accounting	(240,000)			130,909	109,091	0
Information Systems		(176,000)		88,000	88,000	0
Vendor Relations			(58,000)	22,361	35,639	0
Totals	$0	$0	$0	$663,270	$518,730	$1,182,000

Q4: How is the step-down method used to allocate support costs to operating departments?
In the step-down method, some recognition, but not full recognition, is given to the fact the support departments use each others' services. This method begins by making a determination as to which support department's costs will be allocated first. Any reasonable method for making this determination is acceptable. For example, the support departments could be ranked according to the dollar amount of support department costs before allocation, with the highest cost support department's costs being allocated first. The text and this study guide rank the

support departments according to the level of service provided to other support departments. The support department that provides the largest percentage of its services to other support departments has its costs allocated first.

After determining the cost allocation order for the support departments, the first support department's costs are allocated to all support and operating departments that use its services. Then the costs of the second support department are allocated to all support and operating departments that use its services, except that no costs are allocated to the first support department. The rest of the support departments' costs are allocated in the same manner, with no costs being allocated to any support department that has had its costs already allocated.

Demonstration problem-Allocating support department costs using the step-down method
This demonstration problem uses the same given information for Phil's Phiner Phoods. The information is repeated below, except that the information about the cost allocation bases (number of employees, etc.) has been converted to percentages to ease the ranking of the support departments. Notice that the number of employees in the Accounting Department was ignored when computing the percent of services that Accounting provides, the number of computers in the Information Systems Department was ignored when computing the percent of services that Information System provides, and the number of vendors for the Vendor Relations Department was ignored when computing the percent of services that Vendor Relations provides.

| | Support Departments | | | Operating Departments | | | Total % of Services Rendered to Other Service Dept's |
	Acc-ounting	Infor-mation Systems	Vendor Relations	Perish-able Goods	Non-perishable Goods	Total	
Total dep't costs	$240,000	$176,000	$58,000	$422,000	$286,000	$1,182,000	
Acctg (# of empl)		11.905%	9.524%	42.857%	35.714%	100.000%	21.429%
Inf Sys (# of comp)	28.571%		28.571%	21.429%	21.429%	100.000%	57.143%
Vnd Rel (# of vndrs)	4.762%	16.190%		30.476%	48.571%	100.000%	20.952%

Required:
Use the step-down method to allocate support department costs.

Solution to demonstration problem:
The first thing required is to determine the order of the allocation. Information Systems provided 57.143% of its services to other service departments, so its costs will be allocated first. Then the Accounting Department's costs will be allocated, and the costs of the Vendor Relations Department will be allocated last.

solution continues on next page →

Solution to demonstration problem continued:

	Support Departments			Operating Departments		
	Acc-ounting	Infor-mation Systems	Vendor Relations	Perishable Goods	Non-perishable Goods	Total
Total department costs	$240,000	$176,000	$58,000	$422,000	$286,000	$1,182,000
Information Systems	50,286	(176,000)	50,286	37,714	37,714	(0)
Accounting	(290,286)		31,382	141,220	117,683	0
Vendor Relations			(139,668)	53,848	85,820	0
Totals	$0	$0	$0	$654,782	$527,217	$1,182,000

The Accounting Department is allocated $50,286 of costs from Information Systems. This is computed as 4/(21-7) x $176,000, because there are 21 – 7 = 14 computers in departments other than Information Systems. Note that 4/14 = 28.571%, the same percentage shown in the given information on the prior page. Recompute the Information Systems cost allocation to Vendor Relations and the 2 operating departments to make sure you understand where the figures came from.

When costs are next allocated out of the Accounting Department, the Accounting Department's costs are now $290,286, not $240,000. In the step-down method, no Accounting Department costs are allocated to Information Systems because the Information Systems has already had its costs allocated out of the department. The costs allocated out of the Accounting Department and into Vendor Relations are now based on the number of employees in Vendor Relations and the 2 operating departments. For example, the Accounting Department costs allocated to Vendor Relations is 4/(45-3-5) x $290,286 = 4/(4+18+15) x $290,286 = 4/37 x $290,286 = $31,382. Notice that 4/37 = 9.524%/(100% - 11.905%) = 9.524%/(9.524% + 42.857% + 35.714%). Recompute the Accounting Department cost allocations to the 2 operating departments to make sure you understand the procedure.

When costs are next allocated out of the Vendor Relations Department, the Vendor Relations' costs are now $139,668, not $58,000. The Vendor Relations' costs will be allocated only to the 2 operating departments. The costs allocated out of Vendor Relations and into the 2 operating departments are now based on the number of vendors in just the 2 operating departments. For example, the Vendor Relations costs allocated to Perishable Goods is 32/(108-5-17-3) x $139,668 = 32/(32 + 51) x $139,668 = 32/83 x $139,668 = $53,848. Notice that 32/83 = 30.476%/(30.476% + 48.571%). Recompute the Vendor Relations cost allocation to the Non-Perishable Goods to make sure you understand the procedure.

Q5: How is the reciprocal method used to allocate support costs to operating departments?

The step-down method is a bit more accurate than the direct method because it doesn't ignore all inter-support department services. The reciprocal method is the most accurate of the three methods. All uses of services are taken into account in the allocation. This method first computes the total costs of each support department by using simultaneous equations. Then the support department costs are allocated to all support and operating departments.

Demonstration problem-Allocating support department costs using the reciprocal method
This demonstration problem uses the same given information for Phil's Phiner Phoods. The information is repeated below.

	Support Departments			Operating Departments			Total % of Services Rendered to Other Service Dept's
	Acc-ounting	Infor-mation Systems	Vendor Relations	Perish-able Goods	Non-perishable Goods	Total	
Total dep't costs	$240,000	$176,000	$58,000	$422,000	$286,000	$1,182,000	
Acctg (# of empl)		11.905%	9.524%	42.857%	35.714%	100.000%	21.429%
Inf Sys (# of comp)	28.571%		28.571%	21.429%	21.429%	100.000%	57.143%
Vnd Rel (# of vndrs)	4.762%	16.190%		30.476%	48.571%	100.000%	20.952%

Required:
Use the reciprocal method to allocate support department costs.

Solution to demonstration problem:
First a system of simultaneous equations is set up to compute the total costs of each support department. Let A represent Accounting, IS represent Information Systems, and VR represent Vendor Relations.

A = $240,000 + 28.571%IS + 4.762%VR
IS = $176,000 + 11.905%A + 16.19%VR
VR = $58,000 + 9.524%A + 28.571%IS

Substitute the first equation into the second to get:
IS = $176,000 + 11.905%[$240,000 + 28.571%IS + 4.762%VR] + 16.19%VR
IS = $176,000 + $28,572 + 3.401%IS + 0.567%VR + 16.19%VR
IS = $204,572 + 3.401%IS + 16.757%VR
96.599%IS = $204,572 + 16.757%VR
IS = $211,774 + 17.347%VR

Now substitute the first equation into the third:
VR = $58,000 + 9.524%[$240,000 + 28.571%IS + 4.762%VR] + 28.571%IS
VR = $58,000 + $22,858 + 2.721%IS + 0.454%VR + 28.571%IS
VR = $80,858 + 0.454%VR + 31.292%IS
99.546%VR = $80,858 + 31.292%IS
VR = $81,227 + 31.435%IS

Now substitute the equation for IS in terms of VR from the prior page into the above equation:
VR = $81,227 + 31.435%[$211,774 + 17.347%VR]
VR = $81,227 + $66,571 + 5.453%VR
94.547%VR = $147,798
VR = $156,322

solution continues on next page →

Solution to demonstration problem continued:

Now compute the total costs for IS:
IS = $211,774 + 17.347%[$156,322]
IS = $211,774 + $27,118
IS = $238,892

Finally, compute the total costs for A:
A = $240,000 + 28.571%[$238,892] + 4.762%[$156,322]
A = $240,000 + $68,254 + $7,445
A = $315,699

Now costs are allocated using the service usage percentages in the given information on the prior page, and these total costs just computed are the amounts allocated out of the 3 support departments.

| | Support Departments | | | Operating Departments | | |
	Acc-ounting	Infor-mation Systems	Vendor Relations	Perishable Goods	Non-perishable Goods	Total
Total department costs	$240,000	$176,000	$58,000	$422,000	$286,000	$1,182,000
Accounting	(315,699)	37,583	30,067	135,300	112,750	0
Information Systems	68,255	(238,892)	68,255	51,191	51,191	0
Vendor Relations	7,444	25,309	(156,322)	47,641	75,928	0
Totals	$0	$0	$0	$656,132	$525,868	$1,182,000

Check a few of the allocations by hand, just to make sure you understand where the numbers are coming from. These simultaneous equations can be solved by Excel quite easily. Just set up 3 cells to calculate the total costs of each support department and enter the simultaneous equation formulas into the cells. Make sure that the "Iteration" box is checked under Tools, Options, Calculations or you will get a "circular reference error" message.

PROBLEM SET A (Learning Objectives 1 - 5)

<u>True-False</u>: Indicate whether each of the following is true (T) or false (F) in the space provided.

_____ 1. The allocation order of support department costs does not matter in the reciprocal method.

_____ 2. The allocation order of support department costs does not matter in the direct method.

_____ 3. Support department cost allocation is necessary for the preparation of externally-issued financial statements.

_____ 4. A company may have more than one cost allocation method.

_____ 5. One reason to allocate support department costs is to motivate appropriate behavior of operating department managers.

_____ 6. Support department cost allocations should never be made when the information is to be used to evaluate the performance of an operating department manager.

_____ 7. Each support department may use a different allocation base.

_____ 8. Under the reciprocal method, the total costs allocated out of the support departments exceeds the total costs of the support departments before cost allocation began.

_____ 9. Under the direct method, the total costs allocated out of the support departments exceeds the total costs of the support departments before cost allocation began.

_____ 10. Under the step-down method, the total costs allocated out of the support departments exceeds the total costs of the support departments before cost allocation began.

_____ 11. The direct method is the least accurate support department cost allocation method.

_____ 12. When the order of support department cost allocation must be determined, any reasonable procedure for ranking the support departments is acceptable.

_____ 13. It is possible that, in order to motivate the desired manager behavior, a support department's costs may not be allocated to operating departments.

_____ 14. After support department cost allocation, total costs of the operating departments will equal the total costs of the support departments plus the operating departments before the allocation was made.

_____ 15. The reciprocal method is more likely to cause support department managers to control their use of other support department services than is the direct method.

Matching: Match each term with the appropriate definition or phrase. You may use each term more than once.

Terms

A. Operating department	D. Direct method
B. Support department	E. Step-down method
C. Common cost	F. Reciprocal method

_____ 1. Uses simultaneous equations to determine total support department costs

_____ 2. Total costs allocated out of the department exceeds the total cost before allocation began

_____ 3. Costs of a support department when more than one other department uses its services

_____ 4. Human Resources Department

_____ 5. No allocations of support department costs to other support departments are made.

_____ 6. Produces goods or provides services to customers

_____ 7. The allocation order of support department costs is determined before cost allocation begins

_____ 8. Provides services to operating departments and support departments

_____ 9. Assembly Department

_____ 10. The easiest cost allocation procedure

Exercises: Write your answer in the space provided.
1. The table below provides allocation base information for Sue's Products, Inc.

	Support Departments			Operating Departments		
	Mainten-ance	Cafeteria	Mark-eting	Product A	Product B	Total
Maintenance (sq ft)	1,000	3,000	5,000	17,000	24,000	50,000
Cafeteria (# employees)	5	12	8	22	33	80
Marketing (revenues)		$180,000		$880,000	$990,000	$2,050,000

a) Suppose Sue uses the direct method.

What percent of Maintenance Department costs will be allocated to Product A? _____

What percent of Cafeteria costs will be allocated to Product B? _____

What percent of Marketing costs will be allocated to Product A? _____

b) Suppose Sue uses the step-down method, and determines allocation order the same way as Phil's Phiner Phoods from the demonstration problem on page 8-3. Determine the allocation order.

First _____   Second _____   Third _____

2. The information for Sue's Products, Inc. from Exercise #1, with cost data added, is repeated below:

| | Support Departments | | | Operating Departments | | |
	Mainten-ance	Cafeteria	Marketing	Product A	Product B	Total
Total costs	$125,000	$160,000	$220,000	$510,000	$680,000	$1,695,00
Maintenance (sq ft)	1,000	3,000	5,000	17,000	24,000	50,000
Cafeteria (# employees)	5	12	8	22	33	80
Marketing (revenues)		$180,000		$880,000	$990,000	$2,050,000

a) Complete the cost allocation in the table below, using the direct method.

| | Support Departments | | | Operating Departments | | |
	Maintenance	Cafeteria	Marketing	Product A	Product B	Total
Total costs	$125,000	$160,000	$220,000	$510,000	$680,000	$1,695,000
Maintenance (sq ft)						
Cafeteria (# employees)						
Marketing (revenues)						
Totals						

b) Complete the cost allocation in the table below, using the step-down method.

| | Support Departments | | | Operating Departments | | |
	Maintenance	Cafeteria	Marketing	Product A	Product B	Total
Total costs	$125,000	$160,000	$220,000	$510,000	$680,000	$1,695,00
Maintenance (sq ft)						
Cafeteria (# employees)						
Marketing (revenues)						
Totals						

exercise 2 continues on next page →

c) Compute the total costs to be allocated out of each support department under the reciprocal method by setting up and solving the necessary simultaneous equations.

Maintenance _____

Cafeteria _____

Marketing _____

d) Using the costs you calculated in (c), complete the cost allocation in the table below using the reciprocal method.

	Support Departments			Operating Departments		
	Maintenance	Cafeteria	Marketing	Product A	Product B	Total
Total costs	$125,000	$160,000	$220,000	$510,000	$680,000	$1,695,000
Maintenance (sq ft)						
Cafeteria (# employees)						
Marketing (revenues)						
Totals						

CHAPTER REVIEW: Learning Objectives 6 - 7

Q6: What is the difference between single- and dual-rate allocations?

In the cost allocation examples we've seen so far, only one allocation base was used to allocate costs out of a support department. This is known as *single-rate allocation*. In *dual-rate allocation*, each support department's costs are separated into fixed and variable cost sub-pools, and each cost pool uses a different allocation base. The dual-rate method can be used with the direct, step-down, or reciprocal methods, or any combination of these 3 methods.

Demonstration problem-Allocating support department costs using the dual rate method

Phil's Phiner Phoods is interested in refining the cost allocations performed earlier, and has separated all department costs in to fixed and variable cost pools. Separate cost allocation bases have been determined for each cost pool. This revised information is provided in the table below.

	Support Departments			Operating Departments		
	Acc-ounting	Infor-mation Systems	Vendor Relations	Perishable Goods	Non-perishable Goods	Total
Department fixed costs	$200,000	$120,000	$50,000	$222,000	$186,000	$778,000
Department variable costs	$40,000	$56,000	$8,000	$200,000	$100,000	$404,000
Total department costs	$240,000	$176,000	$58,000	$422,000	$286,000	$1,182,000
Allocation bases for fixed costs:						
A: Dep't costs before alloc'n	$240,000	$176,000	$58,000	$422,000	$286,000	$1,182,000
IS: Network usage hours	6,000	10,000	4,000	3,000	2,000	25,000
VR: A/Pay volume in $	$60,000	$40,000	$20,000	$216,000	$124,000	$460,000
Allocation bases for variable costs:						
A: Number of employees	3	5	4	18	15	45
IS: Number of computers	4	7	4	3	3	21
VR: Number of vendors	5	17	3	32	51	108

Required:

Use the dual-rate method to allocate support department costs to the operating departments. Use the reciprocal method for fixed costs and the step-down method for variable costs. Assume the chosen allocation order for the variable costs is Information Systems first, Accounting second, and Vendor Relations last.

solution to demonstration problem begins on next page →

Solution to demonstration problem:

The allocation percentages for the reciprocal method's allocation of fixed costs are shown below. Recalculate a few of them to make sure you understand where the percentages came from.

| | Support Departments | | | Operating Departments | | |
	Acc-ounting	Infor-mation Systems	Vendor Relations	Perishable Goods	Non-perishable Goods	Total
Allocation bases for fixed costs:						
A: Dep't costs before alloc'n		18.684%	6.157%	44.798%	30.361%	100.000%
IS: Network usage hours	40.000%		26.667%	20.000%	13.333%	100.000%
VR: A/Pay volume in $	13.636%	9.091%		49.091%	28.182%	100.000%

This provides the following simultaneous equations:
A = $200,000 + 40%IS + 13.636%VR
IS = $120,000 + 18.684%A + 9.091%VR
VR = $50,000 + 6.157%A + 26.667%IS

Now, either solve these equations by hand (ugh!) or keypunch the formulas into Excel to get:
A = $289,897
IS = $184,812
VR = $117,132

The final cost allocation is shown below. Recompute a few of the allocations to make sure you understand.

| | Support Departments | | | Operating Departments | | |
	Acc-ounting	Infor-mation Systems	Vendor Relations	Perishable Goods	Non-perishable Goods	Total
Department fixed costs	$200,000	$120,000	$50,000	$222,000	$186,000	$778,000
Department variable costs	$40,000	$56,000	$8,000	$200,000	$100,000	$404,000
Total department costs	$240,000	$176,000	$58,000	$422,000	$286,000	$1,182,000
Allocation of fixed costs:						
A: Dep't costs before alloc'n	($289,897)	$54,163	$17,849	$129,869	$88,016	$0
IS: Network usage hours	$73,925	($184,812)	$49,283	$36,962	$24,642	$0
VR: A/Pay volume in $	$15,973	$10,648	($117,132)	$57,501	$33,010	$0
Allocation of variable costs:						
IS: Number of computers	$16,000	($56,000)	$16,000	$12,000	$12,000	$0
A: Number of employees	($56,000)		$6,054	$27,243	$22,703	$0
VR: Number of vendors			($30,054)	$11,587	$18,467	$0
Totals	$0	$0	$0	$697,163	$484,837	$1,182,000

Q7: What are the limitations of support cost allocation, and how can the quality of information be improved?

Because of the uncertainties surrounding, and the judgment needed for, cost allocations, the cost allocation information may be of poor quality. In addition to the choices that must be made about cost assignment to support departments, allocation bases for support department costs, and the cost allocation method, managers must decide whether to use estimated or actual costs and allocation base measures. To make this decision, managers must consider the purpose of the cost allocation.

- If the cost allocation is being performed because of a contract with a customer, the terms of the contract will provide the cost allocation procedure to be used.

- If the purpose of the cost allocation is to motivate department managers to use the support department services efficiently, then it may be appropriate to use budgeted support department costs in the numerator and budgeted volume of the allocation base in the denominator. Department managers then know the cost per unit of the support department's services at the beginning of the year. Each department would then be charged this budgeted allocation rate times the number of actual units of the support department's services that it uses. If actual costs and allocation volumes are used in the allocation base's computation, then managers will not know the support department's charge per unit of the service until the end of the period. Additionally, the fixed cost portion of the charge per unit of the service will be affected by the quantity of the allocation base consumed by other departments.

- At times, companies may employ the dual-rate method and allocate fixed costs based on a budgeted allocation rate and budgeted usage, and allocate variable costs based on an actual or budgeted allocation rate and actual usage.

A department manager may feel that the support department cost allocation charged to his or her department is not "fair". There are two additional allocation methods that may address this, depending on the circumstances. These methods can be used to share any set of common costs. For example, a student who flies to New York City to interview with 3 different companies will have to determine a method to share travel costs across the 3 companies for expense reimbursement purposes.

- Under the *stand-alone method*, users of the common cost are allocated a portion of the cost, where the portion is determined as a ratio of what the costs would have been if each user had contracted for the service independently.

- Under the *incremental cost allocation method*, one user of the common cost is considered the primary user, and is allocated all of the common cost except the incremental portion that was incurred specifically to benefit the other users.

Demonstration problem-Stand-alone and incremental cost allocation methods
Sally Student is a senior at University of Texas, majoring in finance. She wants to work at a Wall Street firm in New York City, and has arranged an interview with Morgan Freeman Investments. She estimates the air fare to be $360, one night's stay in a hotel to be $100, food to be $40, and taxi fares to be $50, for a total of $550. Morgan Freeman agrees to reimburse her in full for her travel costs. After this is arranged, Dean Martin Investments calls her for an interview, and agrees to pay her travel costs. She will interview with both companies on the same trip, but the Dean Martin interview is a 2-day interview and will add another 2 nights in the hotel, another 2 days worth of meals, and another $20 in taxi fares.

Required:
a) Allocate Sally's total estimated costs of $850 to each company using the stand-alone method.
b) Allocate Sally's total estimated costs of $850 to each company using the incremental cost allocation method, assuming that Morgan Freeman is considered the primary purpose of her visit to New York.

Solution to demonstration problem:
a) If she were to make separate trips for each interview, she will incur the following costs:

	Morgan Freeman	Dean Martin	Total
Air fare	$360	$360	$720
Hotel @ $100/night	100	200	300
Meals @ $40/day	40	80	120
Taxi fares	50	70	120
	$550	$710	$1,260

The stand-alone method allocates costs to Morgan Freeman as (550/1260) x $850 = $371, and Dean Martin is allocated costs of (710/1260) x $850 = $479.

b) If Morgan Freeman is the primary user, she could make the trip for that interview alone for $550, and this method allocates $550 to Morgan Freeman. The additional $300 of costs will be incurred because of the Dean Martin interview.

PROBLEM SET B (Learning Objectives 6 - 7)

Completion: Use the following list of terms to complete each phrase or sentence. You may use each term more than once or not at all.

List of terms	
Budgeted support department costs	Incremental cost allocation method
Actual support department costs	Stand-alone method
Budgeted annual volume of allocation base	Dual-rate method
Actual annual volume of allocation base	Fixed costs
Budgeted usage of allocation base	Variable costs
Actual usage of allocation base	

1. The _____ allocates a support department's fixed and variable costs separately.

2. When using _____, one user of the common cost must be designated as the primary user.

3. Using a budgeted cost allocation rate times _____ should provide an incentive for department managers to use the services of support departments efficiently.

4. When a support department's _____ are allocated based on an actual allocation rate times the operating department's actual usage of the allocation base, the operating department's allocation is affected by the actions of the other department managers.

5. When a support department's _____ are allocated based on a budgeted allocation rate times the actual usage of the allocation base, managers will be more likely to use the support department's services efficiently, and they will know the per-unit cost of the support services in advance.

6. When a support department's _____ are allocated based on an actual allocation rate times the actual usage of the allocation base, managers will be more likely to use the support department's services efficiently, but they won't know the per-unit cost of support services in advance.

7. The calculation of the actual allocation rate is the actual support department costs over

_____.

8. The calculation of the budgeted allocation rate is _____ over the budgeted annual volume of the allocation base.

9. Fixed costs are more likely to be allocated using an allocation rate times

_____ than are variable costs.

10. For a newly created operating department with a small budget that shares mail room costs

with established departments, the _____ is more likely to seem fair.

<u>Exercises</u>: Write your answer in the space provided.
1. The manager of the Engineering Department of Park Industries needs to purchase 8 personal computers for her staff. The cost is $700 each. If 10 or more of these computers were to be purchased, however, the cost per computer would be $600. The Engineering manager emails the other department managers to see if they need any personal computers. The Marketing Department manager replies that he would like to purchase 3 of them. An order for 11 personal computers, totaling $6,600 is placed.

a) Calculate the portion of the $6,600 allocated to each department using the stand-alone method.

Engineering _____   Marketing _____

b) Calculate the portion of the $6,600 allocated to each department using the incremental cost allocation method, assuming that Engineering is considered the primary user.

Engineering _____   Marketing _____

2. Dak and Bleker is a small engineering consulting firm specializing in bridge engineering and other consulting as well. The owners of the firm are interested in the relative profitability of bridge work consulting versus other consulting. The firm has a car that cost $3,500 to operate this year. The car was used for bridge consulting projects for 80 days, and 20,000 miles were put on the car. The car was used for non-bridge consulting projects for 130 days, and 15,000 miles were put on the car. When an employee needs the car but it is not available, the firm either rents a car for $35 per day (with unlimited mileage), or pays the employee $0.20 per mile to use his or her own car, whichever is less.

a) Calculate the portion of the $3,500 allocated to each type of consulting if mileage is used as an allocation base.

Bridge _____   Non-bridge _____

b) Calculate the portion of the $3,500 allocated to each type of consulting if number of days is used as an allocation base.

Bridge _____   Non-bridge _____

c) Calculate the portion of the $3,500 allocated to each type of consulting if the stand-alone method is used, where the stand-alone costs are based on each service line's cheapest alternative to using the company car.

Bridge _____   Non-bridge _____

3. ABC Industries makes 2 products in 2 operating departments and has 3 support departments. Information about allocation bases and department costs is given in the table below.

	Support Departments			Operating Departments		
	Mainten-ance	Human Resources	Account-ing	Product A	Product B	Total
Department fixed costs	$41,000	$120,000	$185,000	$320,000	$280,000	$946,0
Department variable costs	$4,000	$12,000	$8,000	$480,000	$350,000	$854,0
Total department costs	$45,000	$132,000	$193,000	$800,000	$630,000	$1,800,0
Allocation bases for fixed costs:						
M: Square feet	400	2,200	1,500	2,000	2,500	8,6
HR: Total payroll	$36,000	$100,000	$170,000	$580,000	$450,000	$1,336,0
A: Total revenue				$2,500,000	$1,800,000	$4,300,0
Allocation bases for variable costs:						
M: # of requests for service	2	5	3	44	21	75
HR: # of employees	2	4	5	19	15	45
A: # of employees	2	4	5	19	15	45

a) Convert the allocation base information to percentages and complete the table below.

	Support Departments			Operating Departments		
	Mainten-ance	Human Resources	Account-ing	Product A	Product B	Total
Allocation bases for fixed costs:						
M: Square feet						
HR: Total payroll						
A: Total revenue						
Allocation bases for variable costs:						
M: # of requests for service						
HR: # of employees						
A: # of employees						

exercise 3 continues on the next page →

b) Compute the total fixed costs to be allocated out of each support department by setting up and solving the appropriate simultaneous equations (or use Excel).

Maintenance _____   Human Resources _____   Accounting _____

c) Compute the total variable costs to be allocated out of each support department by setting up and solving the appropriate simultaneous equations (or use Excel).

Maintenance _____   Human Resources _____   Accounting _____

d) Allocate support department costs in the table below using the dual-rate method. Use the reciprocal method for allocating both fixed and variable costs.

	Support Departments			Operating Departments		
	Mainten-ance	Human Resources	Account-ing	Product A	Product B	Total
Department fixed costs	$41,000	$120,000	$185,000	$320,000	$280,000	$946,000
Department variable costs	$4,000	$12,000	$8,000	$480,000	$350,000	$854,000
Total department costs	$45,000	$132,000	$193,000	$800,000	$630,000	$1,800,000
Allocation of fixed costs:						
M: Square feet						
HR: Total payroll						
A: Total revenue						
Allocation of variable costs:						
M: # of requests for service						
HR: # of employees						
A: # of employees						
Totals						

END OF CHAPTER EXERCISES

<u>Multiple choice</u>: Write the letter that represents the best choice in the space provided.

_____ 1. The allocation method that ignores all services rendered between support departments is
   a.   the direct method
   b.   the step-down method
   c.   the reciprocal method
   d.   the dual-rate method

_____ 2. The allocation method that ignores some, but not all, services rendered between support departments is
   a.   the direct method
   b.   the step-down method
   c.   the reciprocal method
   d.   the dual-rate method

_____ 3. The allocation method that accounts for all services rendered between support departments is
   a.   the direct method
   b.   the step-down method
   c.   the reciprocal method
   d.   the dual-rate method

_____ 4. The allocation method that allocates fixed and variable costs separately is
   a.   the direct method
   b.   the step-down method
   c.   the reciprocal method
   d.   the dual-rate method

_____ 5. The allocation method that can manipulate the costs allocated by changing the order of the support department cost allocation is
   a.   the direct method
   b.   the step-down method
   c.   the reciprocal method
   d.   the dual-rate method

_____ 6. To avoid passing on inefficiencies of the support departments, support department costs should be allocated using
   a.   a budgeted cost allocation rate
   b.   an actual cost allocation rate
   c.   only fixed costs per unit of service
   d.   only variable costs per unit of service

Use the following information for questions 7 – 10:
Trucker industries provides the following information about departmental consumption of allocation bases for its 3 support and 2 operating departments:

	Support Departments			Operating Departments	
	Personnel	Cafeteria	Maintenance	Machining	Assembly
Personnel		10%	20%	30%	40%
Cafeteria	10%		10%	40%	40%
Maintenance	10%	20%		50%	20%

_____ 7. For the direct method, what proportion of the Personnel's costs will be allocated to the Machining Department?
    a. 30%
    b. 10%
    c. 42.9%
    d. 14.3%

_____ 8. For the step-down method, what proportion of the Maintenance Department's costs will be allocated to the Assembly Department if the allocation order is Personnel, Cafeteria, and Maintenance?
    a. 20%
    b. 28.6%
    c. 42.9%
    d. 30%

_____ 9. For the step-down method, what proportion of the Cafeteria's costs will be allocated to the Maintenance Department if the allocation order is Personnel, Cafeteria, and Maintenance?
    a. 11.1%
    b. 10%
    c. 0%
    d. 30%

_____ 10. For the reciprocal method, what proportion of the Personnel Department's costs will be allocated to the Machining Department?
    a. 30%
    b. 42.9%
    c. 20%
    d. 28.6%

Use the following information for questions 11 – 14:
Arthur Henderson, LLC is a CPA firm that has a printing department that makes copies for its two departments, Audit and Tax. The Printing Department's budget for 2005 showed budgeted fixed costs of $40,000 plus variable costs of 2 cents per copy. At the beginning of 2005, the Audit Department budgeted its usage at 80,000 copies and the Tax Department budgeted its usage at 50,000 copies. However, actual usage was 70,000 copies and 60,000 copies made by the Audit and Tax Departments, respectively.

_____ 11. Under the single-rate method, what is the total budgeted costs for the Audit Department?
    a. $1,600
    b. $1,400
    c. $26,215
    d. $22,938

_____ 12. Under the dual-rate method, what amount of cost is allocated to the Audit Department if budgeted fixed costs are allocated based on budgeted usage and budgeted variable costs are allocated based on actual usage?
    a. $26,015
    b. $22,938
    c. $26,215
    d. none of the above

_____ 13. Under the dual-rate method, what amount of cost is allocated to the Audit Department if budgeted fixed costs are allocated based on budgeted usage and budgeted variable costs are allocated based on budgeted usage?
    a. $26,015
    b. $22,938
    c. $26,215
    d. none of the above

_____ 14. Under the dual-rate method, what amount of cost is allocated to the Tax Department if budgeted fixed costs are allocated based on budgeted usage and budgeted variable costs are allocated based on budgeted usage?
    a. $17,667
    b. $16,385
    c. $19,661
    d. none of the above

<u>Use the following information for questions 15 – 17:</u>
The cost of a taxi ride from O'Hare airport to downtown Chicago is $22 plus $1 per person in the cab plus $1 for each luggage item in the trunk. George is on a trip with a business associate from another department. George has one luggage item and his associate has three.

_____ 15. Compute the portion of the taxi fare allocated to George using the stand-alone method.
a. $13.44
b. $24.00
c. $14.56
d. $4.00

_____ 16. Compute the portion of the taxi fare allocated to George using the incremental cost allocation method if George is considered the primary user.
a. $2.00
b. $24.00
c. $4.00
d. $28.00

_____ 17. Compute the portion of the taxi fare allocated to George using the incremental cost allocation method if George's associate is considered the primary user.
a. $2.00
b. $4.00
c. $28.00
d. $14.56

<u>Exercises</u>: Write your answer in the space provided.
1. Badger Bonanza (BB) owns a mini shopping center in Wichita Falls TX with only two stores. BB also maintains office space in the shopping center in order to manage the center as well as BB's other businesses. BB provides the utilities and a part-time security guard for the center. Actual utility costs are charged to the stores and to BB based on the square feet of space each store occupies. Security costs are allocated to BB and the 2 stores based on the average monthly inventory reported by the stores for insurance purposes. The monthly rental on the two stores combined is $8,000 and this is shared between the 2 stores each month based on their relative sales as reported on their sales tax returns. In October the utilities totaled $2,000 and the security costs were $660, so that $10,660 of costs were allocated to the two stores.

In order to make the allocation, you are given the following information for October:

	Store 1	Store 2	BB	Total
Floor space (sq feet)	9,000	6,600	400	16,000
Inventory values	$425,000	$220,000	$15,000	$660,000
Sales revenue	$612,500	$440,000	$0	$1,052,500

a) Determine the total rent, utilities, and security costs charged to each store for October.

Store 1 _____   Store 2 _____

b) Determine the total utilities and security costs allocated to BB for October. _____

c) What might be troublesome about this arrangement to the 2 stores?

_____

_____

_____

_____

_____

2. CIM, Inc. is a fabricator of specialty steel products. Department costs, excluding direct materials and direct labor, as well as information about cost allocation bases is in the table below.

| | Support Departments | | | Operating Departments | | |
	Person-nel	Buildings & Grounds	Repairs & Mainten-ance	Fabric-ation	Assembly	Total
Total department costs	$240,000	$109,750	$157,750	$800,000	$400,000	$1,707,500
Space occupied	600	400	1,000	6,000	4,000	12,000
Employees	10	15	15	125	165	330
R&M hours				6,000	3,000	9,000

Personnel (P) provides services for all employees. Building & Grounds (B&G) provides cleaning and building maintenance services to all departments. Repairs & Maintenance (R&M) provides repairs for the factory equipment.

a) Use the direct method to allocate support department costs in the table below.

| | Support Departments | | | Operating Departments | | |
	Personnel	Buildings & Grounds	Repairs & Mainten-ance	Fabrication	Assembly	Total
Total department costs	$240,000	$109,750	$157,750	$800,000	$400,000	$1,707,500
Personnel						
Buildings & Grounds						
Repairs & Maintenance						
Totals						

b) Determine the allocation order under the step-down method, using the same criterion as the demonstration problem for the step-down method.

First _____   Second _____   Third _____

exercise continues on next page →

2. continued
c) Use the step-down method to allocate support department costs in the table below.

	Support Departments			Operating Departments		
	Personnel	Buildings & Grounds	Repairs & Mainten-ance	Fabrication	Assembly	Total
Total department costs	$240,000	$109,750	$157,750	$800,000	$400,000	$1,707,500
Personnel						
Buildings & Grounds						
Repairs & Maintenance						
Totals						

d) Set up and solve simultaneous equations (or use Excel) to determine the total costs to be allocated out of each department

Personnel _____ B&G _____ R&M _____

e) Use the reciprocal method to allocate support department costs in the table below.

	Support Departments			Operating Departments		
	Personnel	Buildings & Grounds	Repairs & Mainten-ance	Fabrication	Assembly	Total
Total department costs	$240,000	$109,750	$157,750	$800,000	$400,000	$1,707,500
Personnel						
Buildings & Grounds						
Repairs & Maintenance						
Totals						

3. Chico's Tacos sells tacos and quesadillas. Fixed costs are $4,000 per month. You are given the following information for the months of March and April:

	Tacos	Quesadillas	Total
Sales for March	$3,000	$2,400	$5,400
Sales for April	$3,000	$1,900	$4,900

a) Compute the amount of fixed costs allocated to tacos and quesadillas in March if actual sales are used as the allocation base.

Tacos _____   Quesadillas _____

b) Compute the amount of fixed costs allocated to tacos and quesadillas in April if actual sales are used as the allocation base.

Tacos _____   Quesadillas _____

c) Taco sales didn't change from March to April. Compare the cost allocations to the two product lines for March and April and explain the difference.

_____

_____

_____

_____

_____

SOLUTION TO PROBLEM SET A

<u>True-False:</u>

1. T
2. T   The allocation order only matters in the step-down method.
3. F
4. T   One cost allocation might be for pricing decisions and another might be for evaluating the performance of department managers.
5. T
6. F   One of the purposes of support cost allocation is to provide incentives for managers to efficiently use support department services. To see whether they have done so, we would have to allocate support department costs.
7. T   Each support department should use a different allocation base. Otherwise, the costs of the 2 support departments could have been pooled into one cost pool
8. T   See for example the reciprocal demonstration problem. The total cost of the 3 support departments determined by the simultaneous equations exceeds the total of the pre-allocation support department costs.
9. F
10. F   The total costs allocated out of the support departments exceeds the total support department costs before the allocation began in the reciprocal method.
11. T
12. T
13. T   If the objective is to motivate reluctant department managers to use the services of a newly created support department, it may be appropriate to not allocate that support department's costs until it becomes accepted by the other department managers.
14. T
15. T   The direct method does not allocate support department costs to other support departments, so it provides no incentive for support department managers to efficiently use the services of other support departments because those services are essentially free.

<u>Matching:</u>

1. F
2. E
3. C
4. B
5. D
6. A
7. E
8. B
9. A
10. D

Exercises:

1. a) Maintenance Department costs allocated to product A: 17/(17+24) = 17/41 = 41.46%
   Cafeteria costs allocated to product B: 33/(22+33) = 33/55 = 60%
   Marketing costs allocated to product A: 880,000/(880,000+990,000) = 880/1870 = 47.06%

   b) First convert the allocation base information to percentages for ease of comparison.

	Support Departments			Operating Departments		
	Mainten-ance	Cafeteria	Mark-eting	Product A	Product B	Total
Maintenance (sq ft)		6.122%	10.204%	34.694%	48.980%	100.000%
Cafeteria (# employees)	7.353%		11.765%	32.353%	48.529%	100.000%
Marketing (revenues)	0.000%	8.780%		42.927%	48.293%	100.000%

   The cafeteria provided 7.353%+11.765% = 19.118% of its services to other support departments, and will be allocated first. The Maintenance Department provided 6.122%+10.204% = 16.324% of its services to other support departments and will be allocated second. The Marketing Department provided 0%+8.78% = 8.78% of its services to other support departments and will be allocated last.

2. a) The table below contains the cost allocation for the direct method.

	Support Departments			Operating Departments		
	Mainten-ance	Cafeteria	Marketing	Product A	Product B	Total
Total costs	$125,000	$160,000	$220,000	$510,000	$680,000	$1,695,000
Maintenance (sq ft)	(125,000)			51,829	73,171	0
Cafeteria (# employees)		(160,000)		64,000	96,000	0
Marketing (revenues)			(220,000)	103,529	116,471	0
Total	$0	$0	$0	$729,358	$965,642	$1,695,000

   b) The table below contains the cost allocation for the step-down method.

	Support Departments			Operating Departments		
	Mainten-ance	Cafeteria	Marketing	Product A	Product B	Total
Total costs	$125,000	$160,000	$220,000	$510,000	$680,000	$1,695,000
Cafeteria (# employees)	11,765	(160,000)	18,824	51,765	77,646	0
Maintenance (sq ft)	(136,765)		14,866	50,543	71,355	0
Marketing (revenues)			(253,690)	119,383	134,306	0
Total	$0	$0	$0	$731,691	$963,307	$1,695,000

c) The table below converts the allocation base information into percentages.

	Support Departments			Operating Departments		
	Mainten-ance	Cafeteria	Marketing	Product A	Product B	Total
Maintenance (sq ft)		6.122%	10.204%	34.694%	48.980%	100.000%
Cafeteria (# employees)	7.353%		11.765%	32.353%	48.529%	100.000%
Marketing (revenues)	0.000%	8.780%		42.927%	48.293%	100.000%

These percentages are used to create the simultaneous equations, letting M=Maintenance, C=Cafeteria, and MK=Marketing:

M = $125,000 + 7.353%C
C = $160,000 + 6.122%M + 8.78%MK
MK = $220,000 + 10.204%M + 11.765%C

Solve these equations by hand, or use Excel, to get:

M = $139,048
C = $191,050
MK = $256,665

d) The table below contains the cost allocation for the reciprocal method.

	Support Departments			Operating Departments		
	Mainten-ance	Cafeteria	Marketing	Product A	Product B	Total
Total costs	$125,000	$160,000	$220,000	$510,000	$680,000	$1,695,000
Maintenance (sq ft)	(139,048)	8,513	14,189	48,241	68,105	0
Cafeteria (# employees)	14,048	(191,050)	22,476	61,810	92,715	0
Marketing (revenues)	0	22,536	(256,665)	110,179	123,950	0
Totals	$0	$0	$0	$730,230	$964,770	$1,695,000

SOLUTION TO PROBLEM SET B

Completion:

1. dual-rate method
2. Incremental cost allocation method
3. actual usage of allocation base (because a department's allocated costs increase as it uses more of the support department's services)
4. fixed costs (because low usage by one department will increase the allocation rate charged to other departments)
5. variable costs (managers know the cost per unit of support department service in advance because a budgeted allocation rate is being used, and managers watch their consumption of the allocation base when charged based on actual usage)
6. variable costs (this is the same as #5, but managers don't know the exact rate in advance because an actual allocation rate is used)
7. actual annual volume of allocation base
8. budgeted support department costs
9. budgeted usage (because fluctuations in usage will not change the total fixed costs)
10. incremental cost allocation method (because a newly formed department with a small budget is probably not using the mail room's services as much as established departments, and its small budget doesn't allow it much room to absorb the fixed costs of the mail room that existed before it was created)

Exercises:

1. a) Engineering should be allocated $4,800 of the costs and Marketing should be allocated $1,800 of the costs. If they each purchased the computers independently, the would cost $700 each. Engineering would spend 8 x $700 = $5,600 and Marketing would spend 3 x $700 = $2,100. This total is $5,600 + $2,100 = $7,700. Engineering takes 5600/7700 x $6,600 and Marketing takes 2100/7700 x $6,600. This is of course the same as each department paying $600 per unit for its computers.

    b) Engineering would have paid $5,600 (8 x $700) for the computers anyway, so as primary user it would be allocated $5,600. The additional $1,000 would be allocated to Marketing.

2. a) Bridge consulting put on 20,000 miles out of the 35,000 miles, so it would be allocated 20/35 x $3,500 = $2,000. Non-bridge consulting would be allocated 15/35 x $3,500 = $1,500.

b) Bridge consulting used the car 80 out of 210 days, so it would be allocated 80/210 x $3,500 = $1,333. Non-bridge consulting would be allocated 130/210 x $3,500 = $2,167.

c) If Bridge consulting were to use employees cars, it would cost 20,000 miles x $0.20/mile = $4,000. However, Bridge consulting could have rented a car for 80 days, at a cost of $35/day x 80 days = $2,800. If there were no company car, the cheapest alternative for Bridge consulting would be to rent a car for $2,800.

If Non-bridge consulting were to use employees cars, it would cost 15,000 miles x $0.20/mile = $3,000. Or, Non-bridge consulting could have rented a car for 130 days, at a cost of $35/day x 130 days = $4,550. If there were no company car, the cheapest alternative for Non-bridge consulting would be to use employees cars for $3,000.

The sum of the two stand-alone costs is $2,800 + $3,000 = $5,800. Bridge consulting should be allocated 2800/5800 x $3,500 = $1,690. Non-bridge consulting should be allocated 3000/5800 x $3,500 = $1,810.

3. a) The allocation base information converted to percentages is shown below:

	Support Departments			Operating Departments		
	Mainten-ance	Human Resources	Account-ing	Product A	Product B	Total
Allocation bases for fixed costs:						
M: Square feet		26.829%	18.293%	24.390%	30.488%	100.00◖
HR: Total payroll	2.913%		13.754%	46.926%	36.408%	100.00◖
A: Total revenue	0.000%	0.000%		58.140%	41.860%	100.00◖
Allocation bases for variable costs:						
M: # of requests for service		6.849%	4.110%	60.274%	28.767%	100.00◖
HR: # of employees	4.878%		12.195%	46.341%	36.585%	100.00◖
A: # of employees	5.000%	10.000%		47.500%	37.500%	100.00◖

b) The simultaneous equations for the total fixed costs to be allocated out of the support departments are:

M = $41,000 + 2.913%HR
HR = $120,000 + 26.829%M
A = $185,000 + 18.293%M + 13.754%HR

Solving by hand or with Excel the total fixed costs to be allocated out of the support departments are:

M = $44,846
HR = $132,032
A = $211,363

c) The simultaneous equations for the total variable costs to be allocated out of the support
departments are:

M = $4,000 + 4.878%HR + 5.0%A
HR = $12,000 + 6.849%M + 10.0%A
A = $8,000 + 4.11%M + 12.195%HR

Solving by hand or with Excel the total fixed costs to be allocated out of the support
departments are:

M = $5,142
HR = $13,336
A = $9,838

d) The dual-rate cost allocation is in the table below.

	Support Departments			Operating Departments		
	Mainten- ance	Human Resources	Account- ing	Product A	Product B	Total
Department fixed costs	$41,000	$120,000	$185,000	$320,000	$280,000	$946,000
Department variable costs	$4,000	$12,000	$8,000	$480,000	$350,000	$854,000
Total department costs	$45,000	$132,000	$193,000	$800,000	$630,000	$1,800,000
Allocation of fixed costs:						
M: Square feet	($44,846)	$12,032	$8,203	$10,938	$13,672	$0
HR: Total payroll	$3,846	($132,032)	$18,160	$61,957	$48,070	$0
A: Total revenue	$0	$0	($211,363)	$122,886	$88,478	$0
Allocation of variable costs:						
M: # of requests for service	($5,142)	$352	$211	$3,100	$1,479	$0
HR: # of employees	$651	($13,336)	$1,626	$6,180	$4,879	$0
A: # of employees	$492	$984	($9,838)	$4,673	$3,689	$0
Totals	$0	$0	$0	$1,009,733	$790,267	$1,800,000

SOLUTION TO END OF CHAPTER EXERCISES

<u>Multiple choice:</u>

1. A
2. B
3. C
4. D
5. B
6. A   Using a budgeted rate means that any excessive support department expenditures will not be passed on to the user departments
7. C   30%/(30%+40%) = 42.9%
8. B   If Maintenance's costs are allocated last, then its costs will go only to Machining and Assembly. 20%/(20%+50%) = 28.6%
9. A   If Cafeteria is allocated second, its costs will go to Maintenance, Machining and Assembly: 10%/(10%+40%+40%) = 11.1%
10. A   For the reciprocal method, we can read the percentages right from the table of given information.
11. C   Total budgeted costs = $40,000 + $0.02 x (80,000 + 50,000 copies) = $42,600. The single-rate allocation is at $42,600/130,000 copies = $0.3277/copy. Since the Audit Department budgeted 80,000 copies, its total budgeted copy costs are 80,000 copies x $0.3277/copy = $26,215
12. A   The budgeted fixed cost allocation rate is $40,000/130,000 copies = $0.30769/copy. The amount of cost allocated to the Audit Department is $0.30769/copy x 80,000 copies + $0.02/copy x 70,000 copies = $26,015
13. C   The budgeted fixed cost allocation rate is $0.30769/copy and the budgeted variable cost allocation rate is $0.02/copy. Since both the fixed costs and the variable costs are being allocated based on budgeted usage, the amount of cost allocated to the Audit Department is $0.30769/copy x 80,000 copies + $0.02/copy x 80,000 copies = $26,215
14. B   The budgeted fixed cost allocation rate is $0.30769/copy and the budgeted variable cost allocation rate is $0.02/copy. Since both the fixed costs and the variable costs are being allocated based on budgeted usage, the amount of cost allocated to the Tax Department is $0.30769/copy x 50,000 copies + $0.02/copy x 50,000 copies = $16,385
15. A   The total cost of the taxi ride is $22 + $1 for George + $1 for associate + $1 for George's bags + $3 for associates bags = $28. If George took a taxi by himself it would cost $22 + $1 + $1 = $24. If the associate took a taxi by himself it would cost $22 + $1 + $3 = $26. The sum of these two stand-alone costs is $50. George would be allocated 24/50 x $28 = $13.44
16. B   If George is the primary user, he would be allocated what he would have paid if he took a taxi by himself
17. A   If the associate is the primary user, the associate would be allocated what he would have paid if he took a taxi by himself, which is $26. The extra $2 would be allocated to George.

Exercises:

1. a) Store 1 would be allocated $6,206 of the $10,660 and Store 2 would be allocated $4,389, as shown in the table below.

	Store 1	Store 2	BB	Total
Rent	$4,656	$3,344		$8,000
Utilities	1,125	825	50	2,000
Security	425	220	15	660
Total	$6,206	$4,389	$65	$10,660

b) BB would be allocated $65 as shown in the table above.

c) The costs of rent and security are based on the actions of the other store. For example, if Store 2 has a bad month, then Store 1 would have to pick up a larger share of the rent, even if its revenues had not increased. Additionally, one of the managers of the stores might decide to manipulate inventory levels just before the count is taken for the purposes of sharing the utility costs.

2. a) The direct method cost allocation is shown in the table below.

	Support Departments			Operating Departments		
	Personnel	Buildings & Grounds	Repairs & Mainten-ance	Fabrication	Assembly	Total
Total department costs	$240,000	$109,750	$157,750	$800,000	$400,000	$1,707,500
Personnel	(240,000)			103,448	136,552	0
Buildings & Grounds		(109,750)		65,850	43,900	0
Repairs & Maintenance			(157,750)	105,167	52,583	0
Totals	$0	$0	$0	$1,074,465	$633,035	$1,707,500

b) First, convert the allocation base information to percentages to ease the comparison of support services provided, as shown in the table below.

	Support Departments			Operating Departments		
	Personnel	Buildings & Grounds	Repairs & Mainten-ance	Fabrication	Assembly	Total
Space occupied (B&G)	5.172%		8.621%	51.724%	34.483%	100.000%
Employees (P)		4.688%	4.688%	39.063%	51.563%	100.000%
R&M hours (R&M)				66.667%	33.333%	100.000%

B&G will be allocated first because it provided 5.172% + 8.621% = 13.793% of its services to other support departments. Personnel will go next, because it provided 4.688% + 4.688% = 9.376% of its services to other support departments. R&M will be allocated last.

c) The step-down method cost allocation is shown in the table below.

| | Support Departments | | | Operating Departments | | |
	Personnel	Buildings & Grounds	Repairs & Mainten-ance	Fabrication	Assembly	Total
Total department costs	$240,000	$109,750	$157,750	$800,000	$400,000	$1,707,500
Buildings & Grounds	5,677	(109,750)	9,461	56,767	37,845	0
Personnel	(245,677)		12,082	100,687	132,907	0
Repairs & Maintenance			(179,294)	119,529	59,765	0
Totals	$0	$0	$0	$1,076,984	$630,516	$1,707,500

d) The simultaneous equations and their solutions are below.

P = $240,000 + 5.172%B&G
B&G = $109,750 + 4.688%P
R&M = $157,750 + 8.621%B&G + 4.688%P

P = $246,274
B&G = $121,294
R&M = $179,750

e) The reciprocal method cost allocation is shown in the table below.

| | Support Departments | | | Operating Departments | | |
	Personnel	Buildings & Grounds	Repairs & Mainten-ance	Fabrication	Assembly	Total
Total department costs	$240,000	$109,750	$157,750	$800,000	$400,000	$1,707,500
Personnel	(246,274)	11,544	11,544	96,201	126,985	0
Buildings & Grounds	6,274	(121,294)	10,456	62,738	41,826	0
Repairs & Maintenance	0	0	(179,750)	119,834	59,916	0
Totals	$0	$0	$0	$1,078,773	$628,727	$1,707,500

3. a) Tacos would be allocated 3000/5400 x $4,000= $2,222. Quesadillas would be allocated 2400/5400 x $4,000 = $1,778.

b) Tacos would be allocated 3000/4900 x $4,000.= $2,449. Quesadillas would be allocated 1900/4900 x $4,000 = $1,551.

c) The total fixed cost of $4,000 is allocated to the 2 products. Since April was a poor month for quesadilla sales, Tacos had to absorb more fixed costs even though its sales didn't change.

Chapter 9

Joint Product and By-Product Costing

√ **Study Checklist - Monitor your progress**
1. Read the chapter in the text
2. Review the learning objectives below
3. Read the overview of the chapter
4. Read the chapter review for learning objectives 1 - 4
5. Do Problem Set A and check your answers
6. Read the chapter review for learning objectives 5 - 7
7. Do Problem Set B and check your answers
8. Do the End of Chapter Exercises in this study guide
9. Do the homework assigned by your instructor

CHAPTER LEARNING OBJECTIVES

After studying this chapter, you should be able to answer the following questions:
Q1. What is a joint process, and what is the difference between a by-product and a main product?
Q2. How are joint costs allocated?
Q3. What factors are considered in choosing a joint cost allocation method?
Q4. What information is relevant for deciding whether to process a joint product beyond the split-off point?
Q5. What methods are used to account for the sale of by-products?
Q6. How does a sales mix affect joint cost allocation?
Q7. What are the uses and limitations of joint cost information?

OVERVIEW OF CHAPTER

Often a production process yields multiple products. Examples include the lumber and food processing industries and crude oil refining. These production costs are then common costs for the products produced. Allocation of these joint costs to the individual products is not necessary for internal decision making but it is necessary for the preparation of financial statements, tax returns, and other external reports. In some production processes, managers need to decide at what stage of processing the products should be sold. Joint costs are not relevant to this decision. This chapter covers methods for allocating joint costs to products and how to make sell or process further decisions.

CHAPTER REVIEW: Learning Objectives 1 - 4

Q1: What is a joint process, and what is the difference between a by-product and a main product?
In some production processes, costs are incurred before several distinct products become recognizable. When multiple products emerge from the same production process, they are called *joint products*. The production costs incurred to produce the products are called *joint costs*. Meat processing produces several different cuts of meat and the lumber industry produces several different wood products from a single tree. These are examples of joint production processes. If a joint product has a high sales value compared to other joint products, it is called a *main product*. Products that have a low sales value relative to other joint products are called *by-products*.

The joint costs are all the production costs (direct materials, direct labor, and overhead incurred) to the point where the different products become recognizable; this point is known as the *split-off point*. In many, if not most, joint production processes, additional costs must be incurred past the split-off point to continue production on one or more of the products. Costs incurred past the split-off point that are identifiable with the individual products are known as *separable costs*.

Q2: How are joint costs allocated?
There are several methods for allocating of joint costs to the joint products, and they fall into two broad categories.

- Physical output methods. These methods allocate the joint cost to the joint products based on some measure of the units of output. For example, if Product A's output is 20% of the physical output of all of the joint products, then Product A would be allocated 20% of the joint production costs.

- Market-based methods. All of these methods allocate the joint costs to the joint products based on some measure related to the selling prices of the products. There are 3 distinct methods in this category.

    o Sales value at split-off point method. Joint costs are allocated to the products based on their relative sales values at the point of split off.

    o Net realizable value (NRV) method. *Net realizable value* is the final sales value less the costs to complete production. This method allocates joint costs to the products based on their relative NRVs, and can only be used when one or more of the products is incurs additional processing costs beyond the split-off point.

    o Constant gross margin (GM) NRV method. This method first calculates the combined GM for all products as the final sales value of all products less total joint costs less costs to complete (separable costs) for all products. Then the combined GM percentage (combined GM over total sales value) is computed. Finally, joint costs are allocated to all products so that each product has the same GM percentage as the combined GM percentage. If there is no processing beyond the split-off point, this method is the same as the sales value at split-off method.

Demonstration problem-Allocating joint costs using 4 different methods
SoyBeans of Texas processes bushels of soybeans for sale in the final market. At the split-off point, 3 products become recognizable: bean sprouts, bean curd, and soy nuts. This year, it expects to process 100,000 bushels of soybeans. The joint costs for processing these 100,000 bushels is $300,000. Information as to the yield from these 100,000 bushels, and the selling prices at split-off, is given below.

Product	Pounds Produced	Selling Price per Pound	Total Sales Value at Split-Off
Bean sprouts	250,000	$0.60	$150,000
Bean curd	150,000	$0.80	$120,000
Soy nuts	100,000	$1.40	$140,000
	500,000		$410,000

The company has the option of processing the products further. Special seasonings and sauce can be added to the bean sprouts so that they can be sold as a stir-fry mix. The bean curd can be processed further into soy milk, and soy oil can be rendered from the soy nuts. Information about the additional processing costs and final sales values for the products is given below.

Product	Separable Costs	Final Sales Value
Stir-fry	$50,000	$220,000
Soy milk	$40,000	$180,000
Soy oil	$60,000	$190,000
	$150,000	$590,000

Required:
a) Allocate the joint costs to the products, assuming they are sold at the split-off point, using the physical output method.
b) Allocate the joint costs to the products, assuming they are sold at the split-off point, using the sales value at split-off method.
c) Allocate the joint costs to the products, assuming they are processed beyond the split-off point, using the NRV method.
d) Allocate the joint costs to the products, assuming they are processed beyond the split-off point, using the constant GM NRV method.

solution begins on next page →

Solution to demonstration problem:

a) The physical output method's allocation of the $300,000 in joint costs is shown below.

Product	Pounds Produced	Relative Production	Joint Cost Allocation
Bean sprouts	250,000	50.0%	$150,000
Bean curd	150,000	30.0%	$90,000
Soy nuts	100,000	20.0%	$60,000
	500,000	100.0%	$300,000

b) The sales value at split-off method's allocation of the $300,000 in joint costs is shown below.

Product	Total Sales Value at Split-Off	Relative Sales Value at Split-Off	Joint Cost Allocation
Bean sprouts	$150,000	36.6%	$109,756
Bean curd	$120,000	29.3%	$87,805
Soy nuts	$140,000	34.1%	$102,439
	$410,000	100.0%	$300,000

c) The NRV method's allocation of the $300,000 in joint costs is shown below.

Product	Final Sales Value	Separable Costs	NRV	Relative NRV	Joint Cost Allocation
Stir-fry	$220,000	$50,000	$170,000	38.6%	$115,909
Soy milk	$180,000	$40,000	$140,000	31.8%	$95,455
Soy oil	$190,000	$60,000	$130,000	29.5%	$88,636
	$590,000	$150,000	$440,000	100.0%	$300,000

d) The constant GM NRV method's allocates $117,797 to stir-fry, $97,288 to soy milk, and $84,915 to soy oil as shown below. For this method, the total column is first completed and the GM percentage computed. Then the other columns are solved "backwards". For example, if the GM percentage for soy milk is set at 23.729%, then its GM must be $45, 085 ($190,000 x 23.729% = $45,085). Then, sales minus joint costs minus separable costs must equal $45,085, and the required figure for the soy oil joint cost allocation is "plugged".

	Stir-fry	Soy milk	Soy oil	Total
Total revenues	$220,000	$180,000	$190,000	$590,000
Less: Joint costs	($117,797)	($97,288)	($84,915)	($300,000)
Separable costs	($50,000)	($40,000)	($60,000)	($150,000)
Gross margin	$52,203	$42,712	$45,085	$140,000
Gross margin %	23.729%	23.729%	23.729%	23.729%

Q3: What factors are considered in choosing a joint cost allocation method?
It is important to know that the allocation of joint costs to joint products is arbitrary. Therefore, decisions about an individual product line's profitability can never be made using the joint cost allocations. In order to process bean curd, for example, SoyBeans of Texas has to purchase the bushels of soy beans. The joint products are inseparable.

- The physical output method, when output is measured in pounds, allocates the most joint costs to the product that weighs the most, which may cause these products to appear to have a negative gross margin. When the various products' selling prices are reflective of their weights, then this method is less arbitrary.

- The market-based methods allocate joint costs so that each product appears to have the same relative profitability up to the split-off point, and these methods are generally preferred. If most products are sold at split-off, then the sales value at split-off method can be chosen, and the other 2 market based methods are used when one or more products are processed beyond the split-off point.

Q4: What information is relevant for deciding whether to process a joint product beyond the split-off point?
This decision is very similar to the decisions discussed in Chapter 4. The quantitative analysis for this decision just compares the incremental revenue from further processing to the incremental costs of the additional processing. As we learned in Chapter 4, qualitative considerations can often outweigh the quantitative considerations. Examples of qualitative considerations for these types of decisions include:

- the reliability of the cost and revenue estimates

- potential changes in customer demand for products processed beyond split-off

- changes in technology that will affect joint production or beyond split-off processing

- whether the decision to process one product further will affect sales of the other products

Demonstration problem-Determining whether to sell or process further

Information about SoyBeans of Texas products (from the prior demonstration problem) is repeated below:

Product	Total Sales Value at Split-Off	Final Sales Value	Separable Costs
Bean sprouts/stir-fry	$150,000	$220,000	$50,000
Bean curd/soy milk	$120,000	$180,000	$40,000
Soy nuts/soy oil	$140,000	$190,000	$60,000
	$410,000	$590,000	$150,000

The chief operating officer (COO) is responsible for making the sell at split-off versus process further decisions for each product. While gathering the above information, she also talks to the marketing department. They tell her they believe that customer demand for bean sprouts, bean curd, and soy nuts is strong enough that they can sell all of this upcoming year's planned production of these products. However, their information about customer demand for the 3 refined products is not as reliable because fewer customers were surveyed for information about these products. The stir-fry product would be a new one for SoyBeans of Texas, and the marketing people believe this to be a high risk because they are unsure if they will be able to break into the market for this product. Also, marketing believes that sales of soy nuts could diminish demand for bean curd because the products are often seen as substitutes for vegetarians looking for sources of protein.

Required:

a) Perform the quantitative analysis for the sell or process further decision for all three products.

b) Consider the qualitative issues and make the sell or process further decision for all 3 products.

Solution to demonstration problem:

a) The quantitative analysis is below.

Product	Total Sales Value at Split-Off	Final Sales Value	Separable Costs	Incremental Revenue	Incremental Profit if Process Further	Process Further?
Bean sprouts/stir-fry	$150,000	$220,000	$50,000	$70,000	$20,000	Yes
Bean curd/soy milk	$120,000	$180,000	$40,000	$60,000	$20,000	Yes
Soy nuts/soy oil	$140,000	$190,000	$60,000	$50,000	($10,000)	No
	$410,000	$590,000	$150,000	$180,000		

b) The quantitative analysis shows that profit will increase by $20,000 if bean sprouts are processed into stir-fry. However, there is a great deal of uncertainty surrounding this according to the marketing department. If the additional processing is done, and the company is unable to break into the stir-fry market, then it loses the opportunity to earn revenues of $150,000 from bean sprouts. It seems like this is not worth the risk. Soy nuts and bean curd should not both be produced because customers seem to desire one or the other, but not both. Therefore, the soy nuts should not be processed further (in agreement with the quantitative analysis), and the bean curd should be processed into soy milk.

PROBLEM SET A (Learning Objectives 1 - 4)

Matching: Match each term with the appropriate definition or phrase. You must use each term only once.

Terms	
A. Joint costs	G. Net realizable value
B. Joint product	H. Net realizable value method
C. By-product	I. Split-off point
D. Sales value at split-off method	J. Separable costs
E. Physical output method	K. Constant gross margin NRV method
F. Gross margin	L. Market-based methods

_____ 1. Distinct products become recognizable

_____ 2. Products with more measurable output receive a greater proportion of the allocated joint costs

_____ 3. Relates the joint cost allocation in some way to the revenue the products generate

_____ 4. Best used when products are not processed past the split-off point, and relates the joint cost allocation to the revenue the products generate

_____ 5. Revenue less joint costs less separable costs

_____ 6. Revenue less costs to complete

_____ 7. The joint cost allocation is based on the relative product revenues less costs to complete the product

_____ 8. Costs that can be identified with a particular product

_____ 9. Production costs that cannot be specifically identified with a single product

_____ 10. Produced from a single production process

_____ 11. Produced from a single production process, and has low relative sales value

_____ 12. Used when products are processed past split-off; each product will have the same gross margin percentage under this method

<u>True-False</u>: Indicate whether each of the following is true (T) or false (F) in the space provided.

_____   1. If incremental revenues of processing a product further exceed its separable costs, then the product should always be processed further.

_____   2. If products are not processed beyond split-off, then all 3 market based methods are the same.

_____   3. The physical output method is the only method that can provide a joint cost allocation such that a particular product has a negative gross margin.

_____   4. Separable costs are the same thing as the incremental costs of further processing.

_____   5. Joint costs include direct materials and direct labor, but exclude manufacturing overhead.

_____   6. Joint costs include direct materials and direct labor, but exclude selling expenses.

_____   7. If the net realizable value of a product is negative, then a company is most likely to decide to sell it at split-off, rather than processing it further.

_____   8. Joint costs should never be used to make any decision about an individual product's profitability.

_____   9. Joint cost allocations are arbitrary assignments of joint costs to joint products.

_____   10. Joint costs should never be used to make any decision about whether to keep or drop a product line.

<u>Exercises</u>: Write your answer in the space provided.
1. From a single production process, a company produces three products, Yuk, Gluk, and Muk. The production process costs $1,000,000 and yields 12,000 gallons of Yuk, 14,000 gallons of Gluk, and 22,000 gallons of Muk. Yuk, Gluk & Muk sell for $20/gallon, $40/gallon, and $70/gallon, respectively.

a) Use the physical output method to allocate the joint costs to the 3 products.

Yuk _____   Gluk _____   Muk _____

b) Compute the gross margin percentage for each product using the joint cost allocations from part (a)

Yuk _____   Gluk _____   Muk _____

2. From a single production process, a company produces three products, Yuk, Gluk, and Muk. The production process costs $1,000,000 and yields 12,000 gallons of Yuk, 14,000 gallons of Gluk, and 22,000 gallons of Muk. Yuk, Gluk & Muk sell for $20/gallon, $40/gallon, and $70/gallon, respectively.

a) Use the sales value at split-off method to allocate the joint costs to the 3 products.

Yuk _____   Gluk _____   Muk _____

b) Compute the gross margin percentage for each product.

Yuk _____   Gluk _____   Muk _____

c) Compare your answers to exercise 1(b) and exercise 2(b) and discuss the differences. Is there any action that the company needs to take that you can see from these computations?

_____

_____

_____

_____

_____

_____

_____

_____

3. From a single production process, a company produces three products, A, B, and C. The joint costs of the production process are $300,000. However, the three products are not sold at split-off. Rather, they are processed further into AA, BB, and CC. The final sales value for the three refined products totals $100,000, $180,000, and $210,000, respectively. The separable costs for the three products are $10,000, $40,000, and $60,000, respectively.

a) Compute the joint costs allocated to each product under the NRV method.

AA _____   BB _____   CC _____

b) Compute the GM percentage for each product under the NRV method.

AA _____   BB _____   CC _____

c) Compute the joint costs allocated to each product under the constant GM NRV method.

AA _____   BB _____   CC _____

4. Three Stooges Productions makes 4 products from a single production process, W, X, Y and Z. Each product can be further processed into WW, XX, YY, and ZZ. However, the company cannot choose to process both W and Z further because this uses the same equipment. If the company chooses to process W further, the marketing department recommends that X is also processed further because WW and XX are complementary products.

Product	Sales Value at Split-Off	Final Sales Value	Separable Costs
W; WW	$320,000	$420,000	$40,000
X; XX	$120,000	$150,000	$32,000
Y; YY	$180,000	$290,000	$60,000
Z; ZZ	$90,000	$110,000	$2,000
	$710,000	$970,000	$134,000

a) Perform the quantitative analysis for each product line, ignoring for now the product interactions. Should each product be processed further according to this level of analysis? Write "yes" or "no" in the spaces below.

W _____   X _____   Y _____   Z _____

b) Now consider the other issues about production restrictions and product interactions and determine if each product should be processed further. Write "yes" or "no" in the spaces below.

W _____   X _____   Y _____   Z _____

c) Explain your decisions in part (b).

_____

_____

_____

_____

_____

CHAPTER REVIEW: Learning Objectives 5 - 7

Q5: What methods are used to account for the sale of by-products?

In some cases, by-products have zero sales value and are simply disposed of. Here, there is no accounting for by-products issue to consider. Other times, by-products have zero sales value but a positive disposal cost (e.g. hazardous materials). In this instance, the disposal costs of the by-product increases the joint production costs for the main joint products. It is only when by-products have a positive net sales value that we need to determine an accounting method for by-products. The only issue is when the value of the by-product should be recognized.

- Recognize by-product value at the time of production. This is known as the *net realizable value approach* or the *offset approach*. Under this method, the NRV of the by-product decreases the joint production costs at the time of production. Essentially, the NRV of the by-product is placed in an inventory account. When the by-product is eventually sold, the inventory account is decreased. Revenue is not recognized when the by-product is sold. This method is theoretically the most appropriate method because it provides the best matching of revenues and expenses for the main products.

- Recognize by-product value at time of by-product's sale. This is known as the *realized value approach* or the *income approach*. Revenue from the sale of by-products is recognized when the by-products are sold. Although theoretically inferior to the above method, the sales value of by-products is, by definition, relatively small, so this method is acceptable. Under this method, there is no accounting for the by-product until it is sold. Upon sale, it is included in revenue on the income statement.

Demonstration problem-Accounting for by-products

Cleo Manufacturing produces 2 products from a joint process, the main product and a by-product. The main product sells for $7 per unit and the by-product sells for $1 per unit. The joint costs of production total $170,000. Non-manufacturing expenses total $200,000. Information about Cleo's production and sales of each product for this year is shown below.

	Information in Units of Each Product			
	Beginning Inventory	Production	Sales	Ending Inventory
Main product	0	100,000	95,000	5,000
By-product	0	20,000	17,000	3,000

Required:
a) Prepare an income statement that recognizes the by-product value at time of production (the NRV approach). What is the value of ending inventory that would be shown on the year-end balance sheet?
b) Prepare an income statement that recognizes the by-product value at time of the by-product's sale (the realized value approach). What is the value of ending inventory that would be shown on the year-end balance sheet?

solution to demonstration problem begins on next page →

Solution to demonstration problem:

a) First compute the net production costs and production costs per unit for the main product:

Production costs	$170,000
Less: NRV of by-product	20,000
Net joint product cost	$150,000

Net product cost per unit	$1.50

Next, prepare the income statement:

Revenue: 95,000 units at $7/unit	$665,000
Cost of goods sold: 95,000 units at $1.50/unit	142,500
Gross margin	522,500
Less: nonmanufacturing expenses	200,000
Operating income	$322,500

Finally, compute the value of ending inventory for the balance sheet:

Main product: 5,000 units at $1.50	$7,500
By-product: 3,000 units at $1	3,000
Value of ending inventory for balance sheet	$10,500

b) First compute the production costs per unit for the main product:

Production costs	$170,000

Net product cost per unit	$1.70

Next, prepare the income statement:

Revenue: 95,000 units at $7/unit	$665,000
By-product sales: 17,0000 units at $1/unit	17,000
Total revenue	682,000
Cost of goods sold: 95,000 units at $1.70/unit	161,500
Gross margin	520,500
Less: nonmanufacturing expenses	200,000
Operating income	$320,500

Finally, compute the value of ending inventory for the balance sheet:

5,000 units of the main product at $1.70 = $8,500

Q6: How does a sales mix affect joint cost allocation?

Under each of the methods of joint cost allocation that we learned, the actual or expected product mix is incorporated into the calculations. To see how a change in product mix will affect the joint cost allocation, you need to recalculate the allocation under the revised product mix assumptions.

Q7: What are the uses and limitations of joint cost information?

Joint cost allocation is required for financial statement preparation only if production does not equal sales. In other words, if the joint products are sold in different proportions to how they are made, the joint cost allocation will affect the breakdown of production costs between inventory values reported on the balance sheet and cost of goods sold figures reported on the income statement. Joint cost allocation is required for tax return purposes as well, for the same reason.

In the joint cost allocation, much of the information used to do the allocation is usually an estimate, so the joint cost allocation is only as good as these estimates. Examples of estimates used in joint cost allocations include the quantities of each product that can be produced from the joint process, the sales value at the split-off point of the individual products, the final sales value if processed further, and the separable costs related to further processing.

PROBLEM SET B (Learning Objectives 5 - 7)

<u>True-False</u>: Indicate whether each of the following is true (T) or false (F) in the space provided.

_____ 1. A by-product has a small relative sales value compared to the main product(s).

_____ 2. Under the net realizable value method of accounting for by-products, the by-product has no value on the balance sheet.

_____ 3. Under the realized value approach of accounting for by-products, the by-product has no value on the balance sheet.

_____ 4. The per-unit processing cost of the main product is higher under the net realizable value method of accounting for by-products than it is under the realized value method.

_____ 5. The realized value method of accounting for by-products provides better matching of revenues and expenses than the net realizable value method of accounting for by-products.

_____ 6. If there is no beginning inventory of any of the main products or by-products, the difference in income between the two methods of accounting for by-products is equal to the difference in reported ending inventory values.

_____ 7. The net realizable value of a by-product is equal to its selling price if the by-product is not processed past the split-off point.

_____ 8. Cost of goods sold under the net realizable value method of accounting for by-products will always be higher than under the realized value method of accounting for by-products.

_____ 9. If there was no beginning inventory of any products, ending inventory under the net realizable value method of accounting for by-products will always be lower than under the realized value method of accounting for by-products.

_____ 10. The net realizable value method of accounting for by-products recognizes the value of the by-product before the realized value method does.

<u>Exercise</u>: Write your answer in the space provided.

Willy's Widgets produces only one type of widget and metal shavings are a by-product. The widgets sell for $7.50 each and Willy sells the metal shavings to a scrap dealer for $0.80 per pound. There were no beginning inventories of either product this year. During the year, Willy produced 80,000 widgets and 6,000 pounds of metal shavings. Widget sales were 65,000 units this year, and 5,000 pounds of metal shavings were sold to the scrap dealer. This year's joint costs totaled $400,000.

a) Compute the product cost per widget under the net realizable value method of accounting for by-products.

   Cost per widget _____

b) Compute the product cost per widget under the realized value method of accounting for by-products.

   Cost per widget _____

c) Compute the ending inventory value to be reported under the net realizable value method of accounting for by-products.

   Ending inventory value _____

d) Compute the ending inventory value to be reported under the realized value method of accounting for by-products.

   Ending inventory value _____

e) Compute cost of goods sold under the net realizable value method of accounting for by-products.

   Cost of goods sold _____

f) Compute cost of goods sold under the realized value method of accounting for by-products.

   Cost of goods sold _____

g) Compute gross margin under the net realizable value method of accounting for by-products.

   Gross margin _____

h) Compute gross margin under the realized value method of accounting for by-products.

   Gross margin _____

END OF CHAPTER EXERCISES

<u>Multiple choice</u>: Write the letter that represents the best choice in the space provided.

_____ 1. Costs incurred to process joint products beyond a split-off point are called
    a. by-products
    b. joint costs
    c. separable costs
    d. fixed costs

_____ 2. Suppose 2 products, X and Z, are produced simultaneously in a joint process. If the sales value at split-off method is used to allocate joint costs, then the joint cost allocated to product X will increase when
    a. the sales value of Z increases
    b. the sales value of Z decreases
    c. the sales value of X decreases
    d. the separable cost of Z increases

_____ 3. Assume the total final sales value of a set of joint products exceeds the total joint costs, and that the incremental revenue from processing each product further exceeds the separable costs. Which joint cost allocation method could not result in the reporting of a loss for some products and a profit for others?
    a. net realizable value method
    b. physical output method
    c. sales value at split-off method
    d. constant gross margin net realizable value method

_____ 4. Suppose a by-product is created continuously and sold for cash at the end of each day. If the proceeds of the by-product sales are used to reduce the joint production costs, an increase in the by-products sales value will
    a. increase the profit reported for by-product sales
    b. decrease the profit reported for by-product sales
    c. decrease the gross margin reported by the main products
    d. increase the gross margin reported by the main products

_____ 5. In order to make the most profitable sell-or-process-further decisions, one should consider
    a. the increase in the cost of further processing
    b. the increase in sales value due to further processing
    c. the increase in sales value due to further processing less the joint costs of processing less the separable costs of processing
    d. the increase in sales value due to further processing less the separable costs of further processing

_____   6.   Joint costs consist of
             a.   direct materials costs only
             b.   direct materials and direct labor costs only
             c.   direct materials, direct labor, and variable manufacturing overhead costs
                   only
             d.   direct materials, direct labor, and all manufacturing overhead costs

_____   7.   Items produced from a joint process with a small sales value or a negative
             value are called
             a.   separate products
             b.   by-products
             c.   waste
             d.   garbage

_____   8.   Which joint cost allocation method may show a loss for a product with a large
             separable cost?
             a.   sales value at split-off method
             b.   realized value method
             c.   net realizable value method
             d.   none of the above

_____   9.   Suppose a joint process yields 3 main products and one by-product that has
             no sales value and is disposed of in the normal garbage. Which of the
             following is appropriate in accounting for the by-product?
             a.   describe it in a footnote to the financial statements
             b.   allocate a portion of the joint cost to the by-product and show the amount
                   in a loss account on the income statement
             c.   allocate a portion of the joint cost to the by-product and show the amount
                   as a reduction of the processing costs of the main products
             d.   none of the above – no accounting treatment is necessary

_____   10.   Which of the following is the most important reason to allocate joint costs?
             a.   accurate product costs are necessary to make product mix decisions
             b.   accurate product costs are necessary to make product pricing decisions
             c.   production costs must be allocated to inventory and cost of goods sold
                   for financial statement and tax reporting reasons
             d.   none of the above – joint cost allocation is arbitrary

_____   11.   A company incurs joint costs of $700 to produce 100 units of product A, 300
             units of product B, and 500 units of product C. The 3 products sell for $1, $2,
             and $3 each, respectively. What amount of joint cost is allocated to product A
             if the sales value at split-off method is used?
             a. $100.00
             b. $77.78
             c. $31.82
             d.   none of the above

Use the following information for questions 12 – 15:
A joint process has total costs of $1,200 and yields 50 units each of two main products and 10 units of by-product that can be sold for $2.50 each.

_____ 12. Under the realized value approach to accounting for by-products
    a.   the $25 is revenue in the time period that the by-product is sold
    b.   the $25 is revenue in the time period that the by-product is produced
    c.   the $25 is revenue in the time period that the main products are produced
    d.   the $25 is revenue in the time period that the main products are sold

_____ 13. Under the net realizable value approach to accounting for by-products
    a.   the $25 is recognized in the time period that the by-product is sold
    b.   the $25 is recognized in the time period that the by-product is produced
    c.   the $25 is recognized in the time period that the main products are produced
    d.   the $25 is recognized in the time period that the main products are sold

_____ 14. Under the realized value approach to accounting for by-products, what is the per unit cost of a main product if the physical output method of allocating joint costs is used?
    a. $12.00
    b. $24.00
    c. $11.75
    d. $23.50

_____ 15. Under the net realizable value approach to accounting for by-products, what is the per unit cost of a main product if the physical output method of allocating joint costs is used?
    a. $12.00
    b. $24.00
    c. $11.75
    d. $23.50

Use the following information for questions 16 – 20:

The Great Foods Company processes milk into skim milk and butter. This year 70,000 gallons of will be processed, costing $40,000. If processed to the split-off point, this will yield 40,000 gallons of skim milk and 10,000 pounds of butter. Skim milk is sold to distributors for $1/gallon and butter is sold for $0.75/pound. Great Foods has the option of processing the two products further. Skim milk can be processed into canned, sweetened, condensed skim milk and sold for $0.80 per can. One gallon of skim milk makes 2 cans of condensed milk. To process 40,000 gallons of skim milk will cost $18,000. Butter can be processed into cake frosting, sold in containers for $2 each. One pound of butter goes into each container of frosting. The cost of processing 10,000 pounds of butter into frosting costs $15,000.

_____ 16. What is the per-unit joint cost allocated to skim milk and butter if the sales value at split-off method is used?
   a. $0.8421/gallon and $0.6316/pound
   b. $1/gallon and $0.75/pound
   c. $0.381/gallon and $0.9524/pound
   d. $0.7619/gallon and $0.9524/pound

_____ 17. What is the per-unit joint cost allocated to condensed milk and frosting if the sales value at split-off method is used?
   a. $0.8421/can and $0.6316/container
   b. $0.42105/can and $0.6316/container
   c. $0.381/can and $0.9524/container
   d. $0.7619/can and $0.9524/container

_____ 18. What is the per-unit joint cost allocated to condensed milk and frosting if the net realizable value method is used?
   a. $1.64608/can and $0.7157/container
   b. $0.82304/can and $0.7157/container
   c. $0.90196/can and $0.3922/container
   d. $0.45098/can and $0.3922/container

_____ 19. What is the per-unit joint cost allocated to condensed milk and frosting if the constant gross margin net realizable value method is used?
   a. $1.470248/can and $0.2381/container
   b. $0.94048/can and $0.2311/container
   c. $0.69524/can and $1.7381/container
   d.   none of the above

_____ 20. What is the per-unit joint cost allocated to condensed milk and frosting under the physical output method if the number of units of output after further processing is used to measure output?
   a. $0.69524/can and $1.7381/container
   b. $0.4444/can and $0.4444/container
   c. $1.3905/can and $1.7381/container
   d.   none of the above

<u>Exercises</u>: Write your answer in the space provided.
1. Quigley's Quarry mines rocks for landscaping. The two main products are large decorative rocks and driveway stones. This year Quigley processed 200,000 pounds of rocks, 60% of which were large decorative rocks. Processing costs were $500,000. Large decorative rocks sell for $5/pound and driveway stones sell for $2/pound. There were no beginning or ending inventories.

a) Compute the joint cost per pound allocated to each product using the physical output method.

Large decorative rocks _____   Driveway stones _____

b) Compute the gross margin percentage for each product using the physical output method.

Large decorative rocks _____   Driveway stones _____

c) Compute the joint cost per pound allocated to each product using the sales value at split-off method.

Large decorative rocks _____   Driveway stones _____

d) Compute the gross margin percentage for each product using the sales value at split-off method.

Large decorative rocks _____   Driveway stones _____

2. Quigley's Quarry mines rocks for landscaping. The two main products are large decorative rocks and driveway stones. This year Quigley processed 200,000 pounds of rocks, 60% of which were large decorative rocks. Processing costs were $500,000. Large decorative rocks sell for $5/pound and driveway stones sell for $2/pound. There were no beginning or ending inventories. Quigley has the opportunity to process each product further. Large decorative rocks can be processed into smaller patio rocks, which sell for $8/pound. Because of losses in the crushing process, each pound of large decorative rocks yields only 0.9 pounds of patio rocks. Driveway stones can be processed into concrete mixture. One bag of concrete mixture contains 20 pounds of driveway stones and sells for $50. It costs $0.50/pound of large decorative rocks to process them into patio rocks. The costs of processing a bag of concrete are $2/bag.

    a) Compute the joint cost per unit allocated to each product using the net realizable value method.

    Patio rocks _____   Concrete mixture _____

    b) Compute the gross margin percentage for each product using the net realizable value method.

    Patio rocks _____   Concrete mixture _____

    c) Compute the joint cost per unit allocated to each product using the constant gross margin net realizable value method.

    Patio rocks _____   Concrete mixture _____

    d) Compute the increase (or decrease) in profits from processing each original product further.

    Large decorative rocks/   Driveway stones/
         Patio rocks   _____   Concrete mix   _____

3. Larry's Leather makes purses and wallets. Scraps of leather are a by-product and sold for $1/pound. Purses sell for $25 and wallets sell for $10. This year Larry incurred $500,000 in joint costs to produce 30,000 purses, 20,000 wallets, and 4,000 pounds of leather scraps. The separable costs for processing the 30,000 purses and 20,000 wallets were $20,000 and $12,000, respectively. Sales this year were 24,000 purses, 15,000 wallets, and 2,500 pounds of leather scraps. Total administrative expenses this year were $200,000.

This year's beginning inventories consisted of 2,000 purses, 4,000 wallets, and 1,000 pounds of leather scraps. Last year's production costs were exactly 90% of this year's production costs, but leather scraps have sold for $1/pound for years. Larry uses the FIFO inventory method and allocated joint costs using the physical output method (based on number of units of output).

   a) Prepare an income statement using the net realizable value method of accounting for by-products.

   b) Compute the ending inventory value for the balance sheet under the NRV method of

   accounting for by-products. _____

exercise continues on next page →

3. continued

c) Prepare an income statement using the realized value method of accounting for by-products.

b) Compute the ending inventory value for the balance sheet under the realized value method

of accounting for by-products. _____

SOLUTION TO PROBLEM SET A

Matching:

1. I
2. E
3. L
4. D
5. F
6. G
7. H
8. J
9. A
10. B
11. C
12. K

True-False:

1. F   If you said true, then you forgot about qualitative considerations
2. T
3. F   The NRV method can also allocate costs so that a product (with relatively high separable costs) may show a negative gross margin.
4. T
5. F
6. T
7. T
8. T
9. T
10. T

Exercises:

1. a) The joint cost allocation using the physical output method is below.

	Gallons	Physical Volume Method Joint Cost Allocation
Yuk	12,000	$250,000
Gluk	14,000	$291,667
Muk	22,000	$458,333
	48,000	$1,000,000

b) The gross margin percentage for each product, under the physical output method is below.

	Gallons	Physical Volume Method Joint Cost Allocation	Selling Price per Gallon	Revenue at Split Off	GM Under Physical Volume Method	GM% Under Physical Volume Method
Yuk	12,000	$250,000	$20	$240,000	($10,000)	-4.167%
Gluk	14,000	$291,667	$40	$560,000	$268,333	47.917%
Muk	22,000	$458,333	$70	$1,540,000	$1,081,667	70.238%
	48,000	$1,000,000		$2,340,000	$1,340,000	

2. a) The joint cost allocation using the sales value at split-off method is below.

	Gallons	Revenue at Split Off	Sales Value at Split-Off Method Joint Cost Allocation
Yuk	12,000	$240,000	$102,564
Gluk	14,000	$560,000	$239,316
Muk	22,000	$1,540,000	$658,120
	48,000	$2,340,000	$1,000,000

b) The gross margin percentage for each product, under the sales volume at split-off method is below.

	Gallons	Revenue at Split Off	Sales Value at Split-Off Method Joint Cost Allocation	GM Under Sales Value at Split-Off Method	GM% Under Sales Value at Split-Off Method
Yuk	12,000	$240,000	$102,564	$137,436	57.265%
Gluk	14,000	$560,000	$239,316	$320,684	57.265%
Muk	22,000	$1,540,000	$658,120	$881,880	57.265%
	48,000	$2,340,000	$1,000,000	$1,340,000	

c) Product Yuk is 25% of the output in gallons, and gets allocated 25% of the joint costs under the physical output method. However, Yuk has the lowest selling price per gallon of the 3 products. The large joint cost allocation under the physical output method causes Yuk to have a negative gross margin, and hence a negative gross margin percent. The sales value at split-off method allocates joint costs according to their relative sales values, and the products end up with the same gross margin percentage under this method.

3. a) The joint cost allocation using the sales value at split-off method is below.

	Final Sales Value	Separable Costs	NRV	Relative NRV	Joint Cost Allocation Under NRV Method
AA	$100,000	$10,000	$90,000	23.684%	$71,053
BB	$180,000	$40,000	$140,000	36.842%	$110,526
CC	$210,000	$60,000	$150,000	39.474%	$118,421
	$490,000	$110,000	$380,000	100.000%	$300,000

b) The gross margin percentage for each product, under the NRV method is below.

	Final Sales Value	Separable Costs	NRV	Relative NRV	Joint Cost Allocation Under NRV Method	GM Under NRV Method	GM% Under NRV Method
AA	$100,000	$10,000	$90,000	23.684%	$71,053	$18,947	18.947%
BB	$180,000	$40,000	$140,000	36.842%	$110,526	$29,474	16.374%
CC	$210,000	$60,000	$150,000	39.474%	$118,421	$31,579	15.038%
	$490,000	$110,000	$380,000	100.000%	$300,000	$80,000	

c) The joint cost allocation under the constant GM NRV method is below.

	Final Sales Value	Separable Costs	GM%	GM	Joint Cost Allocation Under Constant GM NRV Method
AA	$100,000	$10,000	16.327%	$16,327	$73,673
BB	$180,000	$40,000	16.327%	$29,388	$110,612
CC	$210,000	$60,000	16.327%	$34,286	$115,714
	$490,000	$110,000		$80,000	$300,000

4. a) .The quantitative analysis is below.

Product	Sales Value at Split-Off	Final Sales Value	Separable Costs	Incre-mental Revenue	Incre-mental Profit
W; WW	$320,000	$420,000	$40,000	$100,000	$60,000
X; XX	$120,000	$150,000	$32,000	$30,000	($2,000)
Y; YY	$180,000	$290,000	$60,000	$110,000	$50,000
Z; ZZ	$90,000	$110,000	$2,000	$20,000	$18,000
	$710,000	$970,000	$134,000	$260,000	$126,000

According to the quantitative analysis, products W, Y, and Z should be processed further

b) When the other issues are taken into consideration, W, X, and Y should be processed further but Z should not.

c) The company must choose between W and Z, even though the quantitative analysis says that both should be processed further. Since the incremental profit from processing W further is $60,000 and the incremental profit from processing Z further is only $18,000, the company should process W further but not Z. The net benefit of processing W further instead of Z is $60,000 - $18,000 opportunity cost of not processing Z further = $42,000. Although the quantitative analysis shows that Y should be processed further and X should not, the advice from marketing is that the sell or process further decision for these products should go in the same direction. Therefore, both X and Y should be processed further, for an incremental net profit of $50,000 - $2,000 = $48,000.

SOLUTION TO PROBLEM SET B

True-False:

1. T
2. F
3. T
4. F
5. F   The NRV approach provides better matching because the benefit of the by-product is matched against the costs of production of the main product to which it is related.
6. T   See the demonstration problem on by-products for an example of this.
7. T
8. F   If the beginning inventories are zero, the NRV method would show a lower cost of goods sold than the realized value method.
9. T
10. T

Exercise:

a) $400,000 joint cost less value of by-product of $4,800 [6,000 pounds at $0.80] = $395,200 production costs. $395,200 divided by 80,000 units = $4.94/unit.

b) $400,000 joint cost divided by 80,000 units = $5.00/unit.

c) Widget value = 15,000 x $4.94 plus by-product value = 1,000 pounds at $0.80/pound = $74,100 + $800 = $74,900.

d) Widget value = 15,000 x $5 = $75,000.

e) Cost of goods sold = 65,000 x $4.94 = $321,100.

f) Cost of goods sold = 65,000 x $5 = $325,000.

g) Gross margin = [$7.50/unit - $4.94/unit] x 65,000 units = $166,400.

h) Gross margin = $7.50/unit x 65,000 units + $0.80 x 5,000 units less cost of goods sold of $325,000 = $487,500 + $4,000 - $325,000 = $166,500.

SOLUTION TO END OF CHAPTER EXERCISES

Multiple choice:

1. C
2. B   If the sales value of Z decreases, then the relative sales value of X increases.
3. B   Under the assumptions described, the NRV method could not show a product's gross margin to be negative.
4. D   A and B cannot be right because the discuss the profit reported for by-product sales, and the NRV method of accounting for by-products does not show any revenue for the by-product sales. The NRV method will decrease the production costs for the main products, which will decrease cost of goods sold, which will increase the gross margin for the main products.
5. D
6. D
7. B
8. C
9. D
10. C
11. C   The total revenue at split-off is $100 for A + $600 for B + $1,500 for C = $2,200. The joint costs allocated to A = (100/2,200) x $700 = $31.82.
12. A
13. B
14. A   There were 100 main products produced: $1,200/100 units = $12/unit.

15.   C $1,200 joint costs less $25 value of by-product = $1,175 net production costs. $1,175/100 units = $11.75/unit.

16.   A   The sales value of the skim milk is 40,000 gallons x $1/gallon = $40,000. The sales value of the butter = 10,000 pounds x $0.75/pound = $7,500, for a total sales value at split-off of $47,500. The amount allocated to skim milk is (40,000/47,500) x $40,000 = $33,684, or $33,684/40,000 gallons = $$0.8421/gallon. The amount allocated to butter is (7,500/47,500) x 10,000 pounds = $6,316, which is $6,316/10,000 pounds = $0.6316/pound.

17.   B   Since the sales value at split-off method is being used, the allocations of cost from question 16 still hold. The condensed milk is allocated $33,684, which is $33,684/80,000 cans = $0.42105/can. The frosting is allocated $6,316, which is $6,316/10,000 containers = $0.6316/container. If you chose C or D, one of the errors you made was to base the allocation of the final sales value rather than the sales value at split-off.

18.   D   The NRV for condensed milk is $0.80/can x 80,000 cans less separable costs of $18,000 = $64,000 - $18,000 = $46,000. The NRV for frosting is $2/container x 10,000 containers less separable costs of $15,000 = $20,000 - $15,000 = $5,000. This is a total NRV for the 2 products of $51,000. Condensed milk is allocated (46,000/51,000) x $40,000 = $36,078, which is $36,078/80,000 cans = $0.45098/can. Frosting is allocated (5,000/51,000) x $40,000 = $3,922, which is $3,922/10,000 containers = $0.3922/container.

19.   A   The final sales value is $64,000 + $20,000 = $84,000. Gross margin = $84,000 − ($18,000 + $15,000) separable costs - $40,000 joint costs = $11,000. The gross margin percentage is $11,000/$84,000 = 13.0952%. Therefore, the gross margin for condensed milk must be 13.0952% x $64,000 = $8,381, and the joint cost allocation to condensed milk = $64,000 - $18,000 - $8,381 = $37,619 [which is $0.47024/can]. The gross margin for frosting must be 13.0952% x $20,000 = $2,619, and the joint cost allocation to frosting = $20,000 - $15,000 - $2,619 = $2,381 [which is $0.2381/container].

20.   B   There are 80,000 cans of milk and 10,000 containers of frosting, which is 90,000 total units. The joint costs allocated to condensed milk = (80,000/90,000) x $40,000 = $35,556, which is $0.44445/can. The joint costs allocated to frosting = (10,000/90,000) x $40,000 = $4,444, which is $0.4444/container.

Exercises:

1. a) Let LDR = large decorative rocks and DS = driveway stones. LDR is 60% of the physical output so it is allocated 60% x $500,000 = $300,000, which is $300,000/120,000lbs = $2.50/lb. DS is allocated 40% x $500,000 = $200,000 which is $200,000/80,000 lbs = $2.50/lb.

    b) The revenue for LDR = $5/lb x 120,000 lbs = $600,000. Gross margin for LDR = $600,000 - $300,000 joint costs = $300,000. The gross margin percentage for LDR = $300,000/$600,000 = 50%. The revenue for DS = $2/lb x 80,000 lbs = $160,000. Gross margin for DS = $160,000 - $200,000 joint costs = ($40,000). The gross margin percentage for DS = ($40,000)/$160,000 = (25%).

    c) The total revenue at split-off is $600,000 + $160,000 = $760,000. The joint costs allocated to LDR = (600,000/760,000) x $500,000 = $394,737, which is $394,737/120,000 lbs = $3.2895/lb. The joint costs allocated to DS = (160,000/760,000) x $500,000 = $105,263, which is $105,263/80,000 lbs = $1.31579/lb.

    d) The GM for LDR = $600,000 - $394,737 = $205,263, so the GM percentage for LDR = $205,263/$600,000 = 34.211%. The GM for DS = $160,000 - $105,263 = $54,737, so the GM percentage for LDR = $54,263/$160,000 = 34.211%.

2. a) The 120,000 lbs of LDR will yield 90% x 120,000 lb = 108,000 lbs of patio rocks (PR). The 80,000 lbs of DS will yield 80,000 lbs/20 lbs per bag = 4,000 bags of concrete mix (CM). The NRV for each product is computed below:

	Final Sales Value	Sep-arable Costs	Net Realiz-able Value	
Patio rocks	$864,000	$60,000	$804,000	80.723%
Concrete mix	$200,000	$8,000	$192,000	19.277%
Total	$1,064,000	$68,000	$996,000	

    PR is allocated 80.723% x $500,000 = $403,615, which is $403,615/108,000 lbs = $3.7372/lb. CM is allocated 19.277% x $500,000 = $96,385, which is $96,385/4,000 bags = $24.0963/bag.

    b) The GM % for each product is computed below.

	Patio Rocks	Concrete Mix
Revenue	$864,000	$200,000
Joint costs	$403,614	$96,386
Separable costs	$60,000	$8,000
Gross margin	$400,386	$95,614
Gross margin %	46.341%	47.807%

    c) The joint cost allocation is computed below, where the Total column is computed first, then the GM for each product, and the joint cost for each product if the last cell computed.

	Patio Rocks	Concrete Mix	Total
Revenue	$864,000	$200,000	$1,064,000
Joint costs	$401,233	$98,767	$500,000
Separable costs	$60,000	$8,000	$68,000
Gross margin	$402,767	$93,233	$496,000
Gross margin %	46.617%	46.617%	46.617%

The joint cost per pound of PR is $401,233/108,000 lbs = $3.7151/lb. The joint cost per bag of CM is $98,767/4,000 bags = $24.69175/bag.

d) The incremental revenue from further processing for PR = $864,000 - $600,000 revenue if sold at split-off = $264,000. Subtract separable costs of $60,000 to get an increase in profit from processing LDR into PR of $204,000. The incremental revenue from further processing for CM = $200,000 - $160,000 revenue if sold at split-off = $40,000. Subtract separable costs of $8,000 to get an increase in profit from processing DS into CM of $32,000.

3. a) First note the inventory levels:

	Information in Units of Each Product			
	Beginning Inventory	Production	Sales	Ending Inventory
Purses	2,000	30,000	24,000	8,000
Wallets	4,000	20,000	15,000	9,000
By-product	1,000	4,000	2,500	2,500

Next, compute the production costs per unit for this year and last year (last year's costs were 90% of this year's costs). Notice that the usage of the physical output method to assign costs means that purses and wallets will be assigned the same per-unit cost.

Net product cost per unit $9.92 ($496,000/50,000 units)

Last year's product cost/unit $8.928

Now prepare the income statement, remembering that Larry uses the FIFO method, so the first units sold are the beginning inventory units with last year's costs attached:

Revenue: (24,000 @ $25 + 15,000 @ $10) $750,000	
Cost of goods sold:	
[2,000+4,000]@$8.928+[(24,000+15,000)- (2,000+4,000)]@$9.92	380,928
Gross margin	369,072
Less: nonmanufacturing expenses	200,000
Operating income	$169,072

b) Ending inventory:

Main products: 17,000 units at $9.92	$168,640
By-product: 2,500 units at $1	2,500
Value of ending inventory for balance sheet	$171,140

c) First, compute the production costs per unit for the 50,000 wallets and purses produced this year as well as last year's costs (last year's costs were 90% of this year's costs).

Production costs	$500,000
Net product cost per unit	$10.00
Last year's product cost/unit	$9.00

Now prepare the income statement, remembering that Larry uses the FIFO method, so the first units sold are the beginning inventory units with last year's costs attached:

Revenue: (24,000 @ $25 + 15,000 @ $10)	$750,000
By-product sales: 2,5000 units at $1/unit	2,500
Total revenue	752,500
Cost of goods sold:	
[2,000+4,000]@$9+[(24,000+15,000)- (2,000+4,000)]@$10	384,000
Gross margin	368,500
Less: nonmanufacturing expenses	200,000
Operating income	$168,500

d) Ending inventory:

Main products: 17,000 units at $1.70	$170,000

Chapter 10

Static and Flexible Budgets

√ **Study Checklist – Monitor your progress**

1. Read the chapter in the text
2. Review the learning objectives below
3. Read the overview of the chapter
4. Read the chapter review for learning objectives 1, 2 & 7
5. Do Problem Set A and check your answers
6. Read the chapter review for learning objectives 3 - 6
7. Do Problem Set B and check your answers
8. Do the End of Chapter Exercises in this study guide
9. Do the homework assigned by your instructor

CHAPTER LEARNING OBJECTIVES

After studying this chapter, you should be able to answer the following questions:

Q1. What are the relationships among budgets, long-term strategies, and short-term operating plans?
Q2. What is a master budget, and how is it prepared?
Q3. What are budget variances, and how are they calculated?
Q4. What are the differences between static and flexible budgets?
Q5. How are budgets used to monitor and motivate performance?
Q6. What are other approaches to budgeting?
Q7. How is the cash budget developed? (Appendix 10A)

OVERVIEW OF CHAPTER

Budgets are a way for the management of an organization to communicate and promote the organization's long-term and short-term goals, and motivate the appropriate performance of its employees. When budgets are compared to actual results, management can monitor the performance of its business segments.

CHAPTER REVIEW: Learning Objectives 1, 2 & 7

Q1: What are the relationships among budgets, long-term strategies, and short-term operating plans?

A *budget* is a formalized financial plan for an organization's operations for some specified future period. A budget is a translation of an organization's strategies, and is one method of communicating the organization's goals and strategies to managers. Budgets also help define areas of responsibility and decision-making authority, or *decision rights*. The series of steps that an organization follows to develop and use budgets is known as a *budget cycle*.

Q2: What is a master budget, and how is it prepared?

An organization's budget has several subsidiary budgets, and the collection of all of them is known as the *master budget*. The master budget is usually prepared for the upcoming year, but could prepared for a longer period. It is based on predictions of sales and production volumes, operating costs, and selling prices. The collection of these predictions is known as the *budget assumptions*. The subsidiary budgets of the master budget fall into two main categories.

- Operating budgets. The *operating budget* consists of budgets for revenues, production, and operating costs.

- Financial budgets. The *financial budgets* include plans for cash flows, long-term financing, and capital expenditures.

The operating budget's subsidiary budgets are prepared in this order:
1. revenue budget
2. production budget
3. direct materials budget
4. direct labor budget
5. manufacturing overhead budget
6. inventory and cost of goods sold budget
7. support department budgets
8. budgeted income statement

Demonstration problem-Preparing revenue, production, direct material, direct labor, and overhead budgets

Handbroak, Inc. makes a product used by orthopedic surgeons. It expects to sell 10,000 units in April and 12,000 units in May. Budgeted fixed manufacturing overhead is $64,000. Handbroak prefers to end each period with an ending finished goods inventory equal to 10% of the next period's sales in units and a direct materials inventory equal to 15% of the direct materials required for the next period's production. Assume that Handbroak Handbroak never has any beginning or ending work-in-process inventories, and that budgeted production for May is 10,200 units. Other budgeted information follows.

Budgeted selling price per unit	$132.00
Direct materials required per unit	2 lbs
Direct material cost	$3.00 /lb
Direct labor required per unit	1.5 hrs
Direct labor cost	$11.00
Beginning finished goods inventory for April	1,000 units
Beginning direct materials inventory for April	1,400 hrs
Budgeted variable overhead per DL hour	$4.00 /DL hr

Required:
a) Prepare the revenue and production budgets for April.
b) Prepare the direct materials, direct labor, and manufacturing overhead budgets for April.

Solution to demonstration problem

a) Revenue budget

Budgeted sales in units this period	10,000
Budgeted selling price per unit	$132.00
Budgeted revenues	$1,320,000

Production budget

Budgeted sales in units this period	10,000
Desired ending FG inventory	1,200
Total units required	11,200
Less: beginning FG inventory	(1,000)
Required production in units	10,200

b) Direct materials budget

Required production in units	10,200
DM required per unit, in pounds	2
Total DM required, in pounds	20,400
Less: Beginning DM inventory	(1,400)
Plus: Desired ending DM inventory	3,060
Required DM purchases in pounds	22,060
Budgeted DM cost per pound	$3.00
Budgeted cost of DM	$66,180

Direct labor budget

Required production in units	10,200
DL required per unit, in hours	1.5
Total DL hours required	15,300
Budgeted cost per DL hour	$11.00
Budgeted cost of DL	$168,300

Manufactuirng overhead budget

Total DL hours required	15,300
Budgeted variable overhead per DL hour	$4.00
Total budgeted variable overhead	$61,200
Budgeted fixed overhead	64,000
Total budgeted overhead	$125,200

Demonstration problem-Preparing ending inventory, cost of goods sold, & support department budgets and budgeted income statement

Use the information about Handbroak, Inc., from the prior demonstration problem. Assume the costs attached to April's beginning direct materials and finished goods inventory, respectively, are $4,074 and $33,719. You are given the additional information below.

Total budgeted costs for administration	$187,000
Budgeted fixed costs for distribution	$35,000
Budgetd variable costs for distribution	$1.90 /unit
Total budgeted costs for research & development	$281,000
Budgeted fixed costs for marketing	$94,000
Budgeted variable costs for marketing	12% of sales revenue
Income tax rate	28%

Required:

a) Prepare the ending inventories budget and the cost of goods sold budget for April.
b) Prepare the support department budgets for April.
c) Prepare a budgeted income statement for April.

Solution to demonstration problem:

a)
Ending inventories budget

Budgeted cost of DM purchases	$66,180
Beginning DM inventory	4,074
DM available for use	70,254
Budgeted cost of desired ending DM inventory:	
[10,020 units x 2 lbs/unit] x 15% x $3/lb	9,180
Budgeted cost of DM to be used	$61,074

Budgeted cost of DM to be used	$61,074
Budgeted cost of DL	168,300
Total budgeted overhead	125,200
Total budgeted manufacturing costs	$354,574
Required production in units	10,200
Budgeted manufacturing cost per unit	$34.7622
Budgeted ending FG inventory in units	1,200
Budgeted cost of ending FG inventory	$41,715

Cost of goods sold budget

Beginning FG inventory	$33,719
Total budgeted manufacturing costs	354,574
Cost of goods available for sale	388,293
Less: budgeted ending FG inventory	41,715
Budgeted cost of goods sold	$346,578

solution to demonstration problem continues on next page →

Solution to demonstration problem continued

b) Support department budgets

Administration		$187,000
Distribution: Fixed costs	$35,000	
Variable costs	19,000	54,000
Research & development		281,000
Marketing: Fixed costs	$94,000	
Variable costs	158,400	252,400
Total budgeted support department costs		$774,400

c) Budgeted income statement

Sales revenue		$1,320,000
Cost of goods sold		346,578
Gross margin		973,422
Operating costs:		
Administration	$187,000	
Distribution	54,000	
Research & development	281,000	
Marketing	252,400	774,400
Net income before taxes		199,022
Income taxes		55,726
Net income		$143,296

Q7: How is the cash budget developed? (Appendix 10A)

A *cash budget* is prepared after the operating budgets. It includes three types of cash flows:

- Cash receipts. Operating cash receipts are computed based on sales and a company's knowledge about the timing of the collection of accounts receivable collections from customers. Other sources of cash (such as from the sale of used equipment) come from other portions of the budget.

- Cash disbursements. Operating cash disbursements are computed based on the direct materials, direct labor, manufacturing overhead, and support department budgets, combined with a company's knowledge about the timing of its cash disbursements and payments of accounts payable to its suppliers. Other cash disbursements (such as interest payments) come from other portions of the budget.

- Short-term borrowings or investments. After preparing the cash receipts and disbursement budgets, a company will know if and when it will need short-term loans, as well as when any loan repayments can be made or whether it will have excess funds for temporary investments.

Demonstration problem-Preparing the cash budget

Digital Products has already completed its operating budgets, and asks for your help in preparing its cash budgets. They tell you that all sales are on account, and that they collect 75% of accounts receivable in the quarter the sale occurs, and 25% in the following quarter. Accounts payable represents amounts owed to suppliers for direct materials only. The company pays 60% of its accounts payable in the quarter the direct materials are purchased, and pays the remaining 40% in the subsequent quarter. If necessary, the company can get short-term loans (with terms of 90, 120, or 210 days) from the bank, in increments of $10,000. The interest rate is 5% per year. The company repays any such borrowings in the first possible quarter. All direct labor, variable manufacturing overhead, fixed manufacturing overhead, fixed general and administrative costs, and fixed marketing costs are paid in the quarter they are incurred. Variable marketing costs and shipping costs are paid in the quarter after they are incurred. The beginning accounts receivable balance is $37,000, the beginning accounts payable balance is $18,000, and the beginning balance in the cash account is $29,000. You are given the following additional information:

Beginning accounts receivable balance	$37,000
Beginning accounts payable balance	$18,000
Beginning cash balance	$29,000
Variable marketing costs accrued as of beginning of year	$11,000
Shipping costs accrued as of beginning of year	$4,500
Quarterly dividend	$40,000

Information from the operating budget:

	Quarter				
	First	Second	Third	Fourth	Total
Sales	$300,000	$450,000	$600,000	$150,000	$1,500,000
Direct labor	56,400	84,600	112,800	28,200	282,000
Direct material purchases	69,000	103,500	138,000	34,500	345,000
Variable manufacturing overhead	15,600	23,400	31,200	7,800	78,000
Fixed manufacturing overhead	35,500	35,500	35,500	35,500	142,000
Fixed general & administrative costs	50,000	50,000	50,000	50,000	200,000
Fixed marketing costs	25,000	25,000	25,000	25,000	100,000
Variable marketing costs	24,000	36,000	48,000	12,000	120,000
Shipping costs	12,000	18,000	24,000	6,000	60,000

Required:

a) Prepare a cash receipts budget.
b) Prepare a cash disbursements budget.
c) Prepare a cash flow budget.

solution to demonstration problem begins on next page →

Solution to demonstration problem

a) Recall that all sales are on account, and 75% of accounts receivable is collected in the quarter the sale occurs, with the remaining 25% collected in the following quarter.

Cash receipts budget	Quarter				
	First	Second	Third	Fourth	Total
Collections from last year's sales	$37,000				$37,000
Collections from 1st quarter sales	225,000	75,000			300,000
Collections from 2nd quarter sales		337,500	112,500		450,000
Collections from 3rd quarter sales			450,000	150,000	600,000
Collections from 4th quarter sales				112,500	112,500
Total budgeted cash receipts	$262,000	$412,500	$562,500	$262,500	$1,499,500

b) Recall that direct labor, variable manufacturing overhead, fixed manufacturing overhead, fixed general and administrative costs, and fixed marketing costs are paid in the quarter they are incurred; variable marketing costs and shipping costs are paid in the quarter after they are incurred; and 60% of direct materials purchases are paid for in the quarter of the purchase with the remaining 40% paid in the following quarter.

Cash disbursements budget	Quarter				
	First	Second	Third	Fourth	Total
Costs paid as incurred :					
Direct labor	$56,400	$84,600	$112,800	$28,200	$282,000
Variable manufacturing overhead	15,600	23,400	31,200	7,800	78,000
Fixed manufacturing overhead	35,500	35,500	35,500	35,500	142,000
Fixed general & administrative costs	50,000	50,000	50,000	50,000	200,000
Fixed marketing costs	25,000	25,000	25,000	25,000	100,000
Variable marketing costs	11,000	24,000	36,000	48,000	119,000
Shipping costs	4,500	12,000	18,000	24,000	58,500
Payments on account payable:					
Prior quarter's DM purchases	18,000				18,000
First quarter's DM purchases	41,400	27,600			69,000
Second quarter's DM purchases		62,100	41,400		103,500
Third quarter's DM purchases			82,800	55,200	138,000
Fourth quarter's DM purchases				20,700	20,700
Nonoperating cash disbursements:					
Quarterly dividend	40,000	40,000	40,000	40,000	160,000
Total budgetd cash disbursements	$297,400	$384,200	$472,700	$334,400	$1,488,700

solution continues on next page →

Solution to demonstration problem continued

c) Note that the cash flow budget below shows that the company needs to borrow $10,000 at the end of the first quarter, but is able to pay it back, with interest, at the end of the second quarter.

Cash flows budget	Quarter			
	First	Second	Third	Fourth
Beginning cash balance	$29,000	$3,600	$21,775	$111,575
Budgeted cash receipts	262,000	412,500	562,500	262,500
Budgeted cash disbursements	(297,400)	(384,200)	(472,700)	(334,400)
	(6,400)	31,900	111,575	39,675
Required short-term borrowing	10,000			
Payback short-term loan		(10,125)		
Budgeted ending cash balance	$3,600	$21,775	$111,575	$39,675

PROBLEM SET A (Learning Objectives 1, 2, & 7)

True-False: Indicate whether each of the following is true (T) or false (F) in the space provided.

_____ 1. The master budget is a collection of subsidiary budgets.

_____ 2. The revenue budget is the first of the operating budgets prepared.

_____ 3. All budgeted information in the operating budget is in dollars.

_____ 4. All budgeted information in the cash budget is in dollars.

_____ 5. The budgeted income statement is the last operating budget prepared.

_____ 6. A budget is a method of communicating of an organization's strategies to managers and employees.

_____ 7. The operating budget is short-term in nature.

_____ 8. The cash budget is part of the operating budget.

_____ 9. The cost of goods sold budget is a financial budget.

_____ 10. Some financial budgets include longer-term plans than the operating budget.

Exercises: Write your answer in the space provided.
1. Gundiwa Enterprises expects to sell 1,000 units of its product in January and 1,500 in February. Beginning finished goods inventory on January 1 is 120 units. Gundiwa would like to begin each month with a finished goods inventory equal to 15% of the estimated sales for the month. The product sells for $25 per unit.

a) Compute the budgeted revenues for January. _____

b) Compute the budgeted production, in units, required for January. _____

2. Kirkland, Inc has a new division that sells two products, Pings and Pongs, and April will be the first month of its operations. The budgeted selling price per unit for Pings and Pongs is $30 and $20, respectively. It is expected that cash sales will represent 30% of total sales with the rest on account. Kirkland believes that it will collect 50% of credit sales in the month following the sale because it is offering a 2% sales discount to credit customers who pay within this time frame. The company expects the division to collect 47% of credit sales in the month following the sale, with 3% of credit sales being uncollectible. The sales forecast, in units, for the next three months, follows:

	Pings	Pongs
April	11,200	22,500
May	12,600	25,500
June	15,400	30,000

a) Compute the budgeted sales revenues for April, May and June for the new division.

April _____   May _____   June_____

b) Compute the expected cash receipts for April, May, and June for the new division.

April _____   May _____   June_____

3. Max & Rex, Inc. makes large designer cat scratching posts and sells them to pet stores. It expects to sell 28,000 units in June and 30,000 units in July. Budgeted fixed manufacturing overhead is $94,000. Max & Rex prefer to end each period with an ending finished goods inventory equal to 10% of the next period's sales in units and a direct materials inventory equal to 5% of the direct materials required for the next period's production. Max & Rex never have any beginning or ending work-in-process inventories. Assume that budgeted production for July is 30,000 units. Other budgeted information follows.

Budgeted sales in units for June	28,000 units
Budgeted sales in units for July	30,000 units
Budgeted selling price per unit	$45.00
Direct materials required per unit	1.4 lbs
Direct material cost	$2.10 /lb
Direct labor required per unit	0.6 hrs
Direct labor cost	$12.00
Beginning finished goods inventory in June	2,100 units
Beginning direct materials inventory in June	2,500 lbs
Desired FG as % of next period's sales	10%
Desired DM as % of next period's needs	5%
Budgeted variable overhead per DL hour	$2.00 /DL hr

a) Prepare the revenue budget for June.

b) Prepare the production budget for June.

exercise 3 continues on next page →

3. continued

   c) Prepare the direct materials budget for June.

   d) Prepare the direct labor budget for June.

   e) Prepare the manufacturing overhead budget for June.

4. This exercise is a continuation of exercise 3. Before beginning this exercise, check your answers for exercise 3 and correct any errors you made. Use the budgets you prepared for exercise 3. Assume that the costs attached to June's beginning direct materials and finished goods inventories, respectively, are $5,093 and $29,714.

a) Prepare the ending inventories budget for June.

b) Prepare the cost of goods sold budget for June.

5. This exercise is a continuation of exercises 3 & 4. Before beginning this exercise, check your answers for those exercises and correct any errors you made. Use the budgets you prepared for those two exercises and the additional information below.

Total budgeted costs for administration	$56,000
Budgeted fixed costs for distribution	$12,000
Budgetd variable costs for distribution	$0.40 /unit
Total budgeted costs for information systems	$72,000
Budgeted fixed costs for marketing	$37,000
Budgeted variable costs for marketing	10% of sales revenue
Income tax rate	25%

a) Prepare the support department budget for June.

b) Prepare the budgeted income statement for June.

CHAPTER REVIEW: Learning Objectives 3 - 6

Q3: What are budget variances, and how are they calculated?

In order to monitor operations and motivate appropriate performance, managers compare actual operating results to the budget. Any differences are called *budget variances*. If actual revenues exceed the budget or actual costs are lower the variance is said to be *favorable*. If the opposite is true, the variance is *unfavorable*.

After computing budget variances, managers investigate the reasons they occurred. Reasons for favorable variances may give insight as to how this performance might be replicated in future periods or in other segments of the business. Reasons for unfavorable variances are investigated so the cause may be eliminated, if possible. Of course, budgets are merely forecasts of the future and causes for variances might be out of the realm of responsibility of a particular manager or employee. Additionally, an investigation into budget variances might uncover flaws in the information gathering process used to create the budget.

Q4: What are the differences between static and flexible budgets?

A budget prepared for only one level of sales volume is called a *static budget*. However, using the CVP assumptions from Chapter 3, a budget can be prepared for several possible sales levels within the relevant range. This is called a *flexible budget*. Although a company is likely to prepare a series of flexible budgets at the beginning of the period, the budget for one volume level will be designated as the static budget. At the end of the year, when actual results are compared to budgeted results, any variances from the static budget are called *static budget variances*. Also at the end of the year, a flexible budget that is based on the actual output volume is prepared and variations of actual results from this budget are called *flexible budget variances*.

Demonstration problem-Preparing flexible budgets

Cleo Corporation asks for your help preparing its budget. The budget assumptions are as follows:

Budgeted selling price per unit	$24.00
Budgeted variable production costs per unit	$6.00
Budgeted fixed production costs	$11,200
Budgeted variable nonmanufacturing costs per unit	$2.00
Budgeted fixed nonmanufacturing costs	$9,800

Required:

Prepare a series of flexible budgets for 1,600, 1,700, and 1,800 units of sales.

solution to demonstration problem begins on next page →

Solution to demonstration problem

Sales in units	1,600	1,700	1,800
Revenues	$38,400	$40,800	$43,200
Variable production costs	9,600	10,200	10,800
Variable non-manufacturing costs	3,200	3,400	3,600
Contribution margin	25,600	27,200	28,800
Fixed production costs	11,200	11,200	11,200
Fixed nonmanufacturing costs	9,800	9,800	9,800
Operating income	$4,600	$6,200	$7,800

Q5: How are budgets used to monitor and motivate performance?

Very often the best available information comes from the individuals whose performance may be judged by a comparison of budgeted to actual results. When these people are involved in the budget process, this is called *participative budgeting*. The advantage of this is the potential for better budget information and the likelihood of individuals agreeing that the budget is "fair". The disadvantage is hopefully clear; there is an incentive for individuals to misrepresent the budgetary information. By setting revenue targets low or cost targets high, favorable budget variances will be easier to achieve. If this occurs, it is called *budgetary slack*.

As organizations age, it is possible the department managers "get used to" their budgets, which decreases the incentive for them to find ways to cut costs. Under *zero-based budgeting*, each manager must justify each cost line item in the budget every time a budget is prepared, as opposed to an approach where a manager might merely need to justify increases in the budget from last year.

If budget variances are used to assess managerial performance, it is important to use the right budget variances. For fixed costs, static budget variances equal the flexible budget variances. This is not true for variable costs or for revenues, however. If the actual sales volume is substantially lower than planned in the static budget, a manager's static budget variances may possibly be favorable, even if the manager did a poor job of controlling those variable costs.

It is important to use budget variances to assess managerial performance only for areas where the manager has control of the cost or revenue. Make sure you review Exhibit 10.6 in the text; it is an excellent summary of some of the challenges that can occur when using budget variances for performance assessment.

Demonstration problem-Computing flexible and static budget variances

After your assistance with the flexible budgets at the beginning of the year, the owner of Cleo Corporation designated the budget column for 1,700 units of sales as the static budget. At the end of the year, Cleo comes to you again for help in comparing the actual results shown below to the budget.

	Actual Results
Sales in units	1,590
Revenues	$37,800
Variable production costs	10,100
Variable non-manufacturing costs	3,000
Contribution margin	24,700
Fixed production costs	11,400
Fixed nonmanufacturing costs	10,200
Operating income	$3,100

Required:
a) Compute the static budget variances for all budget line items.
b) Explain to Cleo why some of the variances are favorable even though actual operating income was only half what was budgeted in the static budget.
c) Compute the flexible budget variances for all budget line items.
d) Explain the differences in all of the static budget and flexible budget variances to Cleo.

Solution to demonstration problem
a)

	Actual Results	Static Budget	Static Budget Variance	
Sales in units	1,590	1,700		
Revenues	$37,800	$40,800	$3,000	Unfavorable
Variable production costs	10,100	10,200	100	Favorable
Variable non-manufacturing costs	3,000	3,400	400	Favorable
Contribution margin	24,700	27,200	2,500	Unfavorable
Fixed production costs	11,400	11,200	200	Unfavorable
Fixed nonmanufacturing costs	10,200	9,800	400	Unfavorable
Operating income	$3,100	$6,200	$3,100	Unfavorable

b) The static budget variances for the two variable costs are favorable because the actual costs were lower than the budgeted costs. However, actual sales volume was much lower than budgeted, so one would expect variable costs to be lower. The favorable variances do not show whether or not these costs were managed well. For this, Cleo needs to look at the flexible budget variances.

solution to demonstration problem continues on next page →

Solution to demonstration problem continued

c)

	Actual Results	Flexible Budget	Flexible Budget Variance	
Sales in units	1,590	1,590		
Revenues	$37,800	$38,160	$360	Unfavorable
Variable production costs	10,100	9,540	560	Unfavorable
Variable non-manufacturing costs	3,000	3,180	180	Favorable
Contribution margin	24,700	25,440	740	Unfavorable
Fixed production costs	11,400	11,200	200	Unfavorable
Fixed nonmanufacturing costs	10,200	9,800	400	Unfavorable
Operating income	$3,100	$4,440	$1,340	Unfavorable

d) The basic difference between static and flexible budget variances is that variations due solely to sales volume are excluded from the flexible budget variances. This is why the static budget variances (SBVs) for the fixed costs are the same as the flexible budget variances (FBVs). For example, the SBV for revenues of $3,000 unfavorable shows that actual revenues were $3,000 less than budgeted. This is partially due to that fact that actual sales were 110 units below what was planned, but it also could include the effects of an average selling price that differs from the $24 budgeted selling price. The FBV for revenue of $360 unfavorable, on the other hand reflects only that the average selling price was less than the budgeted selling price. Note that the average selling price was $37,800/1,590 units = $23.7736/unit. The FBV can be calculated as [$24 - $23.7736]/unit x 1,590 units.

The SBV for variable production costs was favorable, but when the effect of the volume difference is removed, the FBV was $560 unfavorable. This tells Cleo that the average variable production costs were higher than the budgeted cost of $6/unit. In fact, the average actual variable production costs per unit were $10,100/1,590 units = $6.3522/unit, and the FBV can be calculated as [$6.3522 - $6]/unit x 1,590 units.

The SBV for variable non-manufacturing costs was favorable, and even after the effect of the volume difference is removed, the FBV was $180 favorable, so Cleo knows that the average variable non-manufacturing costs were lower than the budgeted cost of $2/unit. The average actual variable production costs per unit were $3,000/1,590 units = $1.8868/unit, and the FBV can be calculated as [$2 - $1.8868]/unit x 1,590 units.

For a fair assessment of a manager's performance the flexible budget that is created for comparison to actual results may contain adjustments other than volume adjustments. For example, if a supplier increased its prices (and if negotiating these prices is not the manager's responsibility), then the increased cost may be used.

Q6: What are other approaches to budgeting?

Other approaches to budgeting include:

- Long term budgets. Companies prepare budgets for periods longer than one year in order to plan how to best meet long-term strategic goals.

- Rolling budgets. A *rolling budget* is prepared frequently (monthly or quarterly). As each period's actual results are compared to the budget, the next period's budget incorporates any necessary changes.

- Activity-based budgets. The simple budgets prepared for Cleo Corporation in the demonstration problem used only a few budget lines, with only the number of units as the cost driver for variable cost. *Activity-based budgets* use more cost pools of the costs of activities, with each activity cost pool having its own cost driver.

- Kaizen budgets. In *kaizen costing*, cost reductions are planned over time. For example, a company may expect increasing labor efficiency and decreasing cost of inputs in the future. The company may budget that each period's raw materials costs will be 90% of the costs of the prior period, and that each period's labor costs will be 95% of the prior period.

- Extreme programming. Some large and or long-term projects are difficult to budget because costs or available technology change so quickly. *Extreme programming* is often used to manage information technology (IT) projects. Under extreme programming, the IT project begins without much up-front planning, and the project, and its budget, change as new choices, project objectives, or technology arise.

PROBLEM SET B (Learning Objectives 3 - 6)

<u>Matching</u>: Match each term with the appropriate definition or phrase. You may use each term more than once.

Terms	
A. Favorable	H. Unfavorable
B. Static budget variance	I. Flexible budget variance
C. Participative budgeting	J. Budgetary slack
D. Static budget	K. Flexible budget
E. Zero-based budgeting	L. Rolling budget
F. Activity-based budget	M. Kaizen budgets
G. Long-term budgets	N. Extreme programming

_____ 1. Each consecutive budget shows decreasing costs

_____ 2. Budget shows costs higher than it should so that favorable budget variances are easy to attain

_____ 3. A budget variance where actual revenues are higher than budgeted revenues

_____ 4. Budgets are prepared "bottom-up"

_____ 5. Budget prepared at the beginning of the period for one volume level

_____ 6. Budget prepared at the beginning of the period for several volume levels

_____ 7. Budget prepared that covers several periods

_____ 8. Managers must justify every cost each budget period

_____ 9. The difference between actual results and budgeted results where the budget is at a different volume level than was actually achieved

_____ 10. The difference between actual results and budgeted results where the budget is at the same volume level as was actually achieved

_____ 11. Little up-front planning

_____ 12. Each successive period's budget is updated with information gained from the last period's comparison of budgeted and actual results

_____ 13. A budget variance where actual costs are higher than budgeted costs

_____ 14. A budget with more cost pools and cost drivers than traditional budgets

_____ 15. Under this type of budgeting, the total budgeted cost of a project is not known when the project begins

_____ 16. A budget prepared at the end of the period for a volume level equal to the level actually achieved

_____ 17. This could cause budgetary slack

_____ 18. This may help managers and employees to "buy-in" to the budget

_____ 19. For fixed costs, this is the same as the flexible budget variance

_____ 20. Used in industries where producers expect increased efficiency or decreasing input costs

<u>True-False</u>: Indicate whether each of the following is true (T) or false (F) in the space provided.

_____ 1. If actual volume exceeds the static budget volume, then all static budget variances will be unfavorable.

_____ 2. If actual volume exceeds the static budget volume, then the static budget variance for revenues will be favorable.

_____ 3. If actual volume exceeds the static budget volume, then the static budget variance for fixed costs will be unfavorable.

_____ 4. The static budget variance equals the flexible budget variance for fixed costs if actual volume exceeds the static budget volume.

_____ 5. The static budget variance equals the flexible budget variance for fixed costs if actual volume is lower than the static budget volume.

_____ 6. If actual volume exceeds the static budget volume, then the static budget variance for variable costs will be unfavorable.

_____ 7. An unfavorable flexible budget variance for revenues means that the average actual selling price per unit was lower than the budgeted selling price per unit.

_____ 8. An unfavorable flexible budget variance for variable costs means that the average actual variable cost per unit was higher than the budgeted variable cost per unit.

_____ 9. Suppose the static and flexible budget variances for revenue are both favorable. Then actual volume exceeded the static budget volume and the average actual selling price per unit exceeded the budgeted selling price per unit.

_____ 10. Suppose the static budget variance and the flexible budget variance for variable costs are both favorable. Then actual volume exceeded the static budget volume and the average actual variable cost per unit was lower than the budgeted variable cost per unit.

<u>Exercises</u>: Write your answer in the space provided.
1. You are given the following budgeted information for Tuck's Treasures:

Budgeted selling price per unit	$38.50
Budgeted variable production costs per unit	$7.00
Budgeted fixed production costs	$167,000
Budgeted variable nonmanufacturing costs per unit	$3.50
Budgeted fixed nonmanufacturing costs	$46,000

Prepare a series of flexible budgets for 10,000, 11,000, and 12,000 units of sales.

2. You were recently hired by Martha Manufacturing. When you move into your new office vacated by the recently fired accountant, you find it to be a disaster, with papers and empty fast food containers everywhere. Martha asks you a question about the budget, and all you can find is a budget prepared at the beginning of the year that has ketchup smeared all over it.

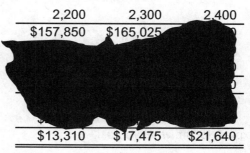

Sales in units	2,200	2,300	2,400
Revenues	$157,850	$165,025	
Variable production costs			
Variable non-manufacturing costs			
Contribution margin			
Fixed production costs			
Fixed nonmanufacturing costs			
Operating income	$13,310	$17,475	$21,640

Martha recalls that budgeted variable production costs were $27.80 per unit and that budgeted fixed production costs were $57,120. Use the techniques you learned in Chapter 2 to compute the following:

Budgeted variable non-manufacturing costs per unit _____

Budgeted fixed non-manufacturing costs _____

3. A bookkeeper for Medina Corporation prepared the following performance report for the last period:

	Actual Results	Static Budget	Difference
Sales in units	32,000	30,000	
Direct materials	$260,820	$240,000	$20,820
Direct labor	112,700	96,000	16,700
Depreciation	36,000	36,000	0
Indirect materials	17,710	15,000	2,710
Insurance	28,000	28,800	(800)
Indirect labor	53,130	48,000	5,130
Property taxes	44,000	43,200	800
Totals	$552,360	$507,000	$45,360

The factory supervisor goes to lunch with you one day and complains that president of Medina blamed him for the additional $45,000 of costs incurred, and he's thinking of quitting.

a) Prepare an improved performance report to show your friend.

b) Explain to him what you did.

_____

_____

_____

_____

_____

4. This is a continuation of exercise 3, so check your answer to exercise 3 before doing this exercise. After seeing your improved report, your friend is still unhappy. He tells you that there was a 20% increase in the direct materials cost from the supplier, and complains that the purchasing manager accepted this supplier's cost increase without ever negotiating with the supplier. Also, a new union contract signed shortly after the beginning of the year gave a 15% wage hike to all direct and indirect labor employees. Because of these increased costs of his inputs, he reorganized the work flow in the factory to attain better efficiency. He's upset because the president doesn't appreciate his efforts.

a) Revise the report you prepared in exercise 3.

b) Prepare a brief memo to the president to explain the report

_____

_____

_____

_____

_____

_____

_____

_____

END OF CHAPTER EXERCISES

Multiple choice: Write the letter that represents the best choice in the space provided.

Use the following information for questions 1 – 7:

	January	February	March	April
Sales	$26,400	$23,100	$33,000	$25,000
Production in units	990	1,440	1,710	1,200

Sales are 30% cash and 70% on account, and 60% of credit sales are collected in the month of the sale. In the month after the sale, 30% of credit sales are collected. The remainder is collected two months after the sale. It takes 4 pounds of direct material to produce a finished unit, and direct materials cost $5 per pound. All direct materials purchases are on account, and are paid as follows: 40% in the month of the purchase, 50% the following month, and 10% in the second month following the purchase. Ending direct materials inventory for each month is 40% of the next month's production needs. January's beginning materials inventory is 1,080 pounds. Suppose that both accounts receivable and accounts payable are zero at the beginning of January.

_____ 1. Total cash sales for the January – March quarter are
   a. $69,135
   b. $62,700
   c. $24,750
   d. $49,500

_____ 2. The accounts receivable balance at the end of March is
   a. $9,240
   b. $17,325
   c. $15,477
   d. $10,857

_____ 3. The ending direct materials inventory for March is
   a. 1,920 pounds
   b. 6,960 pounds
   c. 2,736 pounds
   d. 6,120 pounds

_____ 4. Material purchases for February are
   a. 8,496 pounds
   b. 6,192 pounds
   c. 5,868 pounds
   d. 5,328 pounds

_____ 5. Cash payments on account for February are
   a. $30,960
   b. $12,384
   c. $30,120
   d. $25,344

_____ 6. The ending balance in accounts payable for March is
   a. $30,120
   b. $65,832
   c. $18,072
   d. $21,168

_____ 7. The net change in cash for the period January – March is
   a. $4,500 decrease
   b. $339 increase
   c. $5,811 increase
   d. $1,222 decrease

_____ 8. Which of the following partial budget sequences is correct?
   a. sales, overhead, direct labor, income statement
   b. production, direct materials, cash, income statement
   c. direct labor, direct materials, overhead, production
   d. cost of goods sold, income statement, cash

_____ 9. Which of the following correctly describes budgeted direct materials purchases?
   a. production needs + desired ending inventory – beginning inventory
   b. production needs + beginning inventory– desired ending inventory
   c. sales + desired production – beginning inventory
   d. beginning inventory + desired production – desired ending inventory

_____ 10. The difference between a static budget and a flexible budget is that
   a. a static budget is for fixed costs and a flexible budget is for variable costs
   b. a static budget is for a fixed time period and a flexible budget is several different time periods
   c. a static budget is prepared for a single volume level and a flexible budget is for several different volume levels
   d. a static budget is prepared for the long-term and a flexible budget is prepared for the short-term

_____ 11. When upper-level management prepares a budget with consultations from managers and employees, the firm has a
   a. participative budget
   b. zero-based budget
   c. flexible budget
   d. activity-based budget

Use the following information for questions 12 – 13:
Bynsel, Inc., a retailer, projects the following purchases and sales of its product for the next 4 months:

	In Units	
Month	Purchases	Sales
1	300	200
2	400	300
3	300	400
4	400	300

Each unit costs $100, and all purchases are on account. Two-thirds of purchases are paid in the month of the purchase and one-third are paid in the month following the purchase.   Bynsel gets a 3% discount whenever it pays in the month of the purchase. The selling price per unit is $200. Sales are 60% cash and 40% on customer credit cards. The bank charges Bynsel a 5% fee for each credit card transaction and transfers the funds to Bynsel's checking account on the same day as the credit card sale.

_____ 12. What are cash receipts for the third month?
  a. $78,400
  b. $58,800
  c. $124,000
  d. $76,000

_____ 13. What are cash disbursements for the third month?
  a. $36,367
  b. $23,033
  c. $33,333
  d. $32,733

_____ 14. Which of the following phrases should not be associated with kaizen budgeting?
  a. participative budgeting
  b. activity-based budgeting
  c. flexible budgeting
  d. budgetary slack

_____ 15. Which of the following phrases should not be associated with participative budgeting?
  a. activity-based budgeting
  b. bottom-up
  c. budgetary slack
  d. top-down

Exercises: Write your answer in the space provided.
1. Misha's Mugs makes decorative beer steins and sells them to pubs. Misha's budget assumptions for the year, and its actual results for the year follow:

	Budgeted			Actual Results
Sales in units	23,000		Sales in units	24,390
Selling price	$21.00	/unit	Revenues	$499,995
Direct materials costs	$4.00	/unit	Direct materials costs	92,682
Direct labor costs	$0.75	/unit	Direct labor costs	26,829
Variable overhead costs	$0.80	/unit	Variable overhead costs	24,390
Fixed manufacturing costs	$87,000		Variable shipping costs	25,610
Variable shipping costs	$1.10	/unit	Variable marketing costs	56,097
Variable marketing costs	$2.20	/unit	Contribution margin	274,387
Fixed administrative costs	$72,000		Fixed manufacturing costs	92,000
Fixed shipping costs	$9,850		Fixed administrative costs	73,000
Fixed marketing costs	$42,000		Fixed shipping costs	7,000
			Fixed marketing costs	35,000
			Operating income	$67,387

a) Prepare a report that compares the static budget to the actual results.

	Actual Results	Static Budget	Static Budget Variance	Favorable or Unfavorable
Sales in units	24,390	23,000		
Revenues	$499,995			
Direct materials costs	$92,682			
Direct labor costs	$26,829			
Variable overhead costs	$24,390			
Variable shipping costs	$25,610			
Variable marketing costs	$56,097			
Contribution margin	$274,387			
Fixed manufacturing costs	$92,000			
Fixed administrative costs	$73,000			
Fixed shipping costs	$7,000			
Fixed marketing costs	$35,000			
Operating income	$67,387			

exercise 1 continues on next page →

1. continued

    b) Prepare a report that compares the actual results to a flexible budget.

	Actual Results	Flexible Budget	Flexible Budget Variance	Favorable or Unfavorable
Sales in units	24,390			
Revenues	$499,995			
Direct materials costs	$92,682			
Direct labor costs	$26,829			
Variable overhead costs	$24,390			
Variable shipping costs	$25,610			
Variable marketing costs	$56,097			
Contribution margin	$274,387			
Fixed manufacturing costs	$92,000			
Fixed administrative costs	$73,000			
Fixed shipping costs	$7,000			
Fixed marketing costs	$35,000			
Operating income	$67,387			

2. This exercise is a continuation of exercise 1. Before beginning this exercise, you should check your answers for exercise 1 and correct any errors you made. Suppose Bob is responsible for the purchase and use of direct materials. What can you say about Bob's performance this last period?

_____

_____

_____

_____

3. Refer to exercise 1. Suppose Sally, the sales manager, is responsible for sales and all marketing costs. This year Sally decreased her people's salaries slightly but increased the commission rate. What can you say about Sally's performance this year?

_____

_____

_____

_____

_____

_____

_____

_____

_____

_____

_____

_____

_____

4. Refer to exercise 1. Suppose Dan is responsible for all distribution costs. This year Dan renegotiated his arrangements with outside shipping agents. What can you say about Dan's performance this year?

_____

_____

_____

_____

_____

SOLUTION TO PROBLEM SET A

True-False:

1. T
2. T
3. F   Some of it is in units, or pounds, or grams, or hours
4. T
5. T
6. T
7. T
8. F
9. F   It is an operating budget
10. T

Exercises:

1. a) 1,000 units x $25/unit = $25,000
   b) The required ending inventory is 15% x 1,500 units of planned sales for February = 225 units. 120 units in BI + required production – 1,000 units of sales = 225 units in ending inventory. Solve for required production to get 1,105 units.

2. a)

	April	May	June	Total
Revenue from Pings	$336,000	$378,000	$462,000	$1,176,000
Revenue from Pongs	450,000	510,000	600,000	1,560,000
	$786,000	$888,000	$1,062,000	$2,736,000

b)

	April	May	June	Total
Cash sales	$235,800	$266,400	$318,600	$820,800
Collections on April's sales		269,598	258,594	528,192
Collections on May's sales			304,584	304,584
	$235,800	$535,998	$881,778	$1,653,576

3. a) Revenue budget

Budgeted sales in units this period	28,000
Budgeted selling price per unit	$45.00
Budgeted revenues	$1,260,000

b) Production budget

Budgeted sales in units this period	28,000
Desired ending FG inventory	3,000
Total units required	31,000
Less: beginning FG inventory	(2,100)
Required production in units	28,900

3. c)   Direct materials budget

Required production in units	28,900
DM required per unit, in pounds	1.4
Total DM required, in pounds	40,460
Less: Beginning DM inventory	(2,500)
Plus: Desired ending DM inventory	2,100
Required DM purchases in pounds	40,060 (30,000 x 1.4 x 5%)
Budgeted DM cost per pound	$2.10
Budgeted cost of DM	$84,126

d)   Direct labor budget

Required production in units	28,900
DL required per unit, in hours	0.6
Total DL hours required	17,340
Budgeted cost per DL hour	$12.00
Budgeted cost of DL	$208,080

e)   Manufactuirng overhead budget

Total DL hours required	17,340
Budgeted variable overhead per DL hour	$2.00
Total budgeted variable overhead	$34,680
Budgeted fixed overhead	94,000
Total budgeted overhead	$128,680

4. a)   Ending inventories budget

Budgeted cost of DM purchases	$84,126
Beginning DM inventory	5,093
DM available for use	89,219
Budgeted cost of desired ending DM inventory:	
[30,000 units x 1.4 lbs/unit] x 5% x $2.10/lb	2,102
Budgeted cost of DM to be used	$87,117

Budgeted cost of DM to be used	$87,117
Budgeted cost of DL	208,080
Total budgeted overhead	128,680
Total budgeted manufacturing costs	$423,877
Required production in units	28,900
Budgeted manufacturing cost per unit	$14.667
Budgeted ending FG inventory in units	3,000
Budgeted cost of ending FG inventory	$44,001

4. b) <u>Cost of goods sold budget</u>

Beginning FG inventory	$29,714
Total budgeted manufacturing costs	423,877
Cost of goods available for sale	453,591
Less: budgeted ending FG inventory	44,001
Budgeted cost of goods sold	$409,590

5. a) <u>Support department budgets</u>

Administration		$56,000
Distribution: Fixed costs	$12,000	
Variable costs	11,200	23,200
Information systems		72,000
Marketing: Fixed costs	$37,000	
Variable costs	126,000	163,000
Total budgeted support department costs		$314,200

b) <u>Budgeted income statement</u>

Sales revenue		$1,260,000
Cost of goods sold		409,590
Gross margin		850,410
Operating costs:		
Administration	$56,000	
Distribution	23,200	
Information systems	72,000	
Marketing	163,000	314,200
Net income before taxes		536,210
Income taxes		134,053
Net income		$402,158

SOLUTION TO PROBLEM SET B

Matching:

1. M
2. J
3. A
4. C
5. D
6. K
7. G
8. E
9. B
10. I
11. N
12. L
13. H
14. F
15. N
16. K
17. C
18. C
19. B
20. M

True-False:

1. F   If actual volume exceeds static budget volume, then most likely (unless the actual average selling price per unit was far below what was budgeted) the SBV for revenue is favorable.
2. F   This is likely to be true, but if the actual average selling price per unit was far below what was budgeted, then it may not be true.
3. F   The SBV for fixed costs is unrelated to sales volume.
4. T   These are both true because the FBV removes the effects of volume
5. T   differences from the SBV, and there is no volume difference for fixed costs.
6. F   This is likely to be true, but if the actual average variable price per unit was far below what was budgeted, then it may not be true.
7. T
8. T
9. T
10. F   It is true that a favorable FBV for variable costs means that the actual average variable price per unit was below what was budgeted. However, a favorable SBV for variable costs does not necessarily imply that actual volume exceeded the static budget volume.

Exercises:

1.

Sales in units	10,000	11,000	12,000
Revenues	$385,000	$423,500	$462,000
Variable production costs	70,000	77,000	84,000
Variable non-manufacturing costs	35,000	38,500	42,000
Contribution margin	280,000	308,000	336,000
Fixed production costs	167,000	167,000	167,000
Fixed nonmanufacturing costs	46,000	46,000	46,000
Operating income	$67,000	$95,000	$123,000

2. By subtracting income from revenue, determine that the total costs at 2,200 units of sales equal $144,540, and that the total costs at 2,300 units of sales equal $147,550. The increase in costs is $147,550 - $144,540 = $3,010. To compute the slope of the total cost line, which is variable costs per unit: slope = $3,010/100 units = $30.10 per unit.

Then use the equation of a line to compute total fixed costs:
$144,540 = $30.10/unit x 2,200 units + total fixed costs
$144,540 = $66,220 + total fixed costs
$78,320 = total fixed costs

Since Martha remembers that budgeted variable production costs were $27.80 per unit, the budgeted variable non-manufacturing costs per unit must be $30.10 - $27.80 = $2.30 per unit.

Since Martha remembers that budgeted fixed production costs were $57,120, the budgeted fixed non-manufacturing costs must be $78,230 - $57,120 = $21,200.

3. a)

	Actual Results	Flexible Budget	Flexible Budget Variance	
Sales in units	32,000	32,000		
Direct materials	$260,820	$256,000	$4,820	Unfavorable
Direct labor	112,700	102,400	10,300	Unfavorable
Depreciation	36,000	36,000	0	
Indirect materials	17,710	16,000	1,710	Unfavorable
Insurance	28,000	28,800	800	Favorable
Indirect labor	53,130	51,200	1,930	Unfavorable
Property taxes	44,000	43,200	800	Unfavorable
Totals	$552,360	$533,600	$18,760	Unfavorable

b) Part of the reason the factory supervisor's performance seemed poor in the report the bookkeeper prepared is that actual volume exceeded the static budget volume by 2,000 units, so of course costs would be higher. The flexible budget variance removes this volume effect.

4. a)

	Actual Results	Adjusted Flexible Budget	Flexible Budget Variance	
Sales in units	32,000	32,000		
Direct materials	$260,820	$307,200	$46,380	Favorable
Direct labor	112,700	117,760	5,060	Favorable
Depreciation	36,000	36,000	0	
Indirect materials	17,710	16,000	1,710	Unfavorable
Insurance	28,000	28,800	800	Favorable
Indirect labor	53,130	58,880	5,750	Favorable
Property taxes	44,000	43,200	800	Unfavorable
Totals	$552,360	$607,840	$55,480	Favorable

b) Memo: A manager's performance should not be based on a comparison of actual results to the static budget. When actual sales volumes exceed the volume of the static budget, variable costs should be expected to be higher than shown in the static budget. This report compares actual results to a flexible budget based on the actual sales volume achieved. Additionally, the supplier of the direct materials increased its prices by 20%, and this is the responsibility of the purchasing manager, not of the factory supervisor. The factory supervisor is also not responsible for the 15% wage increase mandated by the new union contract. This flexible budget is based on these higher costs for materials and labor.

In response to these cost increases, the factory supervisor reorganized the work flow in the factory to improve efficiency. You can see the results of his efforts by noting the favorable variances for direct materials, direct labor, and indirect labor. The total of these variances are $57,190 favorable. If he hadn't done this reorganization, the company's operating income would be $57,190 lower than it was. Since these are the only cost items for which he has control, then he in fact saved the company $57,190. He should be commended and rewarded, rather than reprimanded.

SOLUTION TO END OF CHAPTER EXERCISES

Multiple choice:

1. C   The total sales in the 3 month quarter are $82,500. $82,500 x 30% = $24,750.

2. D   At the end of March, 40% sales for March remain uncollected; this is $33,000 x 70% x 40% = $9,240. Also uncollected at the end of March is 10% of February's credit sales.; this is $23,100 x 70% x 10% = $1,617. The accounts receivable balance at the end of March is $9,240 + $1,617 = $10,857.

3. A   For April, required materials will be 1,200 units x 4 lbs/unit = 4,800 lbs. At the end of March, the desired ending materials inventory will be 40% of this: 4,800 lbs x 40% = 1,920 lbs.

4. B   The beginning materials inventory for February will be 40% of February's needs for production: 1,440 units x 4 lbs/unit x 40% = 2,304 lbs. The ending materials inventory for February will be 40% of March's needs for production: 1,710 units x 4 lbs/unit x 40% = 2,736 lbs. February's production will use 1,440 units x 4 lbs/unit = 5,760 lbs. Beginning inventory of 2,304 lbs + purchases of materials – materials used in production 5,760 lbs = 2,736 lbs ending inventory. Solve for materials purchased to get 6,192 lbs.

5. D   We know from #4 that February material purchases was 6,192 lbs, which cost 6,192 lbs x $5/lb = $30,960. But we also need to know January's purchases. January's ending inventory will be 2,304 lbs (same as the beginning inventory for February computed in #4). January's materials usage will be 990 units x 4 lbs/unit = 3,960 lbs. Beginning inventory of 1,080 lbs + purchases of materials – materials used in production 3,960 lbs = 2,304 lbs ending inventory. Solve for materials purchased to get 5,184 lbs, which will cost 5,184 lbs x $5/lb = $25,920. In February we pay 40% of February's purchases plus 50% of January's purchases: 40% x $30,960 + 50% x $25,920 = $25,344.

6. D   The ending balance in accounts payable for March will be 10% of February's purchases plus 60% of March's purchases, so we need to compute March's purchases. March's beginning inventory will be 2,736 lbs (same as the ending inventory for February computed in #4). March's materials usage will be 1,710 units x 4 lbs/unit = 6,840 lbs. March's ending inventory will be 40% of April's requirements: 1,200 units x 4 lbs/unit x 40% = 1,920 units (computed for #3). Beginning inventory of 2,736 lbs + purchases of materials – materials used in production 6,8240lbs = 1,920 lbs ending inventory. Solve for materials purchased to get 6,024 lbs, which will cost 6,024 lbs x $5/lb = $30,120. The ending balance for accounts payable for March is $30,960x 10% + $30,120 x 60% = $21,168.

7. C   Total sales for the period are $82,500, less the ending accounts receivable balance of $10,857 = $71,643 of cash receipts. Total purchases for January through March = $25,920 + $30,960 + $30,120 = $87,000. Cash disbursements = $87,000 – ending balance in accounts payable $21,168 = $65,832. Net increase in cash = $71,643 receipts - $65,832 disbursements = $5,811.

8. D

9. A
10. C
11. A
12. A   Sales for the third month are 400 units x $200/unit = $80,000. Cash receipts for the third month are 60% x $80,000 cash sales + 40% x $80,000 x 95% credit card sales = $78,400.
13. D   Purchases for the third month will be 300 units x $100/unit = $30,000. Purchases for the second month will be 400 units x $100/unit = $40,000. Cash disbursements for the third month are 2/3 x $30,000 x 97% because of discount + 1/3 x $40,000 = $32,733.
14. D
15. D

Exercises:

1. a)

	Actual Results	Static Budget	Static Budget Variance	
Sales in units	24,390	23,000		
Revenues	$499,995	$483,000	$16,995	Favorable
Direct materials costs	92,682	92,000	682	Unfavorable
Direct labor costs	26,829	17,250	9,579	Unfavorable
Variable overhead costs	24,390	18,400	5,990	Unfavorable
Variable shipping costs	25,610	25,300	310	Unfavorable
Variable marketing costs	56,097	50,600	5,497	Unfavorable
Contribution margin	$274,387	$279,450	$5,063	Unfavorable
Fixed manufacturing costs	92,000	87,000	5,000	Unfavorable
Fixed administrative costs	73,000	72,000	1,000	Unfavorable
Fixed shipping costs	7,000	9,850	2,850	Favorable
Fixed marketing costs	35,000	42,000	7,000	Favorable
Operating income	$67,387	$68,600	$1,213	Unfavorable

1. b)

	Actual Results	Flexible Budget	Flexible Budget Variance	
Sales in units	24,390	24,390		
Revenues	$499,995	$512,190	$12,195	Unfavorable
Direct materials costs	92,682	97,560	4,878	Favorable
Direct labor costs	26,829	18,293	8,536	Unfavorable
Variable overhead costs	24,390	19,512	4,878	Unfavorable
Variable shipping costs	25,610	26,829	1,219	Favorable
Variable marketing costs	56,097	53,658	2,439	Unfavorable
Contribution margin	$274,387	$296,338	$21,951	Unfavorable
Fixed manufacturing costs	92,000	87,000	5,000	Unfavorable
Fixed administrative costs	73,000	72,000	1,000	Unfavorable
Fixed shipping costs	7,000	9,850	2,850	Favorable
Fixed marketing costs	35,000	42,000	7,000	Favorable
Operating income	$67,387	$85,488	$18,101	Unfavorable

2. The $682 unfavorable SBV is not relevant for assessing Bob's performance because Bob is not responsible for the increase in sales levels. The FBV shows that Bob was efficient in his purchasing and use of direct materials, saving the company $4,878.

3. Sally's SBV for revenues was $16,995 favorable, and the FBV was $12,195 unfavorable. The unfavorable FBV shows that the actual average selling price was less than was budgeted. Perhaps Sally told her salespeople to reduce the price in order to sell more units. If so, it was a good move on her part because the loss of revenue from the decreased selling price ($12,915) was small enough that it didn't offset the revenues from the increased number of units sold. Overall, Sally brought in $16,995 more revenues than expected. Notice that it is appropriate to use the SBV to measure Sally's performance, even though we normally use the FBV. This is because Sally is responsible for the changes in volume levels.

Sally's decision to decrease salaries and increase commissions was also a good decision. The decrease in salaries saved $7,000, and the increase in commissions only cost $2,439 more than budgeted. The net savings of this decision was an increase in operating income of $4,561. This decision also may very well be at least partly responsible for the increase in sales levels.

4. Dan's renegotiations were very favorable. He saved the company $2,850 in fixed costs and $1,220 in variable costs for a total savings of $4,070.

Chapter 11

Standard Costs and
Variance Analysis

√ **Study Checklist – Monitor your progress**

1. Read the chapter in the text
2. Review the learning objectives below
3. Read the overview of the chapter
4. Read the chapter review for learning objectives 1 - 4
5. Do Problem Set A and check your answers
6. Read the chapter review for learning objectives 5 - 8
7. Do Problem Set B and check your answers
8. Do the End of Chapter Exercises in this study guide
9. Do the homework assigned by your instructor

CHAPTER LEARNING OBJECTIVES
After studying this chapter, you should be able to answer the following questions:
Q1. How are standard costs established?
Q2. What is variance analysis, and how is it performed?
Q3. How are direct cost variances calculated?
Q4. How is direct cost variance information analyzed and used?
Q5. How are variable and fixed overhead variances calculated?
Q6. How is overhead variance information analyzed and used?
Q7. How are manufacturing cost variances closed?
Q8: Which profit-related variances are commonly analyzed? (Appendix 11A)

OVERVIEW OF CHAPTER
By comparing actual results of operations to budgets, managers are able to monitor operations. Reasons for the variance from budgets are investigated, and managers learn how to improve business processes, as well as budgets for future periods. Individuals responsible for favorable variances may be rewarded if the variance was due to superior performance, in order that the performance will continue in future periods.

CHAPTER REVIEW: Learning Objectives 1 - 4

Q1: How are standard costs established?
When setting standard costs for their goods or services, managers consider the cost of the inputs as well as the quantity of the inputs required. Standards are benchmarks that are useful for monitoring an organization's performance.

Q2: What is variance analysis, and how is it performed?
At the end of the accounting period, actual operating results are compared to the budget, as we saw in Chapter 10. A *standard cost variance* is the difference between a standard cost and an actual cost; *variance ana*lysis includes the calculation of standard cost variances and the investigation into the reasons they occurred.

Q3: How are direct cost variances calculated?
The difference between a standard cost of inputs and the actual cost of inputs is called a *price variance*. For direct materials, the price variance is based on the quantity of inputs purchased.

Direct materials price variance = (Standard price - Actual price) x Quantity purchased
DMPV = (SP – AP) x Quantity purchased

For direct labor, the price variance is based on the quantity of inputs used in production.

Direct labor price variance = (Standard price per hour - Actual price per hour) x Actual hours used
DLPV = (SP – AP) x Actual hours used

The direct materials price variance is computed based on the quantity of materials purchased, rather than the quantity used in production, because purchase occurs before use in production; it is important to isolate variances as quickly as possible so that any necessary corrective action can be taken.

A company may have an unfavorable standard cost variance because the actual price paid for the inputs exceeded the standard price, or because the actual usage of the inputs exceeded expectations. An *efficiency variance* places a dollar value on the difference between the actual usage of the inputs and expected usage.

An efficiency variance compares the *standard quantity for actual output* to the actual quantity of the inputs used. The standard quantity for actual output is the quantity of inputs that should have been used in order to produce the actual output for the period. Since the efficiency variances for both direct materials and direct labor are computed based on the actual quantity of inputs used, they have the same formula.

Efficiency variance = (Standard quantity for actual output - Actual quantity) x Standard price
EV = (SQ – AQ) x SP,

where SQ and AQ are measured in hours if you are computing the direct labor efficiency variance. In the direct materials efficiency variance, both SQ and AQ would be measured in pounds or grams or square yards, for example, depending on the type of materials. In all of these variance formulas, a negative result indicates that the actual quantity or the actual price exceeded the standard. Since we are computing cost variances, a negative result means the variance is unfavorable.

In a standard cost system, variances are recorded in general ledger accounts. For example, there is a Direct Materials Price Variance account in the general ledger. Direct materials price variances are recorded when materials are purchased, and direct labor price variances are recorded when labor costs are incurred. Both efficiency variances are recorded when materials and labor are used in production. (Un)favorable variances have a (debit) credit balance.

Demonstration problem-Computing and journalizing direct cost variances

Puzzles, Inc. manufactures customized wooden puzzles and uses a standard job order costing system. For 2005, they expected to make 1,000 puzzles. There are no 2005 beginning inventories. The company has the following standards for each puzzle:

> Direct materials: 4 square feet @ $4.00/ sq. ft $16.00
> Direct labor: 3 hours @ $6/hour   18.00

Actual production for 2005 was 1,200 puzzles, which used 4,900 square feet of direct materials and 3,500 direct labor hours. Puzzles purchased (on account) 6,000 square feet of lumber for $23,400. The average actual price per hour for the direct labor was $6.20/hour.

Required:
a) Compute the direct materials price and efficiency variances.
b) Compute the direct labor price and efficiency variances.
c) Prepare the journal entry to record the purchase of the direct materials.
d) Prepare the journal entry to record the use of direct materials.
e) Prepare the journal entry to record the use of direct labor, and the accrual of direct labor costs.

Solution to demonstration problem
a) The key to success in variance analysis is making sure that you identified the correct information for the formulas. For direct materials the actual quantity purchased is given as 6,000 square feet. The actual quantity used is also given as 4,900 square feet. The standard price for direct materials is $4/square foot. The actual price for direct materials is not given, but can be quickly computed: $23,400/6,000 square feet = $3.90/square foot. The standard quantity must usually be computed. The standard quantity is the amount of materials that should have been used in order to produce the actual quantity of output. In this problem, the information that Puzzles expected to produce 1,000 units is not relevant. The standard quantity is computed as 1,200 actual units of output x 4 square feet/unit = 4,800 square feet.

DMPV = ($4/square foot - $3.90/square foot) x 6,000 square feet = $600 favorable.
DMEV = (4,800 square feet – 4,900 square feet) x $4/square foot = $400 unfavorable.

b) The actual quantity of direct labor is given as 3,500 hours, and the standard price of direct labor is given as $6/hour. We are told that the actual price of direct labor was $6.20/hour. The standard quantity for direct labor is computed as 1,200 actual units of output x 3 hours/unit = 3,600 hours.

DLPV = ($6/hour - $6.20/hour) x 3,500 hours = $700 unfavorable.
DLEV = (3,600 hours – 3,500 hours) x $6/hour = $600 favorable.

Solution to demonstration problem continues on next page→

Solution to demonstration problem continued

b)	Raw materials inventory (6,000 sq. ft. x $4/sq. ft.)	24,000	
	Direct materials price variance		600
	Accounts payable		23,400
c)	Work in process inventory (4,800 sq. ft. x $4/sq. ft.)	19,200	
	Direct materials efficiency variance	400	
	Raw materials inventory (4,900 sq. ft. x $4/sq. ft.)		19,600
d)	Work in process inventory (3,600 hrs. x $6/hr.)	21,600	
	Direct labor price variance	700	
	Direct labor efficiency variance		600
	Accrued payroll (3,500 hrs. x $6.20/hr.)		21,700

Notice in the demonstration problem that work in process inventory is always debited for an amount equal to the standard price of the inputs times the standard quantity of the inputs.

Q4: How is direct cost variance information analyzed and used?

Managers can learn a great deal by analyzing direct cost variances. By investigating unfavorable variances, managers can learn the reasons for the unfavorable variance and work to correct them. While investigating favorable variances, managers may learn something that can be applied to future operations or other business segments. Using variance analysis information correctly allows managers to motivate employee behavior. Sometimes variance analysis will show that standards are inappropriate, and this can be corrected for the next budget cycle.

Exhibit 11.7 in the text is an excellent summary of some reasons for some direct cost variances. For example, a direct materials price variance may be caused by an unexpected price increase by a supplier, a change in order quantity, or a change in the quality of materials ordered. Some of these may be under the control of the purchasing manager and some may not. Additionally, actions of some employees may affect direct cost variances in other areas. For example, the purchasing manager may decide to purchase lower quality inputs, resulting in a favorable direct materials price variance. These lower quality inputs may be more difficult to work with, causing excessive waste in production. The factory supervisor may end up with an unfavorable direct materials efficiency variance as well as an unfavorable direct labor efficiency variance that are unrelated to his or her actual performance. You should take a moment now to review Exhibit 11.7 before continuing on in this study guide.

PROBLEM SET A (Learning Objectives 1 - 4)

<u>Matching</u>: Match each term with the appropriate definition or phrase. You may use each term more than once or not at all.

Terms		
A.	Price variance	I.	Efficiency variance
B.	Direct materials price variance	J.	Direct materials efficiency variance
C.	Direct labor price variance	K.	Direct labor efficiency variance
D.	Standard cost variance	L.	Actual price
E.	Standard price	M.	Actual quantity purchased
F.	Actual quantity used	N.	Favorable
G.	Unfavorable	O.	Debit
H.	Credit	P.	Work in process inventory

_____ 1. A favorable variance will have this type of balance

_____ 2. If this is unfavorable, then more materials were used in production than was expected

_____ 3. The direct materials price variance is computed as the difference between actual price and standard price times this

_____ 4. When fewer costs are incurred to produce the actual output than would have been budgeted to produce that output, there is this type of variance

_____ 5. In a standard cost system, the debit to this account is always based on the standard price of the input times the standard quantity of the input that should have been used

_____ 6. The direct labor price variance is computed as the difference between actual price and standard price times this

_____ 7. The difference between the costs incurred to produce the actual quantity of outputs and the standard cost that should have been incurred to produce that quantity of outputs

_____ 8. This direct cost variance is computed at an earlier time in the production process than any of the other direct cost variances

_____ 9. The direct materials efficiency variance is computed as the difference between the actual quantity of materials used and the standard quantity of materials that should have been used to produce this output times this

_____ 10. An unfavorable variance will have this type of balance

_____ 11. If direct labor workers spend longer producing output than was budgeted, this variance will be unfavorable

_____ 12. This is a company's expectations for the costs of one unit of input

_____ 13. This is the difference between what the company expected to pay for the inputs and what the company actually paid for the inputs; it is computed differently for direct materials and direct labor.

_____ 14. When a resource is a wasted in production, this will be unfavorable

_____ 15. This account will increase for the costs that should have been incurred to produce the actual output, rather than the costs that were actually incurred

---

<u>True-False</u>: Review Exhibit 11.7 in the text before attempting this exercise. Indicate whether each of the following is true (T) or false (F) in the space provided.

_____   1. It is possible for a purchasing manager to generate a favorable price variance by purchasing an excessive quantity of materials.

_____   2. Bookkeeping errors can cause direct cost variances.

_____   3. Excessive use of direct labor personnel can cause an unfavorable direct materials price variance.

_____   4. It is possible that a favorable direct materials price variance could be the cause of an unfavorable direct labor efficiency variance.

_____   5. It is possible that a favorable direct materials price variance could be the cause of an unfavorable direct labor price variance.

_____   6. It is possible that an unfavorable direct materials price variance could be the cause of a favorable direct materials efficiency variance.

_____   7. In a standard cost system, work in process inventory is debited for the actual costs of the inputs used.

_____   8. A change in government regulation could cause a direct labor price variance.

_____   9. An equipment malfunction could cause an unfavorable direct materials efficiency variance and/or an unfavorable direct labor efficiency variance.

_____   10. In a standard cost system, the direct labor efficiency variance and the direct labor price variance are recorded at the same time.

_____   11. In a standard cost system, the direct materials efficiency variance and the direct materials price variance are recorded at the same time.

_____   12. An unfavorable direct labor price variance could be the cause of a favorable direct labor efficiency variance.

_____   13. A favorable direct labor price variance could be the cause of an unfavorable direct labor efficiency variance.

_____   14. Supervisors with favorable variances associated with their area of responsibility should always be rewarded.

_____   15. All unfavorable variances should be investigated but it is not necessary to investigate favorable variances.

<u>Exercises</u>: Write your answer in the space provided.
1. Akdov Industries expected to make and sell 1,000 units of its product during 2004. In its static budget direct materials costs totaled $142,000, and direct labor costs totaled $78,000. Akdov budgets 4 pounds of direct material and 5 direct labor hours to make one unit. Akdov actually produced 1,200 units in 2004, using 4,500 pounds of direct material and 5,850 direct labor hours. The Company purchased 6,000 pounds after material in 2004 at a total cost of $216,000. Actual direct labor costs were $93,600.

a) Compute the standard price for direct materials. _____

b) Compute the standard price for direct labor. _____

c) Compute the direct materials price variance. _____

d) Compute the direct materials efficiency variance. _____

e) Compute the direct labor price variance. _____

f) Compute the direct labor efficiency variance. _____

2. Corey Company uses a standard cost system to account for the production costs of its sole product. The product is expected to use 0.6 gallons of direct materials per unit and 0.4 hours of direct labor per unit. The standard cost of one gallon of direct materials is $1.20 and the standard cost of an hour of direct labor is $12.40. Corey produced 12,400 units this year. Prepare the journal entries to record the following transactions.

    a) Purchased 8,000 gallons of direct materials for $9,300 on account.

    b) Used 7,200 gallons of direct materials.

    c) Accrued for the use of 5,000 direct labor hours for a total cost of $63,000.

    d) Interpret the direct cost variances computed above.

    _____

    _____

    _____

    _____

    _____

    _____

    _____

    _____

    _____

3. Major Enterprises makes custom leather driving gloves for men. You are given the following information:

Standard cost per unit
Direct materials (2 square feet at $4.10 per square foot) $8.20
Direct labor (1.5 hours at $9.00 per hour) $13.50

This year the purchasing manager changed suppliers and was able to acquire 50,000 square feet of leather at $3.25 per square foot. The company made 11,000 pairs of gloves this year, using 32,000 square feet of leather. There were 16,500 direct labor hours used at a total cost of $132,000.

a) Compute the direct materials price variance. _____

b) Compute the direct materials efficiency variance. _____

c) Compute the direct labor price variance. _____

d) Compute the direct labor efficiency variance. _____

d) Interpret the direct cost variances computed above, and indicate how they might be related. Assess the performance of the purchasing and production managers.

_____

_____

_____

_____

_____

_____

_____

CHAPTER REVIEW: Learning Objectives 5 - 8

<u>Q5: How are variable and fixed overhead variances calculated?</u>
In a standard cost system, overhead allocation rates are computed in the same way as traditional job costing.

$$\text{Standard variable overhead allocation rate} = \frac{\text{Estimated total variable overhead cost}}{\text{Estimated volume of allocation base}}.$$

$$\text{Standard fixed overhead allocation rate} = \frac{\text{Estimated total fixed overhead cost}}{\text{Estimated volume of allocation base}}.$$

In Chapter 5 we learned that allocated overhead costs were computed as the overhead allocation rates times the actual quantity of the allocation base used. Under standard costing, allocated overhead costs are computed as the overhead allocation rates times the standard quantity of the allocation base that should have been used in order to produce the actual quantity of outputs.

The difference between actual variable overhead costs and allocated variable overhead costs is known as the *variable overhead budget variance.* It is also known as the variable overhead *flexible budget variance.* The variable overhead budget variance is the sum of the *variable overhead spending variance* and the *variable overhead efficiency variance.*

$$\text{Variable overhead spending variance} = \left(\text{Standard variable overhead allocation rate} \quad X \quad \text{Actual volume of allocation base} \right) -- \text{Actual variable overhead cost}$$

VOSV = [SR x AQ] – Actual variable overhead cost

$$\text{Variable overhead efficiency variance} = \left(\text{Standard quantity of allocation base} \quad -- \quad \text{Actual volume of allocation base} \right) X \text{Standard variable overhead allocation rate}$$

VOEV = [SQ - AQ] x SR

The variable overhead spending variance is a measure of whether the organization was able to control variable overhead costs; it is based on the actual volume of the allocation base used because variable overhead costs change as volume levels change. The variable overhead efficiency variance measures the increase (decrease) in variable overhead costs that is solely due to consuming more (less) of the overhead allocation base. If the formulae above return a negative answer, then the variance is unfavorable.

The formulae for fixed overhead variances are quite different. There is no fixed overhead efficiency variance, for example. Fixed overhead costs are not expected to increase as consumption of the allocation base increases (within the relevant range). The *fixed overhead spending variance* for fixed overhead is simply a comparison of budgeted fixed overhead to actual fixed overhead. The *production volume variance* is associated only with fixed overhead.

Fixed overhead spending variance = Estimated fixed overhead costs -- Actual fixed overhead costs

FOSV = Estimated fixed overhead costs – Actual fixed overhead costs

Production volume variance = (Standard quantity of allocation base -- Estimated volume of allocation base) x Standard fixed overhead allocation rate

PVV = [SQ – Estimated volume of allocation base] x SR

In both of the above cases, if the formula returns a negative result, the variance is unfavorable.

As in a traditional job costing system like we learned in Chapter 5, the journal entries to record the incurrence of actual overhead costs include a debit to the overhead cost control account, and a credit to cash or accounts payable or other accounts. The journal entry that is required to allocate overhead costs is also the same as learned in Chapter 5; the work in process inventory account is debited and the overhead cost control account is credited. The only difference is that the calculation of allocated overhead in the standard cost system is based on the standard quantity of the allocation base that should have been used to produce the actual outputs, rather than the actual quantity of the allocation base that was used.

There are general ledger accounts for the four overhead variances that we just learned. As before, unfavorable variances are debited to the variance accounts and favorable variances are credited to the variance accounts. When recording these overhead variances, the journal entries are balanced by a debit or credit to the overhead cost control account. Most companies use separate overhead cost control accounts for variable and fixed overhead.

Q6: How is overhead variance information analyzed and used?

The variable overhead budget variance measures the difference between actual variable overhead costs and expected variable overhead costs, given the actual level of output. The variable overhead budget variance can be decomposed into the spending variance portion and the efficiency variance portion. Suppose, for example, that the variable overhead budget variance is unfavorable. This could have been caused by excessive consumption of the variable overhead allocation base, or higher costs for some of the costs included in the variable overhead cost pool, or some combination of the two. You should review Exhibit 11.11 in the text for examples of situations that can cause overhead variances.

- The variable overhead efficiency variance captures the portion of the variable overhead budget variance that is due solely to the difference between actual consumption of the allocation base and the standard quantity of the allocation base that should have been used, given the actual output level.

- The variable overhead spending variance captures the portion of the variable overhead budget variance caused by higher or lower costs in the variable overhead cost pool. This spending variance can be due to higher or lower costs per unit of input, or to efficient or inefficient use of the variable cost items. For example, if indirect labor is an element of the variable overhead cost pool, then either a higher average wage rate for indirect laborers or inefficient use of indirect labor hours could cause an unfavorable variable overhead spending variance.

The variable overhead budget variance is also equal to misapplied variable overhead. An unfavorable variable overhead budget variance indicates that variable overhead was underapplied, and a favorable variable overhead budget variance indicates that variable overhead was overapplied.

The *fixed overhead budget variance* is the difference between actual fixed overhead and allocated fixed overhead, and can also be decomposed into two variances.

- • I The fixed overhead spending variance simply measures the difference between actual fixed overhead and fixed overhead budgeted at the beginning of the year.

- • The production volume variance arises because the creation of a fixed overhead allocation rate inherently treats fixed costs as if they were variable. For example, if the fixed overhead allocation rate is $10 per direct labor hour, then the fixed overhead that is allocated to a job increases as the standard quantity of direct labor hours for the job increases. To a production supervisor who is responsible for the costs of that job, this cost appear to be variable, even though fixed costs in total do not change as volume levels increase within the relevant range. Because of this, the production volume variance should not be used to measure performance in the same way as the other variances.

  - ○ In theory, the production volume variance is also a measure of capacity usage. If the actual output level was lower than expected at the beginning of the year, then the production volume variance is unfavorable, indicating that the company had idle capacity. However, this interpretation of the production volume variance is rather abstract; when the company commits to a level of fixed costs at the beginning of the year, it is really buying a range of capacity. Actual customer demand is not known at the beginning of the year.

The fixed overhead budget variance is also equal to misapplied fixed overhead. An unfavorable fixed overhead budget variance indicates that fixed overhead was underapplied, and a favorable fixed overhead budget variance indicates that fixed overhead was overapplied.

Demonstration problem-Computing overhead variances

The Culebra Corporation manufactures customized widgets and uses a standard job order costing system. The standard cost of a widget includes 5 machine hours of variable factory overhead at $7/hour and 5 machine hours of fixed factory overhead at $28/hour. Budgeted fixed factory overhead is $700,000. Actual output was 4,800 units, and actual variable and fixed factory overhead totaled $190,000 and $720,000, respectively. Actual machine hours for the year were 24,800.

Required:
a) Compute the number of machine hours budgeted at the beginning of the year.
b) Compute and interpret the variable overhead budget variance.
c) Compute and interpret the variable overhead spending variance.
d) Compute and interpret the variable overhead efficiency variance.
e) Compute and interpret the fixed overhead spending variance.
f) Compute and interpret the production volume variance.
g) Prepare the journal entries to record the incurrence of actual overhead costs, the allocation of overhead costs, and to record the fixed and variable overhead variances.

solution to demonstration problem begins on next page →

Solution to demonstration problem

a) The number of machine hours expected at January 1 is the denominator in the estimated fixed overhead allocation rate computation. Therefore, estimated fixed overhead allocation rate = estimated fixed overhead/estimated machine hours budgeted at the beginning of the year. So, $28/machine hour = $700,000/estimated machine hours budgeted at the beginning of the year, or, estimated machine hours budgeted at the beginning of the year = 25,000 hours.

b) First we need to compute the standard quantity of machine hours for the actual output. Note that SQ is *not* the 25,000 machine hours calculated in part (a); this is a common student error. The 25,000 machine hours is based on the beginning of the year's expectations of activity whereas SQ is based on the end of the year's knowledge of actual output. SQ = actual output x expected machine hours per unit = 4,800 units x 5 machine hours per unit = 24,000 machine hours. The allocated variable overhead = $7/hour x 24,000 hours = $168,000. Actual variable overhead was given as $190,000. The variable overhead budget variance equals $168,000 - $190,000 = $22,000 unfavorable. This means that the company spent $22,000 more on variable overhead costs than was expected, given the actual level of output.

c) VOSV = [SR x AQ] – Actual variable overhead cost = $7/hour x 24,800 machine hours - $190,000 = $173,800 - $190,000 = $16,400 unfavorable. This means that $16,400 of the variable overhead budget variance was caused by increased costs of items in the variable overhead cost pool. For example, if the cost of machine oil is an element of variable overhead, then the company either paid more than expected for a quart of machine oil or used more machine oil than should have been expected for the 24,800 actual machine hours.

d) VOEV = [SQ – AQ] x SR, where SQ was computed in (b). VOEV = [24,000 machine hours – 24,800 machine hours] x $7/machine hour = $5,600 unfavorable. This means that $5,600 of the $22,000 unfavorable variable overhead budget variance is due to the increase in expected variable overhead costs solely due to the use of a 800 machine hours beyond what should have been used to produce the 4,800 actual output units.

e) FOSV = estimated fixed overhead costs - actual fixed overhead costs = $700,000 - $720,000 = $20,000 unfavorable. The company's fixed overhead costs exceeded the budget by $20,000.

f) PVV = [SQ - expected machine hours at the beginning of the year] x SR = [24,000 - 25,000] x $28/machine hour = $28,000 unfavorable. Theoretically, the production volume variance measures capacity usage. Since the company's output was less than expected at the beginning of the year, there was idle capacity and the variance is unfavorable.

solution to demonstration problem continues on next page→

Solution to demonstration problem continued

g)   Work in process inventory [($7/hr + $28/hr) x 24,000 hrs]   840,000
             Variable overhead cost control [$7/hr x 24,000 hrs]   168,000
             Fixed overhead cost control [$28/hr x 24,000 hrs]   672,000
      To allocate overhead costs to work in process inventory

      Variable overhead cost control   190,000
      Fixed overhead cost control   720,000
             Accounts payable and other accounts   910,000
      To record actual overhead costs incurred

      Variable overhead spending variance   16,400
      Variable overhead efficiency variance   5,600
             Variable overhead cost control   22,000
      To record variable overhead variances

      Fixed overhead spending variance   20,000
      Production volume variance   28,000
             Fixed overhead cost control   48,000
      To record fixed overhead variances

Q7: How are manufacturing cost variances closed?

In Chapter 5 we learned that using an estimated allocation rate for overhead resulted in misallocated overhead, which was closed to work in process inventory, finished goods inventory, and cost of goods sold at the end of the year. This is also true in a standard costing system, but here we are using estimates (standards) for the direct costs as well as for overhead. These differences are located in the eight production variance accounts (two each for direct materials, direct labor, variable overhead, and fixed overhead).

At the end of the year, these eight variance accounts are closed out to work in process inventory, finished goods inventory, and cost of goods sold. Technically, a portion of the direct materials price variance should also be allocated to raw materials inventory, but the textbook and this study guide ignore this minor complication.

If the combined amounts for these eight variances is considered immaterial, they may be closed out to just the cost of goods sold account. To determine materiality, we use the same 10% rule as the text: if the net amount of these eight variance accounts is less than 10% of the period's total production costs, the amount is considered immaterial.

Demonstration problem-Closing variance accounts
Mesquite Company makes propane barbecues and uses the standard costing system. At the end of 2005, Mesquite's variance accounts were as follows:

Direct materials price variance	$12,800	unfavorable
Direct materials efficiency variance	22,000	favorable
Direct labor price variance	18,200	favorable
Direct labor efficiency variance	24,100	unfavorable
Variable overhead spending variance	4,900	unfavorable
Variable overhead efficiency variance	15,300	unfavorable
Fixed overhead spending variance	2,200	unfavorable
Production volume variance	17,700	unfavorable
Net production variance	$36,800	unfavorable

Mesquite's total production costs in 2005 were $320,000. At the end of 2005, Mesquite's general ledger showed the following:

	Amount	Percent
Work in process inventory	$17,000	5.1%
Finished goods inventory	9,000	2.7%
Cost of goods sold	305,000	92.2%
Total	$331,000	100.0 %

Required:
Prepare the year-end journal entry to close the variance accounts.

Solution to demonstration problem
Note that $36,800/$320,000 = 11.5\%$, so the net production variance is considered material. Recall that unfavorable variance accounts have debit balances, so they must be credited in order to be closed out. Favorable variance accounts have credit balances, so they must be debited when closed out.

Work in process inventory [5.1% x $36,800]	1,877	
Finished goods inventory [2.7% x $36,800]	994	
Cost of goods sold [92.2% x $36,800]	33,929	
Direct materials efficiency variance	22,000	
Direct labor price variance	18,200	
Direct materials price variance		12,800
Direct labor efficiency variance		24,100
Variable overhead spending variance		4,900
Variable overhead efficiency variance		15,300
Fixed overhead spending variance		2,200
Production volume variance		17,700

Q8: Which profit-related variances are commonly analyzed? (Appendix 11A)

Managers analyze other variances besides those for production costs.

- The *revenue budget variance* measures the difference between actual revenues and total revenues budgeted at the beginning of the year. This can arise for two distinct reasons, so this variance has two components.

    o The *sales price variance* is the portion of the revenue budget variance that is due to the actual average selling price per unit differing from the budgeted selling price per unit. SPV = [ASP – BSP] x actual units sold, where SPV = selling price variance, ASP = actual average selling price per unit, and BSP = budgeted selling price per unit.

    o The *revenue sales quantity variance* is the portion of the revenue budget variance that is due to the actual quantity of units sold differing from the budgeted quantity. RSQV = [Actual units sold – Budgeted units to be sold] x BSP, where RSQV = revenue sales quantity variance.

- The *contribution margin budget variance* is the difference between the actual contribution margin and the contribution margin budgeted at the beginning of the year. It also has two components.

    o The *contribution margin variance* is the difference between the actual contribution margin and the budgeted contribution margin, adjusted to actual sales volume. CMV = Σ_i [ACM_i – BCM_i] x Actual units of Product i sold, where CMV = contribution margin variance, ACM_i = actual contribution margin per unit for Product i, and BCM_i = budgeted contribution margin per unit for Product i.

    o The *contribution margin sales volume variance* is the difference between the budgeted contribution margin at the actual sales volume and the contribution margin budgeted at the beginning of the year. CMSVV = Σ_i [Actual units of Product i sold - Budgeted units of Product i to be sold] x BCM_i. For companies that sell multiple products the contribution margin sales volume variance can be decomposed into two additional variances.

        - The *contribution margin sales mix variance* is the portion of the contribution margin sales volume variance that is caused when the actual sales mix differs from the budgeted sales mix.

$$CMSMV = \sum_i \left\{ \begin{pmatrix} \text{actual} \\ \text{units of} \\ \text{Product} \\ \text{i sold} \end{pmatrix} - \begin{pmatrix} \text{total} \\ \text{actual} \\ \text{units} \\ \text{sold} \end{pmatrix} \times \begin{pmatrix} \text{budgeted} \\ \text{sales mix} \\ \text{\% for} \\ \text{Product i} \end{pmatrix} \times \begin{pmatrix} \text{budgeted} \\ \text{contribution} \\ \text{margin per unit} \\ \text{for Product i} \end{pmatrix} \right\}$$

        - The *contribution margin sales quantity variance* is the portion of the contribution margin sales volume variance that is caused when the actual total unit sales differs from the budgeted total unit sales.

$$CMSQV = \sum_i \left\{ \left[\begin{pmatrix} \text{actual} \\ \text{total} \\ \text{units} \\ \text{sold} \end{pmatrix} \times \begin{pmatrix} \text{budgeted} \\ \text{sales mix} \\ \text{\% for} \\ \text{Product i} \end{pmatrix} - \begin{pmatrix} \text{budgeted} \\ \text{unit sales} \\ \text{for} \\ \text{Product i} \end{pmatrix} \right] \times \begin{pmatrix} \text{budgeted} \\ \text{contribution} \\ \text{margin per unit} \\ \text{for Product i} \end{pmatrix} \right\}$$

Demonstration Problem-Computing revenue and contribution margin variances
Kenny Maiket Co. sells 3 sizes of its product. The following information comes from Kenny's static budget:

Product	Budgeted Selling Price Per Unit	Budgeted CM per Unit	Static Budget Unit Sales	Static Budget Revenue	Static Budget Total CM	Static Budget Sales Mix
Large	$25.00	$5.00	2,000	$50,000	$10,000	20%
Medium	$20.00	$3.00	5,000	$100,000	$15,000	50%
Small	$15.00	$4.00	3,000	$45,000	$12,000	30%
			10,000	$195,000	$37,000	100%

Kenny comes to you at the end of the year with the following actual results:

Product	Actual Selling Price Per Unit	Actual CM per Unit	Actual Unit Sales	Actual Revenue	Actual Total CM	Actual Sales Mix
Large	$26.00	$6.00	1,800	$46,800	$10,800	14.01%
Medium	$18.00	$4.00	6,800	$122,400	$27,200	52.92%
Small	$14.00	$3.75	4,250	$59,500	$15,938	33.07%
			12,850	$228,700	$53,938	100.00%

Kenny is pleased with this year's results, and asks you to help him interpret the variances.

Required:
a) Compute the revenue budget variance, the revenue sales quantity variance, and the sales price variance.
b) Compute the CM budget variance, the CM sales volume variance, the CM variance, the CM sales quantity variance, and the CM sales mix variance.
c) Interpret these variances for Kenny.

Solution to demonstration problem
Italicized numbers come directly from the static budget information, and bold numbers come directly from the actual information.
a)

Total Static Budget Revenue	Actual Units Sold Times Budgeted Selling Price	Total Actual Revenue
$195,000	$244,750	**$228,700**

Revenue Sales Quantity Variance	Sales Price Variance
$49,750 Favorable	$16,050 Unfavorable

Revenue Budget Variance
$33,700 Favorable

Note: 1,800 x $25 + 6,800 x $20 + 4,250 x $15 = $244,750.

solution to demonstration problem continues on next page →

Solution to demonstration problem continued

b)

Total Static Budget CM	Actual Total Units Sold Times Static Budget Sales Mix Times Static Budget CM per Unit	Actual Total Units Sold Times Actual Sales Mix Times Static Budget CM per Unit	Actual Total Units Sold Times Actual Sales Mix Times Actual CM per Unit
$37,000	$47,545	$46,400	**$53,938**

CM Sales Quantity Variance	CM Sales Mix Variance
$10,545 Favorable	$1,145 Unfavorable

CM Sales Volume Variance	CM Variance
$9,400 Favorable	$7,538 Favorable

CM Budget Variance
$16,938 Favorable

Computations:
12,850 x 20% x $5 + 12,850 x 50% x $3 + 12,850 x 30% x $4 = $47,545
12,850 x 14.01% x $5 + 12,850 x 52.92% x $3 + 12,850 x 33.07% x $4 = $46,400

c) If Kenney would have sold the actual units that he sold in the actual sales mix he actually did, but sold them at budgeted selling prices per unit, his revenue would have been $244,750, which is $49,750 greater than revenues budgeted in the static budget. However, the actual selling prices for the medium and small products were lower than budgeted. The actual selling price for the large product was higher than budgeted. The effect of these different selling prices was to decrease revenue by $16,050, so that Kenny's net revenue budget variance was only $33,700 favorable. Kenny should not necessarily look poorly upon the $16,050 unfavorable sales price variance. It very well could be that the decrease in the actual selling price per unit was the cause of the increase in the number of units sold for the medium and small products.

If Kenney would have sold the same total number of units as he actually did, but in the budgeted sales mix proportion, and at the budgeted CM per unit, then his adjusted budgeted contribution margin would have been $47,545. The increase in Kenny's contribution margin that is due solely to the increase in the total number of units sold his $10,545. The actual sales mix, however, was different than the budgeted sales mix, which lowered contribution margin by $1,145. The net effect of this was an increase in contribution margin of $9,400.

The actual contribution for the large and medium products was higher than what was budgeted, and the actual contribution margin for the small product was only slightly lower than budgeted. This is positive indeed, especially considering that actual selling prices were lower than budgeted selling prices for two of the products. It seems that Kenny has done a good job of controlling variable costs. The net effect of this is to increase contribution margin by $7,538.

The increase in sales volume, combined with the increase in contribution margin per unit, increased Kenny's contribution margin over the static budget by $16,938.

PROBLEM SET B (Learning Objectives 5 - 8)

<u>True-False</u>: Indicate whether each of the following is true (T) or false (F) in the space provided.

_____   1. If overhead is overapplied, then the entry to close the overhead variance accounts will include a debit to cost of goods sold.

_____   2. If fixed overhead is overapplied, the production volume variance must be favorable.

_____   3. If overhead is overapplied, the fixed overhead budget variance must be favorable.

_____   4. If overhead is overapplied, the variable overhead efficiency variance must be favorable.

_____   5. An unfavorable variable overhead spending variance could be caused by higher costs for the costs included in the variable cost pool, or by an inefficient use of variable overhead resources.

_____   6. Suppose the variable overhead cost allocation base is direct labor hours, and that the direct labor efficiency variance is unfavorable. Then the variable overhead efficiency variance must also be unfavorable.

_____   7. If the variable overhead budget variance is unfavorable, then variable overhead must be underapplied.

_____   8. If the fixed overhead budget variance is unfavorable, then fixed overhead must be underapplied.

_____   9. If a multiple product company sells more units in total than was budgeted at the beginning of the year, then the contribution margin budget variance must be favorable.

_____   10. If a multiple product company sells more units in total than was budgeted the beginning of year, then the revenue budget variance must be favorable.

_____   11. In a two product company, if the contribution margin sales mix variance is favorable, then the company must have sold a greater proportion of the product with the higher contribution margin.

_____   12. In a single product company, a favorable sales price variance, combined with an unfavorable revenue sales quantity variance, may indicate that the company priced its product too high.

_____   13. In a single product company, an unfavorable contribution margin variance indicates that the company did not sell as many units as was budgeted at the beginning of the year.

<u>Exercises</u>: Write your answer in the space provided.
1. Dove Manufacturing uses a standard cost system to account for the production costs of its sole product. The estimated variable overhead allocation rate is $4/machine hour, and the estimated fixed overhead allocation rate is $2/direct labor hour. Each completed unit is budgeted to use 1.5 machine hours and 2.3 direct labor hours. Dove Manufacturing produced 10,000 units this year, even though it expected to produce 12,000 units at the beginning of the year. Actual variable and fixed overhead was $67,200 and $45,000, respectively. The company actually used 14,500 machine hours and 24,500 direct labor hours this year.

a) Prepare the summary journal entry to allocate overhead to work in process inventory.

b) Prepare the summary journal entry to record actual overhead costs.

c) Prepare the journal entry to record the variable overhead variances.

d) Prepare the journal entry to record the fixed overhead variances.

2. This is a continuation of exercise 1, so check your answers to that problem before doing this one. Suppose at the end of the year Dove's balances in work in process inventory, finished goods inventory, and cost of goods sold, were $900,000, $750,000, and $3,200,000, respectively. Prepare the journal entry to close Dove's overhead variance accounts, assuming the net variance is considered material.

3. Lonely, Inc. sells only one product. At the beginning of the year it expected to sell 10,000 units at $7 each. This year Lonely actually sold 9,000 units at $7.50 each.

a) Compute the revenue budget variance _____

b) Compute the revenue sales quantity variance _____

c) Compute the sales price variance _____

4. Omed Corporation sells 3 products, A, B, and C. You are given the following static budget and actual information for 2005:

Product	Budgeted Selling Price Per Unit	Budgeted CM per Unit	Static Budget Unit Sales	Static Budget Revenue	Static Budget Total CM	Static Budget Sales Mix
Product A	$12.00	$6.00	1,500	$18,000	$9,000	17%
Product B	$8.00	$5.00	4,000	$32,000	$20,000	44%
Product C	$11.00	$3.00	3,500	$38,500	$10,500	39%
			9,000	$88,500	$39,500	100%

Product	Actual Selling Price Per Unit	Actual CM per Unit	Actual Unit Sales	Actual Revenue	Actual Total CM	Actual Sales Mix
Product A	$11.50	$5.75	1,800	$20,700	$10,350	25.71%
Product B	$8.20	$4.90	3,000	$24,600	$14,700	42.86%
Product C	$14.00	$2.85	2,200	$30,800	$6,270	31.43%
			7,000	$76,100	$31,320	100.00%

a) Compute the revenue variances.

Revenue
budget variance _____

Revenue sales
quantity variance _____

Sales
price variance _____

b) Compute the contriubtion margin variances.

CM
budget variance _____

CM sales
volume variance _____

CM
variance _____

CM sales quantity variance _____

CM sales mix variance _____

END OF CHAPTER EXERCISES

<u>Multiple choice</u>: Write the letter that represents the best choice in the space provided.

_____ 1. The expected costs per unit of input are called
   a. standard costs
   b. standard prices
   c. standard quantities
   d. standard cost allowed

_____ 2. The variance that theoretically measures the difference between actual capacity used and budgeted capacity is called the
   a. direct labor efficiency variance
   b. fixed overhead efficiency variance
   c. variable overhead efficiency variance
   d. production volume variance

<u>Use the following information for questions 3 – 4:</u>
Bellingham, Inc. incurred the following during a recent period:

	Actual	Standard
Machine hours	1,350	1,425
Units produced	570	570
Variable overhead costs	$2,775	$2,850

_____ 3. The variable overhead efficiency variance equals
   a. $75 Favorable
   b. $150 Favorable
   c. $0
   d. $75 Unfavorable

_____ 4. The variable overhead spending variance equals
   a. $75 Favorable
   b. $150 Favorable
   c. $0
   d. $75 Unfavorable

_____ 5. The contribution margin sales volume variance can be further subdivided into
   a. the contribution margin budget variance and the contribution margin variance
      the contribution margin variance and the contribution margin sales mix
   b. variance
   c. the contribution margin sales quantity variance and the contribution margin sales mix variance
   d. the contribution margin sales quantity variance and the contribution margin budget variance

Use the following information for questions 6 – 8:
Vashon Corporation had the following activity during a recent period:

Standard quantity of direct materials	9,000	pounds
Actual quantity of direct materials purchased and used	8,800	pounds
Efficiency variance	$2,400	favorable
Total direct materials budget variance	$200	favorable

_____ 6. The standard price per pound was
   a. $12.00
   b. $12.25
   c. $12.50
   d. $13.00

_____ 7. The actual price per pound was
   a. $12.00
   b. $12.25
   c. $12.50
   d. $13.00

_____ 8. The direct materials price variance was
   a. $2,200 unfavorable
   b. $2,600 unfavorable
   c. $2,000 favorable
   d. $2,200 favorable

_____ 9. A favorable direct materials price variance could be caused by
   a. the purchasing manager acquiring an excessive quantity of direct
       materials
   b. the purchasing manager acquiring materials of higher quality
   c. the purchasing manager acquiring materials of lower quality
   d. either (a) or (c)

_____ 10. The variance over which management probably has the least control is the
   a. direct labor efficiency variance
   b. direct materials price variance
   c. variable overhead efficiency variance
   d. fixed overhead efficiency variance

_____ 11. Which of the following statements is false?
   a. The actions of a purchasing manager can affect a production manager's
       variances.
   b. The actions of a production manager can affect a purchasing manager's
       variances.
   c. Inefficient use of the fixed overhead cost allocation base will cause an
       unfavorable production volume variance.
   d. Inefficient use of the variable overhead cost allocation base will cause an
       unfavorable variable overhead efficiency variance.

Use the following information for questions 12 – 14:
Anacortes, Inc. uses a standard cost system. At the beginning of the year, it budgeted $50,000 of fixed overhead. The estimated variable overhead allocation rate was $3.30 per machine hour, and machine hours is the cost allocation base for both variable and fixed overhead. The static budget was based on 16,000 units of production and sales, and each unit was expected to use 2.5 machine hours. Actual total overhead was $170,000, and Anacortes produced and sold 15,000 units during the year. Actual machine hours for the year were 36,000.

_____ 12. The variable overhead efficiency variance was
     a. $4,950 favorable
     b. $3,750 favorable
     c. $1,200 unfavorable
     d. $3,125 unfavorable

_____ 13. The production volume variance was
     a. $4,950 favorable
     b. $3,750 favorable
     c. $1,200 unfavorable
     d. $3,125 unfavorable

_____ 14. The combined fixed and variable spending variance was
     a. $4,950 favorable
     b. $3,750 favorable
     c. $1,200 unfavorable
     d. $3,125 unfavorable

_____ 15. The contribution margin sales mix variance will be unfavorable when
     a. actual sales in total units is less than total unit sales in the static budget
     b. the actual contribution margin is less than the static budget contribution margin
     c. the actual sales mix includes a lower proportion of the product with the highest contribution margin per unit than its proportion in the static budget sales mix
     d. the actual average selling price is less than the average selling price in the static budget

_____ 16. The revenue sales quantity variance will be unfavorable when
     a. actual sales in total units is less than total unit sales in the static budget
     b. the actual contribution margin is less than the static budget contribution margin
     c. the actual sales mix includes a lower proportion of the product with the highest contribution margin per unit than its proportion in the static budget sales mix
     d. the actual average selling price is less than the average selling price in the static budget

Use the following information for questions 17 – 23:
A small accounting firm budgets 200 hours of billings for the next month, and 60% of these hours are expected to be for tax return preparation services, with the remaining 40% for bookkeeping services. Tax work is billed at $50/hour and bookkeeping work is billed at $40 per hour. The variable costs for both types of services is $10/hour. During the month, 180 hours were billed, 90 of which were for tax work.

_____ 17. The revenue sales quantity variance was
    a. $720 unfavorable
    b. $540 favorable
    c. $900 unfavorable
    d. $180 unfavorable

_____ 18. The contribution margin sales mix variance was
    a. $720 unfavorable
    b. $540 favorable
    c. $900 unfavorable
    d. $180 unfavorable

_____ 19. The sales price variance was
    a. $720 unfavorable
    b. $540 favorable
    c. $0
    d. $1,200 unfavorable

_____ 20. The contribution margin sales volume variance was
    a. $720 unfavorable
    b. $540 favorable
    c. $900 unfavorable
    d. $1,200 unfavorable

_____ 21. The contribution margin budget variance was
    a. $720 unfavorable
    b. $540 favorable
    c. $900 unfavorable
    d. $1,200 unfavorable

_____ 22. The contribution margin variance was
    a. $720 unfavorable
    b. $540 favorable
    c. $0
    d. $1,200 unfavorable

_____ 23. The contribution margin sales quantity variance was
    a. $720 unfavorable
    b. $540 favorable
    c. $0
    d. $1,200 favorable

Use the following information for questions 24 – 25:
Thurston Corp. uses a standard job cost system with the following standards:

Standard price/lb of direct materials	$4.80
Standard price/hr of direct labor	$15.50
Standard quantity of direct materials allowed for actual output	2,100 lbs
Standard quantity of direct labor allowed for actual output	505 hours

Thurston actually used 2,000 pounds of direct material that cost $10,000 and 500 direct labor hours that cost $7,500.

_____ 24. The entry to record the usage of direct materials would include
    a. a debit to Work in process inventory for $9,600
    b. a credit to Raw material inventory for $10,000
    c. a debit to Work in process inventory for $10,500
    d. a credit to Direct materials efficiency variance for $480

_____ 25. The entry to record the usage of direct labor would include
    a. a credit to Direct labor efficiency variance for $77.50
    b. a debit to Work in process inventory for $7,500
    c. a credit to Accrued payroll for $7,827.50
    d. a debit to Direct labor price variance for $250

Use the following information for questions 26 – 27:
Keyport, Inc. uses a standard job cost system. The standard price for direct material is $15/ounce, and Keyport used 60,000 ounces this period. The standard quantity allowed for direct materials this period was 58,000 ounces. The standard price for direct labor is $9/hour, and Keyport used 5,000 direct labor hours, at an actual cost of $10/hour this period. The standard quantity allowed for direct labor this period was 5,200 hours.

_____ 26. The entry to record the usage of direct materials would include
    a. a debit to Work in process inventory for $900,000
    b. a debit to Direct materials efficiency variance for $30,000
    c. a credit to Raw materials inventory for $870,000
    d. a credit to Work in process inventory for $60,000

_____ 27. The entry to record the usage of direct labor would include
    a. a debit to Direct labor efficiency variance for $1,800
    b. a credit to Work in process inventory for $3,200
    c. a debit to Direct labor price variance for $5,000
    d. a debit to Accrued payroll for $3,200

_____ 28. A credit to Direct materials efficiency variance indicates that
    a. actual usage was greater than the standard quantity
    b. actual price was less than the standard price
    c. actual usage was less than the standard quantity
    d. actual price was greater than the standard price

<u>Exercises</u>: Write your answer in the space provided.
1. Redmond, Inc. sells a single product and prepared the following static budget for the year:

Sales (18,000 units @ $30)	$540,000
Direct materials (9,000 lbs @ $10)	90,000
Direct labor (36,000 hrs @ $6)	216,000
Variable overhead (36,000 DL hrs @ $2)	72,000
Fixed overhead	90,000
Gross margin	$72,000

At the end of the year, the following actual results were achieved:

Sales (20,000 units @ $30)	$600,000
Direct materials (10,500 lbs purchased and used)	99,750
Direct labor ($6.25/hr)	243,750
Variable overhead	76,050
Fixed overhead	87,000
Gross margin	$93,450

a) Compute the direct materials variances.

DM price variance _____   DM efficiency variance _____

b) Compute the direct labor variances.

DL price variance _____   DL efficiency variance _____

c) Compute the variable overhead variances.

VO spending variance_____   VO efficiency variance _____

d) Compute the fixed overhead variances.

FO spending variance_____   Production volume variance _____

2. This is a continuation of exercise 1, so check your answers for that problem before attempting this one. Provide a complete interpretation of all the variances in exercise 1.

    a) Direct material variances:

    _____

    _____

    _____

    _____

    _____

    b) Direct labor variances:

    _____

    _____

    _____

    _____

    _____

    c) Variable overhead variances:

    _____

    _____

    _____

    _____

    _____

    c) Fixed overhead variances:

    _____

    _____

    _____

    _____

    _____

3. Kittitas Company's static budget calls for 15,000 units of output and includes the following standard costs:

Direct materials (9 lbs @ $6/lb)	$810,000
Direct labor (4 hrs @ $9/hr)	540,000
Variable overhead ($1.50 per DL hour)	90,000
Fixed overhead ($5.50 per DL hour)	330,000

Actual results for the period were:

Units produced	14,000
Direct materials purchased and used (124,000 lbs @ $6.25/lb)	$775,000
Direct labor (57,000 hrs @ $8.75/hr)	498,750
Variable overhead	84,560
Fixed overhead	332,000

Prepare the journal entries to record the purchase of direct materials on account, the use of direct materials, the use of direct labor, the incurrence of actual overhead costs, the allocation of overhead costs, and the overhead variances.

4. Gotcha Covered, Inc. makes 3 different styles of canvas tents. You are given the following static budget and actual information:

<u>Static Budget Information</u>

Product	Budgeted Selling Price Per Unit	Static Budget Unit Sales
Pup tent	$45.00	800
2-person tent	$110.00	1,000
4-person tent	$180.00	1,200
		3,000

<u>Actual Results</u>

Product	Actual Selling Price Per Unit	Actual Unit Sales
Pup tent	$48.00	700
2-person tent	$104.00	1,200
4-person tent	$160.00	1,800
		3,700

At the beginning of the year, Gotcha Covered expected the contribution margin ratios for the 3 products to be 60%, 40%, and 30%, respectively. However, at the end of the year, the actual contribution margin ratios for the 3 products was 58%, 42%, and 35%, respectively.

a) Compute the revenue variances.

Revenue
budget variance _____

Revenue sales
quantity variance _____

Sales
price variance _____

b) Compute the contriubtion margin variances.

CM
budget variance _____

CM sales
volume variance _____

CM
variance _____

CM sales quantity variance _____

CM sales mix variance _____

5. This is a continuation of exercise 4, so check your answers for that problem before you do this one. Provide a complete interpretation of all the variances in exercise 4.

   a) Revenue variances

   _____

   _____

   _____

   _____

   _____

   _____

   _____

   _____

   b) Contribution margin variances

   _____

   _____

   _____

   _____

   _____

   _____

   _____

   _____

   _____

   _____

   _____

   _____

   _____

   _____

SOLUTION TO PROBLEM SET A

Matching:

1. H
2. J
3. M
4. N
5. P
6. F or M (for DL, the amount purchased = the amount used)
7. D
8. C
9. E
10. O
11. K
12. E   (standard cost is the expected cost of an <u>output</u>)
13. A
14. I
15. P

True-False:

1. T   By purchasing a larger quantity than normal, the purchasing manager may have received volume discounts.
2. T
3. F   The purchase of direct materials occurs before the use of direct materials, so in general actions of direct labor personnel will not affect the purchase price of direct materials. However, it is possible that a production supervisor could inefficiently schedule production so that direct materials must be acquired quickly, which could affect the purchase price.
4. T   If the purchasing manager acquired less expensive, lower quality direct materials, direct labor personnel may have had to spend more time working with these direct materials than budgeted.
5. T   If the purchasing manager acquired less expensive, lower quality direct materials, the production supervisor may have needed to use his higher skilled, more expensive direct labor personnel.
6. T   More expensive, higher quality direct materials may have led to less waste.
7. F   In a standard cost system, work in process inventory is always debited for the standard price of the inputs times the standard quantity of the inputs allowed.
8. T   A change in minimum wage laws could cause of direct labor price variance.
9. T   A malfunctioning piece of equipment can waste direct materials and direct labor.
10. T
11. F   The direct materials price variance is recorded before the direct materials efficiency variance.
12. T   More expensive, higher skilled workers, might have completed tasks more quickly.

13.   T   Less expensive, lower skilled workers, may have taken longer to complete tasks.

14.   F   If the favorable variance occurred due to something outside the employee's control, then the employees should not be rewarded. Additionally, a favorable variance can arise if standards are set inappropriately.

15.   F

Exercises:

1.   a) If the static budget was based on 1,000 units of output, then it allowed for 1,000 x 4 pounds = 4,000 pounds of direct materials. $142,000/4,000 pounds = $35.50/lb.

   b) If the static budget was based on 1,000 units of output, then it allowed for 1,000 x 5 hours = 5,000 hours of direct labor. $78,000/5,000 hours = $15.60/hour.

   c) First note that AP = $216,000/6,000 lbs = $36/lb.
      DMPV = [SP – AP] x Actual quantity purchased = [$35.50/lb - $36/lb] x 6,000 lbs = $3,000 unfavorable.

   d) First note that SQ for materials = 1,200 units x 4lbs/unit = 4,800 lbs.
      DMEV = [SQ – AQ] x SP = [4,800 lbs – 4,500 lbs] x $35.50/lb = $10,650 favorable.

   e) First note that AP = $93,600/5,850 hrs = $16/hr.
      DLPV = [SP – AP] x Actual quantity used = [$15.60/hr - $16/hr] x 5,850 hrs = $2,340 unfavorable.

   f) First note that SQ for labor = 1,200 units x 5 hrs/unit = 6,000 hrs.
      DLEV = [SQ – AQ] x SP = [6,000 hrs – 5,850 hrs] x $15.60/hr = $2,340 favorable.

2.   First note that AP for DM = $9,300/8,000 gal = $1.1625/gal;
     SQ for DM = 12,400 units x 0.6 gal/unit = 7,440 gal;
     AP for DL = $63,000/5,000 hrs = $12.60/hr; and
     SQ for DL = 12,400 units x 0.4 hrs/unit = 4,960 hrs

   a)   Raw materials inventory (8,000 gal x $1.20/gal)   9,600
           DM price variance ([$1.20/gal - $1.1625/gal] x 8,000 gal   300
           Accounts payable   9,300

   b)   Work in process inventory (7,440 gal x $1.20/gal)   8,928
           DM efficiency variance ([7,440 gal – 7,200 gal] x $1.20/gal   288
           Raw materials inventory (7,200 gal x $1.20/gal)   8,640

   c)   Work in process inventory (4,960 hrs x $12.40/hr)   61,504
        DL price variance ([$12.40/hr - $12.60/hr] x 5,000 hrs   1,000
        DL efficiency variance ([4,960 hrs – 5,000 hrs] x $12.40/hr   496
           Wages payable (3500 hrs. x $6.20/hr.)   63,000

2. continued.
   d) DM: Corey paid $1.1625/gallon compared to the standard cost of $1.20/gallon, creating a favorable price variance of $300. Additionally, Corey used only 7,200 gallons of direct materials compared to the 7,440 gallons allowed for the production of 12,400 units, which created a favorable direct materials efficiency variance of $288.

   DL: Corey's average wage rate was $12.60/hour, which is $0.20/hour higher than the standard price, creating an unfavorable direct labor price variance of $1,000. Corey also used 5,000 hours of direct labor when only 4,960 hours were allowed for the production of 12,400 units, which created an unfavorable direct labor efficiency variance of $496.

3. a) DMPV = [SP – AP] x Actual quantity purchased = [$4.10/lb - $3.25/sq ft] x 50,000 sq ft = $42,500 favorable.

   b) First note that SQ for materials = 11,000 units x 2 sq ft/unit = 22,000 sq ft.
      DMEV = [SQ – AQ] x SP = [22,000 sq ft – 32,000 sq ft] x $4.1/sq ft = $41,000 unfavorable.

   c) First note that AP = $132,000/16,500 hrs = $8/hr
      DLPV = [SP – AP] x Actual quantity used = [$9/hr - $8/hr] x 16,500 hrs = $16,500 favorable.

   d) First note that SQ for labor = 11,000 units x 1.5 hrs/unit = 16,500 hrs.
      DLEV = [SQ – AQ] x SP = [16,500 hrs – 16,500 hrs] x $9/hr = $0.

   e) The purchasing manager was able to acquire direct materials at a substantially lower cost than the standard price, which is good. However, 10,000 more square feet of leather were used than were allowed for the production of 11,000 pairs of gloves. The combination of a large favorable direct materials price variance and a large unfavorable direct materials efficiency variance may be indicative of poor quality leather. If so, the production manager should not be held accountable for the unfavorable direct materials efficiency variance. But poor quality may not be the reason for the unfavorable direct materials efficiency variance. The production manager's average wage rate was $1 per hour less than the standard price and his direct labor efficiency variance was $0. Another explanation for the unfavorable direct materials efficiency variance could be that the production manager used (less expensive) workers with less experience and they did not perform their jobs quickly, ignoring the efficient use of direct materials. More investigation is needed to determine the reasons for these variances.

SOLUTION TO PROBLEM SET B

True-False:

1. F   The entry will include a credit to cost of goods sold.
2. F   Under or overapplied fixed overhead includes the fixed overhead spending
3. F   variance as well as the production volume variance.
4. F   The variable overhead efficiency variance is based on a difference in input usage, not a difference of outputs.
5. T
6. T   If the direct labor efficiency variance was unfavorable thean actual hours exceeded the standard quantity of hours allowed.
7. T
8. T
9. F   Although revenues will be higher, a large increase in variable costs could mean that the contribution margin budget variance is unfavorable.
10. F   If the company sold a lower proportion of the product with the highest selling price per unit, into a higher proportion of the product with the lowest selling price per unit, then the revenue budget variance might not be favorable.
11. T
12. T   Increases in selling prices of units may cause customer demand for the products to fall.
13. F   The contribution margin variance captures only the difference between the actual contribution margin and the budgeted contribution margins of the products.

Exercises:

1. First note that SQ for machine hours = 10,000 units x 1.5 machine hour/unit = 15,000 machine hours, and that SQ for direct labor hours = 10,000 units x 2.3 direct labor hours/units = 23,000 direct labor hours. Also, note that $2/ DL hr = Budgeted fixed overhead/27,600 DL hours (27,600 = 12,000 units x 2.3 DL hrs/unit = DL hours in static budget), so budgeted fixed overhead = $55,200.

a)   Work in process inventory   106,000

     Variable overhead cost control ($4/hr x 15,000 mach hrs)   60,000

     Fixed overhead cost control ($2/hr x 23,000 DL hrs)   46,000

b)   Variable overhead cost control   67,200

     Fixed overhead cost control   45,000

     Accounts payable and other accounts   112,200

c)   VO spending variance ([$4/hr x 14,500 mach hrs] - $67,200)   9,200

     VO efficiency variance ([15,000 – 14,500] mach hrs x $4/hr)   2,000

     Variable overhead cost control   7,200

d)   Fixed overhead cost control   1,000

     Production volume variance ([23,000–27,600]DL hrs x $2/hr   9,200

     FO spending variance   10,200

2. First compute the net amount of the production variance

Variable overhead spending variance	$9,200	unfavorable
Variable overhead efficiency variance	2,000	favorable
Fixed overhead spending variance	10,200	favorable
Production volume variance	9,200	unfavorable
Net production variance	$6,200	unfavorable

Next compute the share of this $6,200 to be allocated to work in process inventory, finished goods inventory and cost of goods sold.

	Amount	Percent
Work in process inventory	$900,000	18.56%
Finished goods inventory	750,000	15.46%
Cost of goods sold	3,200,000	65.98%
Total	$4,850,000	100.0 %

Finally, prepare the journal entry to close the overhead variance accounts.

Work in process inventory [18.56% x $6,200]	1,151	
Finished goods inventory [15.46% x $6,200]	958	
Cost of goods sold [65.98% x $6,200]	4,091	
Fixed overhead spending variance	10,200	
Variable overhead efficiency variance	2,000	
Variable overhead spending variance		9,200
Production volume variance		9,200

3. a) Static budget revenues = 10,000 units @ $7 = $70,000; actual revenues = 9,000 units @ $7.50 = $67,500. The revenue budget variance is $2,500 unfavorable.

   b) [Actual units sold – Budgeted units sold] x Budgeted selling price per unit
      = [9,000 units – 10,000 units] x $7/unit = $7,000 unfavorable.

   c) [Actual selling price per unit – Budgeted selling price per unit] x Actual units sold =
      [$7.50/unit - $7/unit] x 9,000 units = $4,500 favorable.

4. Italicized numbers come directly from the static budget information, and bold numbers come directly from the actual information.

a)

Total Static Budget Revenue	Actual Units Sold Times Budgeted Selling Price	Total Actual Revenue
$88,500	$69,800	**$76,100**

Revenue Sales Quantity Variance	Sales Price Variance
$18,700 Unfavorable	$6,300 Favorable

Revenue Budget Variance
$12,400 Unfavorable

b)

Total Static Budget CM	Actual Total Units Sold Times Static Budget Sales Mix Times Static Budget CM per Unit	Actual Total Units Sold Times Actual Sales Mix Times Static Budget CM per Unit	Actual Total Units Sold Times Actual Sales Mix Times Actual CM per Unit
$39,500	$30,722	$32,400	**$31,320**

CM Sales Quantity Variance	CM Sales Mix Variance
$8,778 Unfavorable	$1,678 Favorable

CM Sales Volume Variance	CM Variance
$7,100 Unfavorable	$1,080 Unfavorable

CM Budget Variance
$8,180 Unfavorable

SOLUTION TO END OF CHAPTER EXERCISES

Multiple choice:

1. B
2. D
3. B   VOEV = [SQ – AQ] x SR = [1,425 hrs – 1,350 hrs] x $2/hr = $150 F
4. D   VOSV = [SR x AQ] – Actual VO = [$2/hr x 1,350 hrs] - $2,775 = $75 U
5. C
6. A   The DMEV is $2,400 favorable, so $2,400 = [9,000 lbs – 8,800 lbs] x SP;
        solve for SP = $12/lb.
7. B   The total DM variance is $200 favorable, so $200 = $2,400 favorable +
        DMPV, so DMPV = $2,200 unfavorable. -$2,200 = [$12/lb – AP] x 8,800 lbs;
        solve for AP = $12.25/lb.
8. A   See the computations for #7 above.
9. D
10. B   A company is least likely to have control over supplier's price increases.
11. C   There is no measure of efficiency for fixed costs
12. A   First note that SQ = 15,000 units x 2.5 hrs/unit = 37,500 hrs.
        VOEV = [SQ – AQ] x SR = [37,500 hrs – 36,000 hrs] x $3.30/hr = $4,950 F
13. D   First note that the # of machine hours in the static budget = 15,000 units x
        2.5 hrs/unit = 40,000 hrs.
        Also the SR for fixed overhead = $50,000/40,000 hrs = $1.25/hr.
        PVV = [37,500 hrs – 40,000 hrs] x $1.25/hr = $3,125 unfavorable.
14. C   VOSV = [SR x AQ] – Actual VO and FOSV = Budgeted FO – Actual FO, so
        VOSV + FOSV = SR x AQ + Budgeted FO – [Actual VO + Actual FO] =
        $3.30/hr x 36,000 hrs + $50,000 - $170,000 = $168,800 - $170,000 =
        $1,200 U.
15. C
16. A
17. C   RSQV = [Actual units sold – Budgeted units to be sold] x BSP, summed for
        all products = [90 hrs – 120 hrs] x $50/hr for tax work + [90 hrs – 80 hrs] x
        $40/hr for bookkeeping work = -$1,500 + $400 = $900 U.
18. D   CMSMV = [180 hrs x 60% x ($50 - $10) + 180 hrs x 40% x ($40 - $10)] –
        [180 hrs x 50% x ($50 - $10) + 180 hrs x 50% x ($40 - $10)] = $6,480 -
        $6,300 = $180 U
19. C   Budgeted selling prices were the same as actual selling prices.
20. C   CMSV = = [200 hrs x 60% x ($50 - $10) + 200 hrs x 40% x ($40 - $10)] –
        [180 hrs x 50% x ($50 - $10) + 180 hrs x 50% x ($40 - $10)] = $7,200 -
        $6,300 = $900 U
21. C   The CMBV = CMSVV + CMV (see #22 below) = $900 U + $0 = $900 U
22. C   The CMV captures the difference between the budgeted CM per unit and
        the actual CM per unit and there were no differences.
23. A   CMSQV = [180 hrs x 60% x ($50 - $10) + 180 hrs x 40% x ($40 - $10)] –
        [180 hrs x 60% x ($50 - $10) + 180 hrs x 60% x ($40 - $10)] = $7,200 -
        $6,480 = $720 U

24. D   The entry is:
        dr. WIP inventory (2,100 lbs x $4.80/lb)   10,080.00
            cr. DMEV ([2,100 lbs – 2,000 lbs] x $4.80/lb)   480.00
            cr. RM inventory (2,000 lbs x $4.80/lb)   9,600.00

25. A   First note that AP for DL = $7,500/500 hrs = $15/hr. The entry is:
        dr. WIP inventory (505 hrs x $15.50/hr)   7,827.50
            cr. DLEV ([505 hrs – 500 hrs] x $15.50/hr)   77.50
            cr. DLPV ([$15.50/hr – $15/hr] x 505 hrs)   250.00
            cr. Wages Payable (given)   7,500.00

26. B   The entry is:
        dr. WIP inventory (58,000 oz x $15/oz)   870,000
        dr. DMEV ([58,000 oz – 60,000 oz] x $15/oz)   30,000
            cr. RM inventory (60,000 oz x $15/oz)   900,000

27. C   The entry is:
        dr. WIP inventory (5,200 hrs x $9/hr)   46,800
        dr. DLPV ([$9/hr – $10/hr] x 5,000 hrs)   5,000
            cr. DLEV ([5,200 hrs – 5,000 hrs] x $9/hr)   1,800
            cr. Wages Payable (5,000 hrs x $10/hr)   50,000

28. C   A credit to a variance account is favorable.

Exercises:

1. a) First note that AP for DM = $99,750/10,500 lbs = $9.50/lb. SP for DM is given as $10/lb. AQ for DM is given as 10,500 lbs. Also note from that static budget that 9,000 lbs were budgeted for 18,000 units, so each unit is expected to use 0.5 lbs. SQ for DM = 20,000 units x 0.5 lbs/unit = 10,000 lbs.

    DMPV = [SP – AP] x Actual quantity purchased = [$10/lb - $9.50/lb] x 10,500 lbs = $5,250 favorable.
    DMEV = [SQ – AQ] x SP = [10,000 lbs – 10,500 lbs] x $10/lb = $5,000 unfavorable.

    b) First note that AP for DL is given at $6.25/hr. Also note from that static budget that 36,000 hrs were budgeted for 18,000 units, so each unit is expected to use 2 hrs. SQ for DM = 20,000 units x 2 hrs/unit = 40,000 lbs. AQ for DL is computed as $243,750/$6.25 per hour = 39,000 hrs.

    DLPV = [SP – AP] x Actual quantity used = [$6/hr - $6.25/hr] x 39,000 hrs = $9,750 unfavorable.
    DLEV = [SQ – AQ] x SP = [40,000 hrs – 39,000 hrs] x $6/hr = $6,000 favorable.

    c) VOSV = [SR x AQ] – Actual VO = [$2/hr x 39,000 hrs] - $76,050 = $1,950 favorable
       VOEV = [SQ – AQ] x SR = [40,000 – 39,000 hrs] x $2/hr = $2,000 favorable

    d) FOSV = Budgeted FO – Actual FO = $90,000 - $87,000 = $3,000 favorable

    To compute the PVV, note that the SR for FO is $90,000/36,000 hrs = $2.50/hr.
    PVV = [SQ – static budget hrs] x SR = [40,000 – 36,000 hrs] x $2.50/hr = $10,000 favorable

2. a) The purchasing manager was able to obtain direct materials at a price lower than the standard price, resulting in a favorable direct materials price variance. However, an additional 500 lbs. of direct materials beyond what should have been required to produce 20,000 units were used in production, resulting in an unfavorable efficiency variance. Overall, the direct materials production variances were $250 favorable.

    b) The production manager used 1,000 direct labor hours less than was allowed to produce 20,000 units, resulting in a $6,000 favorable direct labor efficiency variance. However the average wage rate was $0.25/hr higher than the standard price for direct labor, resulting in an unfavorable direct labor price variance of $9,750. If the production manager's efficiency was attained by using higher skilled, more expensive labor, then this trade-off was not worth it (if you ignore the effects on variable overhead for a moment), because the direct labor production variances net to $3,750 unfavorable.

    c) Because direct labor hours is the cost allocation base for variable overhead, the favorable direct labor efficiency variance will result in a favorable variable overhead efficiency variance. In addition to saving $6,000 in direct labor costs due to this efficiency, the production manager also saved $2,000 in variable overhead costs. The variable overhead spending variance was also favorable, indicating the variable overhead costs were lower than would have been budgeted at 39,000 direct labor hours of activity.

    d) The fixed overhead spending variance was $3,000 favorable, indicating that $3,000 less was spent on fixed overhead costs than was budgeted at the beginning of the year. The production volume variance was $10,000 favorable. This merely indicates that the actual output level was higher than the static budget's output level.

3. First begin by making some initial computations:

    SQ for DM = 14,000 units x 9 lbs/unit = 126,000 lbs.
    SQ for DL (and for overhead) = 14,000 units x 4 hrs/unit = 56,000 hrs.

Raw materials inventory (124,000 lbs x $6/lb)	744,000	
DM price variance ([$6/lb - $6.25/lb] x 124,000 lbs	31,000	
Accounts payable		775,000
To record the purchase of direct materials		

Work in process inventory (126,000 lbs x $6/lb)	756,000	
DM efficiency variance ([124,000 – 126,000] lbs x $6/lb		12,000
Raw materials inventory (124,000 lbs x $6/lb)		744,000
To record the use of direct materials		

Work in process inventory (56,000 hrs x $9/hr)	504,000	
DL efficiency variance ([57,000 hrs – 56,000 hrs] x $9/hr	9,000	
DL price variance ([$9/hr - $8.75/hr] x 57,000 hrs		14,250
Wages payable (57,000 hrs. x $8.75/hr.)		498,750
To accrue wages for the period		

3. continued.

Variable overhead cost control	84,560	
Fixed overhead cost control	332,000	
Accounts payable and other accounts		416,560
To record actual overhead costs		

Work in process inventory	392,000	
Variable overhead cost control ($1.50/hr x 56,000 hrs)		84,000
Fixed overhead cost control ($5.50/hr x 56,000 hrs)		308,000
To allocate overhead costs to work in process		

VO efficiency variance ([56,000 – 57,000] hrs x $1.50/hr)	1,500	
VO spending variance ([$1.50/hr x 57,000 hrs] - $84,560)		940
Variable overhead cost control		560
To record variable overhead variances		

FO spending variance ($330,000 - $332,000)	2,000	
Production volume variance ([56,000–60,000]hrs x $5.50/hr	22,000	
Fixed overhead cost control		24,000
To record fixed overhead variances		

4. a)

Total Static Budget Revenue	Actual Units Sold Times Budgeted Selling Price	Total Actual Revenue
$362,000	$487,500	**$446,400**
Revenue Sales Quantity Variance	Sales Price Variance	
$125,500 Favorable	$41,100 Unfavorable	

Revenue Budget Variance
$84,400 Favorable

b)

Total Static Budget CM	Actual Total Units Sold Times Static Budget Sales Mix Times Static Budget CM per Unit	Actual Total Units Sold Times Actual Sales Mix Times Static Budget CM per Unit	Units Sold Times Actual Sales Mix Times Actual CM per Unit
$130,400	$160,827	$168,900	**$172,704**
CM Sales Quantity Variance	CM Sales Mix Variance		
$30,427 Favorable	$8,073 Favorable		

CM Sales Volume Variance	CM Variance
$38,500 Favorable	$3,804 Favorable

CM Budget Variance
$42,304 Favorable

5. a) The revenue budget variance was $84,400 favorable, indicating that actual revenues were $84,400 greater than anticipated in the static budget. If the company had sold this increased number of units for the budgeted selling price, actual revenues would have been $125,500 greater than the static budget. However, the company attained these larger sales (most likely) by decreasing the selling price of some of its units, which cost $41,100 in revenue. It is true that the decreased selling prices for some of the products caused higher sales, then the sales manager should be applauded for the $84,400 increase in sales.

    b) The contribution margin sales quantity variance was $30,427 favorable. This captures the effect of the increased sales in total units. If the actual total sales in units had been sold at the budgeted sales mix and at the budgeted contribution margin, then sales would have increased $30,427 over the static budget. However, the sales mix did change, which increased the contribution by another $8,073. The net of this is that the increase in total actual units of sales and change sales mix increased contribution margin by $30,500. Finally, the increase in the selling price of some products and the decrease in the variable costs some products increased contribution margin by another $3,804. Actual contribution margin was $42,304 higher than the static budget contribution margin.

Chapter 12

Strategic Investment Decisions

√ **Study Checklist – Monitor your progress**

	1. Read the chapter in the text
	2. Review the learning objectives below
	3. Read the overview of the chapter
	4. Read the chapter review for learning objectives 1 - 5
	5. Do Problem Set A and check your answers
	6. Read the chapter review for learning objectives 6 - 8
	7. Do Problem Set B and check your answers
	8. Do the End of Chapter Exercises in this study guide
	9. Do the homework assigned by your instructor

CHAPTER LEARNING OBJECTIVES

After studying this chapter, you should be able to answer the following questions:

Q1. How are strategic investment decisions made?

Q2. What cash flows are relevant for strategic investment decisions?

Q3. How is net present value (NPV) analysis performed and interpreted?

Q4. What are the uncertainties and limitations of NPV analysis?

Q5. What alternative methods (IRR, payback, and accrual accounting rate of return) are used for long-term decision-making?

Q6. What additional issues should be considered for strategic investment decisions?

Q7. How do income taxes affect strategic investment decision cash flows?

Q8. How are the real and nominal methods used to address inflation in NPV analysis? (Appendix 12A)

OVERVIEW OF CHAPTER

Capital budgeting is a process of analyzing long-term investment alternatives. Because cash flows occur over several periods, the time value of money is an important consideration in these decisions. This chapter looks at the four most commonly used capital budgeting techniques.

CHAPTER REVIEW: Learning Objectives 1 - 5

Q1: How are strategic investment decisions made?
The process that managers use to compare and analyze long-term investment projects with cash flows over several years is called *capital budgeting.* The process involves the following stages:

- Identify all decision alternatives
- Identify the relevant cash flows
- Apply the appropriate quantitative analysis technique(s)
  - methods that consider the time value of money:
    - net present value (NPV) method
    - internal rate of return (IRR) method
  - methods that ignore the time value of money:
    - payback method
    - accounting rates of return method
- Perform sensitivity analysis
- Identify and analyze qualitative factors
- Consider quantitative and qualitative information and make a decision

Q2: What cash flows are relevant for strategic investment decisions?
As we learned in Chapter 1, relevant cash flows are those that occur in the future and differ across the alternatives. In capital budgeting decisions, examples of relevant cash flows include the following:

- incremental cash outflows
  - initial investment
  - future operating costs
  - project closing and cleanup costs
- incremental cash inflows
  - future revenues
  - decreased operating costs
  - salvage value of assets at project's end

Q3: How is net present value (NPV) analysis performed and interpreted?
The NPV of a project is the sum of the projects discounted cash flows.

$$NPV = \sum_{t=0}^{n} \frac{\text{Expected cash flow}_t}{(1+r)^t} \text{, where}$$

t = year of the project's life that the cash flow occurs
n = life of the project
r = discount rate

The interest rate used in the above calculations is also known as the *discount rate.* Some managers may have any minimum rate of return they require for all projects and use this *required rate of return,* or *hurdle rate,* as the discount rate in the NPV calculations. Then, a project with a positive NPV has a rate of return that exceeds this hurdle rate, and is deemed acceptable at this stage of the capital budgeting process. Projects with a negative NPV are considered unacceptable.

Often, decision makers will use the *weighted average cost of capital* (WACC) as the discount rate. The WACC is a weighted average of a company's cost of debt financing and its return on equity. Use of one discount rate for all projects, however, assumes that all projects have equal risk. Some decision makers will use risk-adjusted discount rates, where riskier projects would be assigned a higher discount rate than less risky projects.

Computing the NPV for projects may be used as part of a screening process in capital budgeting, where an organization sorts projects according to whether they are acceptable or not. When limited funds are available for projects, companies may then rank the acceptable projects. Projects of the different sizes and different lives may be ranked and compared according to their *profitability index.*

$$\text{Profitability index} = \frac{\text{Present value of benefits}}{\text{Present value of costs}}$$

Demonstration problem-Computing NPV and the profitability index
Renton, Inc. is evaluating two pieces of equipment for purchase. Machine A costs $83,200 and is expected to save an estimated $20,000 per year in operating costs for seven years. Machine B costs $100,000 and is expected to save $30,000 in operating costs in each of the first two years, $20,000 in operating costs in years three and four, and $10,000 in operating costs for years five through seven. Renton uses a minimum required rate of return of 10%. Ignore income taxes.

Required:
a) Compute the NPV for each machine (use the time value of money tables in Chapter 12 of the text book).
b) Compute the profitability index for each machine.

Solution to demonstration problem
a) Since the savings in operating costs for Machine A are the same amount each year, we can use the present value of an ordinary annuity factor to compute the present value of these savings.

Machine A's NPV = $20,000 x [PV of an ordinary annuity factor, n=7, r=10%] - $83,200
   = $20,000 x 4.868 - $83,200
   = $97,360 - $83,200
   = $14,160.

$$\text{Machine B NPV} = \sum_{t=0}^{n} \frac{\text{Expected cash flow}_t}{(1+r)^t}$$

$$= \frac{-\$100,000}{(1.1)^0} + \frac{\$30,000}{(1.1)^1} + \frac{\$30,000}{(1.1)^2} + \frac{\$20,000}{(1.1)^3} + \frac{\$20,000}{(1.1)^4}$$

$$+ \frac{\$10,000}{(1.1)^5} + \frac{\$10,000}{(1.1)^6} + \frac{\$10,000}{(1.1)^7}$$

solution to demonstration problem continues on next page →

Solution to demonstration problem continued

$$= -\$100,000 + \$30,000 \times \mathbf{0.909} + \$30,000 \times \mathbf{0.826} + \$20,000 \times \mathbf{0.751}$$
$$+ \$20,000 \times \mathbf{0.683} + \$10,000 \times \mathbf{0.621} + \$10,000 \times \mathbf{0.564} + \$10,000 \times \mathbf{0.513}$$
$$= -\$100,000 + \$27,270 + \$24,780 + \$15,020 + \$13,660 + \$6,210 + \$5,640 + \$5,130$$
$$= -\$100,000 + \$97,710$$
$$= -\$2,290.$$

b) Machine A profitability index = $97,360/$83,200 = 1.17, which means that each dollar invested in Machine A returns $1.17, after considering the time value of money.

Machine B profitability index = $97,710/$100,000 = 0.977. Note that Machine B's negative NPV is associated with a profitability index under 1.0, and the bold numbers in the profitability index calculation above are the factors from the present value of $1 table.

Q4: What are the uncertainties and limitations of NPV analysis?
Because capital budgeting analyzes future cash flows, many of the elements in NPV analysis are estimates based on assumptions. There are uncertainties surrounding the amount and timing of cash flows, the project life, and the discount rate, and amount of the uncertainty surrounding each of these elements may be different. For example, the initial investment amount and its timing may be more certain than the salvage value at the end of the project's life.

The use of so many estimates with their underlying assumptions requires a great deal of judgment. These estimates are often created by the individuals who are proposing the project, so capital budgeting decision makers must watch for bias in these estimates. They may perform sensitivity analysis, which looks at how the NPV results change as the input data changes.

Q5: What alternative methods (IRR, payback, and accrual accounting rate of return) are used for long-term decision-making?
The internal rate of return (IRR) method computes the discount rate that would set the project's NPV to zero. Microsoft Excel contains formula dialog boxes for NPV calculations as well as IRR calculations. For projects where the only cash outflow is the initial investment, and cash inflows occur in equal amounts each year, IRR can be quickly calculated using time value of money tables.

Initial investment = Annual cash inflow x [present value of an ordinary annuity factor],

where the present value of an ordinary annuity factor is the unknown in the above equation. Once this factor is computed, the IRR can be determined by locating which interest rate column in which the factor is found.

The *payback method* computes the number of years before the initial investment is recovered. If cash inflows are the same amount each year, the payback period is computed as follows:

Payback period = Initial investment/Annual cash inflow.

For projects where the annual cash inflows are not equal, the payback period is determined by simply counting the number of years required before the initial investment is recovered.

Although the payback method is widely used, it is flawed because it does not consider the time value of money, and ignores cash flows that occur after the payback is achieved. However it may be used in conjunction with NPV or IRR to help assess project risk, where projects with longer payback periods are considered more risky.

The *accrual accounting rate of return method* computes project's rate of return as the increase in average annual operating income divided by the initial investment. This method is also widely used, because the financial accounting information is easily obtained. However, like the payback method, it is flawed because it ignores the time value of money.

Demonstration problem-Computing IRR, payback period, and accrual accounting rate of return.
Renton, Inc. is evaluating two pieces of equipment for purchase. Machine A costs $83,200 and is expected to save an estimated $20,000 per year in operating costs for seven years. Machine B costs $100,000 and is expected to save $30,000 in operating costs in each of the first two years, $20,000 in operating costs in years three and four, and $10,000 in operating costs for years five through seven. Renton uses a minimum required rate of return of 10%. Ignore income taxes.

Required:
a) Compute the IRR for Machine A using the time value of money tables in Chapter 12 of the text book, and compute the IRR of Machine B using Microsoft Excel.
b) Compute the payback period for each machine.
c) Compute the accrual accounting rate of return for Machine A, assuming straight-line depreciation is used.

Solution to demonstration problem
a) To find the IRR for Machine A, set the present value of the savings equal to the initial investment:

$83,200 = $20,000 x [Present value of an ordinary annuity factor, n=7, r=unknown]

[Present value of an ordinary annuity factor, n=7, r=unknown] = 4.16

To find the IRR, scan the present value of an ordinary annuity table, along row n=7, until you locate where 4.16 would be placed. It is found exactly in the r=15% column.

Time period	Cash Flow
0	($100,000)
1	$30,000
2	$30,000
3	$20,000
4	$20,000
5	$10,000
6	$10,000
7	$10,000
IRR =	9.12%

To find the IRR for Machine B, type the cash flows into a Microsoft Excel worksheet, and use the IRR formula

solution to demonstration problem continues on next page →

Solution to demonstration problem continued
b) The payback period for Machine A is $83,200/$20,000 = 4.16 years.

The payback period for Machine B is 4.0 years because $60,000 is recovered in years 1 and 2 and $40,000 is recovered in years 3 and 4. The full $100,000 investment is recovered after 4 years.

c) For Machine A, the depreciation expense per year is $83,200/7 years = $11,886 per year. Therefore, the improvement in operating income due to the purchase of this machine will be $20,000 less $11,886 = $8,114. The accrual accounting rate of return for Machine A is $8,114/$83,200 = 9.75%.

PROBLEM SET A (Learning Objectives 1 - 5)

<u>Matching</u>: Match each term with the appropriate definition or phrase. You may use each term more than once or not at all.

Terms

A. Capital budgeting	F. Discount rate
B. Hurdle rate	G. Weighted average cost of capital
C. Net present value	H. Profitability index
D. Internal rate of return	J. Accrual accounting rate of return
E. Payback period	K. Present value of an ordinary annuity factor

_____   1.   A generic term for the interest rate used in present value computations

_____   2.   This is also known as the required rate of return

_____   3.   If this is larger than 1.0, then the NPV of the project is positive

_____   4.   When this is positive, the project is acceptable

_____   5.   This is based on a company's cost of debt financing and its return on equity financing

_____   6.   This is measured in years

_____   7.   For a project whose only cash outflow is the initial investment, and whose cash inflows are the same each year, this is equal to the payback period

_____   8.   A process for analyzing and comparing alternatives for long-term investments

_____   9.   This method of analyzing potential projects includes the computation of depreciation

_____   10. If this is larger than the discount used in the NPV calculations, the NPV will be positive.

_____   11. If this is less than the hurdle rate used in the NPV calculations, then the project's NPV will be negative

_____   12. If this is large, then it could mean that there is a good deal of uncertainty surrounding the cash flows

<u>True-False</u>: Indicate whether each of the following is true (T) or false (F) in the space provided. Ignore income tax effects in your responses.

_____   1. The payback method is inferior to the NPV and IRR methods, but does have at least one useful place in capital budgeting analysis.

_____   2. The payback method ignores depreciation.

_____   3. The IRR method ignores depreciation.

_____   4. The NPV method ignores depreciation.

_____   5. The accrual accounting rate of return method ignores depreciation.

_____   6. When a project has equal cash inflows and only one cash outflow at the beginning of the project, the payback period is equal to the present value of an ordinary annuity factor used to compute the project's NPV.

_____   7. When a project has equal cash inflows and only one cash outflow at the beginning of the project, the payback period is equal to the present value of an ordinary annuity factor used to compute the project's IRR.

_____   8. The IRR method can only be used for projects that have equal cash inflows over the years and only one initial cash outflow.

_____   9. The accrual accounting rate of return method ignores the time value of money.

_____   10. The NPV method ignores the time value of money.

_____   11. The IRR method ignores the time value of money.

_____   12. The payback method ignores the time value of money.

_____   13. When a project's NPV is negative, its IRR is less than the discount rate used in the NPV calculations.

_____   14. When a project's IRR is greater than the hurdle rate, than the project's NPV will be negative.

_____   15. The accrual accounting rate of return method calculates the discount rate to be used in the NPV method.

Exercises: Write your answer in the space provided.
1. Wattigny Enterprises is considering a project that has annual cash inflows of $10,000/year in years 1 and 2, $20,000/year in year 3, and $50,000/year in years 4 and 5. The initial outlay is $60,000.

    Compute the payback period _____

2. Brent Enterprises is considering a project that has annual cash inflows of $50,000 in year 1, $1,000/year in years 2 through 6, $5,000 in year 7, and $120,000 in year 8. The initial outlay is $60,000.

    Compute the payback period _____

3. Compare the projects in exercises 1 and 2, and comment on the results of the payback period computations.

    _____

    _____

    _____

    _____

    _____

    _____

    _____

    _____

4. Vicki's Victory Banners makes large signs sold mostly to high school athletic departments. Vicki is considering purchasing a new machine to print the banners. The machine costs $40,000, and is expected to last eight years. Vicki believes it will save her $10,000 in operating costs each year. Vicki requires all new investments to have the rate of return of at least 8%.

    a) Compute the machine's NPV._____

    b) Compute the machine's IRR. _____

    c) Compute the machine's accrual accounting rate of return,
       assuming Vicki uses the straight-line method of depreciation. _____

    d) Comment on the uncertainties that Vicki must consider in this decision.

    _____

    _____

    _____

    _____

    _____

    _____

    _____

    _____

    _____

CHAPTER REVIEW: Learning Objectives 6 - 8

Q6: What additional issues should be considered for strategic investment decisions?

We learned in Chapter 4 that qualitative issues are important in decision making and that they sometimes outweigh quantitative factors. This is also true in capital budgeting. Examples of qualitative issues that may arise in capital budgeting decisions include:

- the effects of the decision on society as a whole (such as environmental impact)
- the effects of the decision on the company's reputation
- the effects of the decision on the community where the organization exists
- the effects of the decision on the quality of the company's products or services

After a capital budgeting decision is made to accept a project, the progress of the project must be monitored. A *post-investment audit* can be performed to assess the profitability of the project, as well as the capital budgeting decision-making process.

Q7: How do income taxes affect strategic investment decision cash flows?

For capital budgeting decisions, all cash flows should first be converted to an after-tax amount. Since the initial investment becomes deductible depreciation expense on the tax return, the tax savings from this depreciation is a cash inflow. It is often called the *depreciation tax shield*.

Demonstration problem-Capital budgeting analysis and tax effects.

Renton, Inc. is evaluating two pieces of equipment for purchase. Machine A cost $83,200 and is expected to save an estimated $20,000 per year in operating costs for seven years. Machine B costs $100,000 and is expected to save $30,000 in operating costs in each of the first two years, $20,000 in operating costs and years three and four, and $10,000 in operating costs for years five through seven. Renton uses a minimum required rate of return of 10%. Assume that Renton uses the straight-line method of depreciation for both accounting and tax purposes, and has a tax rate of 30%.

Required:
a) Compute the NPV of each machine.
b) Compute the profitability index for each machine.
c) Compute the IRR for Machine A using the time value of money tables in Chapter 12 of the text book, and compute the IRR of Machine B using Microsoft Excel.
d) Compute the payback period for each machine.
e) Compute the accrual accounting rate of return for Machine A.

Solution to demonstration problem
a) Since the savings in operating costs for Machine A are the same amount each year, we can use the present value of an ordinary annuity factor to compute the present value of these savings. The after-tax cash inflows each year are $20,000 x (1 – 30%) after-tax cash inflows + ($83,200/7 years) x 30% depreciation tax shield = $14,000 + $11,886 x 30% = $14,000 + $3,566 = $17,566.

Machine A's NPV = $17,566 x [PV of an ordinary annuity factor, n=7, r=10%] - $83,200
   = $17,566 x 4.868 - $83,200
   = $85,511 - $83,200
   = $2,311   solution to demonstration problem continues on next page →

Solution to demonstration problem continued

Depreciation on Machine B is $100,000/7 years = $14,286/year. This is a tax savings of $14,286 x 30% = $4,286 in each of the 7 years. The after-tax cash inflows in years 1 and 2 are $30,000 x (1 – 30%) + $4,286 = $25,286. The after-tax cash inflows in years 3 and 4 are $20,000 x (1 – 30%) + $4,286 = $18,286. The after-tax cash inflows in years 5 through 7 are $10,000 x (1 – 30%) + $4,286 = $11,286.

> Machine B NPV = -$100,000 + $25,286 x **0.909** +$25,286 x **0.826** + $18,286 x **0.751**
>   + $18,286 x **0.683** + $11,286 x **0.621** + $11,286 x **0.564** + $11,286 x **0.513**
>   = -$100,000 + $22, 985 + $20,886 + $13,733 + $12,489 + $7,009 + $6,365 + $5,790
>   = -$100,000 + $89,257
>   = -$10,743.

b) Machine A's profitability index = $85,511/$83,200 = 1.03, which means that each dollar invested in Machine A returns $1.03, after considering tax effects and the time value of money.

Machine B's profitability index = $89,257/$100,000 = 0.893.

c) To find the IRR for Machine A, set the present value of the savings equal to the initial investment:

> $83,200 = $17,566 x [Present value of an ordinary annuity factor, n=7, r=unknown]

> [Present value of an ordinary annuity factor, n=7, r=unknown] = 4.736

To find the IRR, scan the present value of an ordinary annuity table, along row n=7, until you locate where 4.736 would be placed. It is found somewhere between the r=10% and r=11% columns. (Using the present values tables is imprecise; computing the IRR in Excel reveals the IRR to be 10.84%.)

Time period	Cash Flow
0	($100,000)
1	$25,286
2	$25,286
3	$18,286
4	$18,286
5	$11,286
6	$11,286
7	$11,286
IRR =	6.03%

To find the IRR for Machine B, type the cash flows into a Microsoft Excel worksheet, and use the IRR formula

d) The payback period for Machine A is $83,200/$17,566 = 4.736 years.

Machine B recovers $25,286 x 2 = $50,572 by the end of year 2, $50,572 + (2 x $18,286) = $87,144 by the end of year 4, and $87,144 + $11,286 = $98,430 by the end of year 5. During year 6, $100,000 - $98,430 = $1,570 remains to be recovered. $1,570/$11,286 = 0.14 is the portion of year 6 that is required to recover the full $100,000. The payback period for Machine B is 5.16 years.

solution to demonstration problem continues on next page →

Solution to demonstration problem continued

d) For Machine A, the depreciation expense per year is $83,200/7 years = $11,886 per year. Therefore, the improvement in operating income due to the purchase of this machine will be $20,000 less $11,886 = $8,114 before tax, and $8,114 x (1 – 30%) = $5,680 after taxes. The accrual accounting rate of return for Machine A is $5,680/$83,200 = 6.83%.

Q8: How are the real and nominal methods used to address inflation in NPV analysis (Appendix 12A)

When the purchasing power of the dollar declines over a time period, it is known as a period of *inflation*. If the purchasing power of the dollar increases over a time period, it is called a period of *deflation*. When an interest rate is used that does not consider changes in purchasing power it is known as the *real rate of interest*. The real rate of interest is the sum of the *risk-free rate* plus a *risk premium*. The risk-free rate is the rate that is paid on long-term government bonds. The risk premium is the additional amount decision makers demand to compensate them for taking risk. The *nominal rate of interest* is the rate of return decision makers demand when inflation or deflation is taken into consideration. The nominal rate and the real rate are related to each other (assuming a period of inflation) as follows:

Nominal rate of interest = (1+ real rate) x (1+ inflation rate) – 1.

In the *real method* of NPV analysis, future cash flows are stated in real dollars (without considering changes in the purchasing power of the dollar) and a real rate of interest is used as the discount rate. Incremental cash inflows and terminal values are already stated in "today's dollars" and will not be adjusted. The depreciation deduction, however, will be taken in future years and must be deflated back to today's dollars.

In the *nominal method* of NPV analysis, incremental cash inflows and the terminal value must be inflated to "future dollars", and then a nominal interest rate is used as the discount rate.

Nominal cash flow = Real cash flow x $(1 + i)^t$, and
Real cash flow = Nominal cash flow/$(1 + i)^t$, where
$\quad\quad$ i = rate of inflation, and
$\quad\quad$ t = number of time periods in the future the cash flow occurs.

The real and nominal methods yield the same NPV if the inflation rate is constant over the project's life.

The following demonstration problem uses the IRS' modified asset cost recovery system (MACRS) to compute the depreciation deduction for tax purposes. Refer to Exhibits 12A.4 and 12A.5 for details on this depreciation method.

Demonstration problem-Real versus nominal NPV methods

Flair Corporation makes cabinetry for recreational vehicles. It is considering the purchase of a new woodworking machine that costs $3.7 million. The machine is expected to reduce direct labor costs by $800,000 per year for 7 years, at which point the machine could be sold for $1.5 million. The machine is classified as 7-year property under the MACRS classification system, so the depreciation method used is the 200% declining balance method, using the half-year convention . The percent of asset cost that may be deducted as depreciation in each of the 7 years is given in Exhibit 12A.5 of the text. Flair's marginal tax rate is expected to be 25% for the entire 7 year period.

The risk-free rate is 3%, and Flair believes that a risk-premium of 4% is appropriate for this investment. The rate of inflation is estimated to be 2% per year over this investment's life.

Required:
a) Compute the NPV of the project using the real method.
b) Compute the NPV of the project using the nominal method.

Solution to demonstration problem
a)

Time period	1	2	3	4	5	6	7
Incremental cash inflows	$800,000	$800,000	$800,000	$800,000	$800,000	$800,000	$800,000
Taxes on incremental cash inflows	($200,000)	($200,000)	($200,000)	($200,000)	($200,000)	($200,000)	($200,000)
Terminal cash flow							$1,500,000
Taxes on gain (see below)							($292,444)
Net incremental cash inflows	$600,000	$600,000	$600,000	$600,000	$600,000	$600,000	$1,807,556
Depreciation tax shield:							
MACRS rate (7 year property)*	14.29%	24.49%	17.49%	12.49%	8.93%	8.92%	4.47%
Depreciation deduction (nominal)	$528,730	$906,130	$647,130	$462,130	$330,410	$330,040	$165,205
Depreciation deduction (real)**	$518,363	$870,944	$609,805	$426,937	$299,263	$293,066	$143,821
Tax savings	$129,591	$217,736	$152,451	$106,734	$74,816	$73,267	$35,955
Total incremental cash flow	$729,591	$817,736	$752,451	$706,734	$674,816	$673,267	$1,843,511

* The half-year convention takes only a half year's worth of depreciation in year 7, the year of disposal.

**This is the nominal depreciation over $(1.02)^t$

Computation of gain on asset disposal:

Asset cost	$3,700,000	Computation of NPV:	
Depreciation taken	$3,369,775	PV of incremental cash flows	$4,627,298
Tax basis of asset	$330,225	Initial investment	($3,700,000)
Proceeds from sale of asset	$1,500,000	NPV	$927,298
Gain on sale	$1,169,775		

solution to demonstration problem continues on next page →

Solution to demonstration problem continued
b)

Time period	1	2	3	4	5	6	7
Incremental cash inflows	$800,000	$800,000	$800,000	$800,000	$800,000	$800,000	$800,00
Inflated incremental cash inflows	$816,000	$832,320	$848,966	$865,946	$883,265	$900,930	$918,9
Taxes on inflated incremental cash inflows	($204,000)	($208,080)	($212,242)	($216,486)	($220,816)	($225,232)	($229,7
Terminal cash flow, inflated							$1,723,0
Taxes on gain (see below)							($335,9
Net incremental cash inflows	$612,000	$624,240	$636,725	$649,459	$662,448	$675,697	$2,076,3
Depreciation tax shield:							
MACRS rate (7 year property)*	14.29%	24.49%	17.49%	12.49%	8.93%	8.92%	4.4
Depreciation deduction	$528,730	$906,130	$647,130	$462,130	$330,410	$330,040	$165,2
Tax savings	$132,183	$226,533	$161,783	$115,533	$82,603	$82,510	$41,3
Total incremental cash flow	$744,183	$850,773	$798,507	$764,992	$745,051	$758,207	$2,117,6

* The half-year convention takes only a half year's worth of depreciation in year 7, the year of disposal.

Computation of gain on asset disposal:

			Computation of NPV:	
Asset cost	$3,700,000			
Depreciation taken	$3,369,775		PV of incremental cash flows	$4,627,298
Tax basis of asset	$330,225		Initial investment	($3,700,000)
Proceeds from sale of asset	$1,500,000		NPV	$927,298
Gain on sale	$1,169,775			

PROBLEM SET B (Learning Objectives 6 - 8)

<u>True-False</u>: Indicate whether each of the following is true (T) or false (F) in the space provided.

_____   1.   The tax effects of depreciation are considered a cash inflow.

_____   2.   A project's NPV when taxes are ignored will always be lower than the project's NPV
               when taxes are taken into consideration.

_____   3.   To compute the after-tax cash inflows, multiply each cash inflow times (1 - the tax
               rate).

_____   4.   The nominal rate of interest will always be larger than the real rate of interest if there
               has been a period of inflation.

_____   5.   The real rate of interest is the nominal rate plus a risk premium.

_____   6.   Under inflation, the nominal rate of interest = risk-free rate + risk premium + rate of
               inflation.

_____   7.   Since annual cash inflows are estimated in today's dollars, no restatement of these
               inflows is necessary under the real method of computing NPV.

_____   8.   The nominal depreciation deduction will always be less than the real depreciation
               deduction when there is inflation.

_____   9.   The real rate of interest will be lower for riskier projects than it would be for less risky
               projects.

_____   10. The real and nominal methods of NPV analysis will always compute the same NPV
               for a project when the rate of inflation is constant over the life of the project.

Exercises: Write your answer in the space provided.
1. Barns, Inc. is considering the development of a new product line. Its manufacturing facility has sufficient space for the production of the new product. The new equipment that would be required costs $80,000 and is expected to last 6 years and have no disposal value. The equipment is considered five-year MACRS property for tax purposes. It is estimated that the new product line will generate $30,000 of cash inflows each year. Barns uses a 12% hurdle rate and has a tax rate of 25%. Use the present value tables, and Exhibit 12A.5, in your text.

a) Compute the NPV of this investment project. _____

b) Compute the IRR of this investment project (use Ecel). _____

c) Compute the profitability index of this investment project. _____

d) Compute the payback period of this investment project. _____

2. Hannah, Inc. is considering the development of a new product line. Its manufacturing facility has sufficient space for the production of the new product. The new equipment that would be required costs $80,000 and is expected to last 6 years and have no disposal value. The equipment is considered five-year MACRS property for tax purposes. It is estimated that the new product line will generate $20,000 of cash inflows in years 1 & 2, and $25,000 of cash inflows in years 3 – 6. Hannah uses a 12% hurdle rate and has a tax rate of 25%. Use the present value tables, and Exhibit 12A.5 in your text.

a) Compute the NPV of this investment project. _____

b) Compute the IRR of this investment project (use Excel). _____

c) Compute the profitability index of this investment project. _____

d) Compute the payback period of this investment project. _____

3. Golden, Inc. is considering the development of a new product line. Its manufacturing facility has sufficient space for the production of the new product. The new equipment that would be required costs $80,000 and is expected to last 6 years and have no disposal value. The equipment is considered five-year MACRS property for tax purposes. It is estimated that the new product line will generate $20,000 of cash inflows in years 1 & 2, and $25,000 of cash inflows in years 3 – 6. The tax-free rate is 4%, and Golden believes that 5% is an appropriate risk premium for this project. The inflation rate is expected to the 3% over the next five years. Use the present value tables, and Exhibit 12A.5 in your text. The tax rate is 30%.

a) Compute the real rate of interest. _____

b) Compute the nominal rate of interest. _____

c) Compute the nominal and the real depreciation deduction for each year.

	Nominal	Real
Year 1	_____	_____
Year 2	_____	_____
Year 3	_____	_____
Year 4	_____	_____
Year 5	_____	_____
Year 6	_____	_____

exercise 3 continues on the next page →

3. continued

d) Compute the nominal and the real incremental cash flows for each year.

	Nominal	Real
Year 1	_____	_____
Year 2	_____	_____
Year 3	_____	_____
Year 4	_____	_____
Year 5	_____	_____
Year 6	_____	_____

e) Compute the NPV using both the nominal and the real methods.

Nominal NPV _____   Real NPV _____

END OF CHAPTER EXERCISES

<u>Multiple choice</u>: Write the letter that represents the best choice in the space provided.

_____ 1. The internal rate of return is that rate which
 a. management wants to earn
 b. equates the cash inflows and outflows
 c. results in a positive NPV
 d. is greater than the hurdle rate

_____ 2. A zero NPV indicates that a project
 a. is unacceptable
 b. has a profitability index less than 1.0
 c. has a payback period equal to its life
 d. has an IRR equal to the discount rate used in the NPV analysis

_____ 3. If project X has a lower IRR than project Y, then project X would tend to have
 a. a shorter payback period
 b. a longer payback period
 c. a higher NPV
 d. a lower NPV

_____ 4. What is the NPV of a project with an initial outlay of $10,000, cash inflows of $1,000 at the end of years 1 – 9, and a cash inflow of $4,000 at the end of year 10? Assume an 8% interest rate.
 a. $(1,438)
 b. $(1,901)
 c. $3,000
 d. $8,909

_____ 5. A company is trying to determine its nominal rate of interest. The real rate of interest is 15% and inflation is estimated at 5%. What is the nominal rate of interest?
 a. 20.00%
 b. 15.75%
 c. 20.75%
 d. 19.25%

_____ 6. Carri Company is negotiating for the purchase of a new machine. The machine is expected to generate operating cost savings of $225,000 per year for 4 years. Carri uses a 12% hurdle rate. What is the most Carri would be willing to pay for this machine? Ignore tax effects.
 a. $683,325
 b. $197,935
 c. $540,450
 d. $380,250

_____ 7. Which capital budgeting method computes the discount rate that sets the NPV to zero?
   a.   accrual accounting rate of return
   b.   IRR method
   c.   NPV method
   d.   payback method

_____ 8. A project has an NPV = 0, and the initial investment is $360,000. If the discount rate is 12%, compute the annual cash inflows, if the project's life is 4 years.
   a. $133,080
   b. $118,538
   c. $82,267
   d. $123,682

_____ 9. Shamus Corp. sold a piece of equipment for $80,000. The asset originally cost $272,000, and accumulated depreciation on the equipment at the date of sale was $174,400. What is the after-tax cash inlow (outflow) from the sale of the equipment, assuming the tax rate is 40%?
   a. $(7,040)
   b. $7,040
   c. $100,800
   d. $87,040

_____ 10. Suppose a project's profitability index is 1.12. Then
   a.   the project's IRR is greater than the discount rate
   b.   the project's IRR is less than the discount rate
   c.   the project's IRR is equal to the discount rate
   d.   the relationship between the IRR and the discount rate cannot be determined without more information

_____ 11. Project A has a payback period of 4 years and Project B has a payback period of 6 years. Which project is more profitable?
   a.   Project A
   b.   Project B
   c.   They are equally profitable
   d.   The relative profitability of the 2 projects cannot be determined without more information.

_____ 12. Which of the following statements is false?
   a.   The discount rate does not need to be determined in advance for the IRR method.
   b.   The discount rate does not need to be determined in advance for the NPV method.
   c.   The discount rate does not need to be determined in advance for the payback method.
   d.   The discount rate does not need to be determined in advance for the accrual accounting rate of return method.

_____ 13. The payback method ignores
   a. the time value of money
   b. the cash flows at the end of the project's life
   c. the initial investment
   d. both (a) and (b)

_____ 14. Using a discount rate of 12%, a company determined the NPV of a project to be $12,300. If the NPV was recomputed using a 10% discount rate
   a. the new NPV would be higher
   b. the new NPV would be lower
   c. the new NPV would be $12,300
   d. the relationship between the old NPV and the new NPV cannot be determined without more information

_____ 15. Wiess Corp. is considering the purchase of a new machine. The machine will generate cost savings of $15,000 in year 1, $22,000 in year 2, and $32,000 in year 3. Wiess uses a hurdle rate of 10%. What is the most that Wiess would be willing to pay for the new machine?
   a. $69,000
   b. $131,411
   c. $55,839
   d. none of the above

Exercises: Write your answer in the space provided.

1. CDM, Inc. uses the accrual accounting rate of return method to analyze investment projects. At CDM, upper-level managers are compensated using a formula that is based on the company's return on assets, which was 8% last year. Charlie is analyzing a proposed investment project with an initial investment in equipment of $120,000. The equipment is expected to last 10 years, have no salvage value, and generate cost savings of $22,000 per year for 10 years. CDM uses straight-line depreciation for all of its assets. Ignore income taxes.

   a) Compute the accrual accounting rate of return for this project _____.

   b) Do you think the upper-level mangers will find this project acceptable? Why or why not?

   _____

   _____

   _____

   _____

   _____

   _____

   _____

   c) Suppose that Charlie is one of the upper-level managers. What issues should CDM consider with respect to the quality of information and related uncertainties?

   _____

   _____

   _____

   _____

   _____

2. This is a continuation of exercise 1, so check your answers for that exercise before beginning this one. CDM, Inc. uses the accrual accounting rate of return method to analyze investment projects. At CDM, upper-level managers are compensated using a formula that is based on the company's return on assets, which was 8% last year. Michelle is analyzing a proposed investment project that is an alternative to the project that Charlie is analyzing. It also has an initial investment in equipment of $120,000. The equipment is expected to last 10 years and have no salvage value. It is expected to generate cost savings of $2,000 per year in years 1 and 2, and $37,000 per year in years 3 through 10. CDM uses straight-line depreciation for all of its assets. Ignore income taxes.

a) Compute the accrual accounting rate of return for this project in year 1 and in year 3.

Year 1 _____   Year 3 _____.

b) Do you think the upper-level managers would prefer Michelle's or Charlie's project? Explain.

_____

_____

_____

_____

_____

c) Which project do you think is better? Explain.

_____

_____

_____

_____

_____

3. Bellevue, Inc is contemplating the purchase of a new machine that costs $50,000. It will have a useful life of 5 years and a salvage value of $4,000. Ignore income taxes in your responses.

a) Compute the payback period if the annual cost savings are $15,000 per year for 5 years.

Payback period _____

b) Compute the payback period if the cost savings are estimated at $20,000, $15,000, $10,000, $8,000, and $5,000 in years 1 – 5, respectively.

Payback period _____

c) Compute the NPV of this investment project if the cost savings are $15,000 per year for 5 years and the discount rate is 8%.

NPV = _____

d) Compute the NPV of this investment project if the cost savings are as stated in (b) and the discount rate is 8%.

NPV = _____

SOLUTION TO PROBLEM SET A

Matching:

1. F
2. B
3. H
4. C
5. G
6. E
7. K
8. A
9. J
10. D
11. D
12. E

True-False:

1. T   A longer payback period may be indicative of higher risk because there is usually more uncertainty about cash flows that are further in the future.
2. T
3. T
4. T
5. F
6. T   Refer to the demonstration problem on pages 12-5 and 12-6.
7. F
8. F   This is easily solved in Excel.
9. T
10. F
11. F
12. T
13. T
14. F   The project's NPV will be positive.
15. F

Exercises:

1. The payback period is 3.4 years. $40,000 is recovered after years 1 - 3, leaving $20,000 more to be recovered in year 4. Since the cash inflow in year 4 is $50,000, it will take $20,000/$50,000 = 0.4 of year 4 to recoup the initial investment.

2. The payback period is 7.0 years. $55,000 is recovered after years 1 - 6, leaving $5,000 more to be recovered in year 7. Since the cash inflow in year 7 is $5,000, it will take the whole year to recover the initial investment.

3. The payback method would rank the first project more highly than the second because of its lower payback period. However, the second project recovers 5/6 of the initial outlay in the first year. Additionally, the payback method ignores any cash flows after the payback period ends, so the second project's $120,000 cash flow in year eight isn't even considered.

4. a) NPV = $10,000 x [Present value of an ordinary annuity factor, n=8, r=8%] - $40,000
         = $10,000 x 5.747 - $40,000
         = $57,470 - $40,000
         = $17,470.

   b) $40,000 = $10,000 x [Present value of an ordinary annuity factor, n=8, r=unknown]
      4.0 = Present value of an ordinary annuity factor, n=8, r=unknown
      Search the present value of an annuity table to find that the IRR is just over 18%.

   c) The annual depreciation is $40,000/8 years = $5,000/year. The increase in income then is $10,000 - $5,000 = $5,000. The accrual accounting rate of return = $5,000/$40,000 = 12.5%.

   d) The initial investment amount probably contains the least amount of uncertainty, but even here she may find that there are set up costs or attachments that she must pay for that she didn't know about. Other questions Vicki may be concerned about could include:
- What will the be quality of the banners produced by the new machine?
- Will her workers be able to operate the new machine with the same efficiency as the old machine?
- How reliable is her estimate of the annual savings?
- Will customer demand for her signs remain strong enough? After all, there will be no cost savings if no units are produced if customer demand dries up.

SOLUTION TO PROBLEM SET B

True-False:

1. T
2. F   When a high discount rate is used, cash flows far into the future are valued much less than early cash flows. If the MACRS accelerated depreciation is large enough in the early years, the NPV when taxes are considered could be higher than the NPV when taxes are not considered because of this depreciation tax shield.
3. T
4. T   The real rate of interest is the *risk-free rate* plus a risk premium.
5. F
6. F
7. T
8. F   The nominal depreciation deduction will always be more.
9. F   The real rate of interest will be higher for riskier projects.
10. T   Refer to the demonstration problem about the real and nominal NPV methods.

Exercises:
1. a & b) The NPV of this investment is $27,269, and the IRR is 23.7%, as shown below:

Time Period	Pretax Cash Flow	After-tax Cash Flow	MACRS Deduction %*	MACRS Deduction %*	iation Tax Shield	Total Cash Flows	PV Factor	PV of Cash Flows
0	($80,000)	($80,000)				($80,000)	1.00000	($80,000)
1	$30,000	$22,500	20.00%	$16,000	$4,000	$26,500	0.89286	$23,661
2	$30,000	$22,500	32.00%	$25,600	$6,400	$28,900	0.79719	$23,039
3	$30,000	$22,500	19.20%	$15,360	$3,840	$26,340	0.71178	$18,748
4	$30,000	$22,500	11.52%	$9,216	$2,304	$24,804	0.63552	$15,763
5	$30,000	$22,500	11.52%	$9,216	$2,304	$24,804	0.56743	$14,074
6	$30,000	$22,500	5.76%	$4,608	$1,152	$23,652	0.50663	$11,983
					IRR =	23.7%	NPV =	$27,269

c) The profitability index is ($80,000 + $27,269)/$80,000 = $107,269/$80,000 = 1.34.

d) After year 2, the project has recovered $26,500 + $28,900 = $55,400, leaving $24,600 yet to be recovered. The cash flow in year 3 is $26,340, so it will take $24,600/$26,340 = 0.93, so the payback period is 2.93 years.

2. a & b) The NPV of this investment is $5,513, and the IRR is 14.4%, as shown below:

Time Period	Pretax Cash Flow	After-tax Cash Flow	MACRS Deduction %*	MACRS Deduction	Depreciation Tax Shield	Total Cash Flows	PV Factor	PV of Cash Flows
0	($80,000)	($80,000)				($80,000)	1.00000	($80,000)
1	$20,000	$15,000	20.00%	$16,000	$4,000	$19,000	0.89286	$16,964
2	$20,000	$15,000	32.00%	$25,600	$6,400	$21,400	0.79719	$17,060
3	$25,000	$18,750	19.20%	$15,360	$3,840	$22,590	0.71178	$16,079
4	$25,000	$18,750	11.52%	$9,216	$2,304	$21,054	0.63552	$13,380
5	$25,000	$18,750	11.52%	$9,216	$2,304	$21,054	0.56743	$11,947
6	$25,000	$18,750	5.76%	$4,608	$1,152	$19,902	0.50663	$10,083
					IRR =	14.4%	NPV =	$5,513

c) The profitability index is ($80,000 + $5,513)/$80,000 = $85,513/$80,000 = 1.07.

d) After year 3, the project has recovered $19,000 + $21,400 + $22,590 = $62,990, leaving $17,010 yet to be recovered. The cash flow in year 4 is $21,054 so it will take $17,010/$21,054 = 0.81, so the payback period is 3.81 years.

3. a) The real rate of interest is 4% + 5% = 9%.

b) The nominal rate of interest is (1.09) x (1.03) −1.0 = 12.27%.

c) The real and nominal depreciation deductions for each year are shown below:

Depreciation tax shield:

MACRS rate (5 year property)	20.00%	32.00%	19.20%	11.52%	11.52%	5.76%
Depreciation deduction (nominal)	$16,000	$25,600	$15,360	$9,216	$9,216	$4,608
Depreciation deduction (real)	$15,534	$24,130	$14,057	$8,188	$7,950	$3,859

3. continued

d & e) The real cash flows are shown in the schedule below, as is the NPV. The real cash flows are in italics.

Time period	1	2	3	4	5	6
Incremental cash inflows	$20,000	$20,000	$25,000	$25,000	$25,000	$25,000
Taxes on incremental cash inflows	($6,000)	($6,000)	($7,500)	($7,500)	($7,500)	($7,500)
Net incremental cash inflows	$14,000	$14,000	$17,500	$17,500	$17,500	$17,500
Depreciation tax shield:						
MACRS rate (5 year property)	20.00%	32.00%	19.20%	11.52%	11.52%	5.76%
Depreciation deduction (nominal)	$16,000	$25,600	$15,360	$9,216	$9,216	$4,608
Depreciation deduction (real)	$15,534	$24,130	$14,057	$8,188	$7,950	$3,859
Tax savings	$4,660	$7,239	$4,217	$2,456	$2,385	$1,158
Total incremental cash flow	*$18,660*	*$21,239*	*$21,717*	*$19,956*	*$19,885*	*$18,658*

Computation of NPV:

PV of incremental cash flows	$89,952
Initial investment	($80,000)
NPV	$9,952

d & e) The nominal cash flows are shown in the schedule below, as is the NPV. The real cash flows are in italics.

Time period	1	2	3	4	5	6
Incremental cash inflows	$20,000	$20,000	$25,000	$25,000	$25,000	$25,000
Inflated incremental cash inflows	$20,600	$21,218	$27,318	$28,138	$28,982	$29,851
Taxes on inflated incremental cash inflows	($6,180)	($6,365)	($8,195)	($8,441)	($8,695)	($8,955)
Net incremental cash inflows	$14,420	$14,853	$19,123	$19,696	$20,287	$20,896
Depreciation tax shield:						
MACRS rate (5 year property)	20.00%	32.00%	19.20%	11.52%	11.52%	5.76%
Depreciation deduction (nominal)	$16,000	$25,600	$15,360	$9,216	$9,216	$4,608
Tax savings	$4,800	$7,680	$4,608	$2,765	$2,765	$1,382
Total incremental cash flow	*$19,220*	*$22,533*	*$23,731*	*$22,461*	*$23,052*	*$22,278*

Computation of NPV:

PV of incremental cash flows	$89,952
Initial investment	($80,000)
NPV	$9,952

SOLUTION TO END OF CHAPTER EXERCISES

Multiple choice:

1. B
2. D
3. D
4. B

Time Period	Cash Flow	PV Factor	PV of Cash Flow
0	($10,000)	1.000	($10,000)
1	$1,000	0.926	$926
2	$1,000	0.857	$857
3	$1,000	0.794	$794
4	$1,000	0.735	$735
5	$1,000	0.681	$681
6	$1,000	0.630	$630
7	$1,000	0.583	$583
8	$1,000	0.540	$540
9	$1,000	0.500	$500
10	$4,000	0.463	$1,853
			($1,901)

{Alternatively, $1,000 x 6.247 PV annuity factor + $4,000 x 0.463 PV of $ factor - $10,000 = ($1,901)}

5. C   (1.15) x (1.05) – 1.0 = 20.75%

6. A $225,000 x [PV ordinary annuity, n=4, r=12%] = $225,000 x 3.037 = $683,325

7. B

8. B   NPV =0 = Annual cash inflow x [Present value of an ordinary annuity factor, n=8, r=8%] - $360,000; so $360,000 = Annual cash inflow x 3.037; solve for annual cash inflow = $118,538.

9. D   The basis of the asset at the time of sale = $272,000 - $174,400 = $97,600. It was sold for $80,000, so the loss is $17,600. This loss will generate tax savings of $17,600 x 40% = $7,040. Add this tax savings to the $80,000 proceeds to get $87,040 cash inflow.

10. A

11. D   The payback method does not address project profitability.

12. B

13. D

14. A   The NPV of an investment is inversely related to the discount rate.

15. C $15,000 x 0.909 + $22,000 x 0.826 + $32,000 x 0.751 = $55,839.

Exercises:

1. a) The annual depreciation is $120,000/10 years = $12,000. The increase in income from this project is $22,000 - $12,000 = $10,000. The accrual accounting rate of return is $10,000/$120,000 = 8.33%.

    b) Yes, the managers would like this project because it will increase the return on assets, which will in turn increase their bonuses.

    c) An organization must always be concerned about the quality of information when it is obtained from someone who has a vested stake in the outcome. However, in this case, upper-level managers are compensated based on the actual return on assets. Charlie, therefore, does not have an incentive to misstate the information merely so that the project will be accepted. The real issue here is whether the project adds value to the company if it is accepted, and the accrual accounting rate of return method is not a good measure of that (which is why it is not the best method to use when analyzing capital budget projects).

2. a) The depreciation is $120,000/10 years = $12,000 per year. The accrual accounting rate of return for year 1 (and for year 2) is ($2,000 - $12,000)/$120,000 = -8.33%. The accrual accounting rate of return for year 3 (and for years 4 - 10) is ($37,000 - $12,000)/$120,000 = 20.83%.

    b) If the upper-level managers have a short-term focus, which is common, they would prefer Charlie's project, because the accrual accounting rate of return is negative in years 1 & 2 and would have a negative impact on their bonuses.

    c) Michelle's project seems to have the higher cash flows, overall, even though they don't occur in the first 2 years. In fact, if we compute the NPV of each project using any interest rate, say 8% for example, we can better compare the projects. The NPV of Charlie's project is $27,622, and the NPV of Michelle's project is $65,859. It is important to design a performance compensation scheme so that managers' incentives are aligned with the organization's long-term goals.

3. a) After year 3, the project has recovered $45,000, leaving $5,000 yet to be recovered. The cash flow in year 4 is $15,000, so it will take $5,000/$15,000 = 0.33, so the payback period is 3.33 years.

    b) After year 3, the project has recovered $45,000, leaving $5,000 yet to be recovered. The cash flow in year 4 is $8,000, so it will take $5,000/$8,000 = 0.625, so the payback period is 3.625 years.

c) The NPV is $9,891, as shown below:

Time Period	Cash Flow	PV Factor	PV of Cash Flow
0	($50,000)	1.00000	($50,000)
1	$15,000	0.92593	$13,889
2	$15,000	0.85734	$12,860
3	$15,000	0.79383	$11,907
4	$15,000	0.73503	$11,025
5	$15,000	0.68058	$10,209
			$9,891

{Of course, this can be done more simply by using the PV of an annuity: $15,000 x 3.99271 - $50,000 = $9,891.}

d) The NPV is ($1,400), as shown below:

Time Period	Cash Flow	PV Factor	PV of Cash Flow
0	($50,000)	1.00000	($50,000)
1	$20,000	0.92593	$18,519
2	$15,000	0.85734	$12,860
3	$10,000	0.79383	$7,938
4	$8,000	0.73503	$5,880
5	$5,000	0.68058	$3,403
			($1,400)

Chapter 13

Joint Management
of Revenues and Costs

√ **Study Checklist – Monitor your progress**
1. Read the chapter in the text
2. Review the learning objectives below
3. Read the overview of the chapter
4. Read the chapter review for learning objectives 1 – 4
5. Do Problem Set A and check your answers
6. Read the chapter review for learning objectives 5 – 8
7. Do Problem Set B and check your answers
8. Do the End of Chapter Exercises in this study guide
9. Do the homework assigned by your instructor

CHAPTER LEARNING OBJECTIVES
After studying this chapter, you should be able to answer the following questions:
Q1. How is value chain analysis used to improve operations?
Q2. What is target costing, and how is it performed?
Q3. What is kaizen costing, and how does it compare to target costing?
Q4. What is life cycle costing?
Q5. How are cost-based prices established?
Q6. How are market-based prices established?
Q7. What are the uses and limitations of cost-based and market-based pricing?
Q8: What additional factors affect prices?

OVERVIEW OF CHAPTER
In addition to managing costs, managers must determine selling prices for products and services. This chapter reviews some cost management techniques as well as some pricing techniques.

CHAPTER REVIEW: Learning Objectives 1 - 4

Q1: How is value chain analysis used to improve operations?
The series of sequential business processes that a company goes through as it researches, designs, creates, markets, distributes, and services its products or services is known as the *value chain*. To manage costs, companies analyze the activities in each of the business processes and categorize them as *value-added* or *non-value-added* activities. Non-value-added activities are unnecessary activities that can be eliminated, without diminishing the value of the product or service to the customer, if the business process is changed in some way.

The inspection of incoming raw materials, for example, is a non-value added activity. It should be possible to find reliable suppliers whose shipments do not require inspection, which would eliminate this non-value added cost. In some cases, companies may determine that an activity is not one of their core competencies, and outsource the activity. The classification of activities as to their added value status, and the subsequent investigations that companies perform in their attempts to eliminate non-value added costs (as well as to reduce value-added costs) is known as *value chain analysis*. When companies look for improvements specifically in activities such as the acquisition of materials, management of inventory levels, distribution channels to customers, and their relationships with their suppliers and customers, this is known as *supply chain analysis*.

One way to reduce costs is to maintain low inventory levels for raw materials and finished goods. Under just-in-time (JIT) production and inventory control systems, raw materials are purchased only as they are needed and are delivered directly to the area of production. Also, units are produced only as the customer demands them. JIT systems rely on new technologies to communicate more quickly with suppliers and customers. These systems reduce costs and improve business efficiency, but risk business stoppages when something goes wrong.

Q2: What is target costing, and how is it performed?
In highly competitive markets, companies may have little or no control over their products' selling prices. In target costing, companies start with these given market prices, and subtract their desired profit margin on the product to arrive at the target cost for a product. Engineers and accountants will work to see if the product can be produced at that cost.

> Target cost = Price - Required profit margin

The target costing process takes place before the final decision to produce a product. It is more likely to be successful when the product design and production processes are complex, the company has flexible relationships with suppliers, and potential customers are likely to be willing to pay for product attributes that will differentiate this product from the competition.

Demonstration problem-Target costing process
Pete's Pool Products is considering the development, production, and distribution of a new diving board for in-ground pools. The selling price of similar diving boards is $100, and Pete hopes to produce and sell 20,000 boards. Pete demands a 20% of selling price margin for all products.

Required:
a) Compute the target cost for the proposed diving board.
b) Suppose Pete gathers a team of production engineers, accountants, production supervisors, and marketing personnel to investigate the feasibility of the new product. The team comes up with estimates of costs for the new product. Discuss the types of issues Pete's team should investigate as it tries to reduce costs to meet the target cost.

Direct materials	$40.00
Direct labor	20.00
Variable manufacturing overhead	8.00
Fixed manufacturing overhead	6.00
Variable selling expenses	7.50
Fixed selling & administrative expenses	6.50
	$88.00

Solution to demonstration problem
a) Target cost = $100 - 20% x $100 = $80/unit.
b) As the team attempts to reduce costs by 10%, they may address some or all of the following questions:
- Can the purchase price of any of the materials be re-negotiated with the supplier(s)?
- Can the product be redesigned so that the quantity of materials and/or labor can be reduced?
- Can the production process be redesigned so that the quantity of materials and/or labor can be reduced?
- Can the design of the product be changed to incorporate features that the customer would be willing to pay for?
- Has an appropriate cost allocation base been used to assign variable overhead to the product?
- Can variable selling expenses, for example, commissions, be reduced on this new product?
- Can more than 20,000 units be produced and sold so that the allocation of fixed costs per unit decreases?

Q3: What is kaizen costing, and how does it compare to target costing?
Kaizen costing is different from target costing in that it takes place after the production process has begun. In kaizen costing, explicit cost reductions over time are planned in advance. The process of working with accountants, engineers, and suppliers to achieve these cost reductions, however, is similar to the target costing process. It is a continuous improvement process that takes place over a longer planning horizon than target costing.

Q4: What is life cycle costing?

For many products, market prices decrease over time. Life cycle costing takes into consideration the product's selling price and its costs over the entire product life, beginning at the time the product is introduced to the marketplace. Life cycle costing can be used for products that are expected to produce losses when first introduced, but increases in sales volumes and decreasing production costs over time are expected. It is especially useful in industries with rapid changes in products or production processes. In life cycle costing, initial production and process design costs will be viewed as costs to be matched against the revenues the product is expected to generate over its entire life, not just as expenses in the period incurred.

PROBLEM SET A (Learning Objectives 1 - 4)

<u>True-False</u>: Indicate whether each of the following is true (T) or false (F) in the space provided.

_____   1. Value-added activities increase the product's value from the customer's perspective.

_____   2. The costs of value-added activities can be reduced with improved efficiency.

_____   3. The cost of raw materials storage is an example of a value-added cost.

_____   4. The value chain is a series of business processes beginning with product development.

_____   5. Target costing and kaizen costing are similar, but kaizen costing begins at the product design stage.

_____   6. Implementing a JIT system will decrease inventory levels.

_____   7. Life cycle costing may take costs normally considered to be an expense of the period and allocate them over the product's entire life cycle.

_____   8. Target costing is longer-term in nature than kaizen costing.

_____   9. Supply chain analysis may involve investigating relationships with materials suppliers, but not with distributors of the company's products.

_____ 10. When a JIT system is implemented, distribution cost are likely to decrease.

_____ 11. Target costing explicitly plans cost reductions for successive periods.

_____ 12. JIT systems face less risk of business stoppages than traditional production systems.

_____ 13. A company with a JIT system will not have a Raw Materials Inventory account in the general ledger.

_____ 14. Kaizen costing and life cycle costing are long-term approaches to product costing.

_____ 15. A JIT system relies less on technology than a traditional system, reducing the chance of network downtime affecting production.

<u>Multiple choice</u>: Write the letter that represents the best choice in the space provided.

<u>Use the following information for questions 1 – 4:</u>
Sportstuff, Inc. is investigating the feasibility of a adding a new skateboard to its line up of products. The marketing department believes that 10,000 units can be sold at $90 each. Sportstuff demands a 25% profit margin (i.e. cost is 75% of selling price) on all products.

_____ 1. To achieve its goal, Sportstuff must keep total costs equal to or below
      a. $225,000
      b. $675,000
      c. $506,250
      d. $900,000

_____ 2. To achieve its goal, Sportstuff must earn revenues on the product of
      a. $225,000
      b. $675,000
      c. $506,250
      d. $900,000

_____ 3. To achieve its goal, Sportstuff must keep per-unit costs equal to or less than
      a. $22.50
      b. $67.50
      c. $50.63
      d. $90.00

_____ 4. If it achieves its goal, Sportstuff will have operating income on this product of
      a. $225,000
      b. $675,000
      c. $506,250
      d. $900,000

_____ 5. Product design, product production, and customer service are business processes that are part of the
      a. supply chain
      b. value chain
      c. distribution channel
      d. management of inventory levels

_____ 6. Value-added costs
      a. must be eliminated
      b. include the costs of repairing defective units of production
      c. are costs that a customer is willing to see incorporated into the product's price
      d. do not need to be monitored because they increase the product's value

_____ 7. Which of the following concentrates on reducing costs at the design phase of a product?
   a. life cycle costing
   b. target costing
   c. kaizen costing
   d. value costing

_____ 8. Which of the following is not likely to be a feature of target costing?
   a. The selling price is taken as given.
   b. Product development time is decreased.
   c. Relationships with suppliers are reviewed.
   d. Product design changes are made to decrease production costs.

_____ 9. Which of the following concentrates on reducing costs at the production phase of a product?
   a. life cycle costing
   b. target costing
   c. kaizen costing
   d. value costing

_____ 10. Which of the following assigns product design costs over several years?
   a. life cycle costing
   b. target costing
   c. kaizen costing
   d. value costing

CHAPTER REVIEW: Learning Objectives 5 - 8

Q5: How are cost-based prices established?
When a product's selling price is based on product cost plus a markup the selling price is known as a *cost-based price*. Cost-based pricing is more useful when the company produces specialized or cost of products. If a product costs $100,000 to produce and the markup is 20%, the selling price will be $120,000. Companies differ in which costs to include in that cost upon which the markup is calculated. Some use only variable costs, some only production costs, and some use all production and non-production costs in the base.

Q 6: How are market-based prices established?
The product's selling price in the marketplace depends on the degree of competition in the market and the degree to which the company's product can be differentiated from competitors' products.

To set a *market-based price*, the company has to estimate customer demand for the product as well as the sensitivity of this demand to changes in product price, which is known as the price elasticity of demand. In order to calculate the price elasticity of demand, the company must have information about quantities of the products sold at various selling prices.

$$\text{Price elasticity of demand} = \frac{\ln(1 + \% \text{ change in quantity sold})}{\ln(1 + \% \text{ change in price})},$$

where ln is the natural logarithm operator. In a competitive marketplace, an increase in price should decrease customer demand for the product, even though each product brings in more revenue.

- When the balance of these two offsetting effects is such that a price increase (decrease) causes total revenue to increase (decrease), customer demand is said to be *inelastic*.

- When the balance of these two offsetting effects is such that a price increase (decrease) causes total revenue to decrease (increase) because of the resultant large decrease (increase) in the quantity of units sold, customer demand is said to be *elastic*.

Under this approach to pricing, the profit-maximizing price is determined as follows:

$$\text{Profit-maximizing price} = \left[\frac{\text{Elasticity}}{(\text{Elasticity}+1)} \right] \times \text{Variable cost}$$

The above formula yields the profit-maximizing price, assuming that changes in quantities sold are due solely to changes in price, which is a rather strong assumption. Other market forces or changes in customer attitudes or the business environment could cause changes in the quantities sold.

Demonstration problem-Market-based pricing
Summerfun Products makes gazebos and asks for your help determining the appropriate selling price of their most popular model. Summerfun has gathered data over the years about the response of customer demand to changes in the product's price and estimates that a 10% increase in the product's price results in a 25% decrease in the number of units sold. The variable costs of the gazebo are $167 per unit. The current selling price is $280, but the product line manager feels that the selling price should be decreased.

Required:
a) Calculate the price elasticity of demand.
b) Calculate the profit-maximizing selling price for the gazebo.
c) Discuss the limitations of your analysis and suggest an approach to determining the selling price.

Solution to demonstration problem
a) The price elasticity of demand = $\ln(1 - 0.25)/\ln(1 + 0.10) = \ln(0.75)/\ln(1.1) = -3.0184$.
b) The profit maximizing price is $[(-3.0184)/(-3.0184 + 1)] \times \$167 = \$249.74$.
c) The data about the responsiveness of customer demand to changes in price was gathered over a period of years. It is likely that many other factors besides price had an impact on customer demand for the gazebo over this time period. Perhaps competition levels have changed, customer tastes have changed, or economic conditions have changed over this period. Additionally, Summerfun should take into consideration how the pricing this model will affect sales of its other gazebo models. Since the calculated profit maximizing price is lower than the current selling price, and because the product line manager's intuition is that the selling price should be lower, one pricing approach is to decrease the selling price in small increments over time, all the while monitoring the sales of all models of gazebos.

Q7: What are the uses and limitations of cost-based and market-based pricing?
Cost-based pricing is inappropriate in highly competitive markets. If the selling price determined is greater than what customers are willing to pay, the volume of products sold will decrease. As sales volumes decrease, product cost increases because each unit must absorb a higher amount of fixed costs. The next time the selling price is determined, cost-based pricing computes an even higher selling price, decreasing sales volumes even further. This is known as the *death spiral*.

The advantage of cost-based pricing is that a company determines its margin on sales before the sale. Even though cost-based pricing is best used when a company produces highly customized products, a big problem with cost-based pricing in these situations is that it does not take into consideration what the customer would be willing to pay for a product. If a product costs $100,000 to produce and the markup is 20%, the selling price will be $120,000.

- If the customer would have paid $150,000 without considering a competitor's product, the company has essentially lost $30,000.

- If the customer was willing to pay only $119,500 for the product, then the company loses the sale and the entire production costs of $100,000 if the product cannot be sold to a different customer.

Market-based pricing is superior to cost-based pricing, but the required information was difficult to obtain in the past. Therefore, cost-based pricing is currently more common than market-based pricing. As new information gathering technologies emerge, we are likely to see increased use of market-based pricing.

Q8: What additional factors affect prices?
Some of the other factors that affect prices include:

- Capacity considerations. The company may change its prices at different times in order to try to influence customer demand. For example, Caribbean vacations are less expensive in the summer than in the winter. This is known as *peak load pricing*.

- Different price elasticities of demand for different customers. When new products are introduced, they sometimes have a higher selling price. Many customers would not consider purchasing at that price, but some would. When the introductory price is high, and then gradually lowered to entice new customers to buy the product, this is known as *price skimming*.

- New product introduction. When a company introduces a product into an established market, they may set a very low price in order to capture market share. When a company does this to reduce customer uncertainty about the product, it is legal and is known as *penetration pricing*. However, when the company's intent is to eliminate all competitors from the marketplace, it is illegal and is known as *predatory pricing*.

- Opportunistic pricing. When prices are set unusually high to take advantage of specific situations, this is known as *price gouging*.

- Interdepartmental pricing. When one segment of an organization provides products or services to another segment of the same organization, a *transfer price* is usually attached to these products or services so that each segment's performance can be measured. Transfer prices are covered in more detail in Chapter 15.

- Not-for-profit organizations. Some not-for-profit organizations provide services based on the customer's ability to pay. When a for-profit organization charges different prices to different customers, this is known as *price discrimination*, and is not legal unless the organization can show that their costs for these customers are different.

- Collaboration with competitors. If companies that sell the same product get together to determine the product selling price, rather than competing with each other on price, this is known as *collusive pricing* and is not legal.

- Foreign-based company sales in the U.S. When a foreign-based company attempts to sell its products in the U.S. for prices lower than in the home country, this is known as *dumping*, and the U.S. government will impose in an antidumping dumping tariff.

PROBLEM SET B (Learning Objectives 5 - 8)

<u>Matching</u>: Match each term with the appropriate definition or phrase. Use each term only once.

Terms

A.	Peak load pricing	G.	Dumping
B.	Price discrimination	H.	Collusive pricing
C.	Predatory pricing	I.	Transfer pricing
D.	Price skimming	J.	Price gouging
E.	Death spiral	K.	Price elasticity of demand
F.	Cost-based pricing	L.	Market-based pricing
		M.	Penetration pricing

_____ 1. Pricing depends on capacity and different prices may be charged at different times

_____ 2. Price is determined as cost plus a markup

_____ 3. Decreases in customer demand cause price increases, which further decreases customer demand

_____ 4. Opportunistic pricing

_____ 5. Pricing the goods and services exchanged within an organization

_____ 6. Pricing a product low in the initial product introduction phase so that customers might try the product, and increasing the price later

_____ 7. Pricing a product low in the initial product introduction phase so that the competition is destroyed, and increasing the price later

_____ 8. Charging different prices to different customers is not illegal if the difference is based on different costs

_____ 9. A foreign-based company sells products in the U.S. at prices lower than the market price of the product in its home country

_____ 10. The sensitivity of customer demand to price changes

_____ 11. Product pricing is initially set high to take advantage of the fact that some customers are willing to pay a high price for this new product. The price is lowered after all of these customers have purchased the product.

_____ 12. Setting product prices while taking into consideration what the customer is willing to pay

_____ 13. Companies meet to set prices to reduce competition

<u>Exercises</u>: Write your answer in the space provided.

1. Happy Kitty makes cat treats. It is trying to determine new selling prices for two of its products. Cat Yums was the company's first product; it comes in a large plastic bucket. The variable costs of a bucket of Cat Yums is $2.10 and the current selling price is $4/bucket. Happy Kitty believes that a 10% increase in the price of Cat Yums leads to a 15% decrease in the number of buckets sold. Recently Happy Kitty introduced a "gourmet" cat treat they call Lucky Kitty. Lucky Kitty comes in small, resealable cylinders with a multi-color image of a large fluffy cat reclining on a designer sofa. The treats are in the shape of little fish. The variable costs of a cylinder of Lucky Kitty are $1.60, and a cylinder currently sells for $5.50. Based on the data collected over this product's short life, Happy Kitty believes that a 10% increase in the price leads to a 30% decrease in the quantity of cylinders sold.

a) Compute the price elasticity of demand for each product.

Cat Yums _____   Lucky Kitty _____

b) Compute the profit maximizing price for each product.

Cat Yums _____   Lucky Kitty _____

c) Compare the price elasticities for the 2 product and discuss how they differently affect the profit maximizing price for each product. Should Happy Kitty use the prices from part (b)? Why or why not?

_____

_____

_____

_____

_____

_____

2. Boycov Industries believes that every 5% decrease in the selling price of its product increases the number of units sold by 9%. The product's variable costs are $52 per unit.

   a) Compute the price elasticity of demand. _____

   b) Compute the profit maximizing price. _____

   c) Suppose that the fixed costs per unit are $18 and that Boycov was using cost-based pricing (with the cost base including fixed and variable costs) to achieve a 20% margin on sales. Compute the selling price under this costing approach.

      Selling price under cost-based pricing _____

   d) Compare the two pricing strategies and discuss the pros and cons of each in this situation.

      _____

      _____

      _____

      _____

      _____

      _____

      _____

      _____

      _____

      _____

END OF CHAPTER EXERCISES

<u>Multiple choice</u>: Write the letter that represents the best choice in the space provided.

_____   1. Which of the following statements is false?
    a. When demand is inelastic, a price increase will have little effect on the number of units sold.
    b. An increase in variable costs will increase the profit-maximizing selling price.
    c. Penetration pricing is illegal.
    d. Kaizen costing is a continuous improvement process that decreases waste and increases production efficiency.

_____   2. Place the following tasks involved in target costing in the correct order.
               A: Determine the target cost
               B: Determine the target selling price
               C: Perform value chain analysis
    a. A B C
    b. B C A
    c. B A C
    d. C B A

_____   3. In cost-based pricing, which costs are appropriately included in the cost base?
    a. variable production costs only
    b. production costs only
    c. all production and non-production costs
    d. any of the above may be used.

_____   4. Which of the following statements about life cycle costing is false?
    a. It is long-term in nature.
    b. It is appropriate in situations where production costs are expected to increase over time.
    c. It is appropriate in situations where a product is initially expected to sell at a loss.
    d. It is appropriate in situations where the product's selling price is expected to decrease over time.

_____   5. Which of the following statements about target costing is false?
    a. It is likely to increase product development time.
    b. It may be performed for a product that is eventually never produced.
    c. The product's selling price is determined after the target cost is computed.
    d. Value chain analysis is used to find the cost reductions necessary to meet the target cost.

_____ 6. Just before the landfall of hurricane Ivan a convenience store manager decided to raise the price on a bottle of water from $1 to $7. This is an example of
   a.   price gouging
   b.   predatory pricing
   c.   penetration pricing
   d.   price skimming

_____ 7. A company with a new product decides to set the initial price low so that customers will try the product. This is an example of
   a.   price gouging
   b.   predatory pricing
   c.   penetration pricing
   d.   price skimming

_____ 8. A company with a new product decides to set the initial price low so that the competition is destroyed. This is an example of
   a.   price gouging
   b.   predatory pricing
   c.   penetration pricing
   d.   price skimming

_____ 9. A company with a new product decides to set the initial price high because there are some customers who will pay this high price for a newly introduced product. This is an example of
   a.   price gouging
   b.   predatory pricing
   c.   penetration pricing
   d.   price skimming

_____ 10. Which of the following statements is the best example of the process known as dumping?
   a.   A company with excess inventory sells it in its home country for a price below cost.
   b.   A company sells its products on foreign soil for less than it sells them at home.
   c.   A company with excess inventory sells it in its home country for a price below the normal selling price.
   d.   A company with a new product sells it in its home country for a price above the normal selling price.

Exercises: Write your answer in the space provided.
1. Charmaster makes 2 styles of propane grills for outdoor use, Regular and Deluxe. Charmaster has gathering data to perform market-based pricing, and is interested in comparing cost-based to market-based pricing. Last year's selling prices and variable costs for each product are listed below.

	Regular	Deluxe
Selling price	$110.00	$150.00
Variable costs:		
Direct materials	38.00	42.00
Direct labor	17.00	21.00
Variable manufacturing overhead	3.00	4.00
Variable selling expenses	5.50	7.50
Total variable costs	63.50	74.50
Contribution margin	$46.50	$75.50

Charmaster sold 10,000 Regular and 5,000 Deluxe grills last year. Total fixed manufacturing overhead last year was $200,000, and is allocated to products based on direct labor costs. Total fixed non-manufacturing costs were $150,000, and are allocated to the products based on relative sales revenue.

a) Compute the selling prices if Charmaster uses all manufacturing and non-manufacturing costs as the cost base and a 50% markup on cost. Use last year's allocations of fixed costs to determine total costs.

Regular _____   Deluxe _____

b) Compute the selling prices if Charmaster uses all variable costs as the cost base and a 65% markup on cost.

Regular _____   Deluxe _____

c) Compute the selling prices if Charmaster uses market-based pricing and the data shows that a 10% increase in price results in a 20% and 25% decrease in unit sales for Regular and Deluxe, respectively.

Regular _____   Deluxe _____

2. This is a continuation of exercise 1, so check your answers for that problem before attempting this one.

    a) Why is the selling price for a Deluxe unit so much higher than a Regular unit in part (a) of exercise 1 when compared to the prices computed in part (b) of exercise 1?

    _____

    _____

    _____

    _____

    _____

    b) Why are the prices for each product computed in exercise 1, part (c) so close to one another, especially when compared to the current selling prices?

    _____

    _____

    _____

    _____

    c) Do you think Charmaster should implement the market-based prices computed in part (c) of exercise 1? Why or why not?

    _____

    _____

    _____

    _____

    _____

    _____

    _____

    _____

SOLUTION TO PROBLEM SET A

<u>True-False:</u>

1. T
2. T   It's not just non-value-added costs that are the target of cost management techniques.
3. F
4. T
5. F   Yes, they are similar but target costing begins at the product design stage, not kaizen costing.
6. T
7. T
8. F   Kaizen costing is longer-term in nature than target costing.
9. F
10. T
11. F   No, the phrase is describing kaizen costing, not target costing.
12. F
13. T
14. T
15. F   It relies more on technology, with greater risk should the technology fail.

<u>Multiple choice:</u>

1. B   [$90 x 10,000] x [1 – 25%] = $675,000
2. D   [$90 x 10,000] = $900,000
3. B $675,000/10,000 units = $67.50/unit
4. A $900,000 revenue - $675,000 costs = $225,000 operating income
5. B
6. C
7. B
8. B
9. C
10. A

SOLUTION TO PROBLEM SET B

Matching:

1. A
2. F
3. E
4. J
5. I
6. M
7. C
8. B
9. G
10. K
11. D
12. L
13. H

Exercises:
1. a) Price elasticity for Cat Yums = ln(1.1)/ln(0.85) = -1.705.
   Price elasticity for Lucky Kitty = ln(1.1)/ln(0.7) = -3.742.

   b) The profit maximizing price for Cat Yums = (-1.705/-0.705) x $2.10 = $5.08.
   The profit maximizing price for Lucky Kitty = (-3.742/-2.742) x $1.60 = $2.18.

   c) It seems that Happy Kitty (HK) thought the impressive packaging and fish-shaped treats would command a higher price. However, customers are much more sensitive to changes in price for Lucky Kitty that they are for Cat Yums. The profit maximizing price for Lucky Kitty is computed to be $2.18, much lower than the current price, because of this sensitivity and the lower variable costs per unit for Lucky Kitty. Customers are much less sensitive to price changes for Cat Yums, so this means that the profit maximizing price can be higher.

   When considering whether to use these price computations, HK must remember that the computations are extremely sensitive to errors in the data, and they have only been collecting data on Lucky Kitty's price sensitivity for a short while. Additionally, it is highly likely that the selling prices of one of the products affects the volume of sales of BOTH products. HK should collect more data about the relationship between the two products and how price changes are related before making a decision to use the market-based pricing formulas.

2. a) Price elasticity = ln(-0.5)/ln(1.09) = -1.68.

   b) The profit maximizing price = (-1.68/-0.68) x $52 = $128.47.

   c) Selling price – ($52 + $18) = 20% x Selling price, so 80% x Selling price = $70, and Selling price = $70/0.8 = $87.50.

   d) Boycov's current cost-based price is much less than the computed profit-maximizing price. If the profit-maximizing price calculations are reliable, then the cost-based formula it has been using has not taken into account the customers' willingness to pay for its product. Boycov should investigate the pricing strategies used in its industry. If they are cost-based strategies, what cost base and what profit margin or markup are Boycov's competitors using? Although the market-based pricing approach takes the customers' willingness to pay for the product into account, the calculations are extremely sensitive to error. Where did Boycov attain the price sensitivity information? The market-based price calculations assume that the price elasticity is constant and that the only thing that affects changes in units sold is the product's price, and these assumptions may have been violated, making the sensitivity data unreliable.

SOLUTION TO END OF CHAPTER EXERCISES

Multiple choice:

   1. C
   2. C
   3. D
   4. B
   5. C
   6. A
   7. C
   8. B
   9. D
   10. B

Exercises:

1. a) The first step is to calculate the total cost of each product, then selling prices are computed at 1.5 times total costs.

	Regular	Deluxe	Total
Total direct labor costs	$170,000	$105,000	$275,000
Percent of total	61.818%	38.182%	100.000%
Fixed manufacturing overhead allocated to each product	$123,636	$76,364	$200,000
Per unit	$12.36	$15.27	
Total revenue	$1,100,000	$750,000	$1,850,000
Percent of total	59.459%	40.541%	100.000%
Fixed nonmanufacturing overhead allocated to each product	$89,189	$60,811	$150,000
Per unit	$8.92	$12.16	
Variable costs per unit	$63.50	$74.50	
Fixed manufacturing costs per unit	12.36	15.27	
Fixed nonmanufacturing costs per unit	8.92	12.16	
Total costs per unit	$84.78	$101.93	
Selling prices (at 1.5 times total cost)	$127.17	$152.90	

b) The selling price for Regular is $63.50 x 1.65 = $104.78, and the selling price for Deluxe is $74.50 x 1.65 = $122.93.

c) Regular: Price elasticity = ln(0.1)/ln(0.8) = -2.34;
   the profit maximizing price = (-2.34/-1.34) x $63.50 = $110.84

   Deluxe: Price elasticity = ln(0.1)/ln(0.75) = -3.018;
   the profit maximizing price = (-3.018/-2.018) x $74.50 = $111.41

2. a) Because the Deluxe unit has higher direct labor costs per unit, the fixed manufacturing costs allocated each Deluxe unit are higher than Regular. Also, the higher selling price last year for a Deluxe unit means that this product gets a higher per-unit allocation of fixed non-manufacturing costs. Higher costs per unit result in higher selling prices per unit under cost-based pricing. The selling prices calculated in part (b) do not have the additional fixed costs allocated to unit.

   b) The variable costs of a Deluxe unit are only $11 per unit higher than the variable costs for a Regular unit, even though last year's pricing had the Deluxe unit priced a great deal higher than the Regular unit. Since the demand for the Deluxe unit is more sensitive to changes in price than the demand for a Regular unit, the Deluxe unit will receive a lower markup over cost.

   c) The selling prices calculated in part (c) of exercise 1 cannot be used as the selling prices for the 2 units if Charmaster is interested in keeping both products alive in the marketplace. Presumably the Deluxe unit has more features than the Regular unit. The calculated selling prices are so close to each other that they are essentially the same price. If these prices are used, (virtually) no customers would buy the Regular unit.

Chapter 14

Measuring and Assigning
Costs for Income Statements

√ **Study Checklist - Monitor your progress**

1. Read the chapter in the text
2. Review the learning objectives below
3. Read the overview of the chapter
4. Read the chapter review for learning objectives 1 – 2
5. Do Problem Set A and check your answers
6. Read the chapter review for learning objectives 3 – 5
7. Do Problem Set B and check your answers
8. Do the End of Chapter Exercises in this study guide
9. Do the homework assigned by your instructor

CHAPTER LEARNING OBJECTIVES

After studying this chapter, you should be able to answer the following questions:

Q1. How are absorption costing income statements constructed?
Q2. What factors affect the choice of production volume measures for allocating fixed overhead?
Q3. How are variable costing income statements constructed?
Q4. How are throughput costing income statements constructed?
Q5. What are the uses and limitations of absorption, variable, and throughput costing income statements?

OVERVIEW OF CHAPTER

Under generally accepted accounting principles, accountants allocate fixed manufacturing overhead costs to inventory; this is known as absorption costing. For internal decision making purposes, however, managers may not wish to treat these fixed costs as product costs. This chapter covers absorption costing, and two other definitions of product cost, variable and throughput costing.

CHAPTER REVIEW: Learning Objectives 1 - 2

Q1: How are absorption costing income statements constructed?
In Chapter 2 we covered *product costs*, also known as *inventoriable* costs, and *period costs.* Product costs are assigned to inventory and are only expensed as the goods they are attached to are sold. Period costs, on the other hand, are expensed in the period in which they are incurred. For a manufacturer, we defined product costs to be direct labor, direct materials, variable manufacturing overhead, and fixed manufacturing overhead. This definition of product costs is known as *absorption costing*, because fixed manufacturing overhead costs are "absorbed" by the units produced. It is the required definition of product costs under generally accepted accounting principles (GAAP).

In Chapter 5 we discussed the allocation of fixed overhead to units of production in a job cost system. The fixed overhead allocation rate is computed as total fixed overhead costs/total quantity of the cost allocation base. Examples of allocation bases used in that chapter include direct labor hours and machine hours.

The traditional format of an absorption costing income statement subtracts cost of goods sold from sales to arrive at gross margin, and then non-manufacturing costs are deducted to arrive at operating income. Since cost of goods sold includes the manufacturing costs attached to the units that are sold, this means that all manufacturing costs expensed in the period are deducted above the gross margin subtotal and that all non-manufacturing costs expensed in the period are deducted below the gross margin subtotal.

Demonstration problem-Absorption costing income statements
The Remy McSwain Company provided the following data pertaining to its operations in 2004 and 2005:

	2005	2004
Beginning FG inventory, in units	20,000	-0-
Units manufactured	80,000	100,000
Units sold	65,000	80,000
Direct materials	$56,000	$70,000
Direct labor	120,000	150,000
Variable manufacturing overhead	56,000	70,000
Variable non-manufacturing costs	32,500	40,000
Fixed manufacturing overhead	100,000	100,000
Fixed non-manufacturing costs	60,000	60,000

Required:
Prepare an absorption costing income statement for both years, assuming that Remy uses the LIFO inventory cost flow assumption, each unit sold for $8 in each year, and that there were no units in beginning or ending work in process inventory in either year.

solution to demonstration problem begins on the next page →

Solution to demonstration problem

One way to approach this problem is to begin by computing the per-unit manufacturing costs for each year, where the per-unit cost is the total cost divided by the number of units produced (not by the number of units sold).

	Per-unit Manufacturing Costs	
	2005	**2004**
Direct materials	$0.70	$0.70
Direct labor	1.50	1.50
Variable manufacturing overhead	0.70	0.70
Fixed manufacturing overhead	1.25	1.00
	$4.15	$3.90

The absorption costing income statements for each year are shown below:

	2005	**2004**
Sales (# units sold @ $8)	$520,000	$640,000
Cost of goods sold (# units sold @ $4.15 or $3.90)	269,750	312,000
Gross margin	250,250	328,000
Non-manufacturing costs ($32,500 + $60,000 in 2005 and $40,000 + $60,000 in 2004)	92,500	100,000
Operating income	$157,750	$228,000

Q2: What factors affect the choice of production volume measures for allocating fixed overhead?

In the above demonstration problem, we did not address actual versus estimated fixed manufacturing overhead allocation rates, and explicitly used the actual manufacturing overhead rate. In fact, we used the actual overhead rate per output unit, rather than a rate per direct labor hour or per machine hour. In this chapter, we will continue to use a rate per output unit, even though overhead is generally allocated using a cost allocation base that is an input measure, in order to focus on the different inventory costing methods displayed in this chapter.

Recall that in Chapter 5, we discussed *actual costing* versus *normal costing* for fixed overhead. In actual costing, the fixed overhead allocation rate used is the actual fixed overhead over the actual quantity of the allocation base. In normal costing, the fixed overhead allocation rate used is the estimated fixed overhead over the estimated quantity of the allocation base. Actual costing, even though it is of course more accurate, is inferior to normal costing for several reasons.

- Information timeliness. Under actual costing neither the total fixed overhead cost (the numerator), nor the total quantity of the allocation base (the denominator), are known until the year is over. Therefore, the fixed overhead allocation rate is not known until the end of the year, and products cannot be costed until the year is over.

- Smoothing effects. Allocating fixed overhead to units of production should be done in a manner that assures each unit absorbs its fair share of fixed overhead. If we were to attempt to use actual costing for a period less than one year, for example one month, then products would absorb a different amount of overhead depending on the month in which they were produced. Using an estimated annual fixed overhead rate avoids this. There are two reasons that using an actual rate for a period of less than one year (one month, for example) would allocate different costs to units produced in different periods.

- o *Numerator reason.* Fixed overhead costs are often not incurred smoothly throughout the year. A unit produced in a month when actual fixed overhead costs were higher than in other months would absorb a disproportionate share of fixed costs only because they were produced in that month.

- o *Denominator reason.* Fixed overhead costs, by definition, do not fluctuate with volume. Therefore, a unit produced in a month with low production volume would absorb a disproportionate share of fixed costs compared to units that were produced in a month with a higher production volume.

Under normal costing, companies must use an estimate of output levels at the beginning of the year in order to determine the fixed overhead allocation rate. In other words, companies must "choose a denominator level". There are four measures of capacity that a company could use to determine its denominator level.

- • *Supply-based capacity levels.* These measures consider only what the company is capable of producing and do not take into consideration the production levels a company may see when customer demand is taken into consideration.

  - o *Theoretical capacity.* This is the maximum production volume (whether measured in output units or some level of inputs required to achieve this output level) that a company could achieve with no downtime for any reason taken into consideration.

  - o *Practical capacity.* This is the maximum production volume (whether measured in output units or some level of inputs required to achieve this output level) that a company could achieve, after normal production interruptions for maintenance, holidays, and the like taken into consideration.

- • *Demand-based capacity levels.* These measures take into consideration anticipated customer demand.

  - o *Normal capacity.* This is the average use of capacity over time.

  - o *Budgeted (or expected) capacity.* This is the anticipated use of capacity for the upcoming period.

When using normal costing, the amount of fixed manufacturing overhead allocated to production can differ from the actual fixed overhead costs because the actual fixed overhead costs were different than what was budgeted (the numerator reason). This is called the spending variance, and it was discussed in Chapter 11. The amount of fixed manufacturing overhead allocated to production can also differ from the actual fixed overhead costs because the actual production level was different from the expected production level used in the calculation of the fixed overhead cost allocation rate (the denominator reason); this is known as the *volume variance*, and it was also covered in Chapter 11. The volume variance is the difference between budgeted fixed overhead and allocated fixed overhead.

In this chapter, we ignore the spending variance, and concentrate on how the volume variance affects absorption costing income statements. However, remember from Chapter 11 that all variances, including the volume variance, are allocated to work in process, finished goods, and cost of goods sold (or just to cost of goods sold if immaterial), so there is virtually no effect on the income statement of the choice of denominator volume.

Before the year is over, managers use normal costing information to make decisions such as product pricing or product emphasis. In these cases, the denominator level that is chosen is important. Most fixed manufacturing costs are related to capacity, so the fixed overhead rate can be considered a cost of supplying this capacity. The choice of denominator level also affects the way the volume variance is interpreted.

- The higher the denominator level chosen, the lower the fixed overhead costs are that are allocated to the units produced. Since theoretical capacity is the largest measure of capacity, it yields the lowest fixed overhead rate, and costs assigned to products are too low. The volume variance will always be unfavorable (unless theoretical capacity was measured incorrectly at the beginning of the year), and it measures only the cost of not using a measure of capacity which was known to be unattainable at the outset. Theoretical capacity is rarely used by businesses for this reason.

- Since practical capacity is an attainable measure of capacity, the fixed overhead rate is a good measure of the cost of supplying capacity. An unfavorable volume variance can be thought of as the cost of supplying capacity that was not used, and a favorable volume variance can be thought of as the benefit of using capacity beyond what was thought to be attainable. The volume variance focuses managers' attention on effective use of the capacity available.

- Normal capacity is a measure of expected capacity over time, so volume variances may be large in one period and small in the next period. The volume variance is less useful information than when practical capacity is used.

- Since budgeted capacity measures the expected capacity usage for this period, any volume variance is directly attributable to the difference between the expected volume of production and sales and the actual volumes.

The choice of denominator level also has implications for monitoring and motivating the performance of managers, but this discussion is reserved for the section of this study guide that addresses learning objective Q5.

The next demonstration problem uses the same information as the prior demonstration problem, except this time the effects of using normal costing (i.e. a predetermined, estimated, fixed overhead rate) are included.

Demonstration problem-Absorption costing income statements
The Remy McSwain Company provided the following data pertaining to its operations in 2004 and 2005:

	2005	2004
Beginning FG inventory, in units	20,000	-0-
Units manufactured	80,000	100,000
Units sold	65,000	80,000
Direct materials	$56,000	$70,000
Direct labor	120,000	150,000
Variable manufacturing overhead	56,000	70,000
Variable non-manufacturing costs	32,500	40,000
Fixed manufacturing overhead	100,000	100,000
Fixed non-manufacturing costs	60,000	60,000

Remy uses normal costing, and chose 100,000 units as the denominator level for fixed overhead in both 2004 and 2005. There was no fixed overhead spending variance in either year. Each unit sold for $8 in both years. There were no units in beginning or ending work in process inventory in either year. Remy uses the LIFO inventory cost flow assumption.

Required:
a) Compute the estimated fixed overhead rate per output unit used for each year.
b) Compute the per-unit costs attached to units for each year.
c) Compute the volume variance for each year.
d) Compute the costs attached to ending finished goods inventory and to cost of goods sold for 2005, before any adjustment for the volume variance). Assume the volume variance is considered material. Then determine the disposition of the volume variance.
e) Prepare an absorption costing income statement for each year.

Solution to demonstration problem
a) Note that there is no spending variance for fixed overhead either year, so budgeted fixed overhead equaled actual fixed overhead.
   The estimated fixed overhead rate for each year = $100,000/100,000 units = $1.00/unit.

b)

	Per-unit Manufacturing Costs	
	2005	**2004**
Direct materials	$0.70	$0.70
Direct labor	1.50	1.50
Variable manufacturing overhead	0.70	0.70
Fixed manufacturing overhead	1.00	1.00
	$3.90	$3.90

solution to demonstration problem continues on next page →

Solution to demonstration problem continued

c)

	2005	2004
Budgeted fixed overhead	$100,000	$100,000
Fixed overhead allocated (units produced x fixed overhead rate)	80,000	100,000
Unfavorable volume variance	$20,000	$0

d)

	2005
Beginning finished goods inventory (20,000 units @ $3.90)	$78,000
Total manufacturing costs assigned to units produced (80,000 @ $3.90)	312,000
Cost of goods available for sale	390,000
Cost of goods sold (65,000 @ $3.90)	253,500
Ending finished goods inventory	$136,500

Since the volume variance is considered material, it must be allocated to work in process, finished goods, and cost of goods sold.

	Total	%	Allocated Volume Variance
Work in process inventory at end of 2005	$0	0.0%	$0
Finished goods inventory at end of 2005	136,500	35.0%	7,000
Cost of goods sold for 2005	253,500	65.0%	13,000
Total	$390,000	100.0%	$20,000

e)

	2005	2004
Sales (# units sold x $8)	$520,000	$640,000
Less: Cost of goods sold	253,500	312,000
Adjustment for volume variance	13,000	0
Gross margin	253,500	328,000
Non-manufacturing costs	92,500	100,000
Operating income	$161,000	$228,000

PROBLEM SET A (Learning Objectives 1 - 2)

True-False: Indicate whether each of the following is true (T) or false (F) in the space provided.

_____   1.   Product costs means the same thing as inventoriable costs.

_____   2.   Absorption costing is required under generally accepted accounting principles.

_____   3.   Both theoretical capacity and practical capacity are measures of capacity that are based on customer demand.

_____   4.   When actual fixed manufacturing overhead costs exceed budgeted fixed manufacturing overhead, there is an unfavorable volume variance.

_____   5.   When the actual production level exceeds the denominator level, there is an unfavorable volume variance.

_____   6.   The volume variance is the difference between budgeted fixed manufacturing overhead and actual fixed manufacturing overhead.

_____   7.   Of all of the denominator levels, theoretical capacity is the largest.

_____   8.   Normal capacity is a denominator level that is based on customer demand.

_____   9.   When allocated fixed manufacturing overhead exceeds budgeted fixed manufacturing overhead, the volume variance is unfavorable.

_____   10.   The fixed overhead rate best measures the cost of supplying capacity when practical capacity is used as the denominator level.

_____   11.   When the volume variance is considered material, an adjusting entry is prepared that effectively adjusts the inventory accounts to the values they would have had if actual costing had been used instead of normal costing.

_____   12.   Under actual costing, there can be no volume variance.

_____   13.   For product pricing decisions, theoretical capacity is the best choice for the denominator level.

_____   14.   Under absorption costing, fixed non-manufacturing overhead is expensed as a period cost.

_____   15.   Under absorption costing, variable manufacturing overhead is expensed as a period cost.

Exercises: Write your answer in the space provided.
1. Fleetwood Mac makes seat covers for recreational vehicles. You are given the following
   information for 2004 and 2005:

	2005	2004
Beginning FG inventory, in units	3,500	0
Units manufactured	12,000	10,000
Units sold	11,000	6,500
Direct materials	$72,000	$60,000
Direct labor	36,000	30,000
Variable manufacturing overhead	24,000	20,000
Variable non-manufacturing costs	11,000	6,500
Fixed manufacturing overhead	56,000	56,000
Fixed non-manufacturing costs	34,000	34,000

Each unit sold for $32 in each year. In 2004, Fleetwood used 10,000 units as its denominator
level and in 2005 it used 12,000 units as the denominator level. Fleetwood uses the LIFO
inventory cost flow assumption. Budgeted fixed overhead equaled actual fixed overhead in each
year.

a) Compute the fixed overhead rate per output unit for each year.

2004 _____   2005 _____

b) Compute the per-unit cost of production for each year using absorption costing.

2004 _____   2005 _____

c) Compute the gross margin for each year using absorption costing.

2004 _____   2005 _____

d) Compute the operating income for each year using absorption costing.

2004 _____   2005 _____

2. This exercise uses the same information as exercise #1, so check your answers to that problem before you attempt this one. Suppose that Fleetwood used 10,000 units as the denominator level in 2005, rather than 12,000 units.

   a) Compute the 2005 volume variance. _____

   b) Assume there was no beginning or ending work in process in either year. Compute the balance in work in process, finished goods, and cost of goods sold for 2005 before any adjustment for the volume variance:

   Finished goods _____   Cost of goods sold _____

   c) Assuming that the volume variance is considered material, compute the distribution of the volume variance to work in process, finished goods, and cost of goods sold.

   Work in process _____   Finished goods _____   Cost of goods sold _____

3. This exercise uses the same information as exercise #2, so check your answers to that problem before you attempt this one. Prepare a 2005 income statement using absorption costing.

CHAPTER REVIEW: Learning Objectives 3 - 5

Q3: How are variable costing income statements constructed?

In Chapter 4 we learned that for many types of decisions, particularly short-term nonroutine decisions, fixed costs are not relevant and decisions should not be made based on costs per unit that include an allocation of fixed costs. Although absorption costing income statements are required under GAAP, for internal decision making managers may define products costs in any fashion that best suits the decision at hand.

In *variable costing*, fixed manufacturing costs are treated as period costs and expensed in the period incurred. They are not treated as product costs. Under variable costing, then, product costs are defined to be direct materials, direct labor and variable manufacturing overhead.

A variable costing income statement not only uses a different definition of product costs, it also has a different format. In absorption costing, costs are categorized by function, with manufacturing costs deducted above the gross margin subtotal and non-manufacturing costs deducted below the gross margin subtotal. A variable costing income statement categorizes costs by their cost behavior. Variable costs (both manufacturing and non-manufacturing) are all deducted from sales to arrive at the contribution margin subtotal. Fixed costs (both manufacturing and non-manufacturing) are deducted below the contribution margin subtotal.

An organization that prepares absorption costing income statements for external users and variable costing income statements for internal use will have different income statements, each showing different incomes, for a given period. This may seem confusing to some individuals within the organization. Because of this, it is important for accountants to be able to reconcile the income amounts determined by the two approaches.

Since the only difference between absorption and variable costing is the allocation of fixed overhead costs to inventory, the two methods produce the same operating income when production equals sales and fixed costs have been stable. When production exceeds sales, and the LIFO inventory cost flow assumption is used, absorption costing income will exceed variable costing income statement because a portion of the year's fixed overhead costs will attach to the units in ending inventory under absorption costing, whereas variable costing expenses all of the year's fixed overhead. The difference in income between the two methods is equal to the increase in absorption costing ending inventory less the increase in variable costing inventory, which also equals the amount of fixed overhead allocated to the units added to ending inventory under absorption costing.

When production is less than sales, absorption costing income will be less than variable costing income because cost of goods sold under absorption costing will include fixed overhead costs from the prior year that were attached to units in beginning inventory, whereas variable costing expensed prior year fixed overhead costs on the prior year's income statement. When fixed production costs have been stable over time, this difference in income is equal to the decrease in absorption costing inventory less the decrease in variable costing inventory, which also equals the prior period's fixed overhead costs allocated to the units removed from beginning inventory during the period.

Demonstration problem-Variable costing income statements; reconciling absorption and variable costing income
Use the information about the Remy McSwain Company provided in the demonstration problem on page 14-2.

Required:
a) Compute the per-units costs under variable costing, and compare it to the per-unit costs under absorption costing shown in the demonstration problem solution on page 14-3.
b) Prepare a variable costing income statement for each year.
c) Prepare a reconciliation of the 2005 variable costing income to the 2005 absorption costing income computed in the demonstration problem solution on page 14-3.

Solution to demonstration problem
a)

	Manufacturing Costs Per Unit	
	2005	**2004**
Direct materials	$0.70	$0.70
Direct labor	1.50	1.50
Variable manufacturing overhead	0.70	0.70
Variable costing per-unit cost	2.90	2.90
Fixed manufacturing overhead	1.25	1.00
Absorption costing per-unit cost	$4.15	$3.90

b)

	2005	**2004**
Sales (# units sold @ $8)	$520,000	$640,000
Less: Cost of goods sold (# units sold @ $2.90)	188,500	232,000
Variable non-manufacturing costs	32,500	40,000
Contribution margin	299,000	368,000
Less: Fixed manufacturing overhead	100,000	100,000
Fixed non-manufacturing costs	60,000	60,000
Operating income	$139,000	$208,000

c)

2005 Beginning units in finished goods inventory	20,000		
2005 units produced	80,000	Variable costing	
Units available for sale in 2005	100,000	operating income	$139,000
Units sold in 2005	65,000	Fixed overhead	
2005 Ending units in finished goods inventory	35,000	included in increased	
2004 Ending units in finished goods inventory	20,000	inventory	18,750
Increase in ending inventory units	15,000	Absorption costing	
Fixed overhead rate per unit in 2005	1.25	operating income	$157,750
Fixed overrhead included in increased inventory	$18,750		

Q4: How are throughput costing income statements constructed?

Managers find variable costing income statements useful for internal decision making purposes because fixed production costs are not allocated to inventory units. In some businesses, direct labor costs and variable overhead costs are not really variable costs in the short-term. For example, a union may have a contract specifying a minimum number of labor hours for the factory workers per month. Then, if variable overhead costs are variable with respect to the number of direct labor hours worked, variable overhead is also not really a variable cost in the short-term. In these situations, assigning direct labor and variable overhead costs to inventory is akin to allocating fixed overhead to inventory. *Throughput costing* (sometimes referred to as *super-variable costing*) defines product costs to include only direct materials. Direct labor, variable manufacturing overhead, and fixed manufacturing overhead are all considered period costs and, as such, are expensed in the period incurred.

The format of a throughput costing income statement is different from that of an absorption costing income statement. It is more similar to that of a variable costing income statement. In a throughput costing income statement, "cost of goods sold" is computed as the direct materials costs attached to the units sold. Sales less this "cost of goods sold" figure is called the *throughput margin*. All non-direct materials costs incurred are expensed below the throughput margin subtotal to arrive at income.

Throughput costing income can be reconciled to absorption costing income using the same approach as reconciling absorption costing income to variable costing income, except for the difference in the definition of product costs between the two methods. Direct labor, variable overhead, and fixed overhead are product costs under absorption costing but are period costs under throughput costing.

Similarly, throughput costing income can be reconciled to variable costing income using the same approach as reconciling absorption costing income to variable costing income, except for the difference in the definition of product costs between the two methods. Direct labor and variable overhead are product costs under variable costing but are period costs under throughput costing.

Demonstration problem-Throughput costing income statements and reconciling to income under absorption and variable costing
Use the information about the Remy McSwain Company provided in the demonstration problems on pages 14-2 and 14-3 (absorption costing) and on page 14-13 (variable costing).

Required:
a) Compute the per-units costs under throughput costing, and compare it to the per-unit costs under absorption costing shown in the demonstration problem solution on page 14-3 and the per-unit costs under variable costing shown in the demonstration problem on page 14-13.
b) Prepare a throughput costing income statement for each year.
c) Prepare a reconciliation of the 2005 throughput costing income to the 2005 absorption costing income computed in the demonstration problem solution on page 14-3.
d) Prepare a reconciliation of the 2005 throughput costing income to the 2005 variable costing income computed in the demonstration problem solution on page 14-13.

Solution to demonstration problem

a)

	Per-unit Manufacturing Costs	
	2005	2004
Direct materials (throughput product cost per unit)	$0.70	$0.70
Direct labor	1.50	1.50
Variable manufacturing overhead	0.70	0.70
Variable costing per-unit cost	2.90	2.90
Fixed manufacturing overhead	1.25	1.00
Absorption costing per-unit cost	$4.15	$3.90

b)

	2005	2004
Sales	$520,000	$640,000
Cost of goods sold-direct materials only	45,500	56,000
Throughput margin	474,500	584,000
Direct labor costs	120,000	150,000
Variable manufacturing costs	56,000	70,000
Variable non-manufacturing costs	32,500	40,000
Fixed manufacturing overhead	100,000	100,000
Fixed non-manufacturing costs	60,000	60,000
Operating income	$106,000	$164,000

Note that these costs are expensed based on units produced, not on units sold.

c)

Increase in ending inventory units	15,000
DL, VO, & FO costs per unit	$3.45
DL, VO & FO in increased inventory	$51,750

Throughput costing income	$106,000
DL, VO, & FO included in increased inventory	51,750
Absorption costing income	$157,750

d)

Increase in ending inventory units	15,000
DL & VO costs per unit	$2.20
DL & VO in increased inventory	$33,000

Throughput costing income	$106,000
DL & VO included in increased inventory	33,000
Variable costing income	$139,000

<u>Q5: What are the uses and limitations of absorption, variable, and throughput costing income statements?</u>

Absorption costing income statements are prepared because they are required under GAAP. Additionally, when practical capacity is used as the denominator level, the volume variance computed under absorption costing may help managers monitor the use of capacity. However, there are many reasons that absorption costing income statements may not provide the appropriate information for internal decision making. We learned in Chapter 4 that fixed costs are irrelevant for many short-term nonroutine decisions.

In general, if inventory levels increase over a period, absorption costing income will be higher than variable costing income. If managers are compensated more as absorption costing income increases, then this provides an incentive to build up inventories, which is most likely contrary to the best interests of the organization.

PROBLEM SET B (Learning Objectives 3 - 5)

True-False: Indicate whether each of the following is true (T) or false (F) in the space provided.

_____ 1. Variable costing treats all variable costs as product costs and all fixed costs as period costs.

_____ 2. Both variable costing and throughput costing income statements can be given to external users as long as it is disclosed that the income statements do not follow generally accepted accounting principles.

_____ 3. In throughput costing, direct labor and variable manufacturing overhead costs are treated as period costs.

_____ 4. Direct materials are treated as product costs in absorption, variable and throughput costing.

_____ 5. There is never a volume variance in variable costing.

_____ 6. There is never a volume variance in throughput costing.

_____ 7. There is always a volume variance in absorption costing.

_____ 8. All three inventory costing methods consider only manufacturing costs to be inventoriable.

_____ 9. Sales commissions are a period cost under all three inventory costing methods.

_____ 10. Both variable costing and throughput costing treat *all* fixed costs as period costs.

_____ 11. Absorption costing income is always higher than variable costing income or throughput costing income.

_____ 12. A company might use throughput costing for internal decision making because it considers direct labor and variable manufacturing overhead to be unrelated to production levels in the short term.

_____ 13. If absorption costing is used to measure managerial performance, there may be an incentive for managers to produce more units than they should.

_____ 14. The choice of denominator level is irrelevant under both variable and throughput costing.

_____ 15. In throughput costing, the only product cost is direct materials.

<u>Exercises</u>: Write your answer in the space provided.
1. Starship Enterprises makes a Christmas ornament for Star Trek fans. The ornament sold for $10 in 2004 and 2005. Starship uses the LIFO inventory cost flow assumption. The denominator level was 90,000 units in both years. There was no work in process inventory at the beginning or ending of either year. You are given the following information for 2004 and 2005:

	2005	2004
Beginning finished goods inventory, in units	10,000	0
Units manufactured	90,000	90,000
Units sold	75,000	80,000
Direct materials	$49,500	$45,000
Direct labor	40,500	36,000
Variable manufacturing overhead	33,300	22,500
Variable non-manufacturing costs	11,250	8,000
Fixed manufacturing overhead	130,000	127,000
Fixed non-manufacturing costs	75,000	72,000

Prepare variable costing income statements, using the appropriate format, for each year.

2. Use the information contained in exercise 1 to prepare throughput costing income statements for each year.

3. This exercise uses your responses to exercises 1 and 2, so check your answers for those problems before attempting this one. Prepare a reconciliation of throughput costing income to variable costing income for each year.

END OF CHAPTER EXERCISES

Multiple choice: Write the letter that represents the best choice in the space provided.

_____ 1. Variable costing will produce a larger net income than absorption costing if
a. fixed overhead decreases
b. production exceeds sales
c. fixed overhead increases
d. sales exceed production

_____ 2. Under absorption costing
a. fixed overhead is not a product cost
b. fixed overhead is expensed in the period incurred
c. fixed overhead is expensed when the inventory is sold
d. fixed overhead is a period cost

_____ 3. When reconciling from variable costing income to absorption costing income, if production exceeded sales and LIFO is used
a. the fixed overhead in the beginning inventory is added
b. the fixed overhead in the beginning inventory is deducted
c. the fixed overhead in the ending inventory is added
d. the fixed overhead in the ending inventory is ignored

_____ 4. Musa Company's inventory balances for the beginning and ending of 2004, using both variable costing and absorption costing, are shown below:

	12/31/04	1/1/04
Variable costing	$1,200	$1,200
Absorption costing	1,420	1,260

Variable costing income for 2004 was $3,460. Musa uses LIFO. If absorption costing had been used, income for 2004 would be
a. $3,420
b. $3,620
c. $3,500
d. $3,660

_____ 5. Which inventory costing method treats direct materials as a product cost?
a. absorption costing
b. variable costing
c. throughput costing
d. all of the above

_____ 6. Which inventory costing method treats direct labor as a product cost?
a. absorption costing
b. variable costing
c. throughput costing
d. both (a) and (b)

_____ 7. Which inventory costing method treats variable overhead as a product cost?
    a. absorption costing
    b. variable costing
    c. throughput costing
    d. both (a) and (b)

_____ 8. Which inventory costing method treats fixed overhead as a product cost?
    a. absorption costing
    b. variable costing
    c. throughput costing
    d. none of the above

_____ 9. Which inventory costing method treats variable selling costs as product costs?
    a. absorption costing
    b. variable costing
    c. throughput costing
    d. none of the above

Use the following information for questions 10 – 12:
Whideby Corporation has budgeted overhead as $100,000 plus $5 per unit for the current year. The denominator capacity is 40,000 units per year. Any volume variance is carried forward quarter by quarter and closed at year-end. The company experienced the following activity during the year:

Quarter	Units Produced	Units Sold
First	10,000	8,000
Second	9,000	9,000
Third	9,000	10,000
Fourth	8,000	6,000

_____ 10. The volume variance for the first quarter was
    a. $0
    b. $5,000 unfavorable
    c. $15,000 unfavorable
    d. $10,000 favorable

_____ 11. The volume variance was unfavorable in quarters
    a. 1 and 4
    b. 3
    c. 1 and 3
    d. 2, 3, and 4

_____ 12. The volume variance for the year was
    a. $17,500 unfavorable
    b. $7,500 favorable
    c. $10,000 unfavorable
    d. $12,500 favorable

Use the following information for questions 13 – 16:
Orca, Inc experienced the following activity and costs during its first three years of operations:

Year	Units Produced	Units Sold	Variable Mfg Cost/Unit	Total Fixed Mfg Costs	Selling Price Per Unit
2003	22,000	18,000	$2.00	$49,500	$10
2004	20,000	19,000	2.25	49,500	10
2005	18,000	18,000	2.50	49,500	10

_____ 13. Net income for 2003 using variable costing was
    a. $94,500
    b. $103,500
    c. $86,500
    d. $126,500

_____ 14. Assuming Orca uses actual costing, net income for 2003 using absorption costing was
    a. $94,500
    b. $103,500
    c. $86,500
    d. $126,500

_____ 15. Assuming a denominator level of 20,000 units, and that Orca closes any volume variance to cost of goods sold, net income for 2003 using absorption costing was
    a. $103,500
    b. $104,400
    c. $99,450
    d. $94,500

_____ 16. Assuming a denominator level of 20,000 units, that Orca uses LIFO and closes any volume variance to cost of goods sold, net income for 2005 using absorption costing was
    a. $103,500
    b. $104,400
    c. $95,400
    d. $85,500

_____ 17. Which of the following statements about the contribution margin format of the income statements is false?
    a. Gross margin is not calculated.
    b. The amount of fixed production costs is clearly displayed.
    c. Variable non-manufacturing costs are deducted as product costs.
    d. Manufacturing and non-manufacturing costs are segregated.

_____ 18. Which of the following statements about the traditional format of the income statements is true?
   a. Contribution margin is clearly displayed.
   b. Only manufacturing costs are deducted from sales to arrive at gross margin.
   c. Fixed costs and variable costs are segregated.
   d. The traditional format is used with variable, but not throughput, costing.

_____ 19. A favorable volume variance occurs when
   a. the denominator level exceeds the number of units produced
   b. the number of units produced exceeds the number of units sold
   c. the number of units sold exceeds the denominator level
   d. the number of units produced exceeds the denominator level

_____ 20. When managers are compensated based on income levels, they may have an incentive to overproduce inventory units if income is computed using
   a. throughput costing
   b. variable costing
   c. absorption costing
   d. managers have an incentive to overproduce under all 3 methods

_____ 21. Some companies use throughput costing for internal purposes because
   a. they believe only direct materials costs are truly variable in the short run
   b. they believe direct labor costs are fixed in the short run
   c. they believe all overhead costs are fixed in the short run
   d. all of the above

_____ 22. When production exceeds sales, and costs from year to year have been stable, which method will compute the highest net income?
   a. throughput costing
   b. variable costing
   c. absorption costing
   d. activity-based costing

_____ 23. The fixed manufacturing overhead rate will be the lowest when
   a. the denominator level used is theoretical capacity
   b. the denominator level used is practical capacity
   c. the denominator level used is normal capacity
   d. the denominator level used is budgeted capacity

_____ 24. A company using absorption costing had an unfavorable volume variance. Which of the following statements is true?
   a. Budgeted fixed overhead costs were less than actual.
   b. Allocated fixed overhead costs were greater than were budgeted.
   c. Income will be higher when the volume variance is charged to cost of goods sold than if it is allocated to cost of goods sold, finished goods, and work in process.
   d. The unfavorable volume variance reduces reported income.

<u>Exercises</u>: Write your answer in the space provided.
1. Olympia, Inc. prepares absorption costing income statements and uses actual costing. Information about its first year of operations is shown below:

	<u>2005</u>
Per unit costs of production:	
Direct materials	$20
Direct labor	18
Fixed overhead	12
Variable overhead	<u>20</u>
	$<u>70</u>
Number of units sold @ $100 each	80,000
Number of units in inventory at 12/31	10,000
Non-manufacturing costs (40% variable)	$2,000,000
Absorption costing income	$400,000

a) Prepare a variable costing income statement for 2005.

b) Prepare a reconciliation of variable costing income to absorption costing income for 2005.

2. Use the information presented for Olympia, Inc. from exercise 1.

a) Prepare a throughput costing income statement for 2005.

b) Prepare a reconciliation of throughput costing income to absorption costing income for 2005.

c) Prepare a reconciliation of throughput costing income to variable costing income for 2005.

3. Bellingham, Inc. had the following activity for its first two years of operations:

	2004	2005
Units sold	13,000	14,000
Units produced	16,000	15,000
Selling price per unit	$25	$25
Variable manufacturing costs per unit	9	9
Variable selling costs per unit	1	1
Fixed manufacturing overhead	60,000	60,000
Fixed administrative costs	20,000	20,000

All variances are closed out to cost of goods sold at year-end. The annual denominator level is 15,000 units. Bellingham uses the LIFO inventory cost flow assumption.

a) Prepare income statements for 2004 and 2005 using absorption costing.

b) Prepare income statements for 2004 and 2005 using variable costing.

c) Prepare a reconciliation of variable costing income to absorption costing income for each year.

SOLUTION TO PROBLEM SET A

True-False:

1. T
2. T
3. F   Theoretical and practical capacity are based on what the company can supply and do not take customer demand into consideration.
4. F   This describes an unfavorable fixed overhead spending variance, not an unfavorable fixed overhead volume variance.
5. F   The volume variance would be favorable.
6. F   This describes the fixed overhead spending variance, not the fixed overhead volume variance. The volume variance is the difference between budgeted fixed overhead and allocated fixed overhead.
7. T
8. T
9. F   When allocated fixed overhead exceeds budgeted fixed overhead, the volume variance is favorable.
10. T
11. T
12. T   True because in actual costing the denominator level is the actual volume level.
13. F   False because the fixed overhead allocated to units would be too small.
14. T
15. F

Exercises:
1. a) 2004: $56,000/10,000 units = $5.60/unit
      2005: $56,000/12,000 units = $4.67/unit

b)

	2004	2005
Direct materials	$6.00	$6.00
Direct labor	3.00	3.00
Variable manufacturing overhead	2.00	2.00
Fixed manufacturing overhead	5.60	4.67
	$16.60	$15.67

c)

	2004	2005
Sales (# units sold @ $32)	$208,000	$352,000
Cost of goods sold (#units sold @ $16.60 and $15.67)	107,900	172,370
Gross margin	$100,100	$179,630

d)

	2004	2005
Gross margin (from above)	$100,100	$179,630
Less: Variable non-manufacturing costs	6,500	11,000
Fixed non-manufacturing costs	34,000	34,000
Gross margin	$59,600	$134,630

2. a) Budgeted fixed overhead $56,000
        Allocated fixed overhead (12,000 x $5.60)   67,200
        Favorable volume variance $11,200

   b) Finished goods inventory at 12/31/04 (3,500 @$16.60) $58,100
       2005 manufacturing costs incurred (12,000 x $15.67)   188,040
       Cost of goods available for sale   246,140
       Cost of goods sold for 2005 (11,000 x $15.67)   172,370
       Ending inventory at 12/31/05 $73,770

   c)

	Total	%	Allocated Volume Variance
Work in process inventory at end of 2005	$0	0.00%	$0
Finished goods inventory at end of 2005	73,770	29.97%	3,357
Cost of goods sold for 2005	172,370	70.03%	7,843
Total	$246,140	100.00%	$11,200

3.   Sales $352,000
     Cost of goods sold $172,370
     Adjustment for favorable volume variance (7,843)   164,527
     Gross margin   187,473
     Variable non-manufacturing costs   11,000
     Fixed non-manufacturing costs   34,000   45,000
     Operating income $142,473

SOLUTION TO PROBLEM SET B

True-False:

1. F   Variable nonmanufacturing costs are period costs.
2. F
3. T
4. T
5. T
6. T
7. F   If the denominator level happens to equal the actual production volume, then the volume variance equals zero.
8. T
9. T
10. T
11. F   If production is less than sales, absorption costing income will be lower.
12. T
13. T
14. T
15. T

Exercises:

1.

	2005	2004
Sales (# units sold @ $10)	$750,000	$800,000
Less: Cost of goods sold (# units sold @ $1.37 and $1.15)	102,750	92,000
Variable non-manufacturing costs	11,250	8,000
Contribution margin	636,000	700,000
Less: Fixed manufacturing overhead	130,000	127,000
Fixed non-manufacturing costs	75,000	72,000
Operating income	$431,000	$501,000

2.

	2005	2004
Sales (# units sold @ $10)	$750,000	$800,000
Cost of goods sold-DM only (# units sold @ $0.55 and $0.50)	41,250	40,000
Throughput margin	708,750	760,000
Less: Direct labor costs incurred	40,500	36,000
Variable manufacturing overhead costs incurred	33,300	22,500
Fixed manufacturing overhead costs incurred	130,000	127,000
Variable non-manufacturing costs incurred	11,250	8,000
Fixed non-manufacturing costs incurred	75,000	72,000
Operating income	$418,700	$494,500

3.

	2005	2004
Ending finished goods inventory in units	25,000	10,000
Beginning finished goods inventory in units	10,000	0
Increase in inventory in units	15,000	10,000
Throughput costing income	$418,700	$494,500
Variable manufacturing overhead costs included in increased ending inventory (increase in inventory x $0.37 and $0.25)	5,550	2,500
Direct labor costs included in increased ending inventory (increase in inventory x $0.45 and $0.40)	6,750	4,000
Variable costing income	$431,000	$501,000

SOLUTION TO END OF CHAPTER EXERCISES

<u>Multiple choice:</u>

1. D
2. C
3. C
4. B   Notice that, although there was no increase in inventory under variable costing, the increase in inventory using absorption costing was $160. This is $160 additional fixed manufacturing overhead that was inventoried under absorption costing, so absorption costing income is higher than variable costing income by $160.
5. D
6. D
7. D
8. A
9. D
10. A   The denominator capacity is 40,000 units per year, or 10,000 per quarter. Since the actual production in the first quarter was 10,000 units, there was no volume variance in the first quarter.
11. D   The volume variance is unfavorable when actual production in a quarter is less than 10,000 units.
12. C   The estimated fixed overhead rate $100,000/40,000 units = $2.50/unit. There were 36,000 units produced, which was 4,000 units less than the denominator level, so the unfavorable volume variance is $2.50 x 4,000 units = $10,000.
13. A   18,000 x ($10 - $2) - $49,500 = $94,500
14. B   The fixed overhead rate is $49,500/22,000 = $2.25/unit, so the total cost per unit is $2.00 + $2.25 = $4.25. 18,000 x ($10 - $4.25) = $103,500.
15. B   The fixed overhead rate is $49,500/20,000 = $2.475/unit. The total cost per unit is $2.00 + $2.475 = $4.475. The volume variance is (22,000 – 20,000) x $2.475 = $4,950 favorable. 18,000 x ($10 - $4.475) + $4,950 = $104,400.
16. D   The fixed overhead rate is $49,500/20,000 = $2.475/unit. The total cost per unit is $2.50 + $2.475 = $4.975. The volume variance is (18,000 – 20,000) x $2.475 = $4,950 unfavorable. 18,000 x ($10 - $4.975) - $4,950 = $85,500.
17. C
18. B
19. D
20. C
21. D
22. C
23. A
24. D

Exercises:

1. a)

Sales (80,000 @ $10)		$8,000,000
Cost of goods sold (80,000 x ($70 - $12))	$4,640,000	
Variable non-manufacturing costs (40% x $2,000,000)	800,000	5,440,000
Contribution margin		2,560,000
Fixed manufacturing overhead (90,000 x $12)	1,080,000	
Fixed non-manufacturing costs	1,200,000	2,280,000
Operating income		$280,000

b)

Variable costing income	$280,000
Fixed manufacturing overhead costs included in increased ending inventory (10,000 x $12)	120,000
Absorption costing income	$400,000

2. a)

Sales (80,000 @ $10)	$8,000,000
Cost of goods sold-DM only (80,000 @ $20)	1,600,000
Throughput margin	6,400,000
Less: Direct labor costs incurred (90,000 @ $18)	1,620,000
Variable mfg overhead costs incurred (90,000 @ $20)	1,800,000
Fixed mfg overhead costs incurred (90,000 @ $12)	1,080,000
Non-manufacturing costs incurred	2,000,000
Operating income (loss)	$(100,000)

b)

Throughput costing operating income (loss)	$(100,000)
Direct labor costs included in increased inventory (10,000 @ $18)	180,000
Variable mfg costs included in increased inventory (10,000 @ $20)	200,000
Fixed mfg costs included in increased inventory (10,000 @ $12)	120,000
Absorption costing income	$400,000

c)

Throughput costing operating income (loss)	$(100,000)
Direct labor costs included in increased inventory (10,000 @ $18)	180,000
Variable mfg costs included in increased inventory (10,000 @ $20)	200,000
Variable costing income	$280,000

3. a)

	2004	2005
Sales	$325,000	$350,000
Cost of goods sold (# units sold @ ($9+$4))	(169,000)	(182,000)
Adjustment for volume variance:		
(16,000 units - 15,000 units) x $4/unit	4,000	
Gross margin	160,000	168,000
Variable selling expenses	(13,000)	(14,000)
Fixed administrative expenses	(20,000)	(20,000)
Net income	$127,000	$134,000

b)

	2004	2005
Sales	$325,000	$350,000
Cost of goods sold (# units sold @ $9)	(117,000)	(126,000)
Variable selling expenses	(13,000)	(14,000)
Contribution margin	195,000	210,000
Fixed manufacturing overhead	(60,000)	(60,000)
Fixed administrative expenses	(20,000)	(20,000)
Net income	$115,000	$130,000

c)

	2004	2005
Variable costing income	$115,000	$130,000
Increase in inventory (2005) @ $4/unit		4,000
Increase in inventory (2004) @ $4/unit	12,000	
Absorption costing income	$127,000	$134,000

Chapter 15

Performance Evaluation and Compensation

√ Study Checklist – Monitor your progress

1. Read the chapter in the text
2. Review the learning objectives below
3. Read the overview of the chapter
4. Read the chapter review for learning objectives 1 – 4
5. Do Problem Set A and check your answers
6. Read the chapter review for learning objectives 5 – 7
7. Do Problem Set B and check your answers
8. Do the End of Chapter Exercises in this study guide
9. Do the homework assigned by your instructor

CHAPTER LEARNING OBJECTIVES

After studying this chapter, you should be able to answer the following questions:

Q1. What is agency theory?

Q2. How are decision-making responsibility and authority related to performance evaluation?

Q3. How are responsibility centers used to measure, monitor, and motivate performance?

Q4. What are the uses and limitations of return on investment, residual income, and economic value added for monitoring performance?

Q5. How is compensation used to motivate performance?

Q6. What prices are used for transferring goods and services within an organization?

Q7. What are the uses and limitations of transfer pricing?

OVERVIEW OF CHAPTER

Organizations must define the authority and responsibilities of managers before their performance can be evaluated. This chapter covers three common measures used to evaluate the performance of managers and business segments. Additionally, the chapter covers methods to determine transfer prices for the transfer of goods and/or services between segments of decentralized organizations in order to motivate the appropriate behavior on the part of the segment managers.

CHAPTER REVIEW: Learning Objectives 1 - 4

Q1: What is agency theory?

In *agency theory*, a *principal* contracts with an *agent* to act on his or her behalf. The principal cannot observe the actions of the agent directly, and can only see the outcomes of the agent's actions. The costs, or lost benefits, that are incurred when the agent does not act in the best interests of the principal are known as *agency costs*. The principal must therefore design incentives to ensure that the agent's actions minimize these agency costs. In corporations, the stockholders are the principals and individuals in top management are the agents. Similarly, lower-level managers and employees are the agents for top management. Exhibit 15-2 in your text summarizes various types, and examples of, agency costs.

Q2: How are decision-making responsibility and authority related to performance evaluation?

Agency costs can be reduced when the decision making authority given to agents is clearly defined and agents are held accountable for their decisions and actions. In a *centralized* organization, decision making authority and responsibility resides with top management. In a *decentralized* organization, decision making authority and responsibility is given to lower levels of management. Which organizational structure is best depends on the type of knowledge that is required to efficiently manage the operations of business segments. Some decisions may be centralized and others decentralized.

When a decision requires *general knowledge*, it is possible for top management to hold responsibility and authority for that decision. However, the segment managers are likely to have better information about the specific operations in their business segments. For example, a business segment manager knows his or her employees and their capabilities better than does top management. When a decision requires *specific knowledge*, it is probably best that the segment manager hold the responsibility and authority for that decision.

The advantages of a centralized organizational structure include greater assurance that the decisions are in line with the interests of the organization and reduced costs of monitoring decisions of segment managers. The disadvantages include longer decision time (because top management may need to get information from the segment managers) and the potential for lower quality decisions (because the specific information of the segment managers may not be easily transferable to top management).

The advantages of a decentralized organizational structure include more timely decisions, the potential for higher quality decisions (because the individuals with the appropriate specific knowledge are making the decisions), and a decreased time commitment from top management, which allows them to focus on organizational strategies. The disadvantages include the potential for the segment managers to make decisions that are good for their segments but not in the best interests of the organizational overall, and lower coordination and cooperation between the business segments (so that the business segments may be duplicating efforts).

<u>Q3: How are responsibility centers used to measure, monitor, and motivate performance?</u>
The performance of managers and business segments should be measured using *responsibility accounting,* which assigns revenues and costs to business segments based on the areas over which the segments' managers have decision making authority and responsibility. There are four general types of *responsibility centers*:

- *Cost centers.* Managers of cost centers have responsibility only for managing the costs of their business segments, subject to meeting certain goals. They are not responsible for generating revenues. The accounting department of an organization is an example of a cost center.

- *Revenue centers.* Managers of revenue centers are responsible for generating revenues and will usually have authority to determine prices, and are also responsible for the volume of sales.

- *Profit centers.* Managers of profit centers are responsible for both revenues and costs. These managers usually have authority to determine prices, sales mix, and inputs.

- *Investment centers.* Managers of investment centers are responsible for revenues, costs, and the asset base used to generate the revenues. These managers usually have the authorities that profit center managers have as well as the authority to make asset acquisition and disposition decisions.

An organization must decide which type of responsibility center each business segment will be, and there is no one correct determination. It is always possible that a segment manger may make a decision that is optimal to his or her business segment but is suboptimal for the organization overall. For example, a production department that is evaluated as a cost center will attempt to minimize costs, which could reduce product quality and eventually sales volume. Top management in each organization must use judgment when making responsibility center determinations.

<u>Q4: What are the uses and limitations of return on investment, residual income, and economic value added for monitoring performance?</u>
There are three commonly used measures for assessing the performance of investment centers.

- *Return on investment (ROI).* In general, ROI is computed as earnings over the investment made. For example, if annual earnings from a $10,000 investment are $600, the ROI is $600/$10,000 = 6%. It usually isn't quite that simple in a corporation, however. "Earnings" and "investment" must be defined. Most often, "earnings" is defined as operating earnings before interest and taxes (EBIT or "operating income") and "investment" is defined as the operating assets used in the production of the goods and services. Operating assets usually include cash, accounts receivable, inventory, and the property and equipment used in production. Investments in other assets (such as investments in securities) are not included in operating assets. Only operating assets under the control of the segment manager should be included. The formula for ROI is, then,

  ROI = Operating income/Average operating assets.

- *Residual income (RI).* Residual income is defined as operating income less some required return on invested assets. It measures the operating income earned that was above what was required.

  RI = Operating income – (Required rate of return x average operating assets).

- *Economic value added (EVA®).*[1] EVA is a residual income calculation that uses specific definitions for operating income (OI), the required rate of return, and operating assets. Under EVA, income is defined as adjusted after-tax operating income, where the adjustments are specific to the organization and its structure and goals. The required rate of return is defined as the weighted average cost of capital (WACC), which is a weighted average of the after-tax cost of long-term debt and the company's return on equity. EVA's definition of operating assets is adjusted total assets less current liabilities. The adjustments to operating assets, similar to the adjustments to operating income, are situation-specific. Adjusted total assets less current liabilities is the same thing as adjusted long-term assets plus working capital.

  EVA = Adjusted after-tax OI – WACC x [Adjusted total assets – current liabilities]

The ROI has a useful decomposition known as *DuPont analysis*. Investment turnover is defined as revenue over average operating assets. It measures how many revenue dollars are brought in by each dollar of investment in operating assets. Return on sales is defined as operating income over revenues (return on sales is also known as the profit margin), and measures what percentage of each revenue dollar makes it to operating income. The DuPont decomposition of ROI is

  ROI = Investment turnover x Return on sales.

When managers are evaluated based on ROI, they have an incentive to increase revenues, decrease costs, and carefully monitor the amount they invest in productive assets. In other words, managers are motivated to get the best return for each dollar of investment in assets. Since ROI is a percentage, the performance of segments of different sizes can be compared. ROI does have a serious drawback, though. When their performance is measured using ROI, managers will reject any new project that has an ROI less than their segments' current ROI, even if the project is good for the organization. For example, a segment that currently has an ROI of 12% will reject a new project with an ROI of 10% because it will reduce the segment's ROI. If the organization considers any project with an ROI of 8% or higher to be a good investment, then the segment manager's rejection of the project was suboptimal.

Both residual income and EVA avoid this disadvantage. Any project that has a rate of return higher than the organization's required rate of return will increase residual income and EVA, so the segment manager who is evaluated using these measures would accept the project. On the other hand, residual income and EVA are absolute measures; larger business segments are likely to have higher residual income and EVA, so these measures cannot be used to rank the performance of business segments. All three measures have a common disadvantage: they are higher when the measure of assets is lower. This could motivate managers to decrease investments in assets that may provide a good return in the long run.

Demonstration problem-ROI, Residual income, & EVA

---

[1] EVA® is a registered trademark of Stern Stewart & Co.

Wichita Industries has two divisions, Shepard and Altus. Wichita has a minimum required rate of return of 10%. You are given the following information about each division:

	Shepard	Altus
Operating income	$100,000	$20,000
After-tax operating income	60,000	12,000
Average operating assets	1,000,000	100,000
Average current liabilities	200,000	18,000
Net sales	1,200,000	50,000

Required:
a) Compute the ROI for each division.
b) Use DuPont analysis to compute the ROI for each division and interpret the results.
c) Altus is currently considering a project that will have an average investment of $20,000 and a pre-tax return of $3,000. Suppose the performance of the divisions is evaluated using ROI. Will the Altus division manager accept or reject the project? Is this decision best for the organization overall?
d) Compute the residual income for each division and discuss the results.
e) Compute the residual income for Altus if it accepts the project mentioned in (c). Would Altus accept the project if divisions are evaluated based on residual income, rather than ROI?
f) Compute the EVA for each division, assuming the weighted average cost of capital is 7%. Discuss.

Solution to demonstration problem
a) Shepard ROI = $100,000/$1,000,000 = 10%.
   Altus ROI = $20,000/$100,000 = 20%.

b)

	Shepard	Altus
Return on sales (ROS)	8.3%	40.0%
Investment turnover (ITO)	1.2	0.5
ROI (ROS x ITO)	10.0%	20.0%

Shepard is making better use of its operating assets than Altus because each $1.00 of operating assets brings in $1.20 in sales. For Altus, each $1.00 of operating assets brings in only $0.50 in sales revenue. However, Shepard's ROI is lower than Altus' because Altus does a much better job of getting operating income from a sales dollar. For each dollar of sales, $0.40 makes it to operating income. For Shepard, only $0.083 of each sales dollar makes it to operating income.

c) The ROI for the project is $3,000/$20,000 = 15%. Since 15% is lower than Altus' current ROI, this project would reduce Altus' ROI [note that ($20,000+$3,000)/($100,000+$20,000) = 19.17%], so Altus would reject this project if its performance is evaluated using ROI. However, this is not consistent with the goals of the organization overall, because any project with an ROI > 10% should be accepted.

d) Shepard residual income = $100,000 – 10% x $1,000,000 = $0.
   Altus residual income = $20,000 – 10% x $100,000 = $10,000.
   It should make sense that Shepard's residual income is zero because its ROI exactly equaled Wichita's minimum required rate of return. Altus' residual income is positive because its ROI exceeded the minimum required rate of return.

solution to demonstration problem continues on the next page →

<u>Solution to demonstration problem continued</u>

e) If Altus accepts the project, its residual income would be:

($20,000 + $3,000) – 10% x ($100,000 + $20,000) = $11,000. Since this is higher than its residual income without the project, Altus would accept the project if divisions are evaluated using the residual income measure.

f) Shepard EVA = $60,000 – 7% x ($1,000,000 - $200,000) = $4,000.

Altus EVA = $12,000 – 7% x ($100,000 - $18,000) = $6,260.

Despite the fact that it is a smaller division than Shepard, Altus' EVA is higher. Usually ROI is the only measure that can be used to compare the performance of business segments of varying sizes, because larger divisions usually have a higher residual income and EVA than do smaller divisions, just because of their size. In this case, though, Altus outperforms Shepard in all three performance measures, despite its smaller size.

PROBLEM SET A (Learning Objectives 1 - 4)

<u>True-False</u>: Indicate whether each of the following is true (T) or false (F) in the space provided.

_____ 1. Investment turnover is calculated as investment over revenue.

_____ 2. In general, the performance of business segments cannot be compared using ROI.

_____ 3. Using ROI to evaluate the performance of business segments may cause managers of extremely profitable segments to make project investment decisions that are inconsistent with the goals of the organization.

_____ 4. If a division's ROI is less than the organization's required rate of return, then the division's residual income will be negative.

_____ 5. DuPont analysis gives managers a method to see ways in which a division can increase its ROI.

_____ 6. In residual income and ROI, divisions are "charged" for their investments in operating assets.

_____ 7. Agency costs are higher in a centralized organization than they are in a decentralized organization.

_____ 8. In agency theory, the principals have specialized knowledge and the agents have general knowledge about the business processes of business segments.

_____ 9. Agency costs occur because the principals must rely on agents and the principals can observe the outcome of the agents' decisions, but not the agents' actions.

_____ 10. Managers of profit centers have responsibility for more elements of operating results than do managers of investment centers.

_____ 11. Managers of profit centers and revenue centers are not responsible for investments in long-term assets.

_____ 12. Responsibility accounting means that each division manager is responsible for his or her own accounting department.

_____ 13. Taxes are not taken into consideration when computing EVA.

_____ 14. The weighted average cost of capital is an average of an organization's return on assets and its before-tax interest rate on long-term debt.

_____ 15. If a division's residual income is positive, then its EVA will also be positive.

Exercises: Write your answer in the space provided.
1. Bowie Division of TXI had average operating assets of $5,600,000 and sales of $7,280,000 last year. Its return on sales was 12%. TXI's minimum required rate of return is 13%.

   a) Calculate Bowie's operating income. _____

   b) Calculate Bowie's ROI. _____

   c) Calculate Bowie's investment turnover. _____

   d) Calculate Bowie's residual income. _____

   e) Bowie has the opportunity to invest in a project. The project's operating income is $140,000 and its average investment in operating assets is $1,000,000. If Bowie is evaluated using ROI, will it invest in the project? Is this decision best for TXI? Why or why not?

   _____

   _____

   _____

   _____

   f) Suppose Bowie is evaluated using residual income. Will Bowie invest in the project mentioned in (e)? Is this decision best for TXI? Why or why not?

   _____

   _____

   _____

   _____

   _____

2. Kamay Division of TXI had average operating assets of $4,400,000, current liabilities of $800,000, and operating income of $900,000 last year. TXI's weighted average cost of capital is 9% and its tax rate is 30%.

    Calculate Kamay's EVA. _____

3. Graham Division of TXI has average operating assets of $1,800,000. The division's contribution margin per unit is budgeted at $60 per unit, and its total fixed costs are budgeted at $600,000. Calculate Graham's necessary sales in units in order for it to earn a 20% ROI. (Hint: use your knowledge of CVP analysis from Chapter 3.)

    Units required to achieve target _____

4. Throckmorton Division of Randlett Enterprises had average operating assets of $4,200,000. The division's operating income was $1,200,000 and its residual income was $864,000. Calculate Randlett's required rate of return.

    Randlett's required rate of return _____

CHAPTER REVIEW: Learning Objectives 5 - 7

Q5: How is compensation used to motivate performance?

Organizations attempt to design the appropriate compensation contracts to motivate manager performance. The contract may include a base salary plus a bonus if certain goals are met. Exhibit 15.5 in the text includes examples of such targets. If the goals are short-term in nature then the organization must realize it is providing an incentive for managers to make decisions that are optimal in the short-term, perhaps at the expense of its long-term goals.

In order to focus on long-term goals, U.S. companies may use compensation contracts that include a base salary plus stock options that allow executives to purchase shares of stock at a specified price beginning at some point in the future. For example, a company may grant options that allow executives to purchase 10,000 shares of stock at $20 beginning 3 years from the grant date. If the market price at the grant date is $20, then executives should be motivated to make decisions that will improve the market price in 3 years. In other countries, stock options are used less frequently than they are in the U.S. and in some countries the use of stock options in compensation contracts is discouraged.

Q6&7: What prices are used for transferring goods and services within an organization? What are the uses and limitations of transfer pricing?

When the segments of an organization transfer goods and/or provide services to each other, the way the transfer is accounted for can affect the performance of each segment. The goods or services transferred are known as *intermediate products*. In order to try to best measure each segment's performance, organizations set *transfer prices* on these goods and services. Several different methods exist for computing these transfer prices.

- *Cost-based transfer prices.* The transfer price may be based on different definitions of the cost of the transferred good or service. For example, a cost-based transfer price may include only variable costs or it may also include an allocation for fixed costs. When the segment transferring the good or service could sell instead to outside customers, this method may lead to suboptimal decisions for the organization. When there are no outside customers for the production of the selling segment, this segment may not have any incentive to reduce its costs if it can simply transfer them to the purchasing segment.

- *Activity-based transfer prices.* This is a version of cost-based transfer pricing. The transfer price is computed based on the unit-level and batch-level costs of the transferred goods, plus a percentage of the producing department's facility-level costs. For example, if the purchasing department's plans to use 15% of the output of the producing department, then the purchasing department would be charged an annual fee of 15% of the production department's facility-level costs. When the annual requirements of the purchasing department are known in advance, the producing department's annual planning is improved.

- *Market-based transfer prices.* Market-based transfer prices are useful when there is a highly competitive market for the intermediate product so that the producing department can opt to sell most or its entire intermediate product to external customers. The producing department then has no incentive to sell intermediate products to internal customers unless the transfer price equals what it can get for the product from these external customers.

- *Dual-rate transfer prices*. In order to motivate the appropriate manager behavior for both the purchasing and the producing departments, an organization may set a selling price for the intermediate product's producing department that is different than the product's purchasing price for the purchasing division. When consolidated financial statements for the organization are prepared, adjustments to eliminate these transfer prices are made so that the correct organizational profit is reported.

- *Negotiated transfer prices*. In this case, the managers of the producing and purchasing departments negotiate the transfer price. This can be a time-consuming exercise, but at least both managers then have full information about each others' needs.

From the perspective of the producing division, the lowest acceptable transfer price is one that covers the variable cost per unit plus the lost contribution margin on the sales not made when the transfer is made:

$$\text{Transfer price} \geq \frac{\text{Variable cost}}{\text{per unit}} + \frac{\text{Total contribution margin on lost sales}}{\text{Number of units transferred}}$$

The contribution margin lost to the producing division of course depends on whether it has sufficient external customers to use its entire capacity. From the perspective of the purchasing division, the transfer price must be less than what it would pay to an external supplier.

Demonstration problem-Transfer pricing

Maverick Manufacturing has several divisions. Versalant Division makes vacuum cleaners and Gearso Division makes metal gears. Gearso's capacity is 10,000 gears per month, its fixed costs per month are $15,000, and the variable cost per gear is $2. The gears sell for $6 each on the open market. Versalant requires 2,000 of these gears per month, but it can acquire them from an external supplier for $5.50.

Required:

a) Compute the transfer price if Gearso charges full absorption cost based on 10,000 units of capacity. Will Versalant accept this transfer price? If Gearso can sell all of its production to external customers, is this decision in the best interests of Maverick?

b) Will Versalant accept a transfer price equal to variable cost? If Gearso can sell all of its production to external customers, is this decision in the best interests of Maverick?

c) Suppose that Gearso can sell 9,000 gears per month to external customers. Compute the minimum transfer price that Gearso would accept. Will Versalant accept this transfer price? Is this decision in the best interests of Maverick?

d) Suppose that Gearso can sell 9,000 gears per month to external customers. What is the minimum and maximum transfer price range if the transfer price is to be negotiated between the managers of Gearso and Versalant?

Solution to demonstration problem

a) Full absorption cost = $2.00/unit + ($15,000/10,000 units) = $3.50/unit. Versalant will accept this transfer price because it is less than what it must pay to an external supplier. The lost contribution margin to Gearso (and to Maverick) is ($6 - $2) x 2,000 units = $8,000. It will cost Versalant $5.50 x 2,000 units = $11,000 to obtain the gears from an external supplier, so Maverick saves $3,000 if the transfer takes place. The transfer is in the best interests of Maverick.

b) Of course Versalant would accept a transfer price of $2 because it must pay $5.50 on the open market. As shown in (a), the transfer would save Maverick $3,000, so it is in the best interests of Maverick for the transfer to take place.

c) If Gearso can sell 9,000 gears to external customers, it will lose sales to 1,000 customers if it transfers 2,000 gears to Versalant. The lost contribution margin on these sales is ($6 - $2) x 1,000 units = $4,000. The minimum transfer price Gearso would accept is $2 + $4,000/2,000 units = $4. Versalant would accept this transfer price because it is less than the $5.50 it must pay an external supplier. The lost contribution margin of $4,000 is less than Versalant's cost on the open market of $11,000. It will save Maverick $7,000 if the transfer takes place.

d) The range for the negotiated transfer price is a minimum of $4 (computed in (c) above) and a maximum of the $5.50 Versalant pays for the gear on the open market.

PROBLEM SET B (Learning Objectives 5 - 7)

<u>True-False</u>: Indicate whether each of the following is true (T) or false (F) in the space provided.

_____ 1. Products transferred between the divisions of an organization are called intermediate products.

_____ 2. Transfer pricing is a methodology for sharing an organization's profits across its business segments.

_____ 3. It is always in the best interests of an organization to have business segments purchase intermediate products from each other, rather than purchasing them externally.

_____ 4. Market-based transfer prices are best used when the transferring division has idle capacity.

_____ 5. Transfer price negotiations take place between corporate headquarters and the division interested in purchasing an intermediate product internally.

_____ 6. Transfer prices are necessary in a decentralized organization but not in a centralized organization.

_____ 7. The purpose of transfer prices is to motivate division managers to make decisions that are in the best interests of the organization.

_____ 8. Opportunity costs should be included in the transfer price computation only when the transferring division has idle capacity.

_____ 9. Activity-based transfer prices are a specific example of cost-based transfer prices.

_____ 10. Dual-rate transfer prices are so-named because they include a variable cost and a fixed cost component.

<u>Exercises</u>: Write your answer in the space provided.

1. The Seaview Company owns and operates a series of sandwich stands on the coast of Washington during the summer. Each stand is operated by a manager who is paid a percentage of the profits earned by the stand. As long as food quality is maintained, each manager may buy food supplies from any reputable supplier. Currently, all stands buy ice cream from Seaview, but a few stands have been approached by a local dairy and ice cream novelty company. This diary proposes to supply high quality ice cream at $1.50 per gallon. Seaview currently charges $1.75 per gallon to the stands.

The production of ice cream by Seaview involves the use of equipment that is rented by the season. As a result, it is relatively easy to determine the cost of producing ice cream. The projected operating information for the remainder of the season (based on production and sales of 10,000 gallons of ice cream, since the equipment was already rented for the season) is as follows:

Sales to sandwich stands	$17,500
Variable costs	10,000
Contribution margin	7,500
Machine and other rental costs	6,000
Operating income	$1,500

a) Should the sandwich stands be allowed to buy ice cream from outside suppliers this season? Explain.

_____

_____

_____

b) Suppose that Seaview, but not the stands, could buy as much ice cream as it needed for $1.40 per gallon. Should Seaview do so and sell it to the stands for $1.75 per gallon next season, or should it continue to make and sell its own ice cream? Explain.

_____

_____

_____

c) If the stands can buy ice cream for $1.65 per gallon from external suppliers next season, then what should be the transfer price? Explain.

_____

_____

_____

_____

2. Burke Manufacturing has an Assembly Division that can purchase Component A, one of its inputs, from another division of Burke called West Texas Productions. West Texas' per-unit cost of producing Component A is $16 in variable costs plus $4 in allocated fixed costs, for a total of $20 per unit. Assembly Division uses 20,000 units of Component A per month, and can buy Component A from an external supplier for $25 each.

a) Suppose that West Texas can sell an unlimited number of units of Component A to external customers for $24 each. What is the minimum and maximum acceptable transfer price that will induce a transfer between the two divisions?

Minimum _____   Maximum _____

b) Suppose that West Texas can sell 30,000 units of Component A to external customers for $24 each, and that West Texas' capacity is 60,000 units of Component A each year. What is the minimum and maximum acceptable transfer price that will induce a transfer between the two divisions?

Minimum _____   Maximum _____

c) Suppose that West Texas can sell 30,000 units of Component A to external customers for $24 each, and that West Texas' capacity is 40,000 units of Component A each year. What is the minimum and maximum acceptable transfer price that will induce a transfer between the two divisions?

Minimum _____   Maximum _____

d) Suppose that West Texas can sell an unlimited number of units of Component A to external customers for $25.50 each. What is the minimum and maximum acceptable transfer price that will induce a transfer between the two divisions?

Minimum _____   Maximum _____

3. Poolhouse Productions makes pumps for pool filtration systems and has two divisions. Davison 1 makes the pump's casing and Division 2 assembles the pump. This year Division 1 made 5,000 casings at a total cost of $550,000. All of the casings were transferred to Division 2. In Division 2, the variable costs of assembling the pumps were $40 and the pumps were sold for $300 each. Division 2's fixed costs this year totaled $120,000.

a) Determine the operating income for each division, and for Poolhouse overall, if the transfer price is set at cost ($110 per casing).

Division 1 _____   Division 2 _____   Poolhouse _____

b) Determine the operating income for each division, and for Poolhouse overall, if the transfer price is set at $90 per casing.

Division 1 _____   Division 2 _____   Poolhouse _____

c) Does the manager of Division 1 really care what transfer is chosen? Why or why not?

_____

_____

_____

_____

4. Betty's Burritos makes frozen burritos that can be heated quickly in the microwave. The Tortilla Division makes tortillas in packages of 100 and incurs variable costs of $1.80 for each package. The allocated fixed costs per package are $0.40. The Tortilla Division can produce 1,000,000 packages per year. It can sell all of these to external customers for $4.20 per package. The Production Division of Betty's requires 400,000 packages of tortillas per year. If it doesn't obtain tortillas from the Tortilla Division, it must purchase the tortillas from an external supplier at $4.20 per package.

a) Compute the operating income of the Tortilla Division if it sells 400,000 packages to the Production Division at $4.20 and the rest of its production to external customers.

Operating income _____

b) Compute the operating income of the Tortilla Division if it sells 400,000 packages to the Production Division at cost of $2.20 and the rest of its production to external customers.

Operating income _____

c) Suppose that Tortilla can sell only 800,000 packages per year to external customers. Compute the minimum transfer price that Tortilla would accept.

Transfer price _____

d) Suppose that Tortilla can sell only 500,000 packages per year to external customers. Compute the minimum transfer price that Tortilla would accept.

Transfer price _____

END OF CHAPTER EXERCISES

<u>Matching</u>: Match each term with the appropriate definition or phrase. Use each term only once.

Terms

A.	Cost center	H.	Return on sales
B.	Investment center	I.	Transfer price
C.	Investment turnover	J.	Principal
D.	Profit center	K.	Agent
E.	Residual income	L.	Responsibility accounting
F.	Return on investment	M.	Weighted average cost of capital
G.	Economic value added	N.	DuPont analysis

_____   1. In agency theory, this entity cannot observe the actions of the other

_____   2. Operating income less the required rate of return for the invested assets

_____   3. Operating income over sales

_____   4. A manager of this is held accountable for revenues, costs, and the investment in assets

_____   5. A manager of this is not held accountable for revenues or investment in assets

_____   6. Use of this allocates an organization's profits to its business segments

_____   7. Use of this holds the managers of business segments accountable only for the aspects of the business segment over which they have authority

_____   8. A manager of this is held responsible for revenues and costs but not investment in assets

_____   9. A version of residual income that accounts for taxes and the business segment's investment in operating assets plus working capital

_____   10. Sales over investment

_____   11. This is a breakdown of return on investment

_____   12. Operating income over investment

_____   13. In agency theory, this entity has specific knowledge about a situation

_____   14. This is an average of an organization's return on equity and its after-tax cost of debt

Multiple choice: Write the letter that represents the best choice in the space provided.

_____ 1. A business segment that has responsibility for both revenues and expenses is called a(n)
    a.   administrative center
    b.   investment center
    c.   profit center
    d.   revenue center

_____ 2. For 2005, Aberdeen's return on sales was 10% and its investment turnover was 2.0. Return on investment for 2005 was
    a.   5%
    b.   10%
    c.   12%
    d.   20%

_____ 3. For 2006, Aberdeen's return on investment was 26% and its investment turnover was 2.0. Return on sales for 2006 was
    a.   10%
    b.   13%
    c.   24%
    d.   26%

_____ 4. Thurston, Inc. experienced a 14% rate of return on average investment of $1,000,000. If the required rate of return is 12%, then residual income is
    a. $20,000
    b. $40,000
    c. $120,000
    d. $140,000

_____ 5. Suppose an office building is owned for which long-term leases have been signed, the tenants pay utilities and operating costs, and straight-line depreciation is taken. The rate of return on the book value of this investment can be expected to
    a.   increase over time
    b.   remain constant over time
    c.   decrease over time
    d.   vary randomly over time

<u>Use the following information for questions 6 – 10:</u>
Bellingham Division has a required rate of return by corporate headquarters of 20%. The weighted average cost of capital is 12%. You are given the following information for Bellingham's operations for a two-year period:

	2005	2004
Current assets	$50,000	$60,000
Long-term assets	200,000	204,000
Accumulated depreciation	60,000	44,000
Current liabilities	40,000	20,000
Long-term debt	100,000	140,000
Operating income for the year	19,000	21,000
Tax rate	40%	40%

_____ 6. The ROI for 2005 was
  a.   9.3%
  b.   10.0%
  c.   3.7%
  d.   20.0%

_____ 7. The residual income for 2005 was
  a.   ($21,000)
  b.   ($22,000)
  c.   ($14,000)
  d. $1,000

_____ 8. The average investment to be used in the EVA computation for 2005 was
  a. $257,000
  b. $227,000
  c. $279,000
  d. $175,000

_____ 9. The after-tax income for 2005 was
  a. $47,500
  b. $11,400
  c. $7,600
  d. $31,667

_____ 10. The EVA for 2005 was
  a.   ($18,600)
  b.   ($12,840)
  c.   ($9,600)
  d.   ($6,600)

Use the following information for questions 11 – 12:
The Machining Division has a capacity of 2,000 units. Its sales and cost data are:

Selling price per unit	$100
Variable manufacturing costs per unit	25
Variable administrative costs per unit	5
Total fixed manufacturing overhead	20,000
Total fixed administrative costs	5,000

_____ 11. The Machining Division is currently selling 1,900 units to outside customers, and the Assembly Division wants to purchase 300 units from Machining. If the transaction takes place, the variable administrative costs per unit on the units transferred to Assembly will be $2/unit, not $5/unit. What should be the transfer price?
  a. $73.67
  b. $76.67
  c. $97.00
  d. $100.00

_____ 12. If the Assembly Division is currently buying from an outside supplier at $98 per unit, what will be the effect on overall company profits if internal sales take place at the optimum transfer price?
  a. $7,000 increase
  b. $7,300 increase
  c. $300 increase
  d. there is no effect

Use the following information for questions 13 – 14:
The Kelso Division produces and sells a product to external and internal customers. Per-unit information about its operations include:

Selling price per unit to external customers	$250
Variable manufacturing costs per unit	115
Fixed manufacturing overhead costs per unit	70

_____ 13. If Kelso is operating at capacity and has unlimited external customer demand, what should be the transfer price for Kelso's product?
  a. $245
  b. $250
  c. $115
  d. $185

_____ 14. If Kelso has sufficient excess capacity to meet internal demand, what should be the transfer price for Kelso's product?
  a. $245
  b. $250
  c. $115
  d. $185

_____ 15. An advantage of centralization is
   a. increased time for upper-level management to focus on the organization's strategic goals
   b. the potential for decreased agency costs
   c. managers of business segments feel more empowered to make decisions
   d. managers of autonomous business segments are more likely to make decisions that are in the best interests of the organization as a whole

Use the following information for questions 16 – 18:
Division X sells flour to Division Y. Division X incurs costs of $0.375 per pound of flour. Division Y makes loaves of bread that sell for $2.50 each. Division Y incurs costs of $1.25 per loaf, excluding the cost of the flour. Each loaf of bread uses ½ of a pound of flour.

_____ 16. What is the operating income per pound of flour for Division X if the transfer price is set at $0.625/lb?
   a. $0.25
   b. $0.4375
   c. $0.625
   d. $0.8125

_____ 17. What is the operating income per loaf for Division Y if the transfer price is set at $0.625 per pound for flour?
   a. $0.6250
   b. $0.9375
   c. $1.2500
   d. $0.8750

_____ 18. What is the operating income for the entire organization if 100,000 loaves of bread are sold?
   a. $93,750
   b. $125,000
   c. $106,250
   d. $87,500

_____ 19. Which of the following performance measures can be used to compare the performance of business segments of varying sizes?
   a. return on investment
   b. residual income
   c. economic value added
   d. all of the above

_____ 20. Aiden's operating income was $100,000 and its ROI was 20%. What are Aiden's average operating assets?
   a. $20,000
   b. $200,000
   c. $500,000
   d. none of the above

_____ 21. An organization's required rate of return is 13%. The ROI of Divisions A and B, respectively, is 10% and 15%. Each Division is considering a project that will have a 12% rate of return. If ROI is used to evaluate divisions, which of the following statements is true?
   a. Both divisions will accept the project.
   b. Both divisions will reject the project.
   c. Division A will accept, and Division B will reject, the project.
   d. Division A will reject, and Division B will accept, the project.

_____ 22. An organization's required rate of return is 13%. The ROI of Divisions A and B, respectively, is 10% and 15%. Each Division is considering a project that will have a 12% rate of return. If residual income is used to evaluate divisions, which of the following statements is true?
   a. Both divisions will accept the project.
   b. Both divisions will reject the project.
   c. Division A will accept, and Division B will reject, the project.
   d. Division A will reject, and Division B will accept, the project.

_____ 23. ROI will decrease if
   a. sales increase
   b. investment turnover increases
   c. return on sales increases
   d. average operating assets increases

_____ 24. Operating income is
   a. net income less taxes less interest expense
   b. net income plus taxes plus interest expense
   c. net income plus taxes
   d. net income less interest expense

_____ 25. What is the difference between the definition of investment for residual income and EVA?
   a. residual income does not include long-term assets
   b. EVA subtracts current liabilities from operating assets
   c. EVA does not include current assets
   d. EVA subtracts long-term debt from operating assets

Exercises: Write your answer in the space provided.
1. Petman Division of Animal Enterprises had sales of $20 million last year, and a pre-tax operating income of $2 million. Its average operating assets were $10 million, and its average current liabilities were $3 million. Animal has a minimum required rate of return of 20% and a weighted average cost of capital of 15%. The tax rate is 40%.

   a) Compute the return on sales and the investment turnover for Petman.

   Return on sales _____   Investment turnover _____

   b) Compute the ROI for Petman. _____

   c) Compute Petman's residual income. _____

   d) Compute Petman's EVA. _____

2. The Price Division of Clayton Industries makes a component for Clayton's electric motors. You are given the following information about Price:

Selling price to external customers	$40
Variable costs per unit	$22
Fixed costs per unit (based on full capacity)	$10
Capacity in units	100,000

The Assembly Division of Clayton Industries uses a component similar to the one produced by Price Division, and it is currently purchasing 10,000 components each year from an external supplier for $38 each.

a) If Price Division has sufficient idle capacity to handle the needs of the Assembly Division, what is the minimum and maximum acceptable transfer price that will induce a transfer between the two divisions?

Minimum _____   Maximum _____

b) If Price Division has unlimited demand for its product from external customers, what is the minimum and maximum acceptable transfer price that will induce a transfer between the two divisions?

Minimum _____   Maximum _____

c) If Price Division has unlimited demand for its product from external customers, and that variable costs of the component will be lower by $4 for the components transferred to the Assembly Division, what is the minimum and maximum acceptable transfer price that will induce a transfer between the two divisions?

Minimum _____   Maximum _____

SOLUTION TO PROBLEM SET A

<u>True-False:</u>

1. F   Investment turnover is revenue over investment
2. F   The performance of business segments of varying sizes cannot be compared using residual income and EVA, but ROI is fine.
3. T   A business segment with a high ROI will reject projects with a lower ROI, even if the projects' ROIs exceed the organization's minimum required rate of return. Similarly, a business segment with a low ROI will accept projects with a higher ROI, even if the projects' ROIs are less than the organization's minimum required rate of return.
4. T
5. T   By looking at the components of return on sales and investment turnover, managers may gain insight into ways to increase a business segment's ROI.
6. T   The subtraction from income used in both residual income and EVA computations is the organization's "charge" to the business segment for the use of its operating assets.
7. F   Agency costs are potentially higher in decentralized organizations because segment managers have more decision-making authority.
8. F   It is the other way around. The agents (managers of business segments) have the specialized knowledge about their business segments.
9. T
10. F   Managers of investment centers are responsible for revenues, costs, and investment in assets, while managers of profit centers are responsible for only revenues and costs.
11. T   Only managers of investment centers are responsible for investment in assets.
12. F
13. F   EVA defines income as "after-tax" income and the weighted average cost of capital used in EVA is an after-tax cost of capital.
14. F   The WACC is an average of an organization's return on *equity* and its *after-tax* cost of debt.
15. F   There is no way to know how residual income and EVA will compare to each other without knowing how the weighted average cost of capital compares to the required rate of return or the amount of current liabilities that will be included in the EVA computation.

Exercises:
1. a) ROS = operating income/sales, so 12% = operating income/$7,280,000. Solve for operating income = $873,600.

   b) ROI = operating income/average operating assets = $873,600/$5,600,000 = 15.6%.

   c) Investment turnover = Sales/average operating assets = $7,280,000/$5,600,000 = 1.3.

   d) Residual income = $873,600 – 13% x $5,600,000 = $145,600.

   e) The project has an ROI of $140,000/$1,000,000 = 14%. Since this is less than Bowie's current ROI of 15.6%, accepting the project will reduce Bowie's ROI. Bowie will reject the project. This is not in the best interests of TXI because TXI would like to accept any projects that have an ROI that exceed its minimum required rate of return of 13%.

   f) When divisions are evaluated using residual income, the division will always accept a project that has an ROI greater than the organization's minimum required rate of return. Notice that Bowie's residual income will be higher if the project is accepted: residual income with the project = ($873,600 + $140,000) – 13% x ($5,600,000 + $1,000,000) = $1,013,600 – 13% x $6,600,000 = $155,600, which is greater than the residual income without the project of $145,600.

2. EVA = $900,000(1 – 30%) – 9% x ($4,400,000 - $800,000) = $306,000.

3. ROI = 20% = operating income/$1,800,00. Solve for the operating income that is necessary to achieve this 20% ROI and get operating income = $360,000. Now use CVP analysis (from Chapter 3) to determine how many units must be sold to achieve that operating income.

   Units required = (total fixed costs + target operating income)/contribution margin per unit
   = ($600,000 + $360,000)/$60 per unit = 16,000 units.

4. Residual income = $1,200,000 – required rate of return x $4,200,000 = $864,000. Solve for the required rate of return and get 8%.

SOLUTION TO PROBLEM SET B

True-False:

1. T
2. T
3. F   When the producing department can sell its production for an amount that exceeds the purchasing departments cost of acquiring the intermediate product, it is in the best interests of the organization for the transfer to not take place.
4. F   Market-based transfer prices are best used when the transferring division is at capacity selling its production to external customers.
5. F   The negotiations would take place between the two divisions.
6. T
7. T
8. F   Opportunity costs should be included in the transfer price computation only when the transferring department does not have sufficient idle capacity to fill the needs of the purchasing department.
9. T
10. F   Dual-rate transfer price is the label given to the situation where the producing department's selling price of the intermediate product is different than the purchasing department's purchase cost of the intermediate product.

Exercises:
1. a) It is not in the best interests of Seaview to allow the stands to purchase the ice cream at $1.50 per gallon this season. Seaview's incremental cost of producing the ice cream this season is the $1/gallon variable costs it incurs (the equipment was already rented this season).

   b) When deciding whether to rent the ice cream equipment next season, the incremental costs per gallon are calculated as ($10,000 variable costs + $6,000 fixed costs)/10,000 gallons = $1.60/gallon. If Seaview can purchase ice cream for $1.40/gallon, it should do that and sell the purchased ice cream to the sandwich stands.

   c) Since Seaview's cost of producing the ice cream is $1.60/gallon, it should not allow the stands to purchase ice cream for $1.65/gallon. Instead, Seaview should rent the ice cream equipment next year and produce the ice cream at a cost of $1.60/gallon. Any transfer price less than $1.65 will induce the stands to purchase ice cream from Seaview. Since Seaview pays the managers of the stands a percentage of the profits of the stand, Seaview should charge the highest amount per gallon that will still provide an incentive for the stand managers to purchase the ice cream from Seaview. The best transfer price for Seaview then is something between $1.64/gallon and $1.65/gallon.

2. a) The minimum acceptable transfer price is set by the producing (transferring) division. Since West Texas can sell all of its production for $24 to external customers, the minimum transfer price is $24. The maximum is $25, because the Assembly division can get the component elsewhere for $25.

b) The minimum acceptable transfer price that West Texas would accept when it has idle capacity is its incremental costs of producing the unit, which is $16. The maximum, as before, is $25.

c) If West Texas is selling 30,000 units to external customers and has capacity of 40,000, it must turn down sales of 10,000 units to external customers. The minimum acceptable transfer price that West Texas would accept is one that covers its incremental costs of producing the units ($16) plus an amount to compensate it for its lost contribution margin when it does the transfer to Assembly Division. The lost contribution margin on these 10,000 units is ($24 - $16) x 10,000 = $80,000. If 20,000 units are being transferred to Assembly, this adds an extra $4 per unit to the transfer price. The minimum acceptable transfer price is $16 + $4 = $20. The maximum, as before, is $25.

d) The minimum acceptable transfer price, since West Texas can sell all of its production for $25.50 to external customers, is $25.50. The maximum, as before, is $25. Since the minimum exceeds the maximum, there is no transfer price that will induce this transfer to take place.

3. a) When the transfer price is equal to Division 1's costs, all of the organization's income is attributed to Division 2.

	Division 1	Division 2	Poolhouse
Sales to external customers		$1,500,000	$1,500,000
Sales to internal customers	$550,000		
Division 1 manufacturing costs	550,000		550,000
Transferred-in costs		550,000	
Division 2 variable costs		200,000	200,000
Division 2 fixed costs		120,000	120,000
Operating income	$0	$630,000	$630,000

b) When the transfer price is greater than Division 1's costs, the organization's income is shared between the two divisions.

	Division 1	Division 2	Poolhouse
Sales to external customers	$0	$1,500,000	$1,500,000
Sales to internal customers	$950,000		
Division 1 manufacturing costs	550,000		550,000
Transferred-in costs		950,000	
Division 2 variable costs		200,000	200,000
Division 2 fixed costs		120,000	120,000
Operating income	$400,000	$230,000	$630,000

c) The manager of Division 1 only cares if Division 1 is evaluated as a profit center. Since all of Division 1's output is transferred to Division 2 (it has no external customers) it might just be easier to evaluate Division 1 as a cost center, in which case the manager of Division 1 does not care about the transfer price.

4. a)

Sales to external customers (600,000 @ $4.20)	$2,520,000
Sales to internal customers (400,000 @ $4.20)	1,680,000
Total sales	4,200,000
Variable costs @ $1.80	1,800,000
Fixed costs	400,000
Total costs	2,200,000
Operating income	$2,000,000

b)

Sales to external customers (600,000 @ $4.20)	$2,520,000
Sales to internal customers (400,000 @ $2.20)	880,000
Total sales	3,400,000
Variable costs @ $1.80	1,800,000
Fixed costs	400,000
Total costs	2,200,000
Operating income	$1,200,000

c) Since Tortilla's capacity is 1,000,000 packages, it cannot satisfy the Production Division's needs and its own customer demand (400,000 packages + 800,000 packages = 1,200,000 packages). In order to transfer 400,000 packages to the Production Division, Tortilla will have to forgo sales of 200,000 packages to its external customers. The lost contribution margin is ($4.20 - $1.80) x 200,000 = $480,000. The minimum transfer price that Tortilla will accept will be its variable costs plus an amount that covers this lost contribution margin. The lost contribution margin adds $480,000/400,000 packages = $1.20 to the transfer price. The transfer price is $1.80 + $1.20 = $3.00/package.

d) In this situation, Tortilla has excess capacity. It will accept any transfer price that exceeds its variable costs of $1.80 per package.

SOLUTION TO END OF CHAPTER EXERCISES

Matching:

    1.   J
    2.   E
    3.   H
    4.   B
    5.   A
    6.   I
    7.   L
    8.   D
    9.   G
  10.   C
  11.   N
  12.   F
  13.   K
  14.   M

Multiple choice:

1. C
2. D   ROI = return on sales x investment turnover; 10% x 2.0 = 20%.
3. B   ROI = 26% = return on sales x 2.0; return on sales = 13%.
4. A   ROI = 14% = operating income/$1,000,000, so operating income = $140,000. Residual income = $140,000 – 12% x $1,000,000 = $20,000.
5. A   As assets are depreciated, the book value decreases over time. Since invested assets are the denominator of the ROI calculation, ROI should increase over time.
6. A   Operating assets at the end of 2004 = $60,000 + $204,000 - $44,000 = $220,000. Operating assets at the end of 2005 = $50,000 + $200,000 - $60,000 = $190,000. Average operating assets = ($220,000 + $190,000)/2 = $205,000. ROI = $19,000/$205,000 = 9.26%.
7. B   Residual income = $19,000 – 20% x $205,000 = ($22,000).
8. D   Operating assets less current liabilities at the end of 2004 = $220,000 - $20,000 = $200,000. Operating assets less current liabilities at the end of 2005 = $190,000 - $40,000 = $150,000. Average operating assets less current liabilities = ($200,000 + $175,000)/2 = $175,000.
9. B   After-tax income = before-tax income times (1 – tax rate) = $19,000 x (1 – 40%) = $11,400.
10. C   EVA = $11,400 – 12% x $175,000 = ($9,600).
11. A   Machining Division only has 100 units of idle capacity. In order to transfer 300 units to Assembly, it will have to forgo sales of 200 units to external customers. The opportunity cost of this is ($100 - $30) x 200 = $14,000, or $14,000/300 units = $46.67/unit. The variable costs of the transferred units are $25 + $2 = $27, so the transfer price is $27 + $46.67 = $73.67.

12. B   The organization saves $98 - $27 = $71 on the 300 units that Assembly doesn't purchase from an external supplier, or a total of $21,300. In order for the transfer to take place, the organization loses $14,000 of contribution margin on the lost sales to external customers for 200 units (as computed in #11 above). The net savings is $7,300. Notice that the transfer price is irrelevant in this computation.

13. B   If Kelso is at capacity, the market price is the best transfer price; it is the minimum transfer price that Kelso will accept.

14. C   If Kelso has idle capacity it will accept any transfer price that exceeds its variable costs.

15. B

16. A $0.625 transfer price less costs of $0.375 = $0.25.

17. D   Division Y makes $2.50 - $1.25 per loaf before the cost of flour is taken into consideration. If the transfer price for flour is $0.625, this cost is $0.375/loaf because each loaf uses ½ pound of flour. The net operating income per loaf is then $1.25 - $0.375 = $0.875.

18. C   The transfer price is irrelevant here. The cost of the flour per loaf = $0.375/2 = $0.1875. The profit per loaf is $2.50 - $1.25 - $0.1875 = $1.0625.

19. A

20. C   ROI = 20% = $100,000/average operating assets. Solve for average operating assets = $500,000.

21. C   Division A will accept the project because it has an ROI greater than Division A's current ROI and will hence increase Division A's ROI. Division B will reject the project because it has an ROI less than Division B's current ROI and will hence decrease Division B's ROI.

22. B   When divisions are evaluated using residual income, it will always be in their best interests to accept any project with an ROI greater than the organization's required rate of return and reject any project with an ROI less than the organization's required rate of return.

23. D   ROI = operating income/average operating assets is decreased if assets increase.

24. B   Operating income is earnings before interest and taxes, so interest and taxes need to be added back in to net income.

25. B

Exercises:
1. a) Return on sales = $2 million/$20 million = 10%.
       Investment turnover = $20 million/$10 million = 2.0 times.

    b) ROI = 10% x 2.0 = 20%.

    c) $2 million – 20% x $10 million = $0.

    d) $2,000,000 x (1 – 40%) – 15% x ($10,000,000 - $3,000,000) = $150,000.

2. a) The minimum transfer price that Price will accept is one that covers its variable costs, or $22. The maximum transfer price that Assembly will accept is what it currently pays to an outside supplier, or $38.

    b) In this case Price will not accept anything lower than $40, and Assembly will not pay anything over $38, so no transfer will occur.

    c) In this case Price will accept what it can get from external customers, less the cost savings associated with the transfer or $36. The maximum that Assembly will pay is, as before, $38.

Chapter 16

Strategic Performance Measurement

√ **Study Checklist – Monitor your progress**

1. Read the chapter in the text
2. Review the learning objectives below
3. Read the overview of the chapter
4. Read the chapter review for learning objectives 1 – 3
5. Do Problem Set A and check your answers
6. Read the chapter review for learning objectives 4 – 6
7. Do the End of Chapter Exercises in this study guide
8. Do the homework assigned by your instructor

CHAPTER LEARNING OBJECTIVES

After studying this chapter, you should be able to answer the following questions:

Q1. What is strategic decision making?

Q2. How are financial and nonfinancial measures used to evaluate organizational performance?

Q3. What is a balance scorecard?

Q4. How is a balanced scorecard implemented?

Q5. What are the strengths and weaknesses of the balanced scorecard?

Q6. What is the future direction of cost accounting?

OVERVIEW OF CHAPTER

This chapter introduces a strategic management system known as the balanced scorecard. The balanced scorecard links the organization's vision and strategic plans to its operations. Financial and nonfinancial measures are used to monitor the organization's progress towards its strategic goals.

CHAPTER REVIEW: Learning Objectives 1 - 3

Q1: What is strategic decision making?

Chapter 1 began with an overview of management decision making. Managers begin by determining the vision of the organization as well as its core competencies. Organizational strategies are based on these determinations and are long-term in nature. Short-term operating plans are developed based on the organizational strategies. In order to monitor the results of actual operations, managers determine specific *performance objectives*. Performance objectives are specific goals, and managers establish methods to measure progress towards these goals. These measurements of the performance objectives are compared to management's expectations, and adjustments are made to either change operations or adjust the organization's longer-term strategies.

Q2: How are financial and nonfinancial measures used to evaluate organizational performance?

Financial measures are measures that are reported in dollars or are ratios of measures that are reported in dollars. For example, sales, net income, or the profit margin are all financial measures. Usually, financial measures come from an organization's accounting information system. Managers also use *nonfinancial measures* (measures that are not reported in dollars) to evaluate organizational performance. Examples of nonfinancial measures include number of customer complaints, number of on-time deliveries, responses to customer or employee surveys, and the like.

When evaluating the organization's performance, managers must use several measures. In for-profit corporations, financial information about profitability will always be important because of management's responsibility to the shareholders. However, if the organizational vision includes the desire to be seen as a provider of high-quality products, information to ensure that product quality is not sacrificed for profits must also be analyzed. The measures chosen will be based on the organization's long-term strategic goals. Exhibit 16.5 in the text provides an example of the performance measures used by Wendy's Restaurants.

Q3: What is a balance scorecard?

The *balanced scorecard* is a method of organizing the financial and nonfinancial measures used to monitor operations. The measures are specifically related to the organization's vision and long-term strategies. They must be measures that are easy for employees to see how their behavior can improve the performance measure. For example, a customer help line might measure the number of minutes it takes to resolve a customer complaint. A customer service representative knows that he or she is evaluated based on this measure and will then strive to resolve customer complaints quickly. However, the balanced scorecard will be most beneficial if it is not treated as merely a stand-alone performance measurement system.

The balanced scorecard is also a method for communicating an organization's strategies throughout the organization and to all of the organization's stakeholders. The strategy is explained in terms of measurable targets. The measures have a cause-and-effect relationship with the strategy, and everyone in the organization is made aware of his or her part in achieving the strategy. For example, when Exxon Mobil implemented the balanced scorecard, even truck drivers were given note cards for their cabs' visors listing the five actions they must take to do their part in achieving the organization's strategic goals. Of course, the compensation of all employees must be tied to whether they achieve their targets in order for this to work.

Most commonly, the balanced scorecard contains four layers of measures. Each layer is supported by the layers below it. In order to be financially successful, an organization must have a good relationship with its customers. Good customer relationships are forged by having the internal business processes necessary to support them. The internal business processes can be improved when the organization is able to maintain an atmosphere that supports learning, growth, and positive change.

- *Financial perspective.* These measures evaluate the organization's progress towards its financial goals. For example, managers may expect a minimum rate of return on investment from the organization's business segments. Or, progress toward the reduction of long-term debt may be measured. Many of the measures in this category may be those that managers have traditionally tracked.

- *Customer perspective.* These measures evaluate the organization's performance from the customers' perspective. After determining customers' needs, managers will locate measures to help determine whether the organization is meeting these needs. For example, customers may desire fast service or longer operating hours or more technical assistance. Market share measures, if increasing market share is part of the long-term strategy, would be included in the customer perspective category.

- *Internal business process perspective.* These measures analyze the production and delivery of goods and services to customers. The series of sequential business processes an organization goes through as it designs, sells, delivers, and supports its goods and services is known as the *value chain*. The first stage of the value chain is the *innovation cycle*, where customer preferences and needs are determined and the products or services are designed. In the next stage, the *operations cycle*, the goods or services are produced and delivered to the customer. The *post-sales service cycle* supports the customer after the sale.

- *Learning and growth perspective.* These measures help determine if the organization is able to change and develop improved strategies. Employee and manager training and development measures may be part of the learning and growth perspective, as may be measures of research and development successes.

In a balanced scorecard, 4 – 5 measures are determined for each layer. The scorecard emphasizes cause-and-effect linkages between the layers. The organization's vision links to strategic goals, which link to strategic objectives, which link to measures designed to monitor progress. For each measure, a long-term target will be specified, as will several shorter-term targets so that progress towards the long-term target can be monitored more frequently. The targets must be realistic or employees will not feel that their efforts will make a difference toward achieving the targets. Upper-level management must also design programs that support employee efforts to achieve their targets.

Organizations may choose different perspectives for their scorecards. For example, Charlotte, North Carolina has a balanced scorecard with five perspectives: Community Safety, Transportation, Preservation of Older Neighborhoods, Restructuring of Government, and Economic Development.

Examples of specific measures for each of these perspectives are shown below.

Financial Perspective	Internal Business Process Perspective
<ul><li>operating income</li><li>profit margin</li><li>return on equity</li><li>sales growth in percent</li></ul> **Customer Perspective** <ul><li>market share</li><li>customer satisfaction survey results</li><li>number of customer complaints</li><li>number of new customers</li><li>customer reorder rates</li></ul> **Learning and Growth Perspective** <ul><li>employee turnover</li><li>number of training days per employee</li><li>employee satisfaction survey results</li><li>employee use of new information system</li><li>number of patents per $10,000 spent on research and development</li></ul>	<ul><li>innovation cycle<ul><li>number of new production technologies developed</li><li>number of new features added to existing products</li><li>number of new products developed</li><li>new product development time</li></ul></li><li>operations cycle<ul><li>defect rates</li><li>efficiency measures</li><li>percent of on-time deliveries</li><li>machine maintenance measures</li></ul></li><li>post-sales service cycle<ul><li>warranty repair time</li><li>warranty-related costs</li><li>customer training hours</li><li>accounts receivable turnover ratio</li></ul></li></ul>

Demonstration problem

Stanislawa is known to her family and friends as a preparer of outstanding Polish cuisine. She recently leased a small restaurant in her neighborhood and wants help in developing performance measures for monitoring her new business. Her vision is for her restaurant, Stasha's Place, to be known as the best place to go for Polish food in Chicago's suburbs and for it to provide sufficient profit for her to support herself and her family in a reasonable lifestyle. To support this vision, she worked with a consultant to determine her core competencies and organizational strategies. Together they developed the following lists:

- Core competencies
    - o Stasha has an extensive knowledge of Polish cuisine and the Polish language and customs.
    - o Stasha's extended family have helped her in the kitchen for years and know her recipes and production processes.
    - o The restaurant's location is in a Polish suburb of Chicago, where many residents speak only Polish.
    - o The two other local Polish restaurants serve only buffet-style dinners and are not open for lunch.

- Organizational strategies
    - o Long-term goal: To become known as the best restaurant for Polish cuisine in Chicagoland.
    - o Organizational structure: Sole proprietorship to start, and incorporation after business takes off, with only family members as stockholders.
    - o Financial structure: Use Stasha's savings initially, and finance growth from profits.

Required:
Identify performance measures that Stasha might use in each of the four balanced scorecard perspectives.

Solution to demonstration problem:
Financial perspective:
- Monthly operating income. Stasha might set an absolute target that will allow her to achieve her financial goals. For example, if she needs a minimum of $1,000/month for living expenses, this could be her starting point, and she could increase this target in increments over time.
- Monthly profit margin. If Stasha expects that her operation will become more efficient as the employees gain experience, she might set an ever-increasing set of targets for the next 5 years.

Customer perspective:
- Number of new customers. Stasha might set a target of 50 new customers per month initially, for example.
- Customer satisfaction ratings. Stashu could survey customers as they leave about their dining experience and create an index for customer satisfaction.

Internal business processes:
- Minutes it takes to prepare the average meal. Stasha may have some initial feeling for this given her past experience in the kitchen. She could then set a target for improved efficiency over time.
- Number of new dishes introduced to the menu. Based on responses to customer surveys, Stash may add items to the menu as demanded by the customers.

Learning and growth:
- Number of employees who attend cooking classes.
- Number of employee suggestions for improving the business.

PROBLEM SET A (Learning Objectives 1 - 3)

<u>Matching</u>: Match each measure with the balanced scorecard perspective it addresses. You may use each perspective more than once; a few of the measures address more than one balanced scorecard perspectives.

Balanced scorecard perspectives

A. Financial perspective
B. Customer perspective
C. Internal business process perspective – innovation cycle
D. Internal business process perspective – operations cycle
E. Internal business process perspective – post-sales service cycle
F. Learning and growth perspective

Measures

_____ 1.   Percent increase in market share

_____ 2.   Number of new patents

_____ 3.   Employee satisfaction ratings

_____ 4.   Number of new customers under age 18

_____ 5.   Number of days to collect accounts receivable

_____ 6.   Number of machine set-ups required in the production process

_____ 7.   Number of customer complaints

_____ 8.   Return on investment

_____ 9.   Direct labor efficiency variance

_____ 10. Percent of production batches completed in the budgeted time

_____ 11. Average number of minutes it takes to resolve customer complaint

_____ 12. Percent of customers who reorder the product

_____ 13. Number of customers who received product training

_____ 14. Residual income

_____ 15. Employee turnover

_____ 16. Profit margin

_____ 17. Number of employees who received a graduate degree

_____ 18. Operating income

_____ 19. Number of new features added to products

_____ 20. Average number of days spent from conception of new products to initial production

<u>True-False</u>: Indicate whether each of the following is true (T) or false (F) in the space provided.

_____ 1. A balanced scorecard is "balanced" when all four scorecard perspectives have the same number of measures assigned to them.

_____ 2. In order to monitor the results of actual operations, managers determine specific performance objectives.

_____ 3. Financial measures are stated in dollars or ratios of dollars.

_____ 4. The results of financial measures come mostly from the accounting information system.

_____ 5. All financial measures are associated with the financial perspective of the balanced scorecard.

_____ 6. Managers determine the organizational vision and its core competencies before they establish the organizational strategies.

_____ 7. Organizational strategies are long-term in nature.

_____ 8. An organization's structure is one of the organizational strategies.

_____ 9. An organization's budget for the upcoming year is one of the organizational strategies.

_____ 10. Employee turnover is an example of a nonfinancial measure that addresses the learning and growth perspective of the balanced scorecard.

_____ 11. The financial perspective of the balanced scorecard is addressed with financial measures and the other 3 perspectives are addressed with nonfinancial measures.

_____ 12. Offering high-quality products that sell for premium prices is an example of an organizational strategy.

_____ 13. Offering acceptable-quality products that sell for low prices is an example of an organizational strategy.

_____ 14. The balanced scorecard is used by for-profit companies but not by nonprofit organizations.

_____ 15. The internal business process perspective of the balanced scorecard includes measures related to the innovation cycle, the operations cycle, and the delivery cycle.

CHAPTER REVIEW: Learning Objectives 4 - 6

Q4: How is a balanced scorecard implemented?

A balanced scorecard implementation includes the following stages:

- Clarify organizational vision, competencies, and strategies.
- Analyze the four perspectives to develop performance objectives and measures. An organization may define slightly different perspectives than the most common perspectives mentioned in the last section of this study guide.
- Communicate the components throughout the organization. Although the balanced scorecard implementation begins with top level management, it is refined by suggestions from others in the organization.
- Establish performance targets and action plans. Usually performance targets are set for a three- to five- year horizon, with shorter term intermediate targets.
- Collect and analyze scorecard data. The scorecard performance measures are compared to the targets.
- Investigate variances and reward employees.
- Provide feedback and refine the balanced scorecard. The information gained during the comparison of the actual performance measures may indicate new approaches are needed in order to meet targets, or it may indicate that the organizational strategies and the balanced scorecard need to be refined.

Q5: What are the strengths and weaknesses of the balanced scorecard?

One of the balanced scorecard's greatest strengths is that it encourages communication of the organization's strategy throughout the organization. It also forces management to clarify the organizational vision and strategies. Since it links employee rewards to performance objectives that are derived from the organization's vision and strategies, short-term and long-term strategies are more likely to be aligned.

As with any tool, the balanced scorecard may not be implemented appropriately, or it may be based on inappropriately defined visions or strategies. The measures used for each perspective may have been chosen because the data was easy to obtain, not because they were the best measures that could be used. If performance measures are unattainable, employees may not buy in to the balanced scorecard. Exhibit 16.15 in the text describes many of the advantages and disadvantages of the balanced scorecard.

Q6: What is the future direction of cost accounting?

Advances in information technology have freed accountants to concentrate on providing management with better information to aid decision making. Instead of spending time preparing routine reports, accountants now need to manage the information available. They need to be aware of and understand emerging management tools (such as the balanced scorecard) in order to best support management.

END OF CHAPTER EXERCISES

<u>Multiple choice</u>: Write the letter that represents the best choice in the space provided.

_____ 1. Suppose an organization's strategic goals include the development of unusual, high-quality products. Which of the following would best support this strategy?
   a. offering products at a lower cost than competitors
   b. offering products that are similar to competitors
   c. advertising campaigns that make customers aware of how the company's products differ from competitors
   d. targets to achieve massive production cost reductions

_____ 2. The balanced scorecard will be least beneficial when
   a. it is considered a stand-alone performance measurement system
   b. it is considered a strategic management system
   c. it leaves the hands of upper-level management
   d. targets are easy to understand

_____ 3. The balanced scorecard's financial perspective is immediately supported by which other perspective?
   a. learning and growth
   b. innovation
   c. internal business processes
   d. customer

_____ 4. The balanced scorecard's customer perspective is immediately supported by which other perspective?
   a. learning and growth
   b. innovation
   c. internal business processes
   d. financial

_____ 5. The balanced scorecard's internal business processes perspective is immediately supported by which other perspective?
   a. learning and growth
   b. innovation
   c. customer
   d. financial

_____ 6. Which of the balanced scorecard's perspectives has three subcategories?
   a. learning and growth
   b. internal business processes
   c. customer
   d. financial

_____ 7. The balanced scorecard emphasizes linkages between the organization's vision and its operations. The vision links down to
   a. strategic goals
   b. strategic objectives
   c. measures
   d. employees

_____ 8. The balanced scorecard emphasizes linkages between the organization's vision and its operations. Strategic objectives link down to
   a. strategic goals
   b. strategic objectives
   c. measures
   d. employees

_____ 9. The balanced scorecard emphasizes linkages between the organization's vision and its operations. Strategic goals link down to
   a. strategic goals
   b. strategic objectives
   c. measures
   d. employees

_____ 10. Midwestern Manufacturing has a strategic objective to become the highest quality manufacturer in its industry. Which of the following measures would best monitor progress toward this objective?
   a. customer satisfaction ratings
   b. number of defective units produced
   c. defect rate per 100 units produced
   d. employee training in quality control

_____ 11. Rex Retailers is using the measure "percent increase in market share". This measure is most likely associated with which of the balanced scorecard perspectives?
   a. financial
   b. customer
   c. internal business processes
   d. learning and growth

_____ 12. Max Manufacturing is using the measure "number of steps in production". This measure is most likely associated with which of the balanced scorecard perspectives?
   a. financial
   b. customer
   c. internal business processes
   d. learning and growth

_____ 13. Stanley's Shoe Company is using the measure "number of employee suggestions". This measure is most likely associated with which of the balanced scorecard perspectives?
   a.   financial
   b.   customer
   c.   internal business processes
   d.   learning and growth

_____ 14. For a company using the traditional 4 perspectives of the balanced scorecard, an appropriate total number of measures is
   a.   4 - 5
   b.   6 - 10
   c.   11 - 15
   d.   16 - 20

_____ 15. The first step in implementing a balanced scorecard is
   a.   to choose the performance measures to be used
   b.   to communicate the strategic plan to the organization
   c.   to clarify the organizational vision
   d.   create the performance reward scheme for employees that meet their targets

Exercises: Write your answer in the space provided.
1. Charman Industries makes propane barbeque grills. It is pursuing a product differentiation strategy in that it wants its grills to be considered the top-of-the-line in the industry. It believes that with the right advertising campaign and quality control efforts, it could be successful with this strategy. Identify at least one measure that it might use for each of the four balanced scorecard perspectives.

_____

_____

_____

_____

_____

_____

_____

_____

2. Manchar Industries makes propane barbeque grills. It is pursuing a strategy that states it will become the low-cost provider of functional grills in the industry. It believes that with the right product placement and improvements in production efficiency, it could be successful with this strategy. Identify at least one measure that it might use for each of the four balanced scorecard perspectives.

_____

_____

_____

_____

_____

_____

_____

_____

SOLUTION TO PROBLEM SET A

Matching:

1. B
2. F or C
3. F
4. B
5. E
6. D
7. B or E
8. A
9. D
10. D
11. B or E
12. B
13. E
14. A
15. F
16. A
17. F
18. A
19. C
20. C

True-False:

1. F
2. T
3. T
4. T
5. F   The direct labor efficiency variance, for example, is most likely associated with the internal business processes perspective.
6. T
7. T
8. T
9. F   An organization's budget is part of the short-term operating plans.
10. T
11. F   Financial measures may be used in all perspectives.
12. T
13. T
14. F   See the discussion of the use of the balanced scorecard by non-profit entities in the text.
15. F   The internal business process perspective includes the innovation cycle, the operations cycle, and the post-sales service cycle.

SOLUTION TO END OF CHAPTER EXERCISES

<u>Multiple choice:</u>

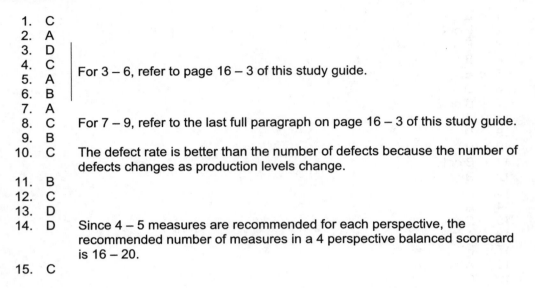

1. C
2. A
3. D
4. C   For 3 – 6, refer to page 16 – 3 of this study guide.
5. A
6. B
7. A
8. C   For 7 – 9, refer to the last full paragraph on page 16 – 3 of this study guide.
9. B
10. C   The defect rate is better than the number of defects because the number of
               defects changes as production levels change.
11. B
12. C
13. D
14. D   Since 4 – 5 measures are recommended for each perspective, the
               recommended number of measures in a 4 perspective balanced scorecard
               is 16 – 20.
15. C

<u>Exercises:</u>

1. Financial: operating income growth from the higher prices charged for the grills
    Customer: market share in the high-quality propane grill market (note that market share in the
        total propane grill market would not be appropriate); customer satisfaction with grill
        performance, quality, and features
    Internal business processes: number of new features added; defect rate
    Learning & growth: number of employees trained in quality control; number of employee
        suggestions for new product features

2. Financial: sales revenue growth from the sale of more grills; operating income growth from
        increased production efficiency
    Customer: market share in the propane grill market; customer satisfaction with grill
        performance and price
    Internal business processes: number of features removed; production time; production
        efficiency measures such as labor or material efficiency variances
    Learning & growth: number of employees trained in production efficiency techniques; number
        of employee suggestions for improvements in the production process